HOW TO CHOOSE WINE

VINCENT GASNIER

PHOTOGRAPHY BY IAN O'LEARY

LONDON • NEW YORK • MUNICH
MELBOURNE • DELHI

For Dorling Kindersley

PROJECT ART EDITOR
Sara Robin

SENIOR EDITOR
Simon Tuite

MANAGING ART EDITOR
Nick Harris

EXECUTIVE MANAGING EDITOR
Adèle Hayward

DTP DESIGNER
Traci Salter

PRODUCTION CONTROLLER
Mandy Inness

WITH CONTRIBUTIONS BY
Ruth Arnold and Gary Werner

Produced for Dorling Kindersley by

cobaltid

The Stables, Wood Farm, Deopham Road,
Attleborough, Norfolk NR17 1AJ
www.cobaltid.co.uk

ART EDITORS
Paul Reid, Lloyd Tilbury, Claire Oldman,
Annika Skoog, Darren Bland

EDITORS
Marek Walisiewicz, Kati Dye,
Louise Abbott, Maddy King

PHOTOGRAPHY ART DIRECTION
Paul Reid

PHOTOGRAPHY
Ian O'Leary, with assistance
from Laura Forrester

First American Edition, 2006
Published in the United States by
DK Publishing, 375 Hudson Street,
New York, NY 10014

06 07 08 09 10   10 9 8 7 6 5 4 3 2 1

A Cataloging-in-Publication record for this book is available from
the Library of Congress.

ISBN-13 978-0-7566-2350-0
ISBN-10 0-7566-2350-2

AD320

DK books are available at special discounts for bulk purchases for sales promotions,
premiums, fund-raising, or educational use. For details, contact: DK Publishing Special
Markets, 375 Hudson Street, New York, NY 10014 or SpecialSales@dk.com

Color reproduction by Colourscan, Singapore
Printed in Singapore by Star Standard

Discover more at
www.dk.com

CONTENTS

FOREWORD

Ever since I was very young, wine has been my passion. Growing up in the Loire Valley, I was surrounded by vineyards, and during my school vacations I would help the local wine producers in return for a few francs—and the benefit of their knowledge and experience in turning the grape into a magical drink! I have made it my life's work not only to learn as much as I can, but also to share in the enjoyment of wine, and to help others to enjoy it to the fullest. Serving my time in restaurants in Paris and in England, I realized that many people would like to know more about wine and try something new, but so often they fear wasting their money, or losing face—or both. So they stick to what they know. This is a shame, since there is so much to enjoy: even though I have been in the wine business now for many years, there are still wines I have yet to try—and I can't wait! One of the great pleasures of wine is that the more you learn and the more you experience, the better it gets, as you gain confidence and enjoyment in comparing wines from different countries, regions, even individual producers, and also begin to compare vintages.

What more does a person need? A little food, some good company with family or friends around them, and one or two wonderful wines to drink, compare, and discuss! I hope that this book will help you to reach that convivial goal—not once, but many times. Santé!

Vincent Gasnier.

Vincent Gasnier

INTRODUCTION

A WINE ODYSSEY

While it's not quite true that wine runs from the faucets in my native land, you can imagine what a culture shock it was for me to relocate from France, where I grew up drinking wines made by our neighbors at every meal, to England—officially not even a wine-producing country at the time—where diners often seemed baffled and intimidated by wine lists, and struggled to recall the flavors of wines they had tasted years ago on vacation. But to my delight, I soon discovered that English wine-drinkers were only too willing to try new taste experiences—far more so, I confess, than many wine-drinkers in France, and indeed in many other European countries. But these would-be wine explorers just weren't sure where to start!

And so began my mission—to take the mystery and uncertainty out of wine. One of my great pleasures in recent years has been to see how wine has become "democratized." Gone is so much of

the snobbishness of the bad old days, and wine has become more popular and accepted as a drink for everyone, young and old, the rich and the not-so-rich—a pleasure for all people, not just a privileged few. Today, we can even buy wine along with the groceries when we go to the supermarket. But the downside of our new wine democracy is that there's often no one around to offer a bit of welcome advice. This breeds its own insecurities: are you right to spend a little more on what looks like a "good brand"? Or will you be laughed at for following the herd? Is that special offer a genuine bargain? And can those New World fizzes *really* be as good as Champagne?

THE WORLD IN A GLASS

Well, this is where I come in. With this book, I aim to help you approach the vast range of wines available today in a way that will start to make sense of them, by grouping similar wines together and comparing their different qualities through tasting. Using this book will not only teach you what to look for, but it will also help you to decide which wines you really like above all others—and why!

I have chosen the wines that fill the pages of this book especially with you, the inquisitive reader and adventurous wine taster, in mind. They are wines that I enjoy myself and that I believe are typical of their particular style. Hopefully, you will enjoy them as much as I do! By using this book, I hope you will enhance your knowledge and your enjoyment of wine. Please remember, though, that almost all wines are alcoholic, and some are quite strong. Too much alcohol is dangerous, and can even ruin people's lives. Make sure you drink sensibly and responsibly, so that you bring only pleasure into your own and other people's lives as a result.

PART 1
WINE STYLES

WHAT IS A STYLE?

YOU ARE WHAT YOU DRINK

Wines are like cars! We all have our favorites; the one we drive every day and feel comfortable with—and the one we dream of owning. Like wines, cars have different styles; a Ferrari is fast, powerful, noisy, and brash (in an expensive way!); a Mercedes is also powerful, but smoother, more quiet and controlled. There are no rights and wrongs, only personal preferences, and, just as you would always test drive a car before buying it, you need to taste wines of many different styles to find your favorites.

Remember, though, that when cars first became available to the general public, there was a simple choice of just one—the Model T Ford—famously available in "any color, so long as it's black." The mind-boggling array of cars for sale today is the result of 200 years of progress. The same is true of wine—though it took not hundreds, but thousands of years before the ordinary wine-drinker could even choose between red or white!

THE FIRST WINEMAKERS

In this book, I describe some 220 different types of wine; and within each type are many different wines from diverse producers, each with its own nuances of style and quality. So how did this extraordinary diversity come into being?

To answer this question, we need to delve into history. In Egypt, tomb paintings dating back to 4000 BCE give us some of the earliest records of winemaking. But this wine was not for everyday drinking: it was offered to the gods and placed in the tombs of the pharaohs to sustain them in the afterlife. Wine also had a ceremonial role in the earliest Greek cultures: in the cult of Dionysus, god of the grapevine, unrestrained drinking inspired frenzied and often violent and bloodthirsty rites. Wine was revered for its intoxicating qualities and for its symbolic connection with the land and fertility; it would have been a very discerning—and foolhardy—reveler who dared mention that he would have preferred something with "more restrained fruit"!

As the ancient Greek and Roman civilizations developed, Dionysian orgies became frowned upon, and were eventually banned. But grape-growing and winemaking spread and flourished around the Mediterranean, and from the ancient Greeks and especially the Romans, we have the first detailed evidence of wine being drunk and enjoyed at all levels of society and of the diversification of wine styles. What did these Roman wines taste like? We know that honey, spices, herbs, and even seawater

EARLY WINEMAKING
Egyptian tomb paintings dating back 5,000 years show grapes being harvested with curved knives, then carried in wicker baskets to acacia wood vats where they were crushed by foot.

MODERN VINEYARD
Many of the classic European vineyard areas, like the Alsace region of northeastern France *(facing page)* and Germany's Mosel Valley, became established under Roman occupation.

were added as preservatives, and that Roman wines were often concentrated by heating, which must have created a style reminiscent of modern port or Madeira. Falerno wine was thought one of the finest: possibly made from the Aglianico grape, still grown today, it was a full, alcoholic wine that was aged for 10 to 20 years—much longer in exceptional vintages. The emperor Augustus loved strong, sweet wines, commanding his vineyard owners to leave their grapes on the vine for as long as possible to concentrate their flavors.

WINE FOR EXPORT

The Romans carried vines and winemaking across the Empire, and eventually all citizens of the provinces—not just Romans—were allowed to make wine. Rome soon began to import wines, notably from Iberia (modern Spain and Portugal) and Gaul (France), and stylistic differences in the wines produced for local tastes, rather than by expatriate Romans, began to be appreciated. But with the fall of the Roman Empire in the 5th century CE, movement of goods between countries

fell away. Monks quietly took over the care of European vineyards, refining their knowledge of viticulture and developing many of the styles of wine we enjoy today. And when Europe emerged from the Dark Ages, wine began to move between countries once more. When the English started importing Bordeaux wines in the 12th century, the commercialization of wine began in earnest, and in the centuries that followed, throughout Europe, tastes for different styles of wine ebbed and flowed, driven by trade alliances, fashion, and politics.

As producers in different regions vied to capture markets for their wines, the idea of offering a guarantee of quality began to take hold, particularly in Bordeaux, which "classified" its wines in 1855. In 1935 France passed its laws of Appellation d'Origine Contrôlée, specifying vineyard area, winemaking methods, grape varieties, maximum crop per hectare, and minimum alcoholic strength. Similar systems of regulation were introduced in Italy, Germany, and Spain, and the idea of *terroir*—that the style of a wine reflects its provenance—gained in commercial significance.

QUALITY TO THE FORE
The 1855 Classification of the wines of Bordeaux established a hierarchy based on the assumption that the wines that sold for the highest prices must be of the finest quality.

HOMAGE TO BURGUNDY
Whether as a tribute to the Old World or a "signpost" to customers, this New World Pinot Noir is packaged in the slope-shouldered bottle traditional to Burgundy.

RAISING A TOAST
According to (oft-disputed) legend, the French monk Dom Pérignon should be thanked for the vinous miracle that is Champagne *(facing page)*.

A NEW WORLD OF WINE

New vineyards and wineries started to grow commercially in the New World after World War II (and the end of Prohibition in the US). In contrast to their European counterparts, New World winemakers, particularly in Australia and California, were not burdened by local tradition; they looked at export markets, identified the styles consumers preferred, and made wines to match. Over the last 60 years, "appellation"-style rules have been introduced and, although New World winemakers still have more scope to make a variety of different styles of wine, the more quality-conscious among them like their wines to show flavors and style that illustrate their provenance.

It's true that globalization has made its mark on wine. Today's winemakers readily share ideas and technology; and while the French Champagne houses set up vineyards as far afield as California and Chile, "flying" Australian and New Zealand winemakers are making their mark in French appellations. Quality control is now so widespread that cheaper wines have generally become more palatable, and there's certainly a plethora of "middle-of-the-road," easy-drinking wines available today. But it's not true, as some cynics say, that wine is "all starting to taste the same." Even where the ubiquitous Chardonnay is concerned, no one could mistake the green steeliness of Chablis for the oaky, exotic fruit fullness of a Californian wine. And remember, too, that for every Cabernet Sauvignon on the shelf, there's another really characterful wine standing nearby, made from distinctive local grape varieties and by producers fiercely proud of their region's traditions. In the following pages, we'll explore just how they do it.

SETTING THE STYLE

Compare a Granny Smith apple to a Cox's Orange Pippin: one is crispy and tart, the other has a floury flesh and a thinner skin. Just like apples, grape varieties have different colors, flavors, and textures, which influence the wine they make. With thousands of different varieties of grape, each with its own personality, that's  a lot of diversity! But this is only part of the story: the same grape variety can make very different wines depending on where it is grown. In a cool climate, Chardonnay produces crisp, dry, refreshing wines like Chablis, but in warmer parts of the world, it makes wines with more pungent and exotic flavors. The winemaker can also influence the style of a wine, adding oak flavors, for example, by aging wines in oak barrels. All these nuances, some subtle, some not so subtle, are what make wine so fascinating.

THE INFLUENCE OF GRAPE VARIETY

HEAVYWEIGHT GRAPES

Wine tastes like the grapes that made it. A simple truism, maybe. But wait! There are more than 4,000 different grape varieties that are used to make wine throughout the world, and each one has its own particular character, in terms of size of berry, color, and flavor, which will affect the taste of the wine it makes.

But don't be put off by that figure of 4,000; of these, just over a dozen rank as the most important for winemaking. The chief white varieties are Riesling, Chardonnay, Sauvignon Blanc, and Sémillon, with Muscat, Gewürztraminer, and Viognier following close behind. Of the red varieties, the most important are Cabernet Sauvignon, Merlot, Grenache, Syrah (or Shiraz), Tempranillo, Sangiovese, and Pinot Noir.

"Feel the oiliness of Sémillon compared with the pungent, refreshing texture of Sauvignon Blanc in Pouilly Fumé."

Rosemount Estates Sémillon *(left)* and Château de Tracy Pouilly Fumé *(right)*

BERRIES BIG AND SMALL

As with many things, size is very important when it comes to grapes. Anyone who has tasted wild strawberries will understand that small fruit often means huge flavor. The principle follows with grapes; generally, the bigger the berry, the lighter the wine will be in both color and structure. The smaller the berry, the more concentrated the resulting wine will be, because although the pulp still contains fruit sugars, it also contains less water to dilute the flavors. Small-berried varieties include Sémillon, Cabernet Sauvignon, Nebbiolo, and Sangiovese. Varieties that produce large berries include Sauvignon Blanc, Riesling, Pinot Noir, and Gamay. The former make full-bodied wines with plenty of concentrated fruit flavors, while wines made from the latter are usually lighter in style, relying on elegance of flavor rather than power.

But, another truism: size isn't everything. It is actually the skin of a grape that contains most of the flavors that set it apart from the rest. Thick-skinned grapes therefore tend to produce wines with very definite, strong flavors, whether they be ripe, fruity flavors in warm climates or green, grassy aromas in cooler climates. Skin color is also

THE TASTE OF SPAIN
Small-berried, thick-skinned Tempranillo produces deeply colored, well-structured wine with the capacity to age well. In Rioja, it produces Spain's premier red wine, but it is increasingly planted elsewhere.

REAPING THE REWARDS
Once, only aficionados knew that white Burgundy owed its greatness to the Chardonnay variety, here being harvested in Puligny-Montrachet *(facing page)*: today, it is a global superstar among grapes.

of paramount importance to the resulting wine. It doesn't always follow that white grapes make white wines and red grapes make reds. If the skins were removed from red or white grapes before pressing, the resulting juice would not be significantly different in color. Color in the wine comes from the skins, and the thicker the skins, the deeper and more concentrated the color.

THE ROLE OF TANNINS

The relative thickness of the grape's skin plays another key role in determining the resulting style of wine, because tannins are located in the skin. Tannins are bitter substances found in bark, wood, roots, and some fruits and vegetables; they are what coats your gums and makes them feel furry after eating spinach. Red winemakers like tannins because they "hold up" a wine, giving it "backbone" and helping it to age (see Taste Test: Tannin, pp.248–9). But the grapes must be ripe: unripe tannin makes stalky, bitter wine that—yes—makes your mouth feel furry. Thick-skinned red grapes generally make intensely colored, richly structured red wines with prominent tannins, while thin-skinned red grapes tend to make lighter, fruitier styles. Winemakers can blend together wines from different grapes to achieve exactly the style and body they want in their wine.

GRAPE CHOICES

Some wines are made from a blend of varieties, while others are the product of a single grape. Both can be great—so how does the winemaker decide which to do? In fact, how do they choose which grape varieties to grow in the first place?

Take, for example, red Burgundy and red Bordeaux wines. To the novice, Burgundy can seem complex and offputting, but actually it's a very simple, single-variety wine—100 percent Pinot Noir. Red Bordeaux, however, is a blend, of principally Cabernet Sauvignon, Cabernet Franc, and Merlot. How did this come about? The answer lies in a complex interrelationship between geography, climate, tradition, and law.

Climate is the most important factor a vinegrower takes into account when deciding which grapes to grow. Big berries with thin skins, such as Pinot Noir, ripen earlier than smaller, thicker-skinned varieties. That is why Pinot Noir is grown successfully in cooler climates with shorter summers. Conversely, Cabernet Sauvignon—a small and thick-skinned grape—needs longer on the vine; and if the weather is not kind and the grower is forced to pick before the grapes reach full ripeness, the resulting wines will taste harsh rather than fruity.

BLOOMING MARVELOUS
Every single grape (facing page) is a miniature wine factory, if the conditions are right. From the ripe flesh comes the sugary juice; the skins contribute color and bodybuilding tannins; and on the surface of the grape, the white "bloom" is composed of wild yeasts that trigger the fermentation process.

CABERNET SAUVIGNON WINE
The berries of Cabernet Sauvignon are small and thick-skinned, and very dark in color. The high proportion of tannin-bearing skins and seeds in the juice gives the wine a rich, warm, deep garnet color.

PINOT NOIR WINE
Thin-skinned Pinot Noir always makes a lighter-colored wine than that from thick-skinned Cabernet Sauvignon. There is a fresher, cherry note to the color, and the wine is also less opaque.

Although it may have warm summers, the Burgundy region lies on quite a northerly latitude—on a par with Zurich, Switzerland, or Budapest, Hungary. Limited, therefore, in their choice of red varieties, the growers have made an art form of the one they grow best—Pinot Noir.

Bordeaux, farther south, has more total hours of sunshine per year than Burgundy, and its maritime position also tempers and softens the climate. This makes it a suitable climate in which to grow long-ripening Cabernet Sauvignon. But in any given year, the weather can be temperamental, and cool, wet conditions often make harvest time stressful. So while Cabernet Sauvignon is the dominant grape here, most producers also grow Merlot and Cabernet Franc. The latter is a close cousin to Cabernet Sauvignon, but it has larger berries and so ripens slightly earlier, giving wine producers a good backup if the harvest-time conditions are difficult. Merlot also has larger berries than

Cabernet Sauvignon, thus ripening earlier. But in addition, it produces a rich, velvety wine, ideal for softening up a blend with Cabernet Sauvignon.

So, it is differences in climate that determined the choices of grapes in Burgundy and Bordeaux—so much so that they have been enshrined in the system of quality and labeling laws that governs all French wine. Red Burgundy must by law be made from Pinot Noir; red Bordeaux may contain Cabernet Sauvignon, Cabernet Franc, and Merlot. Similar laws apply in most of the wine regions of Europe, constraining the choice of varieties grown.

NEW WORLD PIONEERS

In the New World, we see exactly what happens when winemakers are not restricted by local tradition and law. They are free to plant whichever grape varieties they like, and they almost always name their wines after the grapes from which they are made. Inevitably, in the early days, New World growers chose to grow the grapes that made the popular classics of Europe—Chardonnay and Cabernet Sauvignon—although these were by no means copycat wines. As their wine industry evolved, so did their varietal wines, until each took on a distinct personality. Individual regions have become centers of excellence for individual varieties—witness Coonawarra Cabernet and Oregon Pinot Noir—and the best are world-class wines in their own right. And in the meantime, enterprising New World growers have also experimented with every grape variety imaginable to make surprising, exciting wines—Italian Nebbiolo in Australia, for example, or Austrian Blaufränkisch in Washington State.

SINGLE VARIETIES IN DEMAND

Wine drinkers around the world have embraced the labeling of wines by grape variety, rather than by origin, because it seems such an easy way to buy what you like. This approach to labeling is more common in the New World, but some European regions—for example, Alsace and Germany—have always produced and sold their wines by grape variety. But while it's true that the grape variety drives the wine's flavor, its style and perceived quality have as much to do with the sugar levels in the grapes when they are picked. And it's not just a simple equation of longer ripening improving the wine. The grower needs to achieve an optimum degree of ripeness—that is, the best balance possible between sugar and acidity in the grapes—to make a perfectly balanced wine. But as the berries ripen and the sugar content goes up, the acidity reduces, so the winemaker must choose exactly the right moment to harvest.

CONCENTRATED SWEETNESS

In Alsace and in Germany, and in other northerly European vine-growing areas, something else that has traditionally, and fundamentally, affected the

REFRACTOMETER
In the Mosel Valley in Germany, a winemaker uses a refractometer—a device that measures sugar content—to assess the ripeness of his grapes, checking that he is harvesting at the optimum time.

GRENACHE CACHET
Grenache wines from the New World have become so popular that producers in southern France, where the grape has long made wines labeled by region, are now choosing instead to name them after the grape.

FROZEN GRAPES
These frost-blackened white grapes *(facing page)* will be picked, usually in the middle of the night when it is coldest, and rushed to the winery to be pressed before they thaw to make sweet, concentrated "ice wine."

style of wine a grape will make is actually a fungus, albeit a distinguished one. *Botrytis cinerea*, or "noble rot," is a fungus that covers the grape and feeds on the moisture within it. The fungus also consumes almost all of the grape's acidity and up to a third of its sugar content. The affected grapes turn golden through purple to brown as they lose moisture. The juice pressed from grapes with noble rot is more like a sticky syrup and the style of wine is unique—sweet, yes, but with a complexity that only noble rot can give.

Another sweet style of wine is made possible by extremely low temperatures. To make this "ice wine," winemakers bravely leave grapes on the vine well into the winter in the hope that air temperatures will plummet, freezing the grapes on the vine. The water within the grapes freezes, but the sugars and other dissolved solids do not, so when the grapes are pressed, the water can be separated off, leaving behind intensely sweet juice.

"Grapes are just like people, with their different personalities and little idiosyncrasies—it's what makes the world of wine such a fascinating place!"

ALL THINGS CONSIDERED

So, while climate may set some parameters within which a grower must work when determining the grape variety he chooses, he will also take into account the style of wine he wants to make: red or white, obviously, but also sweetness (for whites) or fruitiness, light or full-bodied, as well as a price per bottle. And he must also work with the soil and *terroir* in his vineyard.

CLIMATE AND WEATHER

A TALE OF TWO TREES

I am a proud owner of two apple trees—one in my front yard and one in the back. They are both the same variety (English, of course!) and I planted them myself about five years ago. Both trees are doing very well, and we enjoy a tasty crop of delicious apples every fall. One tree, the one in the front yard, is much smaller than the other, and although it seems to produce smaller apples, they are definitely sweeter and tastier.

Now, I'm no expert on apples, but it's clear to me that the taste of the fruit is affected by the tree's situation. The tree in the back is in the middle of the yard, where it soaks up the plentiful rain and gets the sun all day long; while the tree in the front is sheltered by a wall, and catches only

"Climate determines the grape varieties that can be grown, but both climate and weather influence the style and quality of wine that those grapes make."

the evening sun—its position means that the soil around it is drier, too, and I like to think that its struggle for survival gives it more character than its backyard neighbor.

Grapes behave in exactly the same way. Vines can be grown almost anywhere in the world, but the quality of the grapes they produce is significantly different depending on the climate they enjoy. But it's not simply a matter of how hot or cold it is, or how much rain falls. If I have learned anything so far in my career, it is that nothing to do with vines and wines is that simple!

CLIMATE VERSUS WEATHER

The first distinction to be made is the one between climate and weather. "Climate" refers more to the geographical location of a region—whether it is generally cool or warm; inland or close to the sea; exposed and windy; prone to fog; or in close proximity to any geographical features, such as mountains or forests that can either shelter the region or influence the climatic conditions in any other way. In other words, the climate of a specific region is largely predictable. The weather is another matter altogether. Wherever we live in the world, we all know what the weather should be

SUN-LOVING VINES
All grapes need sun to ripen, but not all need to "bake" like these Barossa Valley vines. Countries as far north as England and Canada have climates in which winemaking is possible—but the weather in any given year can have a marked effect on the quality of the vintage.

CLIMATIC INFLUENCES
Geography and topography play as vital a part as how far north or south a vineyard lies. At Collioures, southwestern France *(facing page, above)*, the vines benefit from the moderating influence of the Mediterranean; in Mendoza, Argentina *(facing page, below)*, mountains shelter the vines.

MAXIMIZING SUNSHINE
On the Côte-Rôtie ("roasted slope") in the upper Rhône, France, vineyards occupy south-facing slopes, the vines aligned top to bottom to minimize the shade they cast on one another.

MAKING A MICROCLIMATE
Planted in rows, vines are carefully trained to create optimum ripening conditions; excess foliage is often trimmed in summer to expose the grapes to the sun *(facing page)*.

like, but experience tells us that we should always expect the unexpected. Too much heat and we complain; too much rain and we're miserable; and if it snows heavily, everything grinds to a halt! And every so often extreme weather conditions, such as hurricanes, heavy rain, or ice storms, completely overwhelm us.

When it comes to climate and weather, vines behave just like humans. They don't cope well with extreme weather, and they too have their climatic preferences: some varieties, such as Riesling, prefer a cooler climate; while others, like Syrah, like it warmer. But the finest grapes always come from a climate that allows them to grow slowly, with a long ripening period. That means a long, warm—not hot—summer and a dry, sunny fall. In these conditions, the grapes ripen with

elegantly complex fruit flavors but remain balanced with good acidity. If it is too hot through the summer and fall, the grapes may ripen too quickly, resulting in jammy, syrupy fruit flavors. Take South Australia as an example; here, the climate is generally warm and sunny but variations within it illustrate the point. The famous Barossa Valley, north of Adelaide, has a hot, dry climate. The land is generally flat and there is little rainfall during the summer months. The resulting Shiraz wines tend to be big and powerful, with lots of jammy fruit. Farther south in Coonawarra, the climate is cooler, helped by a sea breeze that comes off the Southern Ocean. The cooler air slows down the ripening process and the red wines from the region generally have a more elegant fruit quality as a result.

Climate can also differ greatly even within a relatively small vinegrowing region. In the upper reaches of the Rhône Valley in France, the vineyards hug the southeast-facing bank of the river, maximizing the grapes' exposure to sun. In Burgundy's elite Côte d'Or, where the Pinot Noir grape reigns supreme, every possible scrap of land,

WALLED FOR PROTECTION
At the Clos des Menuts estate in St-Émilion near Bordeaux, the vines are surrounded by low stone walls—these are designed to provide shelter from the prevailing winds.

WET FEET
Leafless Cabernet Franc vines in Bourgueil, France, stand in a flooded vineyard *(see facing page)*. When dormant, vines can survive extreme weather that would spell disaster later in the year.

whatever its exposure, is given over to vines: most grow on east-facing slopes, but as the hills curve in and out, some slopes face northeast and some southeast; some have a gentle gradient, while those at the top are steep. Even subtle differences like these can affect the climate within individual vineyards, so that the grapes from one ripen in a different way from those in its next-door neighbor.

WEATHER AND TIMING

Rainfall is a major preoccupation with vine-growers. Grape vines need about 27 in (680 mm) of rain in a year, and growers would prefer most of

that rain to fall during the winter and spring, when the vine is working hard to create buds and bunches of new fruit. We already know that grapes like a long, slow ripening period, so minimal rainfall during the summer and fall is ideal. Rainfall during the summer in a warm climate increases the risk of mildew and mold diseases, and rain at harvest time, whether in a warm or a cool climate, is also problematic: grapes covered in raindrops make diluted wine.

Conversely, at the other end of the growing season, vinegrowers would prefer it not to be too hot during the harvest, either, since the levels of acidity can fall very rapidly as grapes get overripe. Also, the fermentation process is made more difficult if harvested grapes arrive too hot at the winery. In regions where daytime temperatures are still very high during the fall, such as South Africa, Australia, Chile, and parts of southern Europe, grapes are often harvested through the night.

INFLUENCING THE CLIMATE

One major difference between climate and weather is that, while it is not possible to do anything about the weather, vinegrowers can, and often do, influence the climate in their particular vineyard. If conditions are very dry, they may be permitted to irrigate the vines, although they must be careful about how much water they give, and how often. If you water a vine, it will produce more grapes—but the resulting wine will be more dilute. Vines produce their best grapes when made to work hard to produce them; too much water does not encourage the roots to dig deep for nutrients.

And, while a gentle breeze can help keep the air around the vines dry and disease-free, if the climate is too windy, the vinegrower might build a wall or plant a row of tall-growing trees to act as a windbreak. The Rhône vinegrowing region in France suffers from the bitterly cold mistral wind that can reach speeds of up to 90 miles (145 km)

"The heat of the Barossa Valley brings out a richer side in Shiraz compared with wines made by this grape in the Rhône."

Grant Burge Barossa Valley Shiraz *(left)* and Gilles Robin Crozes-Hermitage *(right)*

per hour and is capable of stripping vines bare of their leaves or fruit. The landscape is therefore marked by lines of cypress or poplar trees, planted by vinegrowers to shelter their vineyards from the wind. However, while too much wind can be tempered and too little water can be remedied, unseasonal weather conditions can cause vinegrowers all sorts of problems, and extreme conditions can lead to catastrophe.

SEASONAL DEFENSES

In cooler climates, frost can be a killer! During the winter months, when vines are dormant, they are able to withstand bitterly cold temperatures, as low as –4°F (–20°C). But a hard frost occurring in late spring, when the buds are just breaking or the fruit is "setting"—when the flowers fade and fall away and the tiny grapes begin to form—can devastate a vineyard. Winemakers in the Northern Hemisphere have experienced this many times and have developed a number of different ways to "heat up" their vineyards; they burn bonfires through the night, or use large heaters, similar to the domestic patio heaters many of us have on our decks—these can be seen peppering vineyard landscapes at this crucial time of the year. It was thought in the past that the smoke from traditional braziers and oil burners had a protective effect (rather in the same way that a cloudy night is less

"The finest wines are grown where there is a 'microclimate' that provides the vines with individual and unique growing conditions."

prone to frost than a clear one), but new, higher-tech, smoke-free heating systems have proved this not to be the case. Sometimes (but of course, much more expensively) helicopters are mobilized to hover above the vineyards, keeping the air moving so that frost cannot form. Vinegrowers may also use helicopters and sprinkler systems to spray water on to the vines (as in Chablis), which will freeze rapidly, creating little protective ice cocoons around the buds or grapes.

ANTICIPATING DANGER

So, vinegrowers will exert as much influence as they can on the climatic and weather conditions in their vineyards. They know the climate and will manage their vineyards accordingly, and they will listen to the weather forecast and make attempts to ward off danger from specific events such as spring frosts. What they can't do anything about is severe, one-time occurrences, such as summer rain- or hailstorms. A hailstorm may destroy the vines in one vineyard while those of its neighbor remain unharmed and go on to produce good-quality wines. Localized events such as these create the differences between one vintage and another, or even between wine produced by one part of a vineyard compared with another.

PLANTING WINDBREAKS
This Mediterranean-style landscape is in fact in Washington State, where Seven Hills vineyard has followed the traditional European practice of planting lines of poplars to create natural windbreaks.

PREPARED FOR FROST
The formation of flower buds, and from them grapes, is a critical stage in the vinegrowing year. Frost can result in severe losses, and winemakers mobilize an army of heaters to stand sentinel over the vines *(facing page)*.

FROM THE GROUND UP: SOIL

MINERAL WEALTH

All gardeners know that shrubs, flowers, fruits, and vegetables can be fussy when it comes to soil. Plants might be able to survive across a range of conditions, but will reveal their true beauty or their best flavors only when planted in their favorite soil. Vines are no different.

A vine's roots have the task of taking up water and minerals from the soil. As with many things in life, hard work brings the richest rewards. A vine that grows in a rich, damp soil has to send out only shallow roots to draw up sufficient water and nutrients, feeding a dense growth of leaves and berries. The abundant berries tend to be watery and lacking in nutrient content, and typically make thin, uninteresting wines. In contrast, a vine growing

"Can you taste the soil of the vineyard in a glass of wine? You bet. Try a good northern Rhône red—the earth really speaks to you."

on a poorer, drier soil has to struggle to survive, sending its roots deeper in search of minerals and water. It produces fewer berries, but with a more concentrated and complex juice, which translates into wines with far more potential. There is a limit to how poor the soil can be, however. If it is too dry, the plants will "shut down" to prevent drought damage, and unless the vines are irrigated, the grapes' flavor will not develop to the fullest.

THE TASTE EQUATION

So, the best wines will always come from vines grown on well-drained, moderately fertile soil. If only it were so simple! In Pomerol and St-Émilion in Bordeaux, some of the world's finest vineyards stand on clay—a cold, wet soil, better suited to grape varieties that do not need warmth from the soil to get going. Here, early-ripening Merlot fares very well—much better than Cabernet Sauvignon. And in Germany's Mosel region, top-notch wines are grown on soil consisting almost entirely of shards of rock—but it is well-drained (vital given the heavy winter rains) and also warm: the slate absorbs any heat there is from the sun and releases it through the cold night, keeping the vine cozy. So while good soil has an important role in making good wine, this is clearly only part of the story.

GRAVEL HEATING
The great Bordeaux wines from the Médoc owe part of their character to the region's complex gravelly soils. Gravel acts as a radiator, storing the day's heat and releasing it at night, providing ideal growing temperatures.

TERRA ROSSA
The famous, rich red soil of South Australia's Coonawarra appellation *(facing page)* sits on top of well-drained limestone and produces some outstanding wines. Some parts of Coonawarra have black soil, and produce very different wines, even though they share the same limestone subsoil.

GROWING VINES

PREPARING TO PLANT

Growing vines is all about the fine balance between quality and quantity. The site for a new vineyard is chosen based on its *terroir*—an amalgamation of all the factors discussed on the previous pages: the climate of the region, the exposure of the vineyard itself, and its soil. The winemaker will already have an idea of the style of wine he (or she) wants to make and will accordingly have chosen the grape varieties to plant. How he actually grows the vines will also determine the style of wine produced, but perhaps even more importantly, it will profoundly affect its quality.

In order to produce the best-quality wine possible from his vineyard—whatever its size—the winemaker calculates the optimum yield from the land. He works out the number of vines he should plant: too dense a planting will result in the grapes and the lower leaves being shaded from the sun; too loose a planting and he simply won't grow enough grapes. The width of his rows will depend largely on how he intends to manage the vineyard. If he is going to prune and harvest by hand, the rows may be closer together; if he wants to use a tractor to tend to the vines, he will need to plant the rows with wider gaps between them.

ORIENTING THE VINES

Perhaps even more important than the density of planting is the direction of the rows; we already know that sunshine needs to get to the leaves and fruit to promote optimum ripening. The winemaker

therefore needs to plant his rows so that, as the sun moves during the day, all the vines in the vineyard get their fair share.

Before the vines are planted, the winemaker will also have decided what sort of training or trellising system he is going to use. Again, he must take the *terroir* into account; in a hot climate he may use the "goblet" system, where the vine forms a low bush that shades the grapes from too much heat; on a site where the soil is rich and encourages lots of growth, he might decide on the "Geneva Double Curtain," which trains the vines up and along a horizontal canopy and means that more grapes per vine can be ripened.

TIGHTLY PRUNED
Pinotage vines *(facing page)* at the Perdeberg cooperative in Paarl, South Africa, are grown in a compact "goblet" shape that lets the sun in from all sides while the leafy growth stops the grapes from scorching at midday.

UP AND OVER
At Firestone Vineyard, California *(below)*, the vines grow up and then cascade over overhead trellises, forming a "double curtain" of hanging stems that expose the maximum number of grapes to the sun.

HARDWORKING VINES
Vines close-planted in rows *(above)* in the dry, chalky soil of this area of the Languedoc in France must compete for water and nutrients. This reduces the yield from the vine, and results in grapes with a more concentrated flavor.

CALCULATING THE CROP

All proficient vinegrowers know how many bunches of grapes they intend to grow on each individual vine planted in their vineyard. The smaller the number of bunches per vine, the more complex and well structured the wine will be. This is of particular importance in cooler regions where the climate can impair the ripening process. In order to make consistently high-quality wines every year, the vinegrower must not overestimate the number of grapes he can realistically expect to ripen to perfection on his vines; the fewer grapes he ripens, the more expensive his wine will need to be to cover his costs. In warm regions where there are fewer climatic pitfalls, a larger harvest of ripe grapes can be produced consistently from year to year, allowing prices for the wines to be much more competitive. So it is no surprise that the average number of bunches grown on each individual vine is five in Europe compared with ten in Australia.

To achieve the correct number of bunches per plant, the vines need to be pruned several times during the growing season. Pruning of new shoots takes place in early spring; buds are thinned in late spring; and, most heartbreakingly, whole bunches of grapes are removed during the summer so that the vine can concentrate more energy into the ones that are left. It's a very tricky process; what if there are strong winds just after you have taken off the excess buds, and more buds are lost? Or there could be a hailstorm that affects half of your vineyard, just days after you have removed whole bunches of grapes from the vines. Nobody said growing grapes was a stress-free way of life!

Of course, pruning by hand is labor-intensive and therefore more expensive than machine pruning, adding to the cost of the wine. However, some sites, particularly those situated on slopes rising up from a river—notably the Rhine in Germany or the Rhône in France—are too steep for machines to negotiate.

NO SHORT CUTS
Hand-pruning the vines is a slow, labor-intensive business but is vital to restrict the amount of growth the plants make. Of an abundance of potential shoots, often as few as only two or three per vine are retained to bear the crop.

ALARM SYSTEM
Powdery mildew is a hazard when vines are closely planted in a warm climate. These rose bushes will be the first to show the disease, allowing the vinegrower time to give the vines preventive treatment.

NET GAIN
An ancient, gnarled vine stem holds little appeal for hungry mammals, but these young vine plants (facing page) need "sleeves" of netting to protect them from gnawing rodents and rabbits if they are to mature and bear fruit.

PROTECTING THE VINES

Disease control is another of the vinegrower's preoccupations. Vines are susceptible to all kinds of pests and diseases, ranging from microscopic fungi and bacteria to hungry herbivores. Vinegrowers are troubled by wild boar in parts of Italy, raccoons in California, and kangaroos in Australia! A period of warm, wet weather can induce downy mildew, and dry weather might bring on powdery mildew, both of which are fungal diseases that can be controlled by spraying the vines with fungicide. Rose bushes are even more susceptible to these diseases, so vinegrowers often plant roses at the end of each row of vines; the rose will succumb to mildew before the vines and thus acts as an early warning system for the vinegrower.

Insects can carry disease as well as causing direct damage; around the world, chemical insecticides are increasingly being replaced by more sustainable methods of biological control.

Birds can be another major pest, picking especially on buds and young shoots. Vinegrowers in Chablis often use helicopters to spray their vines with water on cold nights during bud break. The water freezes, creating a little "igloo" around each bud, thus protecting the buds from hungry birds.

TO WATER OR NOT TO WATER?

One of the main causes of stress in any plant is lack of water; on the other hand, too much water results in watery grapes. Until very recently, the irrigation of vineyards was banned in Europe, probably because lack of rainfall has not been a problem year after year and also because wine regulators have understood that quality is more important than quantity. Irrigation is, however, prevalent in the New World, where vinegrowers do not labor under century-old winemaking traditions and regulations. If vineyards in Australia, New Zealand, or California need extra water, they get it—but only under strict controls. The usual method used is drip irrigation; a pipe runs along the length of the row of vines, and a small hole in the pipe delivers water to each vine. The amount of water given to each plant is literally controlled drop by drop, and the humidity of the soil in the vineyard is measured constantly to ensure that the vines are not being overwatered. Witnessing the success of this sort of irrigation in the New World, vinegrowers in the hotter areas of Europe, such as parts of Spain, Italy, and the Douro Valley in Portugal, have successfully fought for the right to water their vines—but only in exceptionally dry years when their vines need help to ripen the grapes.

"The winemaker's skill lies in judging exactly how many grapes to grow— yields that are too high can mean lesser-quality wines."

MACHINE HARVESTING
Using machinery to prune the vines and pick the grapes may lack finesse, but seems to have no effect on the health of the vines. Tractors are a boon when bad weather is forecast and speed of harvest is vital.

HARVESTING BY HAND
These brightly colored plastic crates *(facing page)* are used in many areas in place of the more picturesque pickers' baskets, but the traditional migration of seasonal workers and casual student labor following the vintage from region to region remains unchanged.

BRINGING IN THE CROP

Of course, all the painstaking efforts of the vinegrower are geared toward producing optimum-quality grapes at the harvest. Picking grapes at optimum ripeness is one of the most difficult things for the grower to get right. Weather that is too cool during, or at the end of, the growing season will slow down the ripening process and the resulting wines may be too acidic; too hot a ripening period may result in overripe grapes that produce flabby wines with little structure. The worst-case scenario of all is rain during picking; the grapes will arrive wet at the winery, resulting in diluted grape juice.

As when pruning, the grower will have planted his vines with an idea of whether he intends to hand-pick or machine-harvest his grapes. If his vines are planted on steep slopes, he has no choice other than to hand-pick, but he may choose this option even if his vineyard is on flat ground. Mechanical harvesters are fast, repeatedly hitting the vines so that the grapes, either loose berries or whole bunches, fall off into the machine. However, they cannot select the best grapes on the vine in the same way that trained pickers can. The equation is a simple one: machines provide speed (and therefore less risk) but less quality control at a cheaper price, while humans provide good quality control but at the risk of a longer picking period and at a higher cost.

MAKING WINE

THE WINEMAKER'S ART

Once the freshly picked grapes have arrived at the winery, the winemakers come into their own. Certainly the grapes will already have been chosen with a specific style of wine in mind, and the climate and soil will already have stamped their own authority on the flavors present inside the grapes. But here in the winery, the style of the wine can be influenced still further, by deciding how hard to press the grapes, at what temperature to allow the fermentation, whether to use oak barrels—the options are wide and varied, and the winemaker is in ultimate control.

Wine is essentially fermented grape juice. Grapes contain the sugars fructose and glucose,

"In the California Chardonnay I taste rich, opulent American oak; in the Chablis, the glint of stainless steel."

Stags' Leap Chardonnay *(left)* and Domaine Laroche Chablis *(right)*

and when the skin is broken and the grape juice is left to ferment, these sugars are converted into alcohol. Fermentation is an entirely natural process that is carried out by yeasts—microscopic fungi. Yeasts survive by breaking down sugars to release energy, in the same way that we digest food to sustain life. The key difference is that the waste product of their digestion is alcohol. Yeasts are present in the air, and some winemakers rely on these natural yeasts as the agents of fermentation of their wines; however, most use specially cultured yeasts, which behave more predictably and produce wines of greater consistency.

FROM VINEYARD TO WINERY

Getting the harvested grapes from the vineyard to the winery is a race against time. If the grapes are packed in overly large boxes, the fruit at the bottom of the pile will be crushed under the weight of the rest. While this might not be such a problem for red wines, if the skins of white grapes are split a long time before they reach the winery, essential aromas will be lost and the wine may suffer.

At the winery, the grapes are destemmed (the stalks are removed) and crushed to create a pulpy mixture called "must"; this is then usually

CRUSHING AND STEMMING
Very few wines are trodden by foot today! Most grapes for red wines are lightly crushed and destemmed by machine before being pumped into a vat for fermentation, skins and all.

MODERN WINERY
Large, easy-to-clean stainless steel tanks *(facing page)* with integral temperature control systems are ideal for producing crisp, clean white wines. Hygiene is critical at the winery; if harmful microorganisms enter the wine, they can ruin it.

FERMENTATION TANKS
Oak vats, such as these at the Louis Jadot winery in Burgundy, are traditionally used to ferment wine. However, nowadays many wineries use vats made of stainless steel.

MATURATION IN BARRELS
Many wines are aged in oak barrels *(facing page)*—the smaller the better—which improves the character and complexity of the wine, adding flavors of vanilla and butter.

flash-pasteurized to suppress the growth of wild yeasts and other microorganisms in the grapes that might interfere with the production of the wine. Fermentation can now begin.

THE FERMENTATION PROCESS

As a rule, for white wine, the juice is separated from the skins and seeds and is fermented alone, while for reds, the skins, seeds, and juice are all fermented together. The red grape skins rise to the top of the must and form a "cap." Yeast is added to the juice, and the mixture may be heated to accelerate the conversion of sugars to alcohol— a process that takes from 5 to 15 days. In red-wine production, the juice is regularly pumped from the bottom of the vat and back in at the top over the cap of skins. This increases contact between the juice and the skins so that the maximum amount of color, aroma, and tannin is extracted from the skins. Most rosé wines are made in the same way as reds: red grapes are pressed very lightly, and skin contact with the juice is allowed only until the wine attains the required color.

Temperature is an important factor in fermentation. For red wines, a low temperature means a longer fermentation, which results in delicate but lively and complex wines with fresh fruit character; higher temperatures increase color and tannin extraction to give deeper-colored, richer wines. Most red wines are fermented at between 77°F and 86°F (25–30°C); white wines are fermented at between 50°F and 63°F (10–17°C).

Some winemakers use an alternative method of fermentation, called carbonic maceration, to produce lighter-bodied, fruity red wines. Whole bunches of grapes are put into the vat and carbon dioxide gas is pumped in to blanket them, so that fermentation takes place in the absence of oxygen. The grapes are then pressed and fermented in the normal way to complete the conversion of sugar to alcohol. This method produces light red wines with soft fruit and a telltale pear aroma.

After fermentation, the wine is racked (drawn off) into clean vats or barrels to separate it from the "lees"—the sediment of dead yeast cells and, in red wines, skins and seeds. When making red wines and some fuller styles of white, the winemaker then allows another type of fermentation to take place. In this second or "malolactic" fermentation, appley malic acid in the wine is converted to the softer lactic acid (as found in milk), which gives a rounder, fuller feel to the wine. In white wines especially, it imparts a buttery quality. The winemaker prevents malolactic fermentation when making crisp, white wines by keeping temperatures cool.

BARRELS AND BOTTLES

Some wines are bottled right away, but others undergo deliberate aging, in steel or wooden vats or in old or new oak barrels. Most fine wine is aged in oak barrels or casks to give it an extra layer of complexity. Oak barrels impart flavors of vanilla or toastiness into the wine. The winemaker can control these flavors by specifying the country of origin of the oak used in the barrels, and its level of "toast." When a barrel is made, its interior is heated, or toasted, activating aromatic compounds in the wood that imbue the wine with vanilla and roasted notes. The winemaker orders barrels with a light, medium, or heavy toast, depending on how much oak character he desires.

Before bottling, wine may require blending (where wines from two or more grape varieties are mixed together), filtering (to remove sediment), and stabilizing (adding sulfur dioxide to prevent the growth of residual yeast or bacteria).

"I love the unique and fascinating aromas of fortified wines—each has its own perfect balance of intense, sweet complexity, captured in time."

FORTIFIED WINES

Fortified wines, such as sherry, port, and Madeira, are made in exactly the same way as table wines, but have extra alcohol, usually a grape brandy, added either during the fermentation process or after it has finished, giving them an alcohol content ranging from 14 to 23 percent ABV. Colors may be white, amber, bright red, or dark red. Both cask- and bottle-aging play important roles in realizing the full character of most fortified wines. In Madeira, famously, the wine is heated to caramelize the sugars for a unique flavor.

SPARKLING WINES

Sparkling wines are usually white, but may be red or rosé, and have an alcohol content similar to table wines. In order to have enough "oomph" to carry the bubbles, they are deliberately made with high acidity that would be most unpalatable in a still wine. The winemaking method is the same as for still wines, with one major difference. When grape juice ferments, carbon dioxide gas is released as a by-product; in still wines, this gas simply escapes into the atmosphere, but in sparkling wines, it is kept to provide the essential "fizz." Fermentation must therefore take place in a closed space to keep the gas dissolved in the wine.

Most sparkling wine undergoes a first fermentation as normal to produce a still white wine. It then undergoes a second fermentation, either in the bottle in which it is sold (*méthode champenoise*, also called *méthode traditionnelle* and, in South Africa, *cap classique*), or in a sealed tank, after which it is bottled under pressure (tank method or *cuve close*).

In the *méthode champenoise*, as the wine or blend is bottled, a small dose of a mixture of wine, sugar, and yeast is added. This sets off the second fermentation in the bottle, which, crucially, creates bubbles of carbon dioxide and increases the alcohol content. As the wine matures, the dead yeast cells (lees) impart their flavor—the longer a wine spends on its lees (anything between 15 months and seven years), the better its quality. The yeast sediment is then removed from the bottle using *remuage*, or riddling. In this process, the bottle is turned (by hand or mechanically) very slowly until it is upside down, causing the lees to slip into a plastic cup in the neck, held in place by a crown cap. The sediment is then removed using *dégorgement*— freezing the wine in the bottle neck to take out the sediment—and the bottle is sealed with a cork.

END OF THE LINE
Once the wine is bottled and corked, the neck is encased in a capsule—a sheath of foil or plastic—although nowadays, many producers use a biodegradable wax disk instead.

CHAMPAGNE *PUPITRES*
In these traditional racks, called *pupitres (facing page)*, upended bottles of Cristal Champagne are hand-turned by the *remueur* so that the yeasts gradually gather in the neck of the bottle.

VINE TO WINE

A winemaker's job is never done. Be it winter, spring, summer, or fall, there are always plenty of jobs to be done, either outdoors in the vineyard or indoors in the winery, or even underground in the cellar. Of course, new materials, machinery, and technology have revolutionized the way wine is made, but the  best winemakers still care for their vines and wines as they do their own children. In spring, when the vines are flowering, they sit up all night burning stoves in the vineyard to keep late frosts at bay; once the grapes are gathered and pressed, they keep a round-the-clock vigil in the winery, anxiously watching over the fermentation. And when the time is right, they proudly ask their friends to taste the new vintage, hoping that the young wines they have raised will behave themselves impeccably.

THE WINEMAKER'S YEAR

FROM GRAPE TO BOTTLE

A winemaker's life is governed by the twin demands of his (or her) vineyard and winery. He needs to nurture and protect his vines through their 12-month life cycle, while at the same time creating and raising his wines from previous years in the winery. The following pages describe the typical pattern of activity for a traditional European winemaker. This pattern shifts in phase by six months for winemakers in the Southern Hemisphere, and is of course strongly influenced by differing climates around the world and even different weather patterns from year to year in any one region. Like anyone who makes their living from the soil, the winemaker must always be on the alert and ready to adapt to any situation, foreseen or otherwise, in his bid to produce the best wines he can.

TOPPING OFF
Wine evaporates in barrels, but air spaces must not be allowed to form or the wine may oxidize. The casks rest with their bungs uppermost to permit topping-off.

GATHERING PRUNINGS
Bundles of vine prunings *(facing page)* will make useful bonfires when the vines need protection from frost.

LATE WINTER IN THE VINEYARD

Most vines are dormant during January in the Northern Hemisphere (July in the Southern Hemisphere). The vines are bare, unless the winemaker has left grapes on the plants, hoping for botrytis or for frost or snow to freeze the grapes so that he can make ice wine *(see p.23)*. In February (August down under), the first signs of life appear; as the soil warms up, the vine's roots start taking up water again and the sap rises and "weeps" out of the pruning cuts that were made after harvest. This is the sign for the winemaker to prune the vines before their spring growth. The problem growers face when timing spring pruning is that newly pruned vines are at their most vulnerable to frost. But if the grower waits, and does not prune his vines until after the danger of frost has passed—which can be as late as mid-May—the growth of the vine will be seriously retarded and the ripening period for the grapes will be that much later in the fall, thus exposing them to the dangers of early frost in October.

LATE WINTER IN THE WINERY

Work in the winery during the dark days of winter is concentrated on keeping the barrels containing wine from the last vintage full to the brim to prevent oxidation. In February (July in the Southern Hemisphere), the winemaker begins to rack newly fermented wine off its lees *(see p.51)* and into clean vats or barrels for maturation. As March approaches, the first of the new wines—those not destined to be aged—become ready for filtering, perhaps blending, and bottling. Any extra time in the winery is used to bottle older wines, labeling and packaging them for shipment to customers at home or abroad.

SPRING IN THE VINEYARD

During March or April (September or October in the Southern Hemisphere), buds begin to break on the vines. This happens to different grape varieties at different times, depending on whether they are early or late ripeners, and at different times in different years depending on the weather. The type of soil the vines are planted in also influences the time of budbreak; clay, which is cold, delays it, while warmer sandy soil brings it on earlier.

Pruning continues through March, and the vineyard is plowed between rows to aerate the soil. These are difficult months for the winemaker because the threat of frost is ever-present; vine prunings are often burned in the vineyard at night to try to keep the air surrounding the vines warm and protect the new buds. The buds are also at risk from pests and diseases, and preventive sprays may be used at this time of the year. And as the soil warms up, new vines can be planted in the vineyard to replace any old ones that have had to be grubbed up.

SPRING IN THE WINERY

In the winery, the racking of last year's wines into clean new barrels must be completed before the second, malolactic fermentation *(see p.43)* starts. Many winemakers talk romantically of some mysterious tie between the vines outside and the wines indoors as, when the sap rises in the vines, the wines inside start their second fermentation.

The racking of the new wines signals the start of a relatively quiet time in the winery, although as temperatures rise, the barrels must be topped-off on a daily basis. As much as five percent of the wine can evaporate through the wood of the barrels—the portion of wine that disappears in this way is romantically dubbed "the angels' share."

Any spare time is used for bottling older wines. Bottling lines vary greatly in sophistication from one winery to another—some may have a more rudimentary system requiring labels to be applied by hand, while other wineries have high-tech, mechanized lines and therefore require a minimum number of workers.

LIFE BEGINS AGAIN
Even from the oldest, most gnarled vines, buds break and new shoots grow along the whole length of the stem *(facing page)* as the sap continues to rise.

UNDER THE PLOW
Plowing between the vines aerates the soil and helps it to warm up, and also eliminates the first generation of spring weeds that have germinated.

RACKING NEW WINE
Last year's vintage is carefully transferred out of the barrels in which the alcoholic fermentation took place and into clean casks, leaving the sediments behind.

SPRING TO SUMMER IN THE VINEYARD

May and June (November and December in the Southern Hemisphere) are probably the most stressful months for the winemaker, because this is when the vines flower, determining—in part—the quantity of the vintage. Flowering lasts for about ten days, during which, ideally, sunshine and a light breeze ensure that the flowers are pollinated, fertilization takes place, and the fruit "sets." If there is heavy rain, a sharp frost, strong winds, or, even worse, hail, the vines may lose flowers or embryo bunches, resulting in a reduced or even devastated harvest. Winemakers will not think twice about sitting out in the vineyard all night long at this time of year, burning braziers to keep frost at bay. More affluent growers use helicopters to hover over their vineyards on extremely cold nights. Apart from keeping the neighbors awake, this keeps the air moving and thus prevents the formation of frost on the vines. Unfortunately, no one has yet come up with effective ways to fight the other elements! After the vines have flowered, some of the new shoots are pruned, leaving the best ones to be tied to the training wires. The soil around the vines is turned over again to prevent the growth of weeds, and the winemaker may spray against the fungal disease oidium, familiar to rose growers as powdery mildew, which attacks vine leaves and shoots.

SPRING TO SUMMER IN THE WINERY

All this activity in the vineyard doesn't mean that the winery is quiet: wines from the previous year need to be racked again after the second fermentation is finished. Hopefully the weather outside is warmer now—during the day at least— but this means that, inside, evaporation of the wines in barrels or casks can increase, so extra vigilance is required to keep them all filled to the brim. Some older barrels may show signs of weeping from between the staves and will therefore need to be repaired.

"GREEN" PRUNING
Vines are prolific growers, and left to themselves will produce a tangle of vigorous shoots. The grower must prune unwanted shoots away to concentrate the vine's energy into bearing fruit on those that remain.

VINE FLOWERS
These tiny clumps, correctly known as "embryo bunches," develop into grapes, and are the first indication to the winemaker of the potential yield from his vines this year.

SPRAYING VINES
A preventive spray *(facing page)* at this time helps to minimize the risk of powdery mildew developing later in the season. Also known as oidium, this fungal disease is encouraged by hot, dry weather.

SUMMER IN THE VINEYARD

By the beginning of July (January in the Southern Hemisphere), the fruit set is complete and each tiny berry has started to expand into a recognizable grape. Now is the time that the winemaker can really start to estimate how plentiful the harvest will be. Shoots and leaves are pruned back in order to let air circulate, preventing disease from building up, and to allow maximum sunlight onto the grapes. During August (February in the Southern Hemisphere), when the red grape varieties begin to turn color (the French term for this is *véraison*), some of the bunches of grapes, both red and white, may be removed. This so-called "green harvest" reduces the size of the crop, hopefully resulting in better quality in the grapes that remain. The young grapes can be very tempting for hungry birds at this time of the year, and winemakers may use nets to keep them off the vines.

Many winemakers also use this time for weeding between the rows of vines, to keep their vineyards looking neat and tidy. Others prefer to allow the weeds to grow tall; they then mow them down and plow them back into the soil. This serves to both break up the soil around the vines and provide them with extra nutrients as the weedy growth rots down underground.

As the red grape varieties start to turn from green to red, this serves as a reminder to the winemaker to prepare for harvest: he must check

that all the equipment he needs is in good working order, and also make sure a workforce has been commissioned to be on standby as soon as picking starts. Many producers use the same band of local or migrant grape-pickers year after year.

SUMMER IN THE WINERY

During the summer months, the winery and cellar must be kept as cool as possible to protect the maturing wines. To this end, during a heat wave, cellar doors are shut and, as evaporation is a major danger, the winemaker has to be extra-vigilant that casks of wine are kept full to the brim to prevent oxidation. Since there is a slight lull in the amount of work to do in the vineyard, this is also a good time for the winemaker to work on bottling wines from previous vintages that are still in barrel. To clear the winery floor and allow scrubbing down before the new harvest arrives, the wines from the previous year's vintage will by now have been moved to the "second-year cellar" to join the older wines, staying there for as long as the winemaker decides before being either used as part of a blend or bottled directly from the barrel.

NET GAIN
Birds know as well as the winemaker that the ripening grapes are becoming a sweet and tasty treat, and the vines may need netting *(facing page)*.

CHANGING COLOR
Véraison, the sign that the grapes are ripening, shows that a chemical reaction is taking place inside each grape, increasing the sugar content.

HARVEST TIME

The grapes continue to ripen and change color and are usually ready to be picked in mid- to late September (mid- to late February in the Southern Hemisphere), although the timing varies from year to year depending on the weather. Hordes of temporary workers, all needing food and accommodation, begin to arrive at the winery, ready to pick the grapes. White grapes are harvested before red varieties so that they retain a higher acidity; the whole harvesting process can take up to a month. In October (March in the Southern Hemisphere), after all the grapes have been picked, the vineyard is fertilized, often with the pressed grapeskins, and plowed.

The frenzy of activity in the vineyard is matched by that in the winery at this time of the year. Everything—the pressing vats, the stainless steel fermentation vats, the wooden fermentation barrels, the floors and walls—has been scrubbed, disinfected, and rinsed in preparation for the arrival of the first grapes of the vintage. As the grapes arrive, they are spread on tables or conveyor belts and sorted for quality. Bits of stem, leaves, or stalks are removed, as well as any berries that have not set and swollen properly—as well as any grapes the winemaker just doesn't like the look of! The grapes are then put into the press, and the winemaking process begins. Key winemaking staff may bring their sleeping bags, since they must nurse the new wines through the fermentation process, whatever the time of day or night.

BRINGING IN THE CROP
Red grapes *(facing page)* will be crushed at the winery and can be handled roughly; white grapes may stay in their picking crates in transit to keep them intact.

SORTING GRAPES
Nimble-fingered winery workers sort though the grapes as they arrive, using tiny shears to trim diseased or undeveloped grapes from the bunches.

THE WINEMAKER'S YEAR

WINE STYLES

WINTER IN THE VINEYARD

After all the noise and commotion of the harvest, November (April in the Southern Hemisphere) is a quiet month in the vineyard. As temperatures fall and the days shorten, the vines enter dormancy and the sap stops flowing. If all the grapes have been picked, the vinegrower prunes off the fruited stems and plows again, moving soil over the roots of the vines to protect them from frost. Some growers, however, choose to leave grapes on the vines well into December (May in the Southern Hemisphere) in order to make sweet wines. As the sap stops flowing, any grapes left on the vine begin to dehydrate and the sugar content becomes enhanced. Other growers, in areas where the climate is conducive, will be hoping for the appearance of botrytis or "noble rot" *(see pp.22–3)* on the grapes, which allows them to make sweet wines of greater complexity.

WINTER IN THE WINERY

In the winery, even the biggest red wines from the year's harvest will usually have finished their first fermentation by Christmas, and few winemakers can resist inviting in a few friends for a sneak preview of the new vintage! New wines destined to be drunk young may be prepared for bottling by being "fined" and transferred to a clean vat. Fining involves adding a clarifying agent—traditionally whisked egg white—which sinks through the wine, taking any particles with it as it goes, and arrives at the bottom as sediment, making it easy to draw off the clear young wine.

TASTING FROM THE BARREL
When the alcoholic fermentation is finished, the winemaker begins to form a very definite picture of his new wine and its aging potential.

ALL QUIET IN THE VINEYARD
By midwinter, the vines enter their dormant phase *(facing page)*—they drop their leaves and the sap retreats, leaving them impervious to cold.

FINDING YOUR STYLE

Everything a winemaker does—from choosing where to site his vineyard, and which grape varieties to plant, through to how he makes his wine—goes towards setting the style of wine he produces. When you buy wine, the range of brands and producers can be bewildering; that's why it's useful to identify  the styles of wine that you like, and use these as a starting point to learn more and broaden your horizons. Wherever your tastes lie, they will be affected by occasion; you may enjoy one style of wine—say, a dry Riesling from Australia—with a picnic on the beach, while a big, chunky California Cabernet Sauvignon is your perfect partner with venison on a cold winter evening by the fire. There are no rules when it comes to finding your style; it's down to personal taste, experience, and, above all, having fun!

READING A WINE LABEL

A WORLD OF CHOICE

The international wine trade has blossomed over the past 20 years and—in theory—it has never been easier to buy good wine. If you have deep pockets, a private wine consultant can help you put together a great cellar; and there are plenty of books, magazines, websites, and wine clubs that can guide you to a good bottle. But, inevitably, we still find ourselves in that familiar position—staring at a wall of wine in a store, wondering which to choose. And decoding a wine label is not an easy job, because there is so much variation in the type and amount of information given.

VINTAGE WINES

It is a popular misconception that "vintage" wine means wine of superior quality, and that if a bottle has a year on the label, the wine "must be good." The word "vintage" on a wine label simply means the year in which the grapes were grown—it does

"Sometimes, the more information a winemaker tries to give you on the label, the more confusing it becomes! You need to know just what to look for."

not carry with it any judgment of quality. Good vintages are those years when weather conditions in a particular vine-growing region were just right to produce good wine. In parts of the world with a consistent and predictable climate year on year—Australia or Chile, for example—vintage makes little difference, but elsewhere, the weather can greatly influence the quality of the wine. There are special charts that rank vintages for different regions according to quality, and these—coupled with expert advice—can be a useful guide when buying wines at the upper end of the price range. But they should be used with caution; a localized hailstorm may devastate vines on one side of a valley, but leave the other side untouched. And while a good producer will usually be able to make a fine wine in a "bad" vintage, a bad producer may still struggle in a "good" vintage.

The key, as ever, is to seek out wines made by reputable producers. But this is not information that we all readily have to hand when choosing a wine for dinner. And always sticking to names we know and trust can prevent us from discovering new, perhaps even more enjoyable—occasionally magnificent—wines. So what else can labels tell us about the quality of the wine within the bottle?

WINES FOR KEEPING
Seek advice before investing in wines to "lay down"; the great clarets and Sauternes from Bordeaux command high prices.

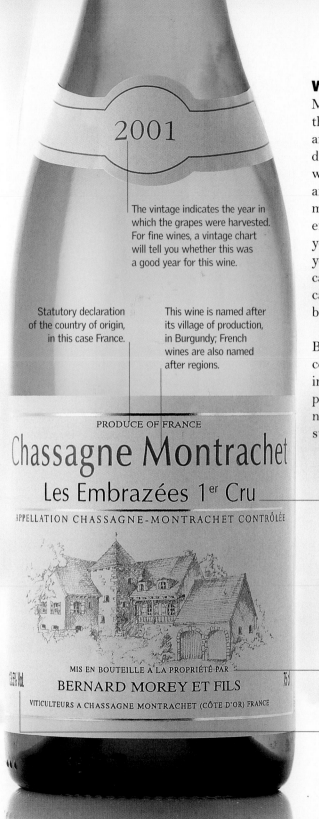

2001

The vintage indicates the year in which the grapes were harvested. For fine wines, a vintage chart will tell you whether this was a good year for this wine.

Statutory declaration of the country of origin, in this case France.

This wine is named after its village of production, in Burgundy; French wines are also named after regions.

PRODUCE OF FRANCE

Chassagne Montrachet

Les Embrazées 1er Cru

APPELLATION CHASSAGNE-MONTRACHET CONTRÔLÉE

MIS EN BOUTEILLE À LA PROPRIÉTÉ PAR

BERNARD MOREY ET FILS

VITICULTEURS A CHASSAGNE MONTRACHET (CÔTE D'OR) FRANCE

Les Embrazées is a designated area within Chassagne Montrachet; 1er (premier) cru means the wine is a "first growth" *(see p.64)*. Below is confirmation that the village has its own appellation and that this wine meets its standards.

Above the name of the producer is confirmation that the wine was bottled at the estate—a good sign.

Alcoholic content, expressed as a percentage of the volume.

WHAT'S IN A NAME?

Many wine-lovers like to think—or pretend—that they know exactly what they are buying, but there are now so many wines on the market that it is difficult even for wine experts to know exactly what lies behind the label, and some wine producers and merchants have become very adept at marketing their wines via a misleading label. For example, many people like Chardonnay, and if you saw an Australian "Colombard Chardonnay," you might be tempted. But the Colombard grape can make up 80 per cent of the blend, and, in that case, the wine will not taste like a typical Chardonnay but will instead be quite neutral in flavor.

There is no global classification of wine quality. But many countries, or regions within those countries, have come to realize that integrity is important for long-term sales and so have put in place a set of rules that define what may and may not be included on the label. Nowhere is this more strictly adhered to than in France.

DECODING A LABEL

Typically, a label will carry the name of the winery or producer, the country and region of origin, the style of the wine, its alcohol content, and details of bottling. It may include the name of the vineyard, the grape variety (or varieties) used to make the wine, and details of the vintage (the year the grapes were grown). It may also carry some form of quality classification, awarded by the government of the country of origin.

READING A WINE LABEL

WINE STYLES

FRANCE

The highest quality classification for French wines is Appellation d'Origine Contrôlée (AOC or AC), which covers about 40 percent of the country's production. If you see AOC on a label, you will know that the wine has been made in a specific named region (the appellation), and according to set quality standards. Depending on the region, AOC wines may have additional designations: Burgundies, for example, carry the titles *grand cru* and *premier cru* to reflect the highest and second-highest quality, respectively, and Bordeaux wines have their own distinct classifications.

The next level of classification is Vin Délimité de Qualité Supérieure (VDQS), which covers just 1 percent of wines, most of which are consumed in France. This classification is commonly seen on wines aspiring to AOC status. Below this is Vin de Pays (VdP; country wine), which covers 25 percent of French production. This classification was established in 1968 to recognize improvements in quality by producers of regional French wines. It allows them to put information on their labels, such as the place of origin and the grape varieties used. The total area covered by each appellation is variable; sometimes it is a large region, such has Vins de Pays d'Oc, which covers four French departments, and sometimes it is a small zone. Many Vin de Pays wines are good for everyday drinking, and some are truly excellent. Look for those made by enthusiastic producers from Australia and elsewhere in the New World, who are using new technology to breathe fresh life into old, established French vineyards, especially in the Languedoc-Roussillon region. The lowest category, Vin de Table (VdT; table wine), covers 28 percent of production, almost all of which is consumed in France. Also known as *vin ordinaire*, this wine is not for keeping, and its robust character means that it is often drunk mixed with water.

There is no doubt that the region around the city of Bordeaux produces some of the great wines of the world. There is no single system that classifies Bordeaux's 57 appellations, and different producers use different terms for wines of similar quality. The famous Bordeaux Classification of 1855 divided red wines, especially those of the Médoc, into five quality classes, or *crus* (growths), the best being the *premiers crus*, the next the *deuxièmes crus*, and so on. Below these were the *crus*

FRENCH COUNTRY WINE

A Vin de Pays may be simple, quaffable, everyday drinking, or it can be a more complex wine that simply does not, geographically, fall within any of the higher French quality regions. This Merlot has been given a flowing, evocative name, but "Merlot" tells you a great deal more about the style of the wine and what flavors to expect.

BORDEAUX CLASSED GROWTH

The words "Grand Cru Classé en 1855" tell you that this, the finest wine of the St-Estèphe appellation, is one of the stars of the original Bordeaux Classification.

VINTAGE CHAMPAGNE

The best Champagne producers "declare" a vintage only in the finest years, making vintage Champagne rarer and thus more expensive than nonvintage. While they do taste different from the same house's nonvintage, they are not "better": nonvintage Champagne, blendng wines from different years, can be superlative.

CHÂTEAU DE MALLES, BORDEAUX
Lying within Sauternes, this château is permitted to produce sweet white wine of that name. Its dry white and red wines fall under the wider Graves appellation.

bourgeois—as the name suggests, not quite aristocratic, but eminently respectable wines, the best being singled out as *superieur*, or, for the real stars, *exceptionel*. The great white wines of Bordeaux were given three classifications: *premier cru classé*, *premier cru*, and *deuxième cru*. And, save for a few changes necessitated by change of ownership, the *crus* have maintained their places in this league ever since, giving them tremendous prestige and value.

Throughout France, terms like *cru classé* and *grand cru classé* are used—albeit more loosely—to denote the best wines of the region.

The French system is a reasonable guide to quality. But there are many VDQS or Vin de Pays wines that you might well enjoy more than an AOC wine, so don't be snobbish. My advice is to first identify the style of table wine you like, then go up a notch in terms of quality, and see whether you like, or even notice, the difference.

ITALY

Like French wines, Italian wines are differentiated primarily by region (or appellation). Chianti is from Tuscany; Barolo and Barbaresco are from Piedmont; Soave, Amarone, Valpolicella, and Bardolino are from the Veneto in northern Italy; and so on. As in France, the wines are classified by quality, the lowliest being Vino da Tavola (VdT, or table wine), which is not required to put the region of origin on the label. Next up is Indicazione Geografica Tipica (IGT, similar in level to the

TUSCAN VINEYARD
Within the broader Chianti DOCG, where these vines grow, the central, *classico* zone generally makes the finest wines.

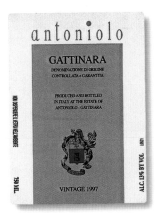

ITALIAN DOCG
The English on this label reveals that this is a wine designed for sale outside Italy, its DOCG quality boldly proclaimed.

ITALIAN DOC
Frascati is a DOC, but has an uneven reputation. This producer makes more of its name—a good one—than that of the wine.

SPANISH DOCA
DOCa Rioja may be red or white; as both red and white Riojas may be aged, they may also be designated *crianza* or *reserva*.

SHERRY
Like Champagne, sherry is a fiercely protected name, valuable for export. "Fino" is the style (light)—it does not mean "fine."

French Vin de Pays). Higher classifications are Denominazione di Origine Controllata (DOC) and the top-rank Denominazione di Origine Controllata e Garantita (DOCG)—wines that adhere to quality standards similar to the French AOC. The wines within this class will also carry either the name of the vineyard or the producer, or both. There may be huge differences in quality within a single appellation; my tip is to look for good producers, rather than putting too much faith in designations.

SPAIN
A Spanish wine labeled Denominación de Origen (DO), like a French AOC, comes from a named area and has been quality-checked by an independent standards committee. It is worth looking for two variants of the DO designation: Denominación de Origen Calificada (DOCa), which identifies the best wines from the regions of Rioja and Priorat; and Denominación de Origen de Pago (DO Pago), which is used for some excellent single-estate wines. Vino de la Tierra identifies some good regional wines (rather like the French Vin de Pays designation) while Vino de Mesa is a basic table wine. Spanish wines can also be classified on the basis of the length of time they are aged; the youngest style is *joven*, which is wine that has not been aged in oak at all and is meant to be drunk within a year. White or rosé *crianza* wines must be aged for a minimum of one year before being released for sale, at least six months of which must be in oak barrels; while *crianza* reds have at least one year in oak but another year in the bottle before release. *Reserva* whites have two years' aging, with at least six months in oak and *reserva* reds have at least three years' aging with at least one in oak. The highest level is *gran reserva*, a name reserved for wines from the very best years. White *gran reservas* require four years' aging with at least six months in oak, and the reds require five years' aging with at least two years in oak.

PORTUGAL
Portugal follows a French-style classification system. Denominação de Origem Controlada (DOC) is the highest category, equivalent to the French AOC; Indicação de Proveniência Regulamentada (IPR) indicates a wine with DOC potential. Vinho Regional (VR) denotes a regional wine from a defined area (like Vin de Pays), while Vinho de Mesa

READING A WINE LABEL

WINE STYLES

TRADITIONAL PORT BOATS
Port is never bottled on the estate, but brought in barrels down the Douro River to the great blending houses.

is a table wine. Sometimes a producer may include the term "Reserva" on his label. This is used to indicate a vintage year of outstanding quality. The wine may come from a demarcated region but, as this is not requisite, it could also be a blend from two different areas.

GERMANY

German wines are graded by the natural sugar content of the grapes used to make them; the more sugar, the higher the quality mark given. This means that the sweetest, most alcoholic wines are given the highest quality grades. There are four basic quality categories. Deutsche Tafelwein is ordinary table wine (with no named vineyard). Landwein is a wine that comes from one of 17 approved regions and must have at least 5.5 percent ABV (alcohol by volume). Qualitätswein bestimmter Anbaugebiet (QbA) is a wine from any

one of 13 approved regions, made only from certain grape varieties, and is at least 7.5 percent ABV; the name of the vineyard may be given if at least 85 percent of the grapes were grown there. Qualitätswein mit Prädikat (QmP) is the top grade; these wines come from a specified region and grape variety. Within this top grade, the QmP wines are quality tested and further subdivided according to their residual sugar level and sweetness. *Kabinett* wines are the lightest and the driest; *Spätlese* wines are slightly sweeter, made from late-picked grapes. *Auslese* wines are sweeter still, made with late-picked grapes and maybe some botrytized grapes *(see p.23)*. Sweeter still is *Beerenauslese*, made entirely from botrytized grapes and with impressive potential alcohol levels of 15.3 to 18.1 percent. The last category is *Trockenbeerenauslese* (TBA)—amber-colored, powerful, and very complex. This intensely,

GERMAN KABINETT

This is a quality QmP German wine. Niersteiner Heiligenbaum is where it was made, from the Riesling grape; *Kabinett* indicates the level of sweetness, emphasized by *"Halbtrocken"*— German for "semidry."

AUSTRIAN TBA

Sweeter wine styles are often sold in half-bottles with a capacity of 375ml, as printed on the bottom left of this label. This is a *Trockenbeerenauslese* from Austria, which uses the same quality system as Germany.

being from grapes grown miles apart, picked on different days, and vinified in different tanks and with different sweetness levels.

THE NEW WORLD

Labels on New World wines tend to emphasize the grape variety and brand name over the region; the label on the back of the bottle also gives much more information than appears on wines from Europe—the precise location of the vineyard, and a description of how the wine has been aged, for example. However, the lack of independent quality standards means that knowledge of good producers is even more important than for European wines. You may see terms like "Reserve" and "Estate," which mean respectively that the wine is the highest quality from that particular vineyard, and that it is bottled on the same estate where it is grown; however, these terms are often used loosely, and are far from a guarantee of quality.

NORTH AMERICA

There is a voluntary appellation system in the US. Each individual state is recognized as its own appellation of origin, as are the smaller counties within it. So, although the label may state an appellation name, there is no guarantee that the district named has met any quality standards. The only rule is that at least 85 per cent of the wine in the bottle is actually from where the label says it's from. The law also requires that the producer's name and address be on the label. In general, the

powerfully sweet wine is made from individually picked, botrytized grapes that have been left on the vine until they have almost completely shriveled.

All German wines classified as QbA or QmP also have on their label an AP (Amtliche Prüfnummer) number. This proves that the wine has passed analytical and tasting tests and that the origin of the grapes is genuine. The number is divided into five sections, and you can use the last two of these to play a fascinating tasting game. The second-last number is the application number and the last number is the year in which that application was made. If you have two bottles of the same wine with exactly the same AP numbers, then you can be sure that the wine inside came from the same cask. But if the application number is different, then the two wines may taste subtly different, being from the same cask but bottled on a different date, or they could taste very different,

"Don't be taken in by an elegantly designed label or cleverly chosen phrases, such as 'old vines'—these tell you nothing about the quality of a wine."

READING A WINE LABEL

WINE STYLES

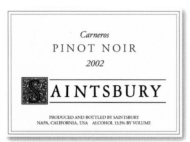

NEW WORLD PINOT NOIR

While the producer—Saintsbury—and the grape variety used to make this wine have top billing on the label, Carneros is one of the best parts of California's Napa Valley for Pinot Noir, and is well worth a mention.

REGIONAL WINE

South African wines with "Wine of Origin Stellenbosch" on the label must be made with grapes grown only in the Stellenbosch region.

Adelaide Hills Chardonnay, then at least 85 percent of the wine must be Chardonnay grown in the GI-defined Adelaide Hills district.

Australian wine labels also tend to have the vineyard name and the grape variety prominently displayed, and sometimes, but not always, a vintage. There is also often a good deal of helpful information on the back label, such as the precise location of the vineyard, whether the wine was aged in oak barrels, and sometimes even tasting notes.

SOUTH AFRICA

South African labels follow patterns similar to those of Australian and American wines. There is no strict appellation system, since the wine industry is still relatively young and undeveloped and new geographical areas for wine production are still opening up. The vineyard name, as well as grape variety, region, and vintage are all displayed on the label, but successfully choosing a good South African wine necessitates knowing something of the winemaker or vineyard.

brand name and the style or grape variety will be the most prominent words on the label. In the case of higher-quality wines, the label will state a year, but if the word "vintage" does not precede this year, then it indicates only that the wine was bottled in that year. If the word "Reserve" appears on the label, you may expect it to indicate that the wine is the best from that particular vineyard. However, my advice would be not to place too much credence in this: less scrupulous producers use it as a marketing tool rather than a real indication of higher quality. Many wines may also be labeled as "Estate" or "Estate Bottled," meaning that the grapes were grown on the same estate where the wine was made and bottled, rather than either grapes or wine being driven for miles across the country to be bottled.

AUSTRALIA

Australia's appellation system, which was enacted only in 2001, does nothing more than define boundaries within a set of Geographical Indications (GIs). Each State is divided into regions, which are then further split into subregions. There is also a simple and straightforward "Label Integrity Program", which rules that if the label states

COLCHAGUA VALLEY VINEYARD, CHILE

South America's winemakers often make grape varieties prominent on labels, like fellow New World winemakers, but Chile and Argentina have broad appellation systems too.

NEW WORLD SUPERSTAR

Once simply an ingredient in the Bordeaux blend, with the popularity of varietal wines, Merlot *(facing page)* has achieved world-class status in its own right.

TRAINING YOUR TASTE

THE FOUR PRINCIPLES OF TASTE

The spectrum of tastes in wine is so vast, and perception of taste varies so greatly, that it is hard to imagine an adequate vocabulary! It is, however, fundamental to analyse the taste of a wine in terms of its balance between four factors: acidity, fruit, alcohol, and, in the case of red wines, tannins.

Acidity is the spine of a wine—especially a white wine. Depending on the grape variety and the climate, it will be more or less pronounced, and affects the style considerably. In red wine, acidity is less perceptible, but it must be there for the wine to age, and well integrated to make sure it doesn't clash with the tannins.

The fruit intensity of a wine gives it complexity of character as well as texture. Fruit should not be confused with sweetness: wines with flavors of sweet, ripe exotic fruit can still be dry—the grapes' sugars all turned into alcohol during fermentation.

It is the tannins in the skin of red grapes and in oak barrels used to age wines that give wines a mouth-drying quality. Tannins are vital to allow red wines to age, and ripe and polished tannins give vital balance to concentrated wines.

The alcohol level in a wine should be in balance with its fruit and structure. To a perfectly balanced wine, the alcohol content brings a touch of oiliness, giving viscosity and roundness on the palate.

You can teach yourself to identify these flavors using a simple exercise *(see below)*. Take four glasses filled with still water, then squeeze lemon into one, stir a spoonful of sugar into another, steep a tea bag in the third, and pour a measure of straight white spirit, such as vodka, into the fourth. Then take a sip of each in turn, rolling the liquid around in your mouth; try to identify where on your tongue each flavor is detected. Finally, pour yourself a glass of wine, and look for the same flavors.

ACIDITY
Acidity, detected on the sides of the tongue, is what gives a wine its refreshing feel. Too much will make the wine sharp and acidic, almost burning. Too little will make the wine flabby and boring.

SWEETNESS
Sweetness is tasted on the tip of the tongue. Dry wine may have sweet fruit flavors; in sweet wines, the sweetness comes from "residual" sugar remaining after the fermentation process.

BITTERNESS
Bitterness is tasted at the back of the tongue. It comes from tannins, astringent substances in grape skins and oak that mellow and soften during the winemaking process and with age.

ALCOHOL
Alcohol is felt as a warming sensation at the back of the throat. Too much alcohol will make a wine feel "porty." Too little will make the wine feel weak and watery.

TASTING WINE

THE ART OF WINE-TASTING

Anyone can drink and enjoy a glass of wine, but tasting wine is an art. It takes experience and a little knowledge of technique to fully appreciate wine's uniquely complex flavors and textures.

Ultimately, wine is a matter of taste, but just because you dislike a wine does not mean it is bad. Such judgments are subjective, and it is crucial to analyze the wine more systematically on the basis of color, aroma, and taste, and whether it is both a good wine—with its acidity, fruit, tannins (for a red), and alcohol finely balanced *(see p.72)*—and a good example of its type. Appreciation of wine grows with experience—the ability to recall, compare, and categorize tastes and aromas—but it starts with a systematic approach to tasting.

I always taste from a plain, thin-walled, stemmed wine glass, rinsing it thoroughly in water before moving from one wine to another. Restricting the

SIPPING AND TASTING
A slight "slurp," drawing some air into your mouth with the wine, releases the flavors, while your mouth "feels" texture and body.

CHECKING THE COLOR
Good natural light shows color accurately. A white background, such as a napkin *(facing page)*, removes distractions.

wines you sample to one style or region is helpful because it helps fine-tune the senses. Ideally, the tasting should take place in a brightly lit room, free from strong odors, such as cigarette smoke and cooking. I like to taste in the morning, before my taste buds become jaded, and I always taste wines at their correct serving temperatures *(see p.308)*.

THE CAT MANTRA

My wine-tasting mantra is "color, aroma, taste"—or CAT. The color of a wine can give you quite a lot of information, even before you have smelled or tasted it. Use something white, like a sheet of paper or a napkin, and examine the color at the rim, and also when looking down on the wine from above. The second step is to swirl the glass to bring the wine in contact with air and release its aromas. Now you can smell the wine. Keep your nose at the rim of the

ANALYZING THE AROMA
A wine's "bouquet" can, literally, translate as a whole bunch of flavors; it takes time to separate and identify them.

glass, take a long sniff, and analyze the aromas. Gently sip a small amount; hold the liquid in your mouth and draw in some air over the wine—this will enhance the flavors. Finally, if you are tasting several wines, spit the wine into a bucket. Make detailed notes of your observations of color, aroma, and taste for each wine you sample.

COLOR

Wines in good condition should be bright, vibrant, and clear. Color often tells you about body—the paler the color, the lighter the wine. Golden tones in a white wine usually indicate that the wine is older, sweeter, or comes from a hotter climate. Red wines range from garnet to a darker ruby red; the richest, densest wines may tend toward purple or even an opaque, inky black.

The color at the rim of the wine is an indicator of age. Young white wine has a silver or green rim, which becomes more golden with age. Young reds have a ruby or purple rim, becoming tile-red with age; a faded orange rim indicates a venerable wine, which can be a good or bad thing! Looking through the edge of the wine, you may detect tiny bubbles; these are acceptable in some still wines, such as Vinho Verde and Muscadet, because of the way they are made, but should not be evident in others. Swirling the wine and then looking above the rim also shows you the wine's viscosity, or "legs." Viscosity is a result of sugar being turned

"We all think of rosé as 'pink' wine, but actually, rosés are hardly ever true pink. Take a look—they range from pinky-blue to salmon pink."

to alcohol; usually, the thicker the legs, the more alcoholic the wine—but it does depend on the temperature of the wine, and how the glass has been washed and polished.

AROMA

The aromas of a good wine should, above all, be clean. A musty smell in a wine usually indicates that it is corked *(see p.316)*. Different grape varieties, *terroir*, and winemaking techniques can produce a huge range of aromas in wine, few of which have anything to do with grapes! Some are easily recognizable, but you may have to rack your brains a little to identify others. Memory can play a large part in pinning down, for example, the smell of new riding tack, or licorice, or the inside of a great-uncle's cigar box. Try sorting smells into their families—fruit, vegetal, spicy, smoky, floral, oaky, mineral, and animal—and keep each family in a separate "box" in your mind. Then you can simply open each box and pick out the aromas that fit best.

TASTE

Most wine-tasting work has already been done before you actually take a sip. It is a little-known fact that we actually "taste" with our noses. When a cold blocks your nose, you also lose your sense of taste; all our tongues can detect is acidity, sweetness, bitterness, salt, and alcohol. So, when you sip the wine, take in some air, too, to send those aromas up into your nose and give you the "flavors," while your mouth analyzes textures and "mouth feel": the refreshingness of the acidity, the ripeness of the fruit, the weight and warmth of the alcohol, and, in red wines, the dryness of the tannins *(see pp.72–3)*. Then take a step back and determine the most important factor—are all of these in balance? Even the cheapest wine will, if well balanced, be pleasant to drink. And if the flavors and impression of balance linger pleasurably in your mouth after swallowing, then you have a wine of some quality. An unbalanced wine, however, is not very well made, or not yet ready to drink, or past its prime.

COLOR AT THE RIM
The warm tone at this wine's rim *(facing page)* indicates some age. The droplets running down the inside of the glass after swirling are the "legs": the slower they travel, the more viscous the wine.

GREEN AROMAS
Green really does have a smell—think of dawn in the backyard on a summer day, just as the sun starts to bring out the fresh, herbaceous aromas of a dewy lawn.

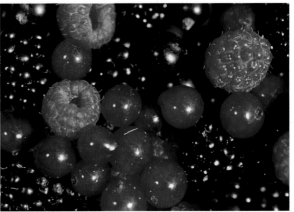

RED SUMMER FRUITS
You can practise distinguishing individual soft fruit flavors by pureeing a little of each fruit, and then tasting them one by one with your eyes closed. Sound easy? Just try it!

GROUPING WINES BY STYLE

THE PERSONALITY OF A WINE

In my job as a sommelier, I find it is not helpful to categorize wines simply in terms of grape variety or by country, unless serving a table of wine experts! When I am helping a client to select a wine to complement the food they have chosen, it is much more informative to find out what style of wine they like, rather than which grape varieties they prefer. If they have chosen fish, do they enjoy light, delicate white wines? If they are eating beef, would they be happy with a smooth, rounded red? Or would they prefer a richer, heavier style?

It worries me when I hear people say, for example, that they "don't like Chardonnay." How can you treat a huge collection of very different wines in such a dismissive way? As I hope this book manages to get across, one grape variety can produce many different styles of wine, depending on where the grapes have been grown and how the wine has been vinified. So simply knowing which variety of grape a wine is made from does not tell you what the wine will taste like.

AN INVITATION TO EXPLORE

By placing wines in categories according to style—based on their flavors, texture, and body—rather than by grape or region, I truly believe that the world of wine is easier to understand. We can all relate to tastes much more easily than we can to technical information. I group white wines into three categories (see below): light, crisp whites; those that are juicy and aromatic; and those that are full and opulent. Red wines (see facing page), I think of as either fruity and lively, ripe and

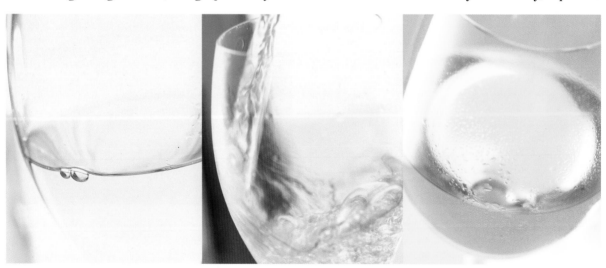

LIGHT, CRISP WHITES
Clean, refreshing flavors are the keystones of this style. These are light, dry, versatile wines, as welcome served on their own as when complementing light dishes.

JUICY, AROMATIC WHITES
These are white wines in a more mouthwatering style. Medium-bodied, with citrus, floral, and grassy aromas, and sweeter fruit flavors, they are nonetheless still dry.

FULL, OPULENT WHITES
I love this voluptuous style—full-bodied, fleshy and long, seductively fragrant wines with a wealth of flavors. But they still manage to maintain their poise with good balancing acidity.

smooth, or rich and dense. That just leaves rosés, sparkling wines, and wines that are sweet or fortified—these categorize themselves!

Armed with these style groupings, I hope to give you the confidence to explore—and in the process experience and enjoy all sorts of wines from all over the world. If you have tried a wine in the past and discovered that you like it—Sancerre, for example—then this book can lead you, via the category that Sancerre falls into, to the whole gamut of wines that are of a similar style.

A SINGLE STEP

So, this book is about providing you with the knowledge you need to find and delve into your favorite styles. What it doesn't do is give you detailed technical advice about specific regions, producers, and vintages. You don't need it! I want to help break the myth that wine is somehow esoteric and exclusive—it is there to be enjoyed. Step one is to find the styles of wine you like; and with that step, the whole world of wine will open up to you.

SWEET AND SPARKLING
The world of sweet and fortified wines is full of luscious, intense experiences. And sparkling wines— dry or sweet, white, rosé, or even red!—are in a class of their own.

FRUITY, LIVELY REDS
Perfumed and elegant or bursting with boisterous sweet fruit, the light, vibrant reds in this category will suit any occasion, from a summer buffet to the fanciest dinner.

RIPE, SMOOTH REDS
The diplomats of the red-wine world, smooth and harmonious, with no sharp edges, but never bland—this category contains truly distinctive and distinguished regional classics.

RICH, DENSE REDS
Delve deeper into the multilayered complexity of dark, intense aromas and flavors that this style can offer, ranging from suavely elegant aristocrats to big, warm, welcoming wines.

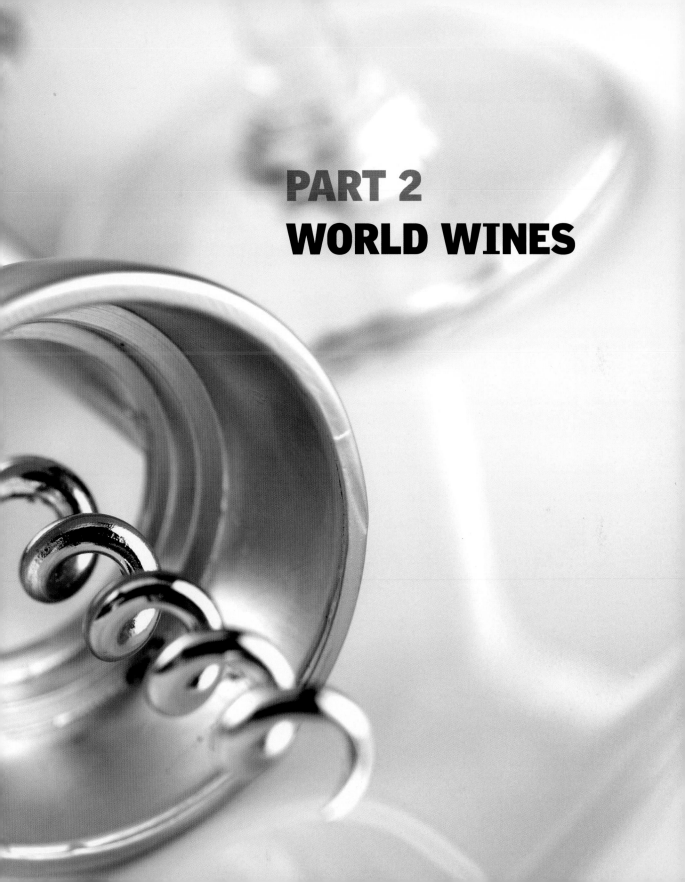

PART 2
WORLD WINES

A TASTING TOUR

FINDING YOUR STYLE

On the following pages, I describe hundreds of different wines from all over the world. Because I believe so strongly that the style of a wine, rather than its place of origin, is the initial key to fixing that wine's identity in the mind, I've dispensed with the usual country-by-country organization in this book, and instead sorted the wines of the world into styles *(see pp.78–9)*, with all the "fruity, lively reds," for example, or "light, crisp whites" together. Having said that, within each style, the wines are arranged by country—and being French, I make no apology for starting each category with the appropriate wines from France! Having done so, it makes sense to then travel around Europe before branching out into the New World. The beauty of this approach is that on any given page, you could find yourself reading about different wines from, say, Austria, Italy, and California—and all would be variations on

a theme. The theme they share is their style, whether full, opulent whites or rich, dense reds, but the differences—their regions of origin and vinification methods—are what really make wine so exciting.

Using these style groupings, I hope I can lead you on tasting tours that will broaden your tastes and introduce you to new wines. Find a wine you already know you like in the directory, then explore other wines within the same style section, enjoying their similarities but also discovering the nuances of aroma, flavor, and texture that reveal just where and how they were made. To start you off, I've included, in each section, two or three comparative tastings—my Taste Tests—that explore a particular aspect of the style—the influence of oak aging in ripe, smooth reds, for example. The particular wines I chose to taste are pictured, but I've recommended others that would make good substitutes.

MY TASTING NOTES FOR EACH WINE

For me, what fundamentally matters about a wine is: how does it look, smell, and taste? So for each of the wines on the following pages, you'll find my CAT mantra— "color, aroma, taste"—giving what I think you might find in a good-quality example of the wine in question, whatever its price bracket. Under Buying, I've listed some (but by no means all) of my favorite producers, ranging from familiar names you'll easily track down, to well-kept secrets you'll have to work a bit harder to obtain. In Enjoying, I've given a handful of serving suggestions—you'll find much more about matching food and wine on pages 318 to 333. And finally, in Branching Out, I've suggested other wines to try that will, I hope, broaden your tasting experience, show you some fascinating comparisons, and above all lead you to discover more wines that you enjoy.

LIGHT, CRISP WHITES

From France's Chablis to Italy's Pinot Grigio and South Africa's Chenin Blanc, there is wonderful variety in light, crisp white wines. Favorites are a matter of personal taste— and may even come down to a memory or mood that a wine conjures up for you. These

wines are fresh and tangy, so you may not like them if you have a sweet tooth or prefer your wine to be oaky (like some Chardonnays) or rich (like the heavier reds). They are pale in color, with shades ranging from lemon to light gold, and can have a green tinge if the wine is of a young vintage. Delicately scented, these wines have aromas of apple, citrus fruits, herbs, and minerals, and are dry and crisp, with just the right balance of acidity to give the wine a refreshing, but not sharp, taste. A measure of the quality of a light, crisp white is its finish, which should be clean and long.

STYLE PROFILE
LIGHT, CRISP WHITES

PERFECT CONDITIONS

The key to a good light, crisp white wine lies in its acidity, which should have enough presence to make the wine refreshing, but not so much as to produce tartness in the taste. The grapes used to make this style (among them Aligoté, Chardonnay, Muscadet, and Pinot Grigio) typically have large berries with thin skins, and ripen earlier than other varieties, so are naturally high in acidity.

When they are grown in cooler climates (such as northern Europe), or in the mountainous regions of hotter countries such as Italy, Portugal, and most parts of the New World, it is important that the berries ripen as early as possible, before they are at risk of being damaged by frost. To ensure that they do, the vines need to be kept warm—

"Far from being boring, crisp, dry whites are fun and youthful—perfect to enjoy with friends on a hot summer day."

witness the flint stones in the soil of the Chablis wine region in France that retain precious heat from the sun. The grapes also need to receive as much sun as possible; it is no coincidence, for example, that the best and most expensive Chablis *premiers crus* and *grands crus* come from vineyards planted on southwest-facing slopes.

KEY TASTES

Light, crisp whites tend to be vinified using modern techniques and stainless steel vats in order to preserve as much of their fresh, crisp fruitiness as possible. The characters of these wines vary according to the particular grower, the region's climate, the soil in the vineyards, and the wine's vintage. The best and most expensive are brilliantly fresh, with a perfect balance between acidity, alcohol, and fruit. They have a complex character that suggests citrus, mineral, and apple aromas, and a deliciously long and refreshing finish. Less expensive light whites may have subtle floral or pear flavors and medium length, and can match very well with strongly flavored, spicy food.

HARDY VINES
Perhaps best known for making full, opulent whites, the versatile Chardonnay grape can thrive in some of the coolest winemaking regions, where it produces refreshing, citrusy, light, dry wines. In France, it is used to make one of the great, classic whites—Chablis.

COOL CUSTOMER
Also known as Muscadet, the Melon de Bourgogne grape resists frost well and ripens early. This variety is used to make light, slightly sparkling Muscadet wines in France's Loire Valley.

TASTE TRAIL

Less expensive light, crisp whites can often lack character and personality, but if you choose carefully, you can find wines that are fresh and clean, with subtle floral and pear flavors, and an acidity that is distinct but not too sharp. For an introduction to this style, try a **MUSCADET** from the Loire Valley, an **ALIGOTÉ** from Burgundy, or a **PINOT GRIGIO** from Italy. If you're willing to spend more, try **CHENIN BLANC** from South Africa, which is full of citrus and apple flavors. At the top of the price range is **CHABLIS**, with its dry flintiness and notes of green apple and grapefruit.

ENJOYING Always serve light, crisp whites well chilled, giving them at least 12 hours in the refrigerator before opening. This style of wine is ideal with light food and makes an excellent companion to the first course of a meal, especially if that course includes seafood. **MUSCADET** and **CHABLIS** are particularly good with fish and charcuterie, while Italian styles, such as **ORVIETO** and **FRASCATI**, go well with light pasta.

The overall style of light, crisp white wines is neutral and dry—but that does not mean that they are bland. Although the dryness is often the first thing to hit the taste buds when we drink a light white, the dry flavors should be something to grow on the palate and to be enjoyed, and should never be confused with sharpness.

DRINK OR STORE?

Light, crisp whites are wines for drinking (rather than laying down): buy the youngest vintage possible and drink it within six to 12 months. Avoid buying the cheapest light, white wines—these often have too much sulfur dioxide added during vinification (to preserve the wine) and some may give you a headache.

WORLD WINES

LIGHT, CRISP WHITES

FRANCE
CHABLIS

I love frosty winter mornings in the country. If I could describe the clean, bracing quality of that air with a wine, it would have to be Chablis. Always pure and refreshing, good Chablis is also one of the best-value buys in Burgundy.

Given its steely nature, many people are shocked to learn that Chablis is 100 percent Chardonnay. It is a world away from the thick, butterscotch-laden Chardonnays that are mass-produced in the Southern Hemisphere for the world's supermarket shelves. The distinctive, stony character of Chablis is a product of fossil-filled limestone soils and a very marginal climate. Sunshine is quite limited in north-central France, and spring frosts can devastate an entire year's production. But that adversity imparts an invigorating, almost magical spark to this wine.

"There really is a flintiness and minerality in Chablis that sets it apart from other Chardonnays."

Chablis has four classifications. The standard Chablis appellation covers most of the production from the vineyards along the Serein River around the town of Chablis. Petit Chablis comes from higher and cooler fringes around the main appellation. Chablis *premier cru* is grown on more favorable, south-facing slopes (including top locations such as Montée de Tonnerre and Vaillons). Finally, there is Chablis *grand cru*—seven sites on one hill to the northeast of the town, all facing south and west for the sun. Les Clos is considered to be the best, although Vaudésir tends to be the most seductive, and Valmur the most classic and austere.

Chablis and Petit Chablis are best in their youth—up to five years old. Good *premier cru* and *grand cru* wines often need five years to reveal themselves, but they can last for up to 20 years.

COLOR Very pale straw yellow; clear, bright, and light.

AROMA Floral, grassy, and minerally; delicate, with green apple.

TASTE Apple, citrus fruits, and minerals, with notes of flint or steel.

BUYING The best of the large producers include Domaine Laroche, Domaine William Fèvre, and Domaine Jean-Marc Brocard. Smaller names worth trying include Vincent Dauvissat and Raveneau.

ENJOYING Chablis is a perfect partner for oysters or simple white fish. Don't serve it too cold: 52°F (11°C) is ideal.

BRANCHING OUT Contrast Chablis with a good Chardonnay from South America or Australia. Chablis is lighter, with "greener," less exotic fruit flavors than New World Chardonnays.

MUSCADET

Muscadet comes from northwestern France, where the Loire River opens to the Atlantic. I grew up in this region, and I know that the best wines are made in the Sèvre-et-Maine district. (Look for it on the label!)

For a top-quality example of this wine, try a Muscadet Sèvre-et-Maine Sur Lie. Those last two words describe a production technique whereby the new wine is left in its fermentation tank for several months to soak up the flavors and aromas of the lees (the natural yeast sediment). It may not sound appealing, but the result is brilliant. The slight fizziness enhances the wine's fresh crispness and orchard fruit flavors.

Most Muscadet is light and lively, and should be consumed while very young; but I have tasted some excellent aged Muscadets with enticing hints of flowers and pineapple.

MUSCADET
Château du Cléray

COLOR Bright; a pale lemon yellow with green tinges.

AROMA Youthful; lemon, pear, and apple, with lime and mineral notes.

TASTE Light, elegant; a lemony acidity and a slightly fizzy feel.

BUYING Many Muscadets are sold in distinctive bottles with long, thin necks, so they are easy to spot. Buy very recent vintages from Château du Cléray, Château la Perrière, Château de Geuline, and the great Domaine de l'Ecu.

ENJOYING Chilled Muscadet goes well with light fish dishes, such as moules marinières, oysters, or grilled sardines.

BRANCHING OUT Compare the subtle flavors and crisp structure of Muscadet with a Chasselas from Switzerland or an Aligoté from Burgundy. Each of these wines is delicate and refreshing.

The Muscadet years: from pocket money to a life in wine

Muscadet means a lot to me. I was brought up in Nantes, and spent many long hours harvesting Melon de Bourgogne grapes to earn a few francs. Even today, the wine's zingy, youthful taste transports me back to those vineyards. It's a real shame for me that Muscadet's reputation has suffered in recent years: true, there has been a lot of overproduction, and some producers have been careless, but it's partly about fashion, too. Today's buyers are more interested in Burgundy's star Chardonnay wines, but they're missing a trick—and a rare bargain—if they overlook Muscadet; the best producers, such as Château de Geuline and du Cléray, are making subtle, stylish wines. My advice: buy now before prices start to rise.

FRANCE
ALIGOTÉ

Try these wines if you have a soft spot for Muscadet or Chablis. Aligotés are often excellent value, and they are becoming more widely available. I think the best ones come from the Burgundy region (especially from around Bouzeron in the Côte Chalonnaise district), but the Aligoté grape is also grown across Eastern Europe and in California. Expect the wine to be very dry, lean, crisp, and refreshing.

COLOR Pale lemon to very pale straw yellow, with silver tinges.

AROMA Lemon and green fruits, such as gooseberry, with a nutty feel.

TASTE Dry and clean, with citrus flavors; straightforward, easy to enjoy.

BUYING Domaine Goisot and Domaine Guy Roulot are top producers of this variety, and their wines are worth paying a little extra for. I would also recommend Domaine Borgeot, as well as the newly created appellation of St Bris—a little-known source of good-quality Aligoté.

ENJOYING Aligoté really comes into its own as an aperitif. Mix it with a splash of crème de cassis—a black currant liqueur—to make a Burgundian Kir.

BRANCHING OUT If you like this wine, try a Mâcon-Villages or a Petit Chablis from France, both of which share its dry, mineral character.

ALIGOTÉ
Domaine Borgeot

SYLVANER

To me, this wine seems rather like Muscadet—but with more flavor, as the Sylvaner grape really thrives in the cool climate of Alsace. Much of the wine is consumed locally, but it has become more widely available in recent years. Sylvaner has fresh and fruity flavors, with some Riesling-like characteristics, although it is neither as elegant as Riesling nor as complex.

COLOR Bright, pale yellow, with green nuances.

AROMA Subtle aromas of pear, lemon, and apple; hints of herbs and beeswax.

TASTE Simple, but amazingly refreshing and zingy, with a long citrusy finish.

BUYING Seek bottles from Alsace, but don't spend too much money. Also, don't lay them down—drink them! Try Domaine Schaetzel or Domaine Ostertag.

ENJOYING Go for the youngest vintage available to enjoy these wines at their fresh and zesty best. Serve well chilled as an aperitif, or with any grilled fish.

BRANCHING OUT Compare one of these wines with a Müller-Thurgau or a Muscadet Sèvre-et-Maine. They have similar bone-dry personalities, with the same flinty, citrusy tones.

PINOT BLANC

Often called the "poor man's Chardonnay," Pinot Blanc is indeed related to the world's most famous white wine. As the name suggests, Pinot Noir and Pinot Gris are close relations, too. But Pinot Blanc has a gentle appeal entirely of its own. Good examples from Alsace have a slightly smoky character. Fresh, clean, flowery, and smooth to the finish, these wines show soft, fruity acidity.

VIN D'ALSACE
APPELLATION ALSACE CONTRÔLÉE
Domaine
MARCEL DEISS
PINOT-BLANC
2001
BERGHEIM
MIS EN BOUTEILLE AU DOMAINE
MARCEL DEISS & FILS VIGNERON
A BERGHEIM • FRANCE
PRODUIT DE FRANCE

PINOT BLANC
Domaine Marcel Deiss

COLOR Very pale straw; clear and light, and very attractive.

AROMA Not deeply aromatic, but soft hints of peach, pear, and flowers.

TASTE Fresh and lively, with white fruits and mineral notes at the finish.

BUYING Look for the words *grand cru*, *clos*, or *special cuvée* on the label, as they signify the very best. Among producers, I particularly like Domaine Marcel Deiss and Domaine Schaetzel.

ENJOYING Pinot Blanc makes an ideal aperitif; but I enjoy it with onion tart—an Alsatian classic. Another great match is with fish, such as pike or trout.

BRANCHING OUT Try these wines alongside a good Muscadet or perhaps a flowery Swiss Chasselas. Each is lean and delicate, but there are clear, if subtle, flavor differences.

BORDEAUX BLANC SEC

For many years, Bordeaux whites were too often semisweet and lacking in character. But new techniques have transformed these wines, and some now represent great value for money. Try the crisp, dry Entre deux Mers (literally "between two rivers") made from Sauvignon Blanc. Also try AOC Bergerac whites: this region is usually associated with sweet wines, but its dry whites are on the rise.

COLOR Pale gold, with silvery tinges; medium intensity.

AROMA Clean and delicate; pear, quince, peach, and flowers.

TASTE Subtle and harmonious, with a refreshing acidity and good length.

BUYING Look for the word *sec* (dry) on the label, and buy recent vintages. Try the châteaux Montdoyen and Thieuley.

ENJOYING You can serve this wine well chilled with a variety of foods, from seafood to white meats, even curry.

BRANCHING OUT Try Bordeaux Blanc Sec with other Sauvignon Blancs: it is richer than many Sancerres, but not as exuberant as New Zealand Sauvignons.

PICPOUL DE PINET

The Picpoul Blanc white grape is grown in Languedoc, southern France. *Piquepoul*, the alternative spelling, meant "lip-stinger" in the local dialect—a reference to the wine's zippy acidity. During the early 20th century, it was used to make potent, aromatic Vermouth; but modern examples from the Pinet appellation offer a refreshing taste of sun-soaked lemons and almonds.

COLOR Bright and light; pale lemon yellow with a silver rim.

AROMA Clean and fresh, with green fruit, peach, and nutty hints.

TASTE Zesty, with a well-defined refreshing character and good length.

BUYING This wine is best purchased straight from the winery while on vacation. The area is heavily influenced by the sea, and vintage matters a lot.

ENJOYING Serve Picpoul with smoked salmon or a Niçoise salad. It also works with roasted vegetables and spicy foods.

BRANCHING OUT Try this wine with an Italian Pinot Grigio. Both have a crisp, clean texture, but the fruit flavors may differ—the latter being peachy. Another similar wine is Italian Soave.

"Picpoul makes fresh and lively white wines; I think it will grow in popularity in years to come."

ITALY
SOAVE

Soave is Italy's most common dry white wine. It is produced around the town of the same name, just northeast of Verona. Pronounced "swah-vay," the name has nothing to do with being "suave"—the wine is too light and fresh for that! Most Soave wine is made from a blend of Garganega and Trebbiano grapes, and it has an earthy character. If Chardonnay is added to the mix, the wine becomes a little softer.

COLOR Straw yellow, occasionally with a touch of green.

AROMA Fresh green and citrus fruits, with delicate hints of almond.

TASTE Delicate and light, with a nutty flavor and a slightly bitter finish.

BUYING Look for the term *classico* on the label, indicating wines from the heart of the region, which are usually the best quality. Top producers include Pieropan and Anselmi.

ENJOYING I love Soave with hors d'oeuvres. Serve it as an aperitif to accompany assorted bruschetta. Soave is also great with simple pasta dishes— try it as a match for seafood linguine.

BRANCHING OUT The best of these wines can compete with a *premier cru* Chablis. If Soave appeals, try some other subtle wines—for example, Verdicchio or Mâcon-Villages, or even a South African Sauvignon Blanc.

LIGHT, CRISP WHITES

WORLD WINES

TASTE TEST: ACIDITY

Try these three styles of white wine to explore the importance of acidity.

❶ ❷ ❸

❶ MUSCADET SÈVRE-ET-MAINE is a breathtakingly fresh, bone-dry white from vineyards around the city of Nantes in France's Loire Valley. Look for a Muscadet with *sur lie* on the label—these are the finest—and be sure to serve it well chilled. **Seek out** Château du Cléray, Domaine de l'Ecu, Pierre Luneau-Papin, Château de la Ragotière.

❷ ALSACE MUSCAT from northeastern France is off-dry and highly perfumed, but with a discreet acidity that makes it a finely balanced wine. Alsace is the main winemaking region producing dry wines from the Muscat grape, thanks to its cool climate. **Seek out** René Muré, Domaine Marcel Deiss, Maison Trimbach, Dopff au Moulin, Zind-Humbrecht, Hugel & Fils.

❸ SÉMILLON grapes, when grown in Australia, make a fresh, elegant wine with an opulent oily texture. Look for any examples from Margaret River in western Australia or the Hunter Valley in New South Wales—these regions produce good-quality wines and so are always a safe buy. **Seek out** Fermoy Estate, Vasse Felix, Brokenwood, McGuigan, Tyrell's.

"The key to the freshness of light, crisp white wines lies in a perfect balance between fruit and acidity."

Acidity in a wine should never be harsh or bitter, or overpower the fruit qualities in the wine—think of it more as the **wine's backbone**. The amount of acidity in a wine depends largely on the **grape variety**, but also on the way that the grapes were grown: acidity is **lower** in grapes grown in **warm climates**, and **higher** in those grown in **cooler climates**.

The first wine in this tasting—the **MUSCADET SÈVRE-ET-MAINE**—is also the **driest**. Muscadet grapes have good resistance to cold and the **pale color** of this wine indicates that it is indeed from a **cool climate**. First, sample the aroma, which is full of **very citrusy green fruit** and **yellow lemons**, leading you to expect something very dry and fresh on the palate. Then take a sip, and you will find that the **acidity** does indeed **dominate your senses**—it's the main factor in this wine—but it is neither sharp nor overwhelming, allowing **delicate lemony flavors** to come through.

Next try the **ALSACE MUSCAT**. Muscat is an off-dry grape variety that is **naturally low in acidity**, so it needs to be grown in cooler climates in order to preserve what acidity it does have. In contrast to the Muscadet, this wine has **floral aromas**, with **hints of honey and apricots**, and these are carried through on the palate. Although the **acidity is quite low**, it is still clearly there, holding the floral flavors together, and it gives the wine a **dry finish**.

SÉMILLON is another grape variety that needs cooler growing conditions in order to **preserve** its natural acidity levels. This wine has a **richer, more oily texture** than Muscadet or Muscat, and so can be **aged in oak** without overpowering the fruit. First, examine the color of the wine—oak-aging has given it a **darker, more golden color** than the other two wines. On the palate, notice the **dry, flinty acidity**, which perfectly balances the wine's **oily texture**.

ITALY
PINOT GRIGIO

This wine is everywhere—it's the new Chardonnay! The Pinot Grigio variety is also grown in Germany (as Grauburgunder), France (as Pinot Gris), New Zealand, the US, and many other countries. Within Italy, the finest expressions of Pinot Grigio originate in the northeast, from Trentino through Veneto to Friuli.

Good Grigio should be light, lively, refreshing, and lots of fun—a profile that has caused an explosion in the wine's popularity over recent years. (Pinot Grigio is now the leading imported wine in the US.) Of course, prices have risen, too, but I'm not sure that this is reflected in higher quality. Mass production has created some wine that is neither offensive nor inspiring. True Italian Pinot Grigio should be crisp and zesty, with exciting fruit flavors.

PINOT GRIGIO
Mezzacorona

COLOR Pale lemon yellow with silvery-gray tinges.

AROMA Youthful and fresh; green fruits, flowers, and hints of minerals.

TASTE Elegant, slightly fleshy, with a subtle texture; lemony at the finish.

BUYING Buy and drink this wine within two years of the vintage. Producers to check out include Mezzacorona, Beltrame, and Lis Neris.

ENJOYING Serve Pinot Grigio well chilled. It's ideal for cocktail receptions, and complements any white fish—I enjoy it with baked cod drizzled in *beurre blanc*.

BRANCHING OUT Pinot Grigio and Pinot Gris are not just alternative spellings for the same grape—they are stylistic statements. Contrast the weight and texture of an Italian Pinot Grigio with a fuller, richer Alsatian Pinot Gris.

Pinot Grigio: a new fashion that's bound to last

Wine, like most other things, follows fashion, and wines move from being "in" for a few years, to "out" again. Twenty years ago, everyone wanted Muscadet, which was then eclipsed by the ubiquitous Australian Chardonnay. Now people are looking for a new alternative, and Pinot Grigio is on the rise. Most Pinot Grigios are quaffing wines, but if you are prepared to pay just a bit more, there are some great examples, matching Chablis in character. In my family we have a small yacht on the River Hamble, in Hampshire, England. My favorite trick is to hang a bottle of PG over the side for an hour and then sit on the back of the boat and enjoy it with a plate of oysters—now that's a fashion that won't change!

TREBBIANO

The Trebbiano grape is a component of many blended Italian whites; it's too neutral in flavor to produce good wine on its own. For this reason, the French (who call this grape Ugni Blanc) use it as a base for brandy. But the finest Trebbiano is from central Italy. Try Trebbiano Toscano, Romagnolo, Soave, and Giallo. The crisp, fresh Trebbiano d'Abruzzo is perhaps the most interesting.

COLOR Bright lemon yellow with highlights of silver.

AROMA Subtle, with green fruits and hints of almond and white flowers.

TASTE Dry; refreshing with a marked acidity and good balance of alcohol.

BUYING Valentini and Thaulero are reliable producers. Whatever the source, I recommend that you buy only the latest vintage. Age does this wine no favors.

ENJOYING Chill the wine well and try it with a spicy risotto or other smoky dishes—delicious. Other successful matches include seafood or even baked goat cheese.

BRANCHING OUT If you like Trebbiano, try a Colombard, a lighter Rioja Viura, or a simple Muscadet, all of which are also light and subtle.

ORVIETO

According to 19th-century Italian poet Gabriele d'Annunzio, this wine is "the sun of Italy in a bottle." Metaphors aside, modern Orvieto seems to delight and disappoint with equal frequency. I personally like good expressions of this wine, but conflicting opinions among my customers make it difficult to recommend.

Orvieto, a Trebbiano-based blend, is the most important white wine in southwestern Umbria (central Italy). In the Middle Ages, Orvieto became a papal favorite. Pope Gregorio XVI allegedly requested that his body be washed in Orvieto before being interred. (This pontiff was clearly someone who enjoyed God's gifts to the full: he also was a champion of the rival wine Frascati!)

Make sure you pay attention to the label when buying Orvieto. To breathe new life into the denomination, some producers have supplemented the most important *secco* (dry) style with less

ORVIETO
Castello della Sala

familiar *abboccato* (semidry or semisweet), *amabile* (medium-sweet), and *dolce* (sweet) versions. It's worth spending extra for the added body and intensity of Orvieto from the *classico* zone. Look for that word on the label.

COLOR A medium-intense straw yellow, with green tinges.

AROMA Delicate; soft flowers with fruits and roasted almonds.

TASTE Fresh, elegant; lemony acidity, medium alcohol, and medium length.

BUYING The younger the better. I recommend Castello della Sala, Luigi Bigi, and Barberani.

ENJOYING Serve Orvieto chilled as an aperitif or drink it with any simple pasta dish. I enjoy it with grilled bruschetta.

BRANCHING OUT Compare the light and simple style of Orvieto with neighboring Frascati. You can also contrast it with the more significant texture and more overt character of Verdicchio.

"Orvieto: laced with fruits, flowers, and roasted almonds. It's fresh and elegant like a Chablis, but with a juicier flavor and a richer texture."

FRASCATI

Produced on the beautiful slopes of the volcanic Alban Hills and within sight of Rome, Frascati is a versatile, easy-going wine with a worldwide reputation. It was a favorite among the ancient Romans, and was later promoted by the church in Italy. Frascati is made from a blend of two grapes—Malvasia and the ubiquitous Trebbiano—and is perfect for summer drinking.

COLOR Straw yellow, sometimes with greenish tinges.

AROMA Citrus fruits, flowers, perhaps with a hint of ripe pear.

TASTE Delicate, with a good balance of citrus and acidity.

BUYING Frascati comes in a variety of styles: *secco* or *asciutto* (both dry), *amabile* (off-dry or sweetish), and *dolce* or *cannellino* (both sweet). There is also a *spumante* (sparkling) style. Great producers are Colli di Catone and Fontana Candida.

FRASCATI
Colli di Catone

ENJOYING This wine is happily matched with any light dish. It is an excellent accompaniment to chargrilled sardines, and goes even better with fresh asparagus Milanese.

BRANCHING OUT Challenge Frascati's somewhat "funky" style with a "posh" Soave, Verdicchio, or Petit Chablis. Their similarly refreshing structures are contrasted by differing fruit characters.

LIGHT, CRISP WHITES

WORLD WINES

ITALY
VERDICCHIO

Verdicchio is grown along the Adriatic coast of east-central Italy. The best-known wines come from the denomination of Verdicchio dei Castelli di Jesi. They have a lemon–lime acidity and a slightly chalky note, rather like Chablis. Wines from the smaller, less well-known district of Verdicchio di Matelica have more body than those of Castelli di Jesi, with a softer texture and a more melonlike flavor.

COLOR Pale gold with sparkling glints of silver; very bright.

AROMA Fresh and light; green apple and lemon; hints of pear or melon.

TASTE Clean and characterful with almond and pear; medium length.

BUYING For higher-quality wines, look for the terms *classico* and *superiore* on the label. Monte Schiavo, Umani Ronchi, and Bucchi are amazing producers.

ENJOYING Enjoy these wines with white-meat dishes or with fish in a light tartare sauce. Verdicchio makes great company for salads, too. Try it in summer with lemon-dressed artichokes.

BRANCHING OUT
It's interesting to compare Verdicchio with a good Orvieto from Umbria or a Gavi from Piedmont. They all share a crisp, stony style, but each is made from a different grape variety.

VERDICCHIO
Monte Schiavo

GREECE
ASSYRTIKO

The finest white wine in Greece! Assyrtiko has excellent structure and vibrant, citrusy flavors. It is normally associated with the Aegean islands, especially Santorini. The Assyrtiko grape has been grown on Santorini for 3,000 years, and the island's volcanic soil brings out its smoky, flinty flavors. But Assyrtiko is now being planted in many of Greece's other vine-growing regions. Look out for it.

COLOR Usually greeny yellow, with medium intensity.

AROMA Delicate, with notes of lemon, green apple, honeysuckle, and minerals.

TASTE Well balanced with a lemony acidity; fresh at the finish.

BUYING Wines from Santorini are the best expressions of this variety. Boutari, the Santorini Co-op, and Hatzidakis are among the best producers.

ENJOYING Give yourself a little taste of Greece: match Assyrtiko with chunks of rich feta cheese with ripe cherry tomatoes and crisp, fresh cucumber—delicious!

BRANCHING OUT
Try it as an alternative to dry French or Italian whites. It's halfway between an Alsatian Riesling and a Pinot Grigio.

ASSYRTIKO
Boutari

RHODITIS

Despite the name, this grape variety does not come from Rhodes, but is native to the Peloponnese. It maintains refreshing acidity even in this hot, southern part of the Greek mainland. The wines show real harmony, and are among the best-quality whites in Greece. Historically, winemakers have produced Rhoditis for the domestic market, but a new generation is now improving the wine, making it easy to recommend for everyone.

COLOR Bright; pale yellow with tinges of gold and straw.

AROMA Complex; lemon, new-mown grass, pineapple, walnut.

TASTE Delicate, well balanced, and subtle; a long, slightly resinous finish.

BUYING As with most light white wines, buy Rhoditis from the most recent vintage. Tsantalis and Boutari are two very reliable producers.

ENJOYING I love this wine with fish, especially grilled sea bream, or mullet in a lemon and olive oil sauce.

BRANCHING OUT Try this bone-dry wine alongside an Italian Verdicchio or Soave. Almond notes on the finish seem to make them part of the same family.

PORTUGAL
VINHO VERDE

Portugal has never been famous for white wine—it's the home of port, after all—but good Vinho Verde is a real treat. Producers in this part of northern Portugal harvest the grapes early to avoid fall rains from the Atlantic, so these whites are fruity and fresh, and low in alcohol.

The name Vinho Verde means "green wine," but the "green" refers to its youthfulness, not its color. The most sought-after Vinhos Verdes are made from the Alvarinho grape. Slightly more expensive than other wines from this region, they have bright fruit flavors and a refreshing sparkle or prickly quality.

COLOR Bright; distinctive pale lemon with green tinges.

AROMA Youthful, fresh, delicate, with green fruits, flowers, and hints of pear.

TASTE Dry, with a slight sparkle on the tongue; refreshing; medium length.

BUYING Drink this wine as young as possible. Any given vintage should be available by the following summer. Among producers, look for Montez Champalimaud, Quinta da Aveleda, and Quinta da Tamariz.

ENJOYING The biting freshness, sherbet fizz, and low alcohol of Vinho Verde make it perfect for drinking with Thai fish soup and lemon chicken.

BRANCHING OUT If you like Vinho Verde, try Spanish Rías Baixas or French Muscadet. All three are sleek, cool, and refreshing wines.

LIGHT, CRISP WHITES

WORLD WINES

MONTEZ CHAMPALIMAUD

PAÇO de TEIXEIRÓ

2004

VINHO BRANCO
White Wine
Vin Blanc

VINHO REGIONAL MINHO

750ml

TASTE TEST: LENGTH

Just what is meant by "length" when tasting wine?

❶ PINOT GRIGIO is the star white of northern Italy, and is an easy-quaffing, light wine with a clean, lemony, and refreshing taste. Look for examples from Veneto or Trentino. **Seek out** Mezzacorona, Livio Felluga, Beltrame.

❷ MUSCADET SÈVRE-ET-MAINE is a wonderful dry white from the Loire Valley. **Seek out** Sauvion, Château de la Placière, Château de la Ragotière, Domaine de l'Ecu. Make sure you choose a wine with *sur lie* on the label.

❸ CHENIN BLANC from South Africa is a refreshing, straightforward white wine. Wines from named regions are the best quality—look for examples from Stellenbosch or Paarl. **Seek out** Simonsig, Kanu, de Trafford, Ken Forrester, Villiera, Fairview.

❹ CHABLIS is a steely, dry French wine made entirely from Chardonnay. **Seek out** Domaine du Chardonnay, La Chablisienne, Domaine Laroche, Jean Durup, or any *premier cru*, especially Montée de Tonnerre.

"Length is one of the most important elements that determine the character of a good-quality wine."

The three aspects to remember when tasting wine are color, aroma, and taste, but the last of these—taste—can also itself be broken down into distinct stages. The initial stage is the **first impression**—the flavor that hits you as soon as the wine is in your mouth; then there is a **second set** of flavors that develop in the mouth, **underlying the first**; and finally there is the **length**—that is, the flavors that **linger in your mouth** after you have swallowed the wine. All styles of wine have

the potential to have **good length**: they don't have to be aromatic or opulent, all they need is to be made with **good-quality fruit**.

The **PINOT GRIGIO** is the first wine in this tasting. It is very **light** on the nose, with a **fresh, crisp** character that reflects its cool-climate provenance. It is very **dry** on the palate and the flavors linger for only a **short time**.

The **MUSCADET SÈVRE-ET-MAINE** is **bone dry** on the nose, with clean, straightforward, **fresh citrus** flavors and a **dry finish**. While the first wine—the Pinot Grigio—can be a little flabby at the end, its flavors dropping off one by one, the Muscadet has a **steely** and very **crisp finish**, although it too **vanishes very quickly**.

The third wine, the **CHENIN BLANC**, is quite **exotic** on the palate with flavors of **peaches and apricots**. It has a **good length** even though this is rather **one-dimensional**; all together, not too different from the Pinot Grigio, but **longer-lasting**.

And finally, the **CHABLIS**. This has a nose full of **fresh citrus fruit** as well as that telltale **flinty, mineral** quality that gives away the wine's provenance. That steeliness is carried through, **intensifying on the palate**, but becomes even more **concentrated** in the wine's **fantastic length**. This wine's finish lasts for more than 20 seconds, the flavors left in the mouth evolving from **citrus** to **mineral** over a long time.

LIGHT, CRISP WHITES

WORLD WINES

SPAIN
VIURA

Most people think of Rioja as a red wine, but this region also produces whites—and they are beginning to develop a great reputation. This success has been due in part to the Viura grape (also known as Macabeo), which is now the most widely planted grape in the region. Viura creates interesting, fruit-driven, citrusy wines. The best are fresh and crisp, with a strong floral character and a distinctive nutty aroma.

COLOR An unusual pale greenish yellow, with tinges of silver.

AROMA Discreet, subtle, and light, with flowers, lime, and hints of nuts.

TASTE Dry, refreshing acidity, balanced alcohol, and a medium finish.

BUYING Look for the name of the grape on the label—it can sometimes be part of a blend. Among producers, I recommend Marqués de Monistrol and Marqués de Riscal.

ENJOYING This is a fun wine. Drink it young to appreciate its refreshing, pungent style. Well chilled, it is ideal with tapas, seafood paella, or a barbecue.

BRANCHING OUT If the restrained, lemony character of this wine appeals, you're also likely to appreciate a good Bordeaux white or a Sauvignon Blanc from the Touraine district of the Loire.

GERMANY
MÜLLER-THURGAU

Robust Müller-Thurgau thrives in even the coolest of wine regions. But a great deal of it forms the basis of characterless, mass-market German wines such as Liebfraumilch and Niersteiner. This is a tragedy, because it is a variety with potential to produce exciting, light-bodied wines with delicate, floral flavors that are well balanced by crisp acidity. Don't let its reputation prevent you from experimenting with this wine.

COLOR Usually straw yellow, sometimes with a delicate touch of green.

AROMA Fresh green and citrus fruits; flowers and almonds.

TASTE Delicate and light, sometimes with a nutty flavor; finish slightly bitter.

BUYING "The younger the better" is the rule with this wine. Try to buy something designated from a single vineyard for more personality. Meersburger and Rudolf Fürst are top producers.

ENJOYING I recommend Müller-Thurgau with a light lunch, perhaps in the German style. Try it, for example, with cold meats or a savory strudel, accompanied by a potato salad.

BRANCHING OUT Müller-Thurgau enthusiasts should try Luxembourg's Rivaner or a glass of Sylvaner—remarkably similar.

SWITZERLAND
CHASSELAS

Swiss Chasselas is known by different names depending upon its region of origin. These include Fendant (the best-known alternative), Dorin, Gutedel, and Perlan. Whatever it's called, this grape produces fresh, fruity wines, low in acidity and high in alcohol. The most elegant and distinctive versions are likely to come from the Lavaux or Chablais districts, both of which are in the Vaud region near Lake Geneva.

CHASSELAS
Rouvinez

COLOR Pale yellow, with a faint sparkle and attractive silvery highlights.

AROMA Young, fresh, and delicate; lightly perfumed with lemon.

TASTE Dry, impressive texture, with good balance, charm, and a long finish.

BUYING Buy the most recent vintage, and look for the Lavaux or Chablais districts on the label. Rouvinez and Hammel are two great producers.

ENJOYING This wine is perfect after a long day's skiing, and also makes a great aperitif. In the summer, try it at lunchtime with barbecued shrimp.

BRANCHING OUT Compare this wine with a basic Chablis or even Pinot Blanc. All share a distinct apple, citrus, and stony character.

SOUTH AFRICA
CHENIN BLANC

South Africa's most prolific variety, Chenin Blanc also has the local name "Steen." It is an extremely versatile grape, and this has led to huge stylistic variation in the wines it produces.

Many producers have introduced fermentation or maturation in new oak barrels for a deep yellow color and a rich, creamy, nutty flavor. However, this is not typical of Chenin, and in my opinion it does not suit the wine at all. Good South African Chenin should be light, fresh, and fruity in style. But note that generic "South African" Chenin can be a little lean and watery, so look for more concentrated wines from specified districts in the Cape region, including Stellenbosch and Paarl.

COLOR Bright; pale lemon yellow with slight tinges of green.

AROMA Young and pleasant, with green fruits and notes of melon.

TASTE Dry, fresh, well structured; well balanced, with a floral finish.

BUYING As South Africa's flagship variety, there are many producers—and some are clearly more dedicated than others. I recommend Kanu, Simonsig, Mulderbosch, and Ken Forrester.

ENJOYING A great party wine, this also works well with river fish, including trout with spring vegetables.

BRANCHING OUT Compare the fruit character and structure of good South African Chenin Blanc with expressions of the same variety as it is grown in the Loire Valley of France—particularly the austere Savennières and Vouvray Sec.

LIGHT, CRISP WHITES

WORLD WINES

JUICY, AROMATIC WHITES

Bursting with loads of fruit and with distinct personalities, juicy, aromatic white wines range from the fresh-mown grassiness of Sauvignon Blanc to the deeply perfumed lychee flavors of Muscat. They vary in color from lemon to pale gold,  depending mostly on vinification technique and the grape varieties used to make them, and they have a slightly thicker viscosity than light, crisp whites. When you taste them, these wines should remind you of ripe peaches—deliciously fresh and juicy, with good acidity to balance the fruit, and a long, pleasant finish. Vibrant, with plenty of exotic fruit to make your mouth water, these are exuberant wines with great all-around harmony. Even though you may soon find a particular favorite, I urge you to keep exploring this style—there is so much to discover!

STYLE PROFILE
JUICY, AROMATIC WHITES

RIPE YET DRY

The most important thing to remember about juicy, aromatic whites is that the word "juicy" does not imply that the wine is sweet. Some of these wines may have sweet aromas, but this is a reflection of the ripe fruit that has gone into the wine and is not a measure of the sweetness of the wine itself. Juicy, aromatic whites are dry, and differences in their styles are like the different characters you would expect in members of the same family. They all share a common bond, but each one is unique. The differences between them, of course, are a result of the grape variety that has gone into the wine, as well as the soil, climate,

> *"The secret of these wines is their gentle exuberance— vibrant fruit matched by delicate lemony acidity, and wonderful length."*

and viticulture that has gone into the winemaking. For example, Muscat wines are naturally aromatic, while in others, such as Gavi di Gavi from Italy, the aromas are brought out by careful vinification.

Juicy, aromatic whites are typically produced in cool, temperate climates. The ideal wine in this style is fresh and clean, but has a pungent, full flavor. The best examples come from those cool vinegrowing areas where a long ripening season gives the grapes plenty of opportunity to develop their fruity character. Regions such as Alsace in northeastern France, New Zealand's South Island, or the mountainous Rueda in Spain present the perfect conditions for creating excellent wines.

STAINLESS STEEL FOR A LIGHT TOUCH
Like many light, crisp whites, wines that are aromatic and juicy are vinified at low temperatures to bring out their fruitiness, usually in stainless steel vats to maintain the wine's freshness.

CHARACTERFUL FLAVORS

Moderately priced juicy, aromatic whites will be fairly light, but they should still have lots of character and expression. The flavors and aromas, although probably not profound or even necessarily obvious, will be lemony and floral, and the wines should have a pleasant, medium length. The more you spend, the more expressive the wines become.

SAUVIGNON BLANC

This classic grape makes great wines around the world, from the Loire region of France—where it makes the superb Sancerre and Pouilly Fumé—to the Marlborough region of New Zealand and parts of Australia and South Africa.

TASTE TRAIL

There are two great classics in this group: Sauvignon Blanc and Riesling. Try **SAUVIGNON BLANC** from the Loire, and move on through Australia and South Africa to New Zealand, particularly the Marlborough region for the most aromatic wines. **RIESLING** is the distinctive, fruity grape from Alsace, Germany, and Austria, and recently Australia and New Zealand. Other superior wines come from grapes such as **ALBARIÑO** (Spain); the up-and-coming **GRÜNER VELTLINER** (Austria); and most aromatic of all, **MUSCAT**.

ENJOYING Enjoyment of these wines lies in their fruitiness. Chilling is essential: the colder the wine, the fruitier it will taste. Seafood is perfect with all these wines. Drier wines, such as French or New Zealand Sauvignon Blanc, are great with fish and salads; richer, fuller wines, such as Australian or Alsace Rieslings, accompany Asian food well. Try aromatic whites with the local food of the wine's origin: goat cheese with Sancerre, for example, is an unbeatable combination.

Good wines have medium weight and a clean, juicy texture; their flavors are fresh, but full of character and with a perfect balance of alcohol and acidity. Their bouquet is complex, intense, and full, immediately making an impact. You will know when you encounter a great wine in this category: it is like walking into a wonderful perfumery!

DRINK OR STORE?

Juicy, aromatic whites are versatile wines: mid-priced examples are generally very reliable, and their refreshing fruitiness suits most people's tastes. With the main exception of Riesling, which has proved its aging potential all over the world, these are not usually wines for aging and are best consumed within two to five years.

FRANCE
SANCERRE / POUILLY FUMÉ

All hail the queen of the Loire Valley! If you enjoy aromatic, refreshing, yet restrained white wines, then this is the place for you. Located in the upper Loire, Sancerre is famed for its whites, although it also produces some rosés and light reds. The style and quality of Sancerre wines can be highly variable, even between adjacent producers. I think the best white Sancerres come from the villages of Bué, Chavignol, Ménétréol, and Verdigny, rather than from the village of Sancerre itself. So when buying Sancerre, look for one of these names on the label.

Sancerre's direct neighbor, just across the Loire River, is Pouilly Fumé, and its smoky and mineral-laden wines offer exceptional quality and value. Both Sancerre and Pouilly Fumé are made

"This classy wine is typically drunk young, to fully savor its wonderfully fresh and zesty character."

from Sauvignon Blanc—instantly recognizable for its piercing aroma. This distinctive scent has been ascribed many descriptions, from gooseberry and nettle to cat pee! But the best Sauvignon Blancs are always fresh and full of life. Sancerre has been called the Sauvignon capital of the world, but this might now be disputed in some wine regions of the Southern Hemisphere. Even so, it's still the best to my mind. Of course, I'm biased—I grew up in the Loire Valley!

COLOR Bright lemon yellow to pale straw, with tinges of green.

AROMA Youthful and aromatic, with green fruit, elderflower, citrus, and grass.

TASTE Intense, with a refreshing, persistent acidity and a long, clean finish.

BUYING Some winemakers exploit the reputation of this area and mass-produce mediocre wines. But there are real stars, too, including Domaine J. C. Chatelain, Domaine Henri Bourgeois, Domaine Didier Dagueneau, Domaine Alphonse Mellot, and Château de Tracy.

ENJOYING Try these wines with creamy goat cheese and a fresh green salad, or with grilled red sweet peppers—again, stuffed with goat cheese!

BRANCHING OUT It's worth tasting this wine alongside a good Sauvignon Blanc from New Zealand or South Africa. The New World examples have more exuberant (even tropical) fruit flavors and more body or weight, while the French wines are more mineral, transparent, and generally refreshing.

POUILLY FUMÉ
Château de Tracy

ALSACE PINOT GRIS

This wine is made from the same grape as light and crisp Pinot Grigio, but that is where the similarities end. At its rich, honeyed, and aromatic best, Pinot Gris can compete with the Pulignys of Burgundy *(see p.132)*. And Pinot Gris from Alsace is making a real comeback. The wine can be kept for five to eight years, mellowing to a spicy, smoky richness.

ALSACE PINOT GRIS
Marc Kreydenweiss

COLOR Bright golden yellow, with a distinct green tinge.

AROMA Complex, dry, and elegant, with crystallized fruit, apricot, and raisins.

TASTE Well balanced, with spicy touches, oak hints, and a long finish.

BUYING Ensure there is no mention of *vendange tardive* or *sélection de grains nobles* on the label, denoting a sweet wine. Marc Kreydenweiss and Domaine Zind-Humbrecht are among the world's best producers.

ENJOYING Pinot Gris is a good match for fish or white meat. Try it with monkfish or even warm truffles. I also like it with foie gras and toasted brioche.

BRANCHING OUT If you like this wine, try Pinot Gris from New Zealand, or an unwooded Australian Chardonnay. Rich fruit flavors come through these wines very nicely indeed.

ALSACE RIESLING

Riesling is the most elegant grape of the Alsace region. However, the wines vary from pricey, world-class *grands crus* down to very undistinguished examples. They also range from bone-dry and steely to more rich and opulent in style. Even so, the best wines are rarely oaked. They are often aged in the bottle, where they develop gunflint acidity and intense fruit.

COLOR Bright yellow, with a silver tinge; pale to medium intensity.

AROMA Very expressive and intense; citrus and exotic fruits, also minerals.

TASTE Well balanced and clean, with complex flavors and texture.

BUYING At a decent price, this wine is worth exploring. However, I find the cheapest ones can give you a headache, due to heavy-handed use of sulfur in the winery. Among producers, I enjoy Domaine Ostertag and Maison Trimbach.

ENJOYING Serve this wine well chilled to reinforce its zesty acidity and pungent, citrus fruit flavors. It works well with both delicate foods and spicy cuisine.

BRANCHING OUT Try this wine alongside a Vouvray Sec or a Loire Valley Savennières. The fruit characters may differ, but you will notice the same minerality and pronounced acidity.

FRANCE
ALSACE MUSCAT

The Muscat grape is associated with the exotic aromas and flavors of sweet wines. Indeed, many of the best dessert wines of southern France and Australia are based on this variety. But Alsace also produces a complex, dry wine from this grape—thanks to its cool, but sunny, climate—that is low in both alcohol and acidity.

COLOR Pale straw or golden yellow, with green highlights.

AROMA Expressive rich scents of flowers, musk, and exotic fruits.

TASTE Dry, light texture; delicate and subtle, underlined by a lemony acidity.

BUYING Capturing the grape's purity requires special care in both vineyard and cellar. For me, Domaine Weinbach and Domaine Rolly-Gassman are the finest.

ENJOYING This variety is best as a sweet wine. The dry version is a great aperitif—ideal for sipping in summer.

BRANCHING OUT The exotic notes that are so typical of Muscat can also be found in a Gewürztraminer, or a Viognier from the Rhône Valley.

"Don't be fooled—Muscat from Alsace is not sweet. It's dry and fresh, rich and inviting, exotic and stimulating."

SAVOIE ROUSSETTE

If you ever visit the Alps, try this wine—perhaps the finest Savoie white. Production is limited due to the location and climate, but most of the wine is drunk locally anyway. Look for the name of a commune after the word Roussette on the label; wines lacking this may be blended with up to 50 percent Chardonnay.

COLOR Pale golden yellow, with a silver tinge.

AROMA Intense; dried apricot, peach, pear, and roasted almond.

TASTE Complex and dry; fleshy with a fresh texture and a mineral touch.

BUYING Only the top producers achieve anything interesting with this variety. I prefer Prieuré St Christophe and Domaine Louis Magnin.

ENJOYING This is a perfect drink with a fondue or a cheese soufflé. It also goes well with Comté cheese melted on toast.

BRANCHING OUT If you like the subtlety of Savoie, try a lightweight Ruländer or even a Picpoul de Pinet.

JURANÇON SEC / PACHERENC DU VIC-BILH

These exotic dry wines from southwestern France both offer a fleshy texture and smoky, mineral flavors. I am a great fan of Jurançon Sec—a blend of three regional grape varieties called Gros Manseng, Petit Manseng, and Courbu. Pacherenc du Vic-Bilh uses the same grapes, along with the more common Sémillon and Sauvignon. These wines are a must-try for anyone out to impress.

PACHERENC
DU VIC-BILH
Château d'Aydie

COLOR Pale, becoming darker with age; gold with green tinges.

AROMA Peach, pineapple, citrus, almond, blossom, and minerals.

TASTE Dense, underlined with lemon acidity; lingering finish.

BUYING Château d'Aydie (Laplace), Domaine Cauhapé, and Château Castera are all top producers. Be careful when choosing a bottle—Jurançon without the word *sec* after it is a sweet wine.

ENJOYING Drink both wines within two or three years of the harvest, and serve them lightly chilled. Enjoy these wines with any fish or white meat—or in your backyard with a bowl of olives.

BRANCHING OUT Distinctive aromas and flavors give these wines their own strong identity. Australian Riesling or a Sémillon from Australia's Hunter Valley get close to the mark.

GAILLAC

The southwestern appellation of Gaillac, one of France's earliest wine-producing areas, has found renewed dynamism in the past decade. Wine production has almost doubled, although most of it is still drunk by locals—and connoisseurs! The main grapes used to make this dry white are the local Len de L'Elh (Gascon dialect for *loin de l'oeil*, meaning "far from sight") and Mauzac. Gaillac is a great buy.

COLOR Pale to medium intensity; golden yellow, with a hint of green.

AROMA Delicate: quince, orange peel, fresh hay, pineapple, blossom, spice.

TASTE Elegant, slightly oily; complex flavors with a refreshing acidity.

BUYING Top producers are Domaine Rotier, Domaine des Tres Cantous, and Domaine de Causse-Marines. Beware when buying Gaillac, since the region also produces a sweet version.

ENJOYING Gaillac wines are best within two or three years of the harvest. They are great with a smoked haddock salad, or with monkfish on a bed of saffron risotto.

BRANCHING OUT
Try Gaillac alongside Savagnin from the Jura, or Muscadet Sèvre-et-Maine or Anjou Blanc from the Loire. All are very dry, with mineral and nutty flavors.

GAILLAC
Domaine Rotier

LANGUEDOC VIOGNIER

The Viognier grape has a rich, blossomy perfume. Its traditional home is the northern Rhône Valley of France, but it is now also popular in New World regions—especially California. Languedoc-Roussillon in southern France also produces Viognier, but the style is different from its Rhône and Californian cousins. It is much drier and more refreshing, with a lighter texture and more citrusy flavors. Nevertheless, this wine retains its aromatic intensity and structure.

COLOR Bright and clear; yellow to light gold.

AROMA Intense, with grapefruit, peach stones, and apricot.

TASTE Fleshy and full; perfect balance of alcohol and acidity; long, clean finish.

BUYING Les Perles de Méditerranée and Vignerons des Trois Terroirs are good sources. The cooperatives of southern France have really improved their work in recent years.

ENJOYING Serve this wine well chilled. Drink it young—after about 18 months it loses its pungent aromas and flavors.

BRANCHING OUT This wine has intense character. Try Gewürztraminer or Muscat, which are similarly exuberant, but have their own personalities.

BELLET

Bellet is produced in the hills around Nice, at the heart of the beautiful French Riviera. This wine is fresh, fruity, and aromatic. Rolle is the main grape variety, and it has distinct floral aromas and a natural citrusy acidity. However, production is very limited— I could not even find a bottle at Nice airport! This means it is expensive, rather like everything else in this part of the world.

COLOR Pale; lemon yellow, with fresh green tinges.

AROMA Expressive, with white flowers, ripe white fruits, and ripe peach.

TASTE Round and delicate, balanced by lemony acidity and a harmonious finish.

BUYING Clos St Vincent and Château Bellet are two very well-known producers. Although this wine is hard to find, I would not keep it for too long— preferably a maximum of three years.

ENJOYING If you are lucky enough to find a bottle of Bellet, save it for a meal with crab or langoustines. It's also great with a Niçoise salad.

BRANCHING OUT Try this wine alongside an Italian Vermentino. Other comparisons include Viognier from the Languedoc or Sauvignon Blanc from Australia, although these wines are usually riper in texture.

TASTE TEST: FRUIT

Four wines, four grape varieties, four very different fruit styles.

❶ SAUVIGNON BLANC makes wines full of citrus and gooseberry flavors, with fantastic expression and exuberance. **Seek out** Château de Maupas, Georges Chavet, Domaine de Loye, Domaine Henry Pellé, or any Loire Sauvignon Blanc.

❷ VERDEJO, a Spanish grape, makes great whites that may also be named after the Rueda DO. **Seek out** José Pariente, Aldor, Marqués de Riscal, Frutos Villar, Agricola Castellana, Con Class de Cuevas de Castilla.

❸ VIOGNIER is a wine for those with a sweeter tooth—make sure it is served very well chilled. **Seek out** Bell or Fetzer from California. Or, substitute a French Condrieu, from the same grape; look for the producers Domaine Chèze or Yves Cuilleron.

❹ RIESLING has found a new home in Australia, where it makes wonderful, juicy whites, especially in the Clare and Eden Valleys. **Seek out** Pewsey Vale, Henschke, O'Leary Walker, Knappstein.

"To me, a 'juicy,' aromatic white wine has loads of fruit character that literally makes your mouth water."

This character may be so **intense** that it hits you like a sledgehammer at the first sniff, or it may be **more subtle**, opening out into a wider spectrum of **fruit complexity** as you smell and taste. It will rarely be accompanied by oak—the fruit is all-important—and will always have a **fresh, dry finish**, leaving your mouth watering, desperate for the next sip.

The **pale lemon** color of the **SAUVIGNON BLANC** belies a pungent nose full of **lemons** and **freshly cut grass**. Take a sip—this wine is **lean, pungent, and straightforward** on the palate, with not much complexity but loads of **lemony, grassy fruit** and a dry, refreshing finish.

VERDEJO, from Spain, is a **more aromatic** grape variety with sweet, elegant, **perfumed** aromas of **peach, apricot, and grapefruit**. This wine has a different level of intensity to the first; the fruit is more **"shy"** with new layers of **complexity** coming out **little by little**, although it too has a deliciously **clean, citrusy, juicy** finish.

VIOGNIER, the third wine to taste, is a **difficult grape to grow** as it can easily overripen and **lose acidity**. But a good Viognier has charming, **complex fruit aromas** of **peach, lychee, white flowers**, and hints of **spice**. It has **greater intensity of fruit** than the Verdejo, with a **fatter** texture, but it also has nice underlying acidity for a **dry finish**.

Finally, pour the **RIESLING** into your glass, and hold it up to the light. The **hints of gold** in its color foretell the **exuberance** of the fruit to come. It has a very **aromatic nose**, similar in intensity to the Sauvignon Blanc but very different in terms of complexity and the variety of aromas. These range from **limes and flinty, smoky petrol** through to sweetish hints of **ripe pineapple**. The palate is fresh and **mouthwatering**, juicy and thirst-quenching, but still with a **dry, clean finish**.

SPAIN
RUEDA

Most people think of Spanish wine as being red. However, the small town of Rueda, northwest of Madrid, has given its name to an excellent white. Produced largely from the local Verdejo grape, Rueda should be drunk young, as its lively aroma is its best feature.

Until the 1970s, the *bodegas* (wineries) in this stretch of the Duero Valley focused on sweet, sherrylike whites. But the arrival of new equipment (mainly stainless steel tanks) showed that Verdejo was capable of creating a great dry wine. I love its fresh character, and I often recommend it over a Sancerre or Pinot Grigio. Stock up!

COLOR Bright, light straw yellow, sometimes with glints of green.

AROMA Intense notes of flowers, cut grass, and lemon zest.

TASTE Clean and crisp, with a refreshing texture and a very long finish.

BUYING Look for very recent vintages and enjoy them young. Among the best Rueda producers, I would recommend Alvarez y Diez, Castilla la Vieja, and José Pariente.

ENJOYING Enjoy this wine on its own or with fish—I suggest grilled sole or pan-fried sea bass dressed with fennel and green vegetables. Such a treat!

BRANCHING OUT Try this wine with a Sancerre, and compare their "green" aromas and clean, refreshing acidity.

GALICIA

In the far northwestern corner of the country, on the border with Portugal, Galicia is Spain's most isolated wine-producing region. Atlantic weather gives it the alternative name of *España Verde*, or "Green Spain." Galician wines are made mainly from the native Albariño grape, which is a variation of the Portuguese Alvarinho, the major component of Vinho Verde. At its best, Albariño produces wines that finely balance fruit flavor and acidity, and that can improve in the bottle (unlike Vinho Verde).

Within Galicia, the denominations of Rías Baixas, Ribeiro, and Ribeira Sacra produce wines that are particularly delicious and aromatic. My personal favorites are the wines from Rías Baixas. Production is limited, but these vineyards produce Galicia's most amazing and most sought-after (and therefore most expensive) wines. Rías Baixas is itself divided into three subzones: Val do Salnes, O Rosal, and Condado do Tea. Among them, I think the wines of Val do Salnes, along the west coast, are the purest form of Albariño. Actually, I feel the wines of Galicia are the most representative of juicy, aromatic whites as a whole. They never cease to amaze me!

GALICIA
Martín Códax

COLOR Bright; straw yellow, with silvery highlights.

AROMA Intense, citrusy, and herbaceous; green apple and flint.

TASTE Full of character; refreshing acidity, with a long, lemony finish.

BUYING Buy and drink these wines in their youth. Among producers, the leading name is Martín Códax; I also recommend Pazo de Señorans and Palacio de Fefiñanes.

ENJOYING Galician wines are ideal well chilled and served alongside fresh, simply prepared seafood: from shrimp, mussels, and oysters through sea bass and cod, to lobster and crab.

BRANCHING OUT The light, fresh nature of Galician wines compares most directly with neighboring Vinhos Verdes from Portugal. Also try them alongside good Muscadet.

"You can almost taste the sea breeze in Galician Albariños! These are wines to rival the grassy Sauvignon Blancs of the Loire Valley."

LA MANCHA

La Mancha is the largest wine region in Europe—but it's a sleeping giant. La Mancha wine is made from the Airén grape, which is particularly suited to the hot, dry climate of central Spain. New producers in this region have started to harvest the grape as early as possible, to capture both the crisp acidity and the fresh fruit flavors. Modern production methods at low temperatures in stainless steel tanks help the wine to maintain its aromatic character.

COLOR Pale intensity; bright lemon yellow, with tinges of green.

AROMA Delicate; pear, lemon, minerals, honey, flowers, and grapes.

TASTE Clean, with good acidity and medium alcohol; apple at the finish.

BUYING Buy and drink La Mancha very young—ideally within six months of the current vintage—for crisp refreshment. Some particularly fine examples are produced by Finca Antigua and Señora del Rosario.

ENJOYING La Mancha is simple, inexpensive, and fun to drink at a barbecue or a picnic with your friends. Alternatively, try it with a plate of tapas or various spicy foods.

BRANCHING OUT Fans of this bone-dry and highly refreshing wine will probably also enjoy an Italian Verdicchio or Orvieto, or perhaps even a Muscadet Sèvre-et-Maine from the Loire Valley, France.

ITALY
ARNEIS

Demand for white wines to complement the famous reds of northwest Italy saved the Arneis grape from virtual extinction—it had almost disappeared by the early 1970s. This local variety is now making first-class wines in an elegant, refreshing style similar to Chablis, but with fruitier aromas. These wines also have an herby, nutty character, although I think their acidity can be a little on the low side.

Arneis is often blended with the powerful Nebbiolo grape variety in order to temper the tannin and acidity of the great red wine Barolo—hence its nickname Barolo Bianco, meaning "white Barolo."

Look for the best Arneis under the denomination Roero Arneis, which is from the hills north of Alba in the Piedmont region. This variety has also started to perform well in Australia, so we might soon see it become more widely appreciated.

COLOR Straw yellow, with green or light amber reflections.

AROMA Herbaceous, with apple, lemon, pear, peach, and almond.

TASTE Dry, with a light, lemony acidity; elegant, with a long, persistent finish.

BUYING Arneis is best enjoyed young—the wine does not have the minerality and acidity required for aging. Good producers include Prunotto, Bruno Giacosa, and Carlo Deltetto.

ENJOYING This is a perfect wine to enjoy in the summer. I think it's excellent chilled with grilled sea bass accompanied by new potatoes and baby leeks.

BRANCHING OUT The delicate charms of Arneis are not obvious—if the lean subtlety appeals to you, try a Gavi di Gavi, or even a Verdicchio.

Stubborn little rascals can grow up to be winners

The first time I ever tasted this lovely wine was when a supplier friend of mine tested me with it in a "blind" tasting. I knew immediately that it was a European, "Old World" wine, and I remember describing it as very elegant, fleshy but dry, with a strong mineral character as well as citrus and apple. I went for a Chablis, probably a well-made one—most likely a *premier cru*. But I was wrong: it was Arneis! Since then, I've been a big fan. *Arneis* means "stubborn little rascal," referring to the fact that the grape is difficult to work with, because it has a delicate skin and a tendency for its vine shoots to break. Arneis is one to watch—I can see this rising star overtaking Pinot Grigio in popularity one day.

VERMENTINO

The Vermentino grape is similar to good Sauvignon Blanc, although it is perhaps more exuberant, and less complex and profound. The most notable Vermentino wines are produced on the island of Sardinia, where the grapes are harvested early to ensure refreshing acidity. The best examples are from the denominations of Vermentino di Gallura and Vermentino di Alghero. You may also find Vermentino from the French island of Corsica.

COLOR Bright; straw yellow, glinting with light green.

AROMA Subtle, aromatic, and floral, with notes of rosemary and sage.

TASTE Intense, with a lemony acidity and a refreshing kick.

BUYING A lot of Vermentino of variable quality is consumed by sun-seeking tourists on Sardinia's popular Costa Smeralda. But two producers whose wines I particularly enjoy are Cantina Gallura and Contini.

ENJOYING Vermentino is best when well chilled and served with simple food, such as grilled or roasted vegetables. Never try it with anything too complicated.

BRANCHING OUT Vermentino's attractive aromas make an interesting comparison with Muscat or Viognier. Sauvignon Blanc from the Touraine district of the Loire Valley, or Verdejo from Rueda, Spain, may also appeal.

GAVI DI GAVI

I love this wine. It's made from the local Cortese grape in the district of Gavi, not far from Genoa and the Italian Riviera. The name "Gavi di Gavi" refers to wines that are produced close to the town of Gavi itself, in the far southeast of the district. This white wine has developed a reputation as one of the finest in Piedmont, and that is no easy feat, since wine and food are nearly a religion in this part of Italy.

GAVI DI GAVI
Broglia "La Meirana"

COLOR Bright; lemon yellow, with highlights of green.

AROMA Medium intensity; notes of pear, golden apple, citrus, and roasted almond.

TASTE Fleshy; ripe peach; harmonious with a long, clean finish.

BUYING I suggest you stick with recommended producers—people who care more for the quality of their wine than just the amount they can make. My own favorites are Broglia "La Meirana," Fontanafredda, and Nicola Bergaglio.

Gavi di Gavi is tangy, zesty, intense, and refreshing. The alternative, called Cortese di Gavi, is made elsewhere in the region, but it tends to be a thinner, rather steely wine.

As Gavi wines have become quite fashionable in Italy, so quantity has become more important than quality for a number of producers. With the introduction of modern winemaking techniques, wineries find it easier to churn out large volumes that are good value and simply refreshing, but that lack genuine character and body. So choose your Gavis carefully.

ENJOYING Don't drink this wine when it is very young. Gavi is often better—meaning richer, with stronger, more mineral flavors—two or three years after its vintage. It's a natural partner for seafood, so try it with grilled tuna steaks. I enjoy it well chilled with a fresh salad of tomatoes, feta cheese, and basil. Delicious!

BRANCHING OUT If you like the fruit character and acidity of Gavi di Gavi, I would recommend trying its neighbor, Arneis, or a good Verdicchio.

"Unpretentious but very popular, Gavi di Gavi wines are tangy, zesty, and refreshing. I absolutely adore them!"

LUXEMBOURG
RIVANER

If you like the idea of aromatic Chablis, then you really should try Rivaner. This wine seems to combine freshness and minerality with slightly richer and more complex aromas. The grape is a cross between Riesling and Sylvaner, which in Germany is known as Müller-Thurgau. In Luxembourg, almost all the wine is consumed locally, and production is in decline, so you may need to hunt around to find a bottle of Rivaner.

COLOR Bright and crisp; pale lemon yellow with silvery tinges.

AROMA Clean; mainly citrus and green fruits, such as apple; also minerals.

TASTE Well structured, elegant, and delicate, with a mellow touch.

BUYING Not many wineries are producing this wine, but two great sources are Domaine Mathis Bastian and Domaine Wormeldange. Some cooperatives are also very good, but taste before you buy!

ENJOYING The best Rivaners are distinctive and delicate, and they are a good accompaniment for any seafood. For a special treat, try a good-quality Rivaner with wild Scottish salmon.

BRANCHING OUT A good Rivaner can be compared to a crisp Grüner Veltliner or minerally Chablis. If you enjoy this style of wine, try an Austrian or German (Mosel) Riesling.

RIVANER *Domaine Mathis Bastian*

JUICY, AROMATIC WHITES

WORLD WINES

❶ SANCERRE from the Loire Valley is made from 100 percent Sauvignon Blanc, and is classy, pure, and clean, with a distinct minerality. If possible, choose a Sancerre from either the village of Bué or Chavignol. **Seek out** Jean-Max Roger, Vincent Pinard, Lucien Crochet.

❷ SOUTH AFRICAN SAUVIGNON BLANC has a great balance between intensity of fruit and fresh acidity. Look for wines from Constantia or Paarl. **Seek out** Buitenverwachting, Vondeling, Springfield Estate, Klein Constantia Estate, Plaisir de Merle.

❸ NEW ZEALAND SAUVIGNON BLANC from Marlborough is an attractive expression of the Sauvignon Blanc grape—full of exotic fruits balanced by the unique citrus acidity of this world-famous grape variety. **Seek out** Blue Ridge (from West Brook Winery), Wither Hills, Jackson Estate, Cloudy Bay, Oyster Bay, Isabel Estate.

TASTE TEST: CLIMATE

Discover the effect of climate in three wines made from the same grape variety.

Sauvignon Blanc vines in Constantia, South Africa

"Clean and crisp or ripe and exotic; climate has a considerable influence on the flavors in a wine."

Sauvignon Blanc is a grape variety that is grown all over the world. It survives well in **cool climates**, producing **clean, crisp** whites, but seems equally at home in **warmer climates,** where the sun induces more **exotic** flavors. The three wines in this tasting, all made from Sauvignon Blanc, look very similar— a clear, pale **straw yellow**, with hints of green. All are aromatic, invigorating wines, with **refreshing acidity**, but in terms of flavor, the Sauvignon Blanc grape is something of a **chameleon**, taking on the characteristics of the region where it is made, and each of the wines reveals a different portfolio of aromas and tastes.

The first wine in this tasting, the **SANCERRE**, is made from Sauvignon Blanc grapes grown in the Loire Valley. It has a distinct nose of **lemon** with **green fruits**. The lemon freshness, together with a **mineral flintiness**, comes through on the palate, although this is quite a **discreet and shy** wine with **subtle fruit** quality. The character of the palate is **narrow** and straightforward, reflecting the **cool climate** in which it is made.

There can be no argument that Constantia in South Africa has a **warmer climate** than Sancerre, and this becomes obvious when you taste the **SOUTH AFRICAN SAUVIGNON BLANC**. This wine is very **aromatic**, with **citrus and pineapple** aromas that are carried through to the palate. There is still some **crisp, fresh acidity**, thanks to the **cooling breeze** that comes off the ocean in Constantia. The

acidity keeps the wine **well structured** but the fruit flavors in this wine are definitely **more exotic** than in the Sancerre.

The third wine in this tasting is a **NEW ZEALAND SAUVIGNON BLANC** from the Marlborough region of the South Island. The climate here is warmer than Sancerre, and **slightly warmer** than Constantia, but again, there is a **cooling onshore breeze**, giving the wine a **balanced acidity**. It has **citrus and pineapple** aromas, but there is also a distinct **tropical** character, with **mango and melon** fruit flavors coming through, as well as hints of **lychee and peach**.

This tasting clearly reveals that **extra warmth** helps induce more **exotic** flavors in a wine. But for Sauvignon Blanc in particular, a **cooling** aspect to the climate is important, to **protect the acidity** levels in the wine.

GERMANY
RIESLING

German Rieslings are some of the world's best white wines—really! The leading region is Mosel-Saar-Ruwer, which makes very delicate wines bursting with juicy fruit and lively acidity. They are also smoky, and with age—they do age very, very well—they show a hint of petrol in the aroma.

Riesling from the historic Rheingau region has a rich texture, with plenty of depth and body. Nearby is the Nahe, where the best Rieslings are pure and crystalline, with flavors of passion fruit, guava, apricot, and minerals. Finally, the wines of the beautiful Pfalz region are dry, full-bodied, and have an essential minerality.

COLOR Clear and bright pale straw yellow, with tinges of green.

AROMA Intense and complex; peach, pineapple, citrus, flint, and smoke.

TASTE Harmonious, deep; great finesse; tangy when young; mineral finish.

BUYING There are many great producers. On the bottle, look for the stylized eagle symbol of the VDP—an association of the best growers. I like Fritz Haag, Dr Loosen, Dönnhoff, Franz Künstler, and Bassermann-Jordan.

ENJOYING Chilled German Riesling goes well with simple pork, chicken, and seafood dishes, and also, I think, with Thai cuisine.

BRANCHING OUT To sample Riesling's versatility, compare the fruit character and weight of good German Riesling with examples from Australia, New Zealand, South Africa, and Alsace in France.

"So sadly underrated, German Rieslings are a great bargain to buy—even in the best restaurants!"

RULÄNDER

The Ruländer grape makes wines with more flesh, but less exuberance, than many other German wines. And with two or three years of bottle aging, they develop exotic, flinty flavors. Grown mostly in the Pfalz and Baden regions (in warmer southwestern Germany), Ruländer needs deep, heavy soils to fulfill its potential for complexity and a full bouquet. Be open to experiment with these wines; you may be pleasantly surprised.

COLOR Pale straw yellow, with lemony highlights.

AROMA Dense and rich, with flowery hints of acacia and freesia.

TASTE Smooth and finely tuned, with a distinct spiciness on the finish.

BUYING A wave of new producers are working hard to raise the profile of this variety. Quality-conscious leaders worth seeking out include R. und C. Schneider and Weinhaus Heger.

ENJOYING I enjoy a chilled glass of Ruländer with lighter dishes, such as grilled shrimp, a simple tuna salad, or even a Niçoise salad.

BRANCHING OUT If you like the aroma and body of this wine, you may enjoy a Pinot Gris from Alsace, a premium-quality Italian Pinot Grigio, or even some Vermentino from Corsica.

HUNGARY
FURMINT

While Furmint is a grape most famous for the sweet wine Tokaji *(see p.289)*, it also produces a dry wine that is intensely aromatic and powerful, with rich flavors of apple, citrus, and smoke. Furmint wines are characterized by high levels of alcohol and acidity, which give them great potential for aging. After a typical two years' maturation in small casks, the wine has a distinctive, spicy aroma and a slightly tart flavor.

FURMINT
Crown Estates

COLOR Intense wheat-gold, with tinges of green.

AROMA Pronounced; grapefruit peel, minerals, and warm bread.

TASTE Dense but harmonious, with marked acidity.

BUYING Crown Estates and Chapel Hill are two leading producers. However, there are excellent examples of Furmint produced just over the border in the Austrian region of Burgenland.

ENJOYING Try Furmint with smoked trout. It also goes well with roast chicken or pork, or even with mushroom risotto.

BRANCHING OUT This bone-dry wine compares well with Chenin Blanc from the Loire Valley, such as Savennières or Saumur Blanc. See also how it measures up against Savagnin from the Jura region of France.

BULGARIA
DIMIAT

Dimiat is used to produce both dry and sweet wines. The dry version is uncomplicated, and when well made is aromatic, fresh, and tangy, with lots of spice. The majority of wines exported from Bulgaria are international varieties, such as Chardonnay, Merlot, and Cabernet Sauvignon; but Dimiat could not be more of a native product. The copper-colored Dimiat grape is grown mainly in the eastern and southern parts of the country, along the coast of the Black Sea.

COLOR Bright; deep gold with a silvery tinge on the rim.

AROMA Intense, deliberately scented; pear, flowers, spice, and mango.

TASTE Subtle, with good balance of alcohol, fruit, and acidity; clean finish.

BUYING Boyar Estates' Blueridge Winery, Lambol, and Suhindol are all reliable producers who are striving to improve the standing of this wine (and Bulgarian wine in general) on the world stage.

ENJOYING Drink Dimiat within two years of the vintage. Try it as an alternative to an Italian or Greek white, with some grilled fish or a salad.

BRANCHING OUT Taste this wine alongside a young, inexpensive Italian Pinot Grigio. Both are free of pretense, and all about refreshment.

DIMIAT
Boyar Estates

JUICY, AROMATIC WHITES

WORLD WINES

AUSTRIA
GRÜNER VELTLINER

This grape variety is the star of Austria's wine scene, and it has created a real stir on the global wine scene, too. Grüner Veltliner ripens late in the year, so its cultivation is unsuitable for the cooler parts of northern Europe. But it flourishes in central Europe, where the summers last for longer and the winters tend to be slightly milder. It thrives in the soils of eastern Austria, and covers more than a third of the country's total vineyard area.

Weinviertel is the largest growing district, and also the first in the country to promote the new national appellation system. As a result, you might see the letters DAC on the label—they stand for *Districtus Austriae Controllaus*—but this designation is so new it doesn't really give much indication of what you are getting in the bottle.

In the opinion of most of us in the wine trade, the best wines come from the districts Wachau, Kamptal, and Kremstal, which lie along the Danube River west of Vienna. During the late 1990s, it seemed as though many leading wineries here were trying to impress the world with big, powerful, concentrated wines. But thankfully, that phase has passed, and these Grüners have now returned to their sleek and sexy former selves. The best Grüner Veltliners are clean, clear, bright, and racy—and in my opinion just fantastic.

Grüner Veltliner is best while still young, although its zesty acidity does lend it the character to age in the bottle. Either way, modern Austrian Grüners are gaining a tremendous reputation, and they are becoming

widely available outside Austria. Some of the world's top restaurants are adding these wines to their lists, so this is definitely one you should try.

COLOR Pale, straw yellow or pale green, perhaps with silvery tinges.

AROMA Complex and subtle; citrus fruits, white flowers, and flint.

TASTE Dry, delicate, and well balanced, with a persistent peppery finish.

BUYING There are so many inspiring producers. Look for Rainer Wess, Bründlmayer, Donabaum, Hirtzberger, Bernhard Ott, and Prager—I wish I had more space! Some of these wines can be expensive, but they're well worth it.

ENJOYING I love Grüner Veltliner chilled and sipped on its own, but it also makes a good accompaniment for light meats or white fish. This superb wine will set off a dinner party on absolutely the right note.

BRANCHING OUT Grüner is an Austrian specialty, so comparisons with other wines may not be obvious; however, Grüner has parallels with racy dry German Riesling, perhaps from the Pfalz region. You might also try it with an edgy white Burgundy, such as Puligny-Montrachet.

"Often marketed as simply GV, and dubbed 'Groovy' in the US, Grüner Veltliners can compete with the best Burgundy Chardonnays."

ENGLAND
BACCHUS

What better name for a grape than the Roman god of wine! Bacchus is the result of crossing two German grapes: Riesling and Sylvaner. The fruit ripens early, so it can produce quality wines even in a cool climate. Good Bacchus is clean, zesty, and aromatic.

COLOR Bright; pale lemon yellow with green highlights.

AROMA Young, intense, and distinct; gooseberry, green apple, and flowers.

TASTE Lean but delicate; refreshing with marked acidity; moderate alcohol.

ROBOLA
Gentilini

BUYING Try Chapel Down or New Wave Wines. Check the label: "English" wines are made from grapes grown in England; "British" wines use imported grape juice, and their quality is difficult to monitor.

ENJOYING I enjoy these wines with seafood, especially crab or fishcakes in a creamy sauce, or with smoked salmon.

BRANCHING OUT Good Bacchus compares well with Sancerre and Pouilly Fumé. Also try it alongside a Rías Baixas.

GREECE
ROBOLA

The Robola grape variety from the Greek island of Cephalonia has achieved enormous success in both the quality and the quantity of the wine that it produces. Now it is becoming widely recognized beyond Greece for its potential to make fine, aromatic wines. At its best, the Robola grape produces wines of vibrant acidity with distinct peachy and lemony characters.

COLOR A soft but bright gold, with green hues.

AROMA Complex; flowers, honey, lemon peel, and peach.

TASTE Moderately rich, with a mineral touch at the finish.

BUYING Many producers make this wine for local consumption, with a bit of sherrylike oxidation. Gentilini, Ktima Mercouri, and the Kefalonian Wine Cooperative concentrate on export markets, with a cleaner and fresher taste.

ENJOYING Robola can be enjoyed when it is still very young, or it can be kept for up to four years. Serve it chilled, perhaps with some squid or octopus, or with a Greek salad.

BRANCHING OUT If you like this wine, you are also likely to enjoy either an Italian Vermentino, a Spanish Verdejo, or a Viognier (Vin de Pays) from France.

JUICY, AROMATIC WHITES

WORLD WINES

AUSTRALIA
RIESLING

I have friends who refuse to buy Riesling on principle, but they just don't know what they're missing! Admittedly, Riesling's reputation has suffered in the past from mass-market wines such as sweet and bland German Liebfraumilch (which, by the way, is not made from Riesling), as well as other similar wines from eastern Europe. But now is an ideal time to discover authentic Riesling from the so-called New World countries of the southern hemisphere.

RIESLING
Pewsey Vale Vineyard

These wines are wonderfully expressive and remarkably versatile, and those from Australia show fabulous potential. I particularly like the juicy style from the Clare Valley. Located just north of Adelaide in the state of South Australia, the Clare Valley is a source of truly exciting wine—drawn in part from some appropriately German and Austrian roots. For example, back in 1851, Jesuits fleeing religious and political persecution in Austria established the valley's oldest winery, Sevenhill Cellars, in order to make their own altar wine.

Today, Clare Valley wineries produce some of Australia's very best Rieslings; their vibrant lime flavors just explode in your mouth. In the warmer climate around the town of Clare itself (at the north end of the region), the wines are full-bodied and round. In the cooler area farther south around Watervale, they are crisp, tangy, and delicate.

The best Clare Rieslings are highly aromatic and racy. These wines also age beautifully and will improve for five years or more. It may be difficult to wait that long, but if you can, you will find rich flavors of lime syrup and toast.

Another great source of Australian Riesling is the nearby Eden Valley. While Clare Valley wines display ripe lime fruit, Eden Valley Rieslings are very floral and sleek. So keep your eyes open (and your glass out) for Australian Riesling! You will not be disappointed.

COLOR Pale straw yellow, with silver and green highlights.

AROMA Intense, delicate, with lime, peach, pineapple, and hints of smoke.

TASTE Dense and rich, underlined with a citrusy and steely acidity; long finish.

BUYING The king of Australian Riesling is Jeffrey Grosset. However, I also look out for the wines of producers such as Leasingham, Tim Adams, Knappstein, Pewsey Vale, and the exciting new venture O'Leary Walker.

ENJOYING Savor the flavor of Australia and drink these wines with barbecued shrimp—which are great on skewers with zucchini. Rieslings are also a good match for crab and other seafood, as well as for light salads made with chicken or bacon.

BRANCHING OUT Compare the crisp acidity and the lime and peach fruit characters of these wines with Rieslings from New Zealand and South Africa. Also try them alongside a Riesling from Austria, and note the firm mineral notes evident in the latter.

SAUVIGNON BLANC

Australia is not the first place that comes to my mind when thinking of good Sauvignon Blanc—even after discounting my bias for the Loire Valley, the original home of Sauvignon. As a general rule, Australian examples of this variety tend to be richly layered with exotic fruit flavors that dominate—and sometimes even eliminate—the grape's racy freshness. This is simply the result of cultivation at high temperatures. When grown in a climate that is too warm, Sauvignon Blanc grapes get overripe, and the wine produced from them is often heavy or oily.

An exception to this is the Sauvignon Blanc produced in the Adelaide Hills wine region—just to the east of Adelaide in South Australia—which has the coolest climate of all the vine-growing areas in the state. Most of the vineyards in the Adelaide Hills are above an altitude of 1,300 ft (400 m). They enjoy the highest rainfall in South Australia, and they also benefit from a strong, cool southerly wind. Together, these conditions promote a long ripening season that enables the grapes to hang on to their zesty freshness—the hallmark of "true" Sauvignon Blanc. High-quality examples of this wine will display distinctive aromas of grasses and citrus fruit, and plenty of full, crisp flavors. Overall, I think the Sauvignon Blanc from this part of South Australia is exceptional.

SAUVIGNON BLANC
Shaw and Smith

Beyond the Adelaide Hills, the Orange district of New South Wales is also well-suited to cultivating Sauvignon grapes. Furthermore, some good Sauvignon–Sémillon blends are made in Western Australia. These wines will never be the central theme of the Australian wine story, but they certainly make a very enjoyable diversion!

COLOR Light straw yellow, with silvery tinges.

AROMA Fresh and pungent, with grass, gooseberry, tropical fruit, and pear.

TASTE Full-flavored and complex, with a long, crisp finish.

BUYING There is a limited range of what I would call benchmark-quality Australian Sauvignon Blanc on the world market, but seek out examples from Shaw and Smith, Nepenthe, and Stafford Ridge. Always buy and drink these wines as young as possible.

ENJOYING I will happily drink this wine well chilled and all on its own, but it is great partnered by light dishes such as grilled white fish, ripe avocado salad, or stir-fried vegetables.

BRANCHING OUT For a fun night in with friends, have a Sauvignon safari! Compare a good Aussie Sauvignon Blanc with examples from New Zealand, South Africa, Chile, and (of course!) the Loire Valley of France. And, if you can find one, Sauvignon from the Austrian region of Styria makes a great comparison, too.

JUICY, AROMATIC WHITES

WORLD WINES

TASTE TEST: AROMATIC WHITES

Discover the difference between fruity, aromatic wines and true sweet wines.

❶ **❷** **❸**

❶ ALBARIÑO is an up-and-coming grape variety from Spain, making aromatic wines that are crisp and fresh on the palate. At its best, its wines can rival the great Sauvignon Blancs from the Loire Valley. **Seek out** Casal Caeiro, Pazo de Señorans, Pazo Pondal, Pazo de Barrantes, Palacio de Fefiñanes.

❷ NEW ZEALAND SAUVIGNON BLANC is a dry white wine with expressive fruit character. The best wines are made in Marlborough, in the far north of New Zealand's South Island. Be sure to serve this wine well chilled, to enhance its

fruity nature. **Seek out** Wither Hills, Oyster Bay, or Jackson Estate. Or, if you prefer, you could use a South African or Chilean Sauvignon Blanc in its place.

❸ RIESLING AUSLESE from Germany is a deliciously sweet wine, but perfectly balanced by the natural acidity of the Riesling grapes. The Pfalz region in southwest Germany produces some of my favorites. This wine can make a great alternative to French dessert wines, such as Monbazillac and Barsac. **Seek out** Freiherr Heyl zu Herrnstein, Dr Loosen, J. L. Wolf, Dönnhoff, Dr Deinhard, Reichsrat von Buhl.

"Sweetness can be found in fruity, aromatic dry wines, but this is a result of fruit quality, not sugar."

There have been many times when I have served a **brilliantly fruity**, aromatic wine to a customer only to be told that **they don't like "sweet" wines**. The thing is, none of the wines that are classified here as "fruity" and "aromatic" are actually sweet. They may have **lots of ripe fruit flavors** but they are **dry wines**—during the fermentation process, all of the sugar in the grapes has been **turned to alcohol**, and so unlike a true sweet wine, they have **no residual sugar**.

I have chosen the **ALBARIÑO** as the first wine in this tasting, because it is a good example of a **fruity, yet very dry** wine. It has aromas of **super-fresh lemons**, and on the palate gives **crispy green apples**. The grapes for this wine are grown at high altitude and thus in a cooler climate, making the wine **high in acidity** but with some **exuberance of fruit**.

Now taste the second wine, the **NEW ZEALAND SAUVIGNON BLANC**. Its aromas will hit you right away—very exuberant, **ripe gooseberries, melon, and kiwi fruit**. There is lots of ripe, juicy fruit on the palate—not exotic fruits but **green fruit**, gooseberries, and kiwi again; the finish is **clean, refreshing** and, above all, **dry**.

In contrast to the other two, the third wine in this tasting—the **RIESLING AUSLESE** from Germany—is a **true sweet wine**. *Auslese* on the label of a German wine means that some, if not all, of the grapes used to make the wine have been **left on the vines** much longer than usual, so that their sugar content is as **high as possible**. The presence of **residual sugar** left over after the fermentation process becomes apparent as soon as you smell the wine. It has exuberant aromas of **orange peel, raisins, honey, and caramelized fruits**. Although the Riesling grape imparts an **oiliness**, the texture is also **syrupy**, coating the tongue. And while the finish is **clean**, it is certainly **not dry**.

NEW ZEALAND
SAUVIGNON BLANC

New Zealand Sauvignon Blanc is sending shock waves through the wine world! Its exuberant character is sweeping away palates everywhere. The epicenter of this New World phenomenon is the Marlborough district on South Island.

Marlborough wines are light, with markedly crisp acidity and powerful flavors of gooseberry, citrus, passion fruit, and herbs. The style is generally similar to that of a French Sancerre, but it is much bolder and juicier. (Maybe it's the hole in the ozone layer down there!)

Sauvignon Blanc has established itself as the flagship of this corner of the wine world—but the prices match its reputation. You will not find good examples in the bargain bins, but they are worth paying a little extra for.

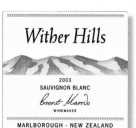

SAUVIGNON BLANC
Wither Hills

COLOR Bright and lively; pale straw yellow with green tinges.

AROMA Powerful, with bags of fruit: citrus, melon, gooseberry, and pineapple.

TASTE Dry, ripe flavors; marked, balanced acidity; clean, infinite length.

BUYING My list of recommended producers could go on and on! A few personal favorites include Wither Hills, Villa Maria, and the world-famous Cloudy Bay. Buy this wine young and drink it young.

ENJOYING Drink these wines well chilled as an aperitif. Alternatively, try them with a goat cheese salad or with grilled trout.

BRANCHING OUT Compare the fruit of N.Z. Sauvignon with a good example from South Africa. Contrast both with the structure and minerality of Sancerre.

Cool-climate wines ideal for hot summer days

New Zealand's fairy-tale landscapes are matched by the country's Sauvignon Blancs—some of which are really out of this world! The key to this grape variety is growing it in a relatively cool climate, which slows the ripening of the grapes and increases the complexity of the wine. I remember trying a Sauvignon Blanc in Hawkes Bay, in central North Island. Although it was very good, the warm climate made it just a little bit flabby. But farther south in Marlborough, in the northern part of South Island, there is a terrific combination of cooler weather, sea breezes, and hills. All of these features combine to give the wine just the right amount of lemony acidity, and ensure that it is not too sharp.

PINOT GRIS

New Zealand's Pinot Gris is a contemporary alternative to unoaked Chardonnay. With richly colored grape skins, Pinot Gris makes attractively golden wine that is also intensely aromatic. New Zealand Pinot Gris is very fruity, but also has a firm mineral or stone character that makes it highly distinctive. It has a fresher taste than Alsace Pinot Gris, although it shares the same characteristic viscous texture.

COLOR Attractive pale gold, reflecting the rich color of the grape.

AROMA Honey, apple, lemon, pear, peach, white flowers, and minerals.

TASTE Fleshy, complex; a ripe texture and a long, aromatic, and clean finish.

BUYING Don't bother looking for mature vintages, since these wines are new to most retail and restaurant lists. Two outstanding wineries are Seresin and Matakana.

ENJOYING New Zealand Pinot Gris is a great summer wine. It's excellent both on its own and with light dishes, such as fettucine in a tomato and basil sauce. It's also great with sushi.

BRANCHING OUT If you have tried and enjoyed this New Zealand wine, I would suggest you also try a Pinot Gris from Alsace, a Viognier from California, or an unwooded Chardonnay from South Africa.

SOUTH AFRICA
SAUVIGNON BLANC

South African Sauvignon Blancs have become fantastically popular. They are richer and more luscious than their French equivalents, but they are less exuberant than those from other parts of the New World: their style lies somewhere between the two. Sauvignon Blanc thrives in the Cape regions of Paarl and Constantia, producing wines of great quality and real expression, thanks to the cooling influence of the Atlantic Ocean.

COLOR Pale lemon yellow, with tinges of luscious green.

AROMA Elegant and expressive; gooseberry, green pepper, pineapple, and passion fruit.

TASTE Refreshing, balanced; lightly structured, but with a citrusy spine.

BUYING Buitenverwachting, Klein Constantia Estate, and Vergelegen are amazing producers and well worth buying. But drink these vibrant wines within two years.

ENJOYING These wines are perfect as an aperitif, but they also go well with a crudité salad, most types of fish or seafood, and many spicy dishes.

BRANCHING OUT If this wine hits the spot, try experimenting with other Sauvignon Blancs from around the world. See how it compares to a Sauvignon from New Zealand or a French Sancerre.

SAUVIGNON BLANC
Buitenverwachting

ARGENTINA
TORRONTÉS

The Spanish word *torrontés* means "torrent," and that's a great name for this variety—the aromas are a tumultuous outpouring of grapey fruit, lychee, and flowers. The scent of this wine reminds me of Muscat or Gewürztraminer, but its flavor reminds me of Sauvignon Blanc. What a combination!

Torrontés is well suited to Argentina's arid climate, where it produces a light-bodied wine with crisp acidity. Nevertheless, this grape variety needs careful handling at the winery to retain its freshness and delicacy, and to avoid overexposure to oxygen, which can rob it of its fabulous character.

Torrontés seems to have been brought to Argentina from Galicia in northwestern Spain, although there is no official evidence to confirm the link between the two. However it arrived, Torrontés has now carved out a niche for itself in the wine world, and it is winning the same level of attention for Argentinian white wines that Malbec has done for the country's reds. Refreshing and vibrant, Torrontés is an exciting find for anyone—give it a try.

COLOR A refined golden yellow, with pale intensity.

AROMA Floral, exotic, and spicy, with fresh grapes, lychee, and flowers.

TASTE Zesty and full of spice, and with a distinctive and refreshing acidity.

BUYING Torrontés is best in its vibrant youth, so buy the most recent vintage you can find. Among producers of Torrontés, I recommend Etchart, Santa Julia, and La Nature.

ENJOYING When well chilled, Torrontés is wonderful for summertime drinking. Try it with a crisp, green salad or alongside a light lunch of grilled chicken.

BRANCHING OUT The elaborate aromas of Torrontés would naturally lead you to also try Gewürztraminer from South America and New Zealand.

TORRONTÉS
Etchart

"Fresh and spicy, with aromas of Muscat and the taste of Sauvignon Blanc, this wine is a 'torrent' of fruit, lychee, and flowers!"

JUICY, AROMATIC WHITES

WORLD WINES

FULL, OPULENT WHITES

With a firm, full structure, subtle texture, and expressive fruit, these wines appeal to millions of wine drinkers in their classic incarnations—the great white wines of Burgundy—and in their "popular" forms, such as New World Chardonnays and 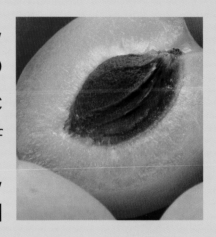 Viogniers. They have such a complex texture that you almost "eat" them. Good examples have a clean, fresh finish and do not leave you with a lifeless, buttery mouth once swallowed. Ranging from pale gold to straw yellow, they should include some beautiful deep honey colors—a pleasure to bring to your lips. Often well defined and expressive, the bouquet can vary from ripe apple, apricot, and peach to pineapple and mango, with hints of smoke, warm bread, and vanilla. Smooth and intense, yet delicate and dry, these wines are perfect to enjoy with food.

STYLE PROFILE
FULL, OPULENT WHITES

WORLD-CLASS WINES

A great full white wine melds finesse and balance with concentration. Its vast, complex, and intense flavors linger, stamping the wine's class into your palate. The full, opulent white category includes some world-famous wines, such as some of the best Burgundies—Chassagne-Montrachet, Puligny-Montrachet, Meursault, and the like—made from the Chardonnay grape. But New World Chardonnays from South Africa or California are now competing with the most renowned Burgundies, giving the French a real headache. Other notable full, opulent whites include Sémillon from Western Australia or the Hunter Valley,

"Full white wines are a real treat, and if you have deep pockets, you can buy yourself a taste of heaven."

Gewürztraminer from Alsace, Viognier from the United States, the more austere Chenin Blancs from the Loire Valley (such as Savennières), and Marsanne from the Rhône Valley.

FAT AND FLAVORSOME

Full whites typically have a firm structure and may feel oily in the mouth, a sensation derived either from the grape variety used—especially Marsanne or Sémillon—or from aging in oak. The grapes used to make full whites, among them Chardonnay, Sémillon, and Viognier, have relatively small berries with thick skins. They are less productive than other grape varieties, yielding less juice, but the result is a wine that is naturally fuller. Generally speaking, with full white wines, the deeper the color, the fuller the wine.

Full white wines often originate in areas with warmer climates—Western Australia, California, and south-central France, for example—or from warmer microclimates in other regions. Their special character is their body, strength, and weight, balanced with fruit and acidity to keep the

FULL OF THE SUN
A traditional grape of the Rhône Valley in France, Viognier is now increasingly grown in California, making wines to rival the biggest Chardonnays in the robustness of their exotic flavors.

NAPA VALLEY GOLD
In this premium Chardonnay-growing county, home to a veritable host of wineries, long days of California sunshine intensify the flavors of the ripening grapes.

TASTE TRAIL

The special character of these wines is their body, strength, and weight, balanced with fruit and acidity. They are often matured in oak, but this should not be overpowering. The classic varieties used to make full, opulent whites are **CHARDONNAY** and **VIOGNIER**, in their complex French and openly fruity New World styles, and **SÉMILLON**, mainly from Australia. There are also spicy varieties, such as **GEWÜRZTRAMINER** from Alsace and New Zealand.

ENJOYING Full white wines often need a little time to "talk"—to make contact with the air and release their flavors. Swirl the wine in a big glass, or oxygenate by pouring into a decanter and, if you wish, back into the bottle. Serve not too cold, at around 50–54°F (10–12°C), to retain the fleshiness of the wine. These whites are perfect companions for delicate food such as fish or seafood, particularly lobster, monkfish, or sea bass. They are also excellent with light meats, such as chicken, or simply to drink on their own.

wine in harmony. Full whites are typically vinified in oak barrels. New oak results in a richer wine than old oak, and toasted oak gives the richest finish of all—sometimes too rich. Generally, the more the oak is toasted, the more pronounced the woody flavor in the wine will be—but it should never mask the subtlety of the wine.

DRINK OR STORE?
Unusually, some of these white wines can be aged. Fine (but expensive) Montrachets and Meursaults benefit from ten years or more before drinking. Gewürztraminer and Viognier, where fruitiness and subtle texture are key, should be drunk younger than the more robust Chardonnay, Sémillon, and Marsanne.

FRANCE
CÔTE DE BEAUNE

If one place can be singled out as the source of the finest Chardonnay—or even the finest white wine—in the world, it is the Côte de Beaune. This small district unfolds around the town of Beaune at the center of the Burgundy region, where the principal white wine appellations are Puligny-Montrachet, Chassagne-Montrachet, Meursault, and Aloxe-Corton.

Puligny-Montrachet produces wines of pure gold, with distinct minerality underlying intense and complex aromas combining citrus, apple, marzipan, and honey. Nearby Chassagne-Montrachet makes balanced, complex whites, with powerful flavors of orchard fruit and honeysuckle, and a steely edge. The wines of Meursault are rich, full, and opulent, with a long, complex, fruity finish. The best vintages of these wines age for up to 15 years. The great Corton-Charlemagne, the *grand cru* wine of Aloxe-Corton, offers deep aromas of baked apple, nuts, butter, citrus fruits, pineapple, and honey. Drink it no younger than five years old; some vintages will age for up to 25 years.

COLOR Pale to deep straw yellow, with green to golden tinges.

AROMA Delicate, with apple, peach, bread, hazelnut, honey, and minerals.

TASTE Round and elegant; balanced, with a persistent, refreshing finish.

BUYING Among my favorite producers are Bernard Morey, Coche-Dury, Chartron et Trébuchet, and J. M. Pillot.

ENJOYING The full flavors of these wines are a superb match for seafood, such as dressed lobster or scallops. They also go well with many French cheeses.

BRANCHING OUT Compare the fruit flavors and prominent structure of these wines to Chardonnays from anywhere else in the world. You will see why these are the benchmark.

CONDRIEU

For me, this is the Rhône Valley's finest white. Made from Viognier grapes, it is intense and unctuous, but balanced by fresh acidity and moderate alcohol. Condrieu is a full-bodied, rich wine that is best enjoyed in its youth.

COLOR Pale to deep golden yellow, with touches of silvery green.

AROMA Unique; roses, apricot, mango, lychee, peach, pineapple, and hazelnut.

TASTE Complex and classy; ripe fruit with refreshing acidity; lingering finish.

BUYING Domaine Georges Vernay and Domaine Cheze are top producers.

ENJOYING Chilled and decanted, this wine is great with seafood and chicken.

BRANCHING OUT Condrieu's subtlety and opulence are the complete opposite of a Sauvignon Blanc. Try them together!

HERMITAGE / CROZES-HERMITAGE

Hermitage is a hill on the east bank of the Rhône River; Crozes is a village on the plateau that surrounds it. White wines from these areas blend the robust Marsanne grape with some Roussanne for subtlety and aroma. Marsanne makes rich wines, full of body and texture and mineral flavors. Some Hermitage whites develop well with age, but I recommend that you drink most Crozes-Hermitage and Hermitage whites when they are young.

COLOR Golden yellow; green to silver highlights; medium to deep intensity.

AROMA Ripe and exotic; minerals, honeydew, flowers, pine, and hazelnut.

TASTE Clean and rich; juicy acidity and an elegant finish; notes of spice and pear.

BUYING Domaine Alain Graillot and Domaine Jean-Louis Chave are two well-known and highly respected names in these appellations.

ENJOYING Try Crozes-Hermitage and Hermitage whites with grilled fish or white meat. If the wine has a bit of bottle age (meaning if it is a few years old), try it with a mature Cheddar or perhaps Comté cheese.

BRANCHING OUT Being very complex and opulent, Hermitage and Crozes-Hermitage wines have clear similarities with Australian Sémillon from the Hunter Valley, and also with white Châteauneuf-du-Pape from France.

FULL, OPULENT WHITES

WORLD WINES

A wine auction with tradition, quality, and style

I have many fond memories of the Côte de Beaune, but perhaps my favorite is the wine auction at the Hospices de Beaune. This institution dates from 1443, and began as a charitable body that cared for the sick and the poor of the town. Since 1859, it has been the center for a major wine auction, selling some of the greatest wines in the world. In my view, these wines are a little overpriced, but I like the tradition and I love to support something that began as a help to the community. Hospices de Beaune has such a fantastic range of AOCs that, if you could afford it, you could stock your entire cellar with wines from this one auction, and still have the complete range of tastes and styles!

TASTE TEST: TEXTURE

What is the texture that defines full, opulent white wines?

❶ **SAVENNIÈRES** is an intense, yet quite reserved white wine made in the Anjou region of France's Loire Valley. **Seek out** Clos de la Marche, Domaine du Closel (Clos du Papillon), Domaine des Baumard, Coulée de Serrant, Château Pierre Bise.

❷ **AUSTRALIAN SÉMILLON** from the Hunter Valley, New South Wales, is distinguished by its intensity and its complex aromas. **Seek out** Brokenwood, Arrowfield, Allandale, Tower Estate, Tyrell's, Chalkers Crossing.

❸ **MARSANNE** from California is full of opulence and individuality. There are few producers of this wine, so it may be hard to find. **Seek out** Qupé. Alternatively, try a French Marsanne from the Rhône Valley, such as Hermitage.

❹ **SOUTH AFRICAN CHARDONNAY** from the Stellenbosch region is a world-class wine and a great rival to Burgundy. **Seek out** Waterford Estate, Rustenberg, Meerlust, Bouchard-Finlayson, Hamilton Russell.

"Opulence conjures up thoughts of richness and smoothness—something that is very exuberant, almost to excess."

Oak-aging can account for some of this opulence, but the winemaker **can only do so much**. Full-bodied white wines are really driven by their **grape variety**.

The first wine in this tasting is our benchmark for comparison—the **SAVENNIÈRES**, made from Chenin Blanc grapes. First, lift your glass and sample the aromas. You will find **quince** and **green apple** and a **mineral, stony quality**. Then, take a sip: the wine is **muscly and tight** rather than opulent, but it is certainly

powerful. Any hints of opulence provided by the quince are **restrained** by the wine's acidity.

Next, try the **AUSTRALIAN SÉMILLON**. Sémillon grapes can produce wine with more **complexity** than Chenin Blanc. This example has been aged in oak, and the **spicy oak aromas** are there on the nose, evenly weighted by **ripe fruit**. The well-structured palate is **dry but powerful**, with **juicy pineapple, pear, peach, and apricot** flavors, and so is more opulent than the Savennières.

Next, try the **MARSANNE**. The aromas are discreet and delicate but complex—**honey and almonds** with **floral overtones** and **hints of caramel**. On the palate this wine is, again, **bone dry**. It too has

been aged in oak, and has loads of refreshing but **powerful fruit** together with an **oiliness** that adds to the opulence and intensity.

The golden color of the final wine, the **SOUTH AFRICAN CHARDONNAY**, reveals that it is the most intense of these wines. It has an open, **pronounced nose**—not as aromatic as the Marsanne but more creamy, with **toasted hazelnuts, exotic fruits**, and hints of **green apple**. With all the promised fruit quality together with an **oaky, buttery toastiness**, the palate has a **clean, refreshing finish**. Fruit and oak are **perfectly balanced**, neither dominating the other, and the texture is **oily but refreshing**—the ultimate expression of a full, opulent white.

FRANCE
CHÂTEAUNEUF-DU-PAPE BLANC

When people talk about Rhône Valley wines, they tend to speak exclusively of reds. However, this extensive wine region produces wines in a range of styles and qualities—among them some excellent whites. Châteauneuf-du-Pape, the star of the southern Rhône and world-famous for its distinguished red wine, also produces a small amount of Châteauneuf Blanc—and I recommend that you try it.

The French have enjoyed Châteauneuf Blanc for many years, but these wines are now gaining rightful recognition throughout the rest of the world. A wine of great charm, Châteauneuf Blanc is big and rich, with a unique character that comes from the "pudding" stones (*galets*) that cover the vineyards. Remnants of the last Ice Age, these stones soak up the heat of the sun in the daytime, and then radiate it back, warming the vines during the night.

This process accelerates the ripening of the grapes. The stones also help the soil to retain moisture.

COLOR Bright; pale golden yellow with greenish tinges.

AROMA Exotic fruits, acacia, honey, citrus, almond, and beeswax.

TASTE Round and creamy; great harmony and depth; long finish.

BUYING Drink Châteauneuf-du-Pape Blanc when it is young—up to three or four years old. I prefer the wines of Château de la Gardine and the great Château de Beaucastel. These wines are not cheap, but they can be very rewarding.

ENJOYING Serve this wine chilled, at around 46°F (8°C), and match it with foie gras, lobster, or Roquefort cheese.

BRANCHING OUT Try this wine alongside Roussanne- or Marsanne-based whites from California or Australia, comparing their rich textures and range of fruit characters. For the same reasons, try it with Viognier.

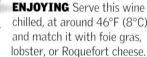

CHÂTEAUNEUF-DU-PAPE BLANC
Château de Beaucastel

"This elegant white, at its best, is so good that locals like to keep it for themselves! If you spot a Châteauneuf Blanc from one of the top producers, snap it up—you are in for a treat."

ALSACE
GEWÜRZTRAMINER

Gewürztraminer is one of the great specialties of the Alsace region of France. The grape is easily identified by its pink berries, and by its powerful aromas of flowers, fruit, and spice. The wine is round and rich, with relatively low acidity. In good-quality examples, the flavors explode in your mouth and have a long, refreshing, and clean finish. Drink it young; once tasted, it is impossible to forget!

COLOR Pale gold to amber, with tinges of green.

AROMA Lychee, pineapple, ginger, white pepper, roasted almond, flowers.

TASTE Big and rich with lots of muscle and explosive flavors; long, clean acidity.

BUYING Look for wines designating single vineyards—they are well worth it. Producers such as Leon Beyer, Chateau d'Orschwihr, and Domaine Zind-Humbrecht are always reliable.

ENJOYING Gewürztraminer is a perfect partner for spicy Asian food. Try it while savoring ginger-spiced pork on herbed rice. It also goes well with Munster—a strong, creamy cheese, also from Alsace.

BRANCHING OUT Any aromatic Gewürztraminer has similarities with wines like Viognier. Muscat is also made in the same style, but aromatic Sauvignon Blancs are in a different taste category due to their marked acidity.

JURA SAVAGNIN

Savagnin grapes, grown mainly in the mountainous Jura region of eastern France, are known for producing *vin jaune* (literally "yellow wine"), a fortified wine rather like sherry. But Savagnin also produces fantastic dry white wine in a fresh, more conventional style. It has distinctive nutty, lemon, and peach aromas, and a clean finish. With a prominent spine of acidity, Savagnin also has a long life span.

COLOR Pale yellow, to more golden with bottle aging.

AROMA Fresh, intense, and full of character; citrus, honey, and dried nuts.

TASTE Dense, marked acidity, medium alcohol, and a nutty finish.

BUYING The specific vintage makes a difference to this wine's complexity and finesse. I recommend Jacques Puffeney, Henri Maire, and Domaine Aviet.

ENJOYING Serve Jura Savagnin well chilled as an aperitif, perhaps with olives to complement its flavor. Over dinner, enjoy it with roast chicken in a creamy mushroom sauce.

BRANCHING OUT If you are a fan of Jura Savagnin, it is a safe bet to try a Savennières from the Loire Valley, or a Fino sherry. A real contrast would be with Muscat!

SAVENNIÈRES

I may be biased, since this wine comes from a village close to my hometown, but in my opinion Savennières is one of the finest of the world's whites—part of an elite group with a real "wow" factor. If you like steely, unoaked Chardonnays or well-made dry Rieslings, then I think you'll agree with me.

Savennières is a complex wine from the Anjou region at the heart of the Loire Valley. The Chenin Blanc grape variety is king here, and distant breezes from the Atlantic combine with the local *terroir* to shape this fruit into wine of remarkable character and quality. Chenin Blanc's high natural sugar content translates into the alcohol that gives Savennières its full body; but the grape also has high levels of acidity, so Savennières is best only after aging for at least seven years. A good, long-aged Savennières will simultaneously suggest velvetlike softness and granitelike hardness, just as it combines bone-dry character with full flavors. You'll just have to try it.

COLOR Pale lemon yellow, to deep golden when aged; good intensity.

AROMA Persistent yet delicate; quince, citrus, smoke, and minerals.

TASTE Complex, powerful; fresh acidity; unforgettable finish.

BUYING Loire Valley vintages vary, so seek your wine merchant's advice. Try wines from Domaine du Closel (Clos du Papillon), Pierre Bise, and Nicolas Joly.

ENJOYING This wine is an ideal partner for goat cheese, simply prepared river fish, smoked eels, or mackerel.

BRANCHING OUT Try Saumur Blanc or Anjou Blanc from the same region. Good examples have the minerality of Savennières, but are noticeably fresher.

The quality of the wine may be written in the stars

At college in the Loire Valley, I was assigned a project on organic wine production, so I went to see the owner of the Coulée de Serrant vineyard, one of the best producers of Savennières. Well, he really put me through my paces! He took out all his books and vineyard records, explained the effect of the sun and the moon, and how he worked at night under the stars. He took me among the vines and showed me the layers of organic manure helping them to grow. He was so utterly against pesticides that at one point I thought he might be mad! In fact, he was one of the first "biodynamic" producers, and today his Savennières is one of the finest expressions of Chenin Blanc in the world, with fantastic complexity.

FULL, OPULENT WHITES

WORLD WINES

AUSTRIA
ZIERFANDLER

With the potential for making elegant and complex wines, Zierfandler is one of the most notable white grape varieties in Austria. The grape (which in some areas is known as Spätrot) is naturally high in acidity, and that makes it great for aging. However, Zierfandler is often blended with another successful white grape called Rotgipfler. Together, they create a wine full of character and strength.

COLOR Deep lemon yellow, with golden highlights.

AROMA Unique and ripe; pineapple, spice, walnut, and apple.

TASTE Powerful and firm; good acidity, well-integrated alcohol; spicy finish.

BUYING A small group of top producers makes truly excellent wine. I enjoy Weingut Stadlmann, Franz Kurz, and G. Schellmann. Also, look out for the name of a subregion on the label—such designations are a sign of higher quality.

ENJOYING Serve Zierfandler with meaty fish, such as tuna or marlin, or any white meat. For a really healthy match, try it with a salad of field mushrooms and green vegetables.

BRANCHING OUT Compare Zierfandler with a Sémillon, Riesling, or Chenin Blanc. This wine is similarly austere and concentrated, but not quite as elegant.

ZIERFANDLER
Weingut Stadlmann

SPAIN
RIOJA / PENEDÈS

While most of Spain's best wines are reds, there are some fine whites, especially those made from the Garnacha Blanca grape. This variety is used as a component of white Riojas, and to a greater extent in the whites of the Penedès region of northeastern Spain. These can be rich and polished, with strong flavors of spice, nuts, pineapple, and pear, and a satisfying lemony finish.

COLOR Mellow, pale golden yellow, with straw tinges.

AROMA Very clean; pineapple, lemon, grapefruit, walnut; hints of spicy oak.

TASTE Rich and opulent, with integrated acidity and alcohol; long, nutty finish.

BUYING Only the best producers really stand out here, and some of my favorites are López de Heredia, Bàrbara Forés, and Torres.

ENJOYING Try these wines with white meats, such as chicken, pork, or veal. They go well with gently spiced dishes, or a mature salty cheese such as Beaufort.

BRANCHING OUT This wine is the opposite of delicate Viognier, although both are big, fruity wines. The best comparisons for me are with a delicious mature Hermitage or a rustic, old-style Meursault.

ITALY
GRECO DI TUFO

Greco di Tufo is a full-bodied, dry white wine made in the Campania region of southern Italy, around the village of Tufo. Greco in this wine's name refers to the grape— a versatile fruit (also used to make sweet wine) originating from Greece. Greco di Tufo is fermented at cool temperatures to preserve its subtle and complex aromas. This is a wine with a low profile, but it's well worth trying.

GRECO DI TUFO
Mastroberardino

COLOR Bright, pale orange-straw; golden tinges when older.

AROMA Delicate, with notes of citrus, peach, honey, spice, hazelnut, and minerals.

TASTE Marked acidity, with balanced alcohol and a firm structure; clean, long finish.

BUYING Mastroberardino, Terredora, and D'Antiche Terra Vega are the star producers here. But don't look for any old vintages—these wines are just too new to most retail and restaurant lists.

ENJOYING Greco di Tufo is good with spicy Chinese food or Mediterranean dishes. To be loyal to Campania, try it with seafood pasta, or indeed with a grilled tuna steak and roasted vegetables.

BRANCHING OUT This wine is similar to Loire Valley Chenin Blanc, but has less citrus and minerality.

ALBANA

Albana is a wine with great potential, and the best examples come from around the town of Forlì, in the Emilia-Romagna region of northern Italy. At its best, Albana is smooth yet crisp, with hints of nuts. It has a long history of popularity, too. In the year 435, in the local village of Bertinoro, it is said that the daughter of Emperor Theodosius tasted Albana and exclaimed, "This should be drunk from a jug made of gold!" In saying so, she gave Bertinoro its name, which means "to drink in gold."

COLOR Straw yellow, with silvery highlights; medium to full intensity.

AROMA Subtle and elegant; fruit, sage, flowers, almond, and green apple.

TASTE Full but lean and dry; marked acidity, medium alcohol, spicy finish.

BUYING Fattoria Paradiso, Commune Zerbina, and Commune di Faenza are all good producers. Also, check the back label to see whether or not the wine has been matured in oak; the styles will be very different in each case.

ENJOYING Serve the wine well chilled. I particularly like to drink it with tapas, or with hummus and bread.

BRANCHING OUT Without meaning to upset the French, I would say that a modest Chassagne-Montrachet is stylistically quite close to this wine, as is a good California Marsanne.

UNITED STATES
VIOGNIER / GEWÜRZTRAMINER

Viognier is a recent arrival in California. Even so, it has made rapid progress: its complexity and depth of character are beginning to rival good local Chardonnays. It produces opulent, full-bodied wines with aromas of flowers, spice, apricot, apple, and peach.

Well-crafted examples have perfectly balanced acidity and fruit. Some are made in stainless steel tanks, which brings out their ripe peach and apricot flavors. Other wines are aged in oak barrels, and this adds layers of vanilla and spice. I think that many California Viogniers are reminiscent of wines from Gewürztraminer, which are also making headway in this state. These wines vary from delicate with a sweet edge in California's warmer regions through to fresh, vibrant citrus flavors from the cooler areas—including lesser-known districts such as Mendocino and Monterey counties.

VIOGNIER *Kendall-Jackson*

COLOR Medium straw-yellow, with tinges of silver.

AROMA Aromatic and youthful; peach, apricot, mango, flowers, and vanilla.

TASTE Delicacy, harmony, balance; fresh and full of flavor, with a perfect finish.

BUYING Names to know include Kendall-Jackson, Joseph Phelps, Navarro, Calera, and Chalone.

ENJOYING Gewürztraminer and Viognier make good partners for spicy Asian food. Try them with beef or a meaty fish in a spicy black bean sauce.

BRANCHING OUT Compare the fruit flavors of these wines with examples from South America.

The memories of childhood, captured in a bottle

When I was a trainee, I made the mistake of asking a top Gewürztraminer producer where his Viognier grapes were, and was told very sharply that they are hardly ever grown in the same region! These two wines are easily confused because they are very similar in character, but the grapes used to make them and the right *terroir* are very different. Both wines take me back to when I was 12, picking peaches for pocket money—the smell of the fruit, the chilly morning breeze, and the smell of summer mornings are all there in their aroma and taste. When drinking Gewürztraminers or Viogniers at home, be sure to decant them, as they benefit from oxygen to release their fruity aromas—but keep them well chilled!

FULL, OPULENT WHITES

WORLD WINES

❸ NAPA VALLEY CHARDONNAY
from the fertile heart of this Californian region, the warm and sheltered valley floor running down from Calistoga to Napa itself, is one of my real favourites. **Seek out** Frog's Leap, Shafer, Beringer, Chalone Vineyard, Clos du Val, Stags' Leap Winery, ZD Wines.

❷ SANTA BARBARA CHARDONNAY
comes from a warm area on the south-central coast of California: its rich, opulent, top-flight Chardonnays and its Pinot Noirs are probably its most successful wines. **Seek out** Au Bon Climat, Cambria, Andrew Murray Vineyards, Firestone Vineyard, Fess Parker, Sage Road Cellars.

❶ CARNEROS CHARDONNAY
comes from a district that straddles the southern tips of Sonoma and Napa counties, with warm sunshine tempered by ocean breezes from the Pacific. **Seek out** Ramey, Kistler, Beaulieu Vineyard ("BV"), Cuvaison, Saintsbury, Acacia. Weather patterns in California vary little from year to year, so any vintage is a safe bet.

TASTE TEST: MICROCLIMATE

The influence of microclimate in three Chardonnays from California.

Early morning mist over a Napa Valley vineyard

"How can three wines made from the same grape variety, and all from California, have such different qualities?"

California, the third-largest US state, is bigger than Germany. Despite its size, its climate is quite **uniform**, but there are slight **regional variations** and these show through in its wines. The wines in this tasting are from three important **winemaking regions** in California, and the subtle differences in **fruit quality** between them are clearly influenced by the **microclimate** in the area in which each wine was made.

The first wine in this tasting is the **CARNEROS CHARDONNAY**. In this part of California, the temperatures are **consistently lower** than in Santa Barbara and the Napa Valley. The grapes

therefore have a **long, cool ripening period** and can be harvested with **higher levels of acidity**. This is reflected in the wine: it has a **dry, oaky** style, not especially buttery, and perhaps more reminiscent of European oaked Chardonnay. On the palate it has **bone-dry acidity** that is very **well balanced** with elegant but **intense yellow-lemon citrus** fruit. The oak flavor is very **discreet**, again giving this wine a European feel, although it does have a **ripeness** of flavor that is typical of its New World provenance.

The first thing to hit you when you smell the **SANTA BARBARA CHARDONNAY** is a big whiff of **new American oak,** overlaying **rich, buttery aromas** that also come through on the palate. Santa Barbara has a **warmer**, more constant climate than Carneros, although **tempered by a sea**

breeze, and the resulting wine has **riper fruit** qualities and slightly **less acidity**. There is some lovely **ripe, exotic fruit** character in this wine, with some nice **clean acidity** underneath the rich **heavy weight** of the oak.

On the nose, the **NAPA VALLEY CHARDONNAY** is different again, offering a much deeper intensity of fruit than the other wines. The Napa Valley is famous for its **morning fog**, which burns off as the sun rises to give **warm, sunny days** during the ripening period. This means that the sugar content of the grapes **increases** during the day, while the **cool nights** preserve the acidity. The resulting wine, when married with oak, has a **greater depth of complexity** than the other two wines. There's loads of **ripe, peachy** exotic fruits on the palate with a **buttery texture** and **clean acidity**—all in the same glass!

UNITED STATES
CALIFORNIA
CHARDONNAY

Chardonnay has for centuries been the source of steely or mineral-laden dry wines from Chablis and the Côte d'Or district of Burgundy. However, there are at least two generations of wine drinkers who associate it most with the soft, fruity, honeyed wines of the New World—especially those from Australia and California. Chardonnay is by far the most important white grape variety in California. There are now countless producers, and there is enormous variation in style. Some wines are crisp and fresh; others are thick with butterscotch and vanilla from aging in new oak; and then there is everything in between.

You might think that, as a Frenchman, I am inclined to be negative about these wines. On the contrary, I am delighted by their quality. I love the rich wines that come from California's North Coast region—particularly from appellations such as Alexander Valley, Russian River Valley, and Chalk Hill—all of which are in Sonoma County. These wines remind me of good Meursault *(see p.132)*.

Of course, other districts draw my attention, too. Carneros is one of them. This appellation overlaps Sonoma and Napa counties, and its cool, fog-shrouded climate leads to wines with a more defined and lemony acidity than others in California. Their combination of elegance, finesse, and dense flavors is almost unique—although I could compare them with Burgundy's famous Puligny-Montrachet *(see p.132)*.

One other region to look for is Monterey, south of San Francisco. The cool sea breezes that move through the valleys here make for bright and expressive wines. In fact, many leading producers based in more famous appellations, such as Napa Valley, have long sourced grapes from Monterey because of their superior quality.

COLOR Bright, golden yellow, with tinges of silver.

AROMA Delicate and elegant, with great complexity; baked apple, pineapple, peach, and hazelnut.

TASTE Opulent, but perfectly balanced by a lemony acidity; long, intense finish.

BUYING Much of California's wine country has consistently good weather, so vintage variation is not the concern it is with many other regions. I especially enjoy the wines of Gallo of Sonoma, Kistler, Marimar Torres, Morgan, Peter Michael, and Sonoma-Cutrer.

ENJOYING California Chardonnay can suit almost any occasion. Enjoy a chilled glass as an aperitif. Many of these wines are delicious with fresh crab or salmon, and also with chicken and lamb. Also try matching them with zucchini tart.

BRANCHING OUT Compare the fruit flavors and structure of a good California Chardonnay with a similar wine from Oregon—particularly from the Willamette Valley—and also from Washington State. Looking outside the US, these wines compare well with good Chardonnays from Western Australia.

WASHINGTON CHARDONNAY

Beyond California, there are excellent Chardonnays produced in the Pacific Northwest of the US—especially in Washington State. Here, the high desert climate of the vast Columbia Valley offers bright sunshine but cold nights, and the wide temperature swings between day and night preserve the lively acidity of the fruit as it ripens. This makes for rich but elegantly balanced wines. Most of them offer good value for money, too.

COLOR Golden yellow, often with highlights of green.

AROMA Complex, intense; mango, red apple; oak-aging gives toast and vanilla.

TASTE Rich; great balance of complex flavors and buttery texture; clean finish.

BUYING My favorite examples of these wines are from producers such as Château Ste Michelle, Columbia Crest, and Columbia Winery.

ENJOYING Have a glass on its own— just socially or as an aperitif. These wines are good partners for seafood and fish, and also for vegetarian dishes.

BRANCHING OUT If you enjoy the richness of this wine, try St Aubin, Meursault, or Western Australia (Margaret River) Chardonnays, or even some of the better Chardonnays produced in Stellenbosch, South Africa.

CHILE CHARDONNAY

You can't really go wrong in choosing a Chilean Chardonnay. Chile offers the Chardonnay grape its perfect growing conditions, particularly in the Central Valley region. There is plenty of sunshine to ripen the fruit, while cool breezes from both the ocean and the mountains meet on the valley floor to build flavor and preserve acidity in the grapes. The result is wine with a great balance between ripeness and refreshment.

CHARDONNAY
Errazuriz

COLOR Typically rich, yellow-green with gold tinges.

AROMA Citrus, apple, exotic fruits (such as pineapple), butter, and vanilla.

TASTE Fruity, with well-balanced fruit, acidity, and alcohol.

BUYING Flavor complexity depends very much on the producer and the region. For the finest, most intense wines, look out for Errazuriz, Casa Lapostolle, and Santa Rita, and generally the Casablanca region.

ENJOYING This wine can be enjoyed on its own as an aperitif, or with light dishes such as salad, grilled fish, or white meat. Avoid anything oily or smoky, as it will destroy the wine!

BRANCHING OUT If you are a fan of Chilean Chardonnay, you are also likely to enjoy Chardonnays from both southeast Australia and South Africa, for around the same price.

AUSTRALIA
SÉMILLON

Australian Sémillon is often seen as part of a blend. Chardonnay is the most common partner, but in Margaret River, Western Australia, it is usually Sauvignon Blanc. Here, blistering heat and cooling sea breezes combine to ripen both varieties with intense, fruity flavors. The resulting wine is rich and full, yet well balanced. Similar to white Bordeaux, this Sémillon–Sauvignon Blanc is dry, crisp, tangy, and herbaceous.

On the opposite side of Australia, in the Hunter Valley of New South Wales, growers produce some exceptional varietal (unblended) Sémillons. Like Margaret River, the Hunter Valley is unusually hot for vine-growing. But the region is also very humid, with low cloud cover during the afternoons. This tempers the evaporation of water from the vines, allowing for ripe, luscious grapes that are bursting with flavor. One of the special characteristics of Hunter Valley Sémillon is that

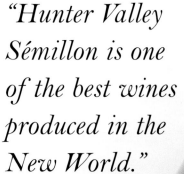

"Hunter Valley Sémillon is one of the best wines produced in the New World."

it is generally unoaked. Yet over time it develops all the richness and complexity of a wine that has been fermented or matured in new oak barrels. It's just amazing!

The best examples from the Hunter Valley will improve with age for between 10 and 20 years, becoming truly rich with flavors of melted butter, honey, and nuts. If you like blockbuster Chardonnays, try a bottle of aged Hunter Valley Sémillon. This wine makes an excellent and refreshing alternative.

COLOR Pale gold to lemon yellow with distinct green tinges; medium to deep intensity.

AROMA Charming and pronounced; pineapple, apple, warm bread, honey.

TASTE Big and rich; amazing complexity, lingering acidity, and "nonstop" length.

BUYING Good Sémillon wines benefit from age, so store younger examples for at least a handful of years. The producers I prefer are Brokenwood, Cullen, Peter Lehmann, and Voyager Estate. The one "must-try" is Tyrell's—in particular their "Vat 1."

ENJOYING Sémillon is a perfect partner for all white meats. Enjoy it with succulent, honey-glazed chicken on a bed of crisp, steamed vegetables, or match it with roast pork drizzled with apple and sage sauce.

BRANCHING OUT Fans of Sémillon–Sauvignon blends will enjoy white Bordeaux. The weight and fruit character of Hunter Valley Sémillon are similar to those of Californian Chardonnay.

SOUTHEAST AUSTRALIA CHARDONNAY

Australian Chardonnay is causing a worldwide sensation. Most of this wine is a good-value blend of fruit sourced from across South Australia, Victoria, and New South Wales. But in my opinion some of the best wine comes from Victoria. These Chardonnays have firmer acidity than many of their counterparts. However, they manage to retain their complex flavors, finesse, and elegance, just as a good Chardonnay should.

COLOR Bright; straw yellow, edged with green.

AROMA Pronounced and exotic; melon, pineapple, warm bread, and quince.

TASTE Rich and heavy, but balanced by a lemony acidity and perfect length.

BUYING Within Victoria, look for wines from the Mornington Peninsula and the Yarra Valley. Two producers that I like are Coldstream and Yarra Yering.

ENJOYING Southeastern Australia wines are generally appealing and "laid-back," and will match a very wide range of dishes and occasions.

BRANCHING OUT Try this wine with a Margaret River Chardonnay from Western Australia, which is much "fattier." You could also compare it with a California Chardonnay—you'll notice that the weights are very different.

Art Series
LEEUWIN ESTATE
2000
MARGARET RIVER
CHARDONNAY
14.0% vol PRODUCE OF AUSTRALIA 750mL.

WESTERN AUSTRALIA CHARDONNAY
Leeuwin Estate

WESTERN AUSTRALIA CHARDONNAY

Another top spot for southern hemisphere Chardonnay is Western Australia—specifically the Margaret River district. The wines produced here are high in alcohol, but the best succeed in balancing this with ripe fruit and crisp acidity. Some wines may be matured in French *barriques* (a special kind of oak barrel) for up to 12 months to round off their flavors with notes of toast and vanilla.

COLOR Golden yellow, with a silver rim.

AROMA Intense, but delicate, with apple, peach, apricot, citrus, and vanilla.

TASTE Unctuous and harmonious, with great intensity and a complex finish.

BUYING Check the label for the sub-regions of Margaret River or Frankland. Among producers, try Leeuwin Estate, Cullen, Vasse Felix, and Cape Mentelle.

ENJOYING These wines are great with lobster, crab, and shrimp, or with barbecued chicken and spicy sausages. The best can age for two to five years; drink cheaper wines within a year.

BRANCHING OUT I enjoy these wines so much because of their complexity, which puts me in mind of a Meursault or Puligny-Montrachet. Try them—it makes for a special (if expensive!) tasting.

FULL, OPULENT WHITES

WORLD WINES

TASTE TEST: OAK-AGING

How much does oak influence the taste of white wines?

❶ **AUSTRALIAN CHARDONNAY** that is unoaked has a fresher and cleaner feel to it than oaked versions. Make sure you choose a wine that has the word "unoaked" or "unwooded" on the front or back label of the bottle. **Seek out** Nepenthe, Yalumba, Redbank, Weighbridge (Peter Lehmann), Chapel Hill, Geoff Merrill.

❷ **GEWÜRZTRAMINER** is the star grape of the Alsace region, in northeastern France. The wines made from it are rarely oaked, but get their heavy, rich texture and big fruit flavors from the grape itself. **Seek out** Château

d'Orschwihr, Hugel & Fils, René Muré, Domaine Marcel Deiss, Dopff au Moulin, Domaine Schaetzel, Domaine Zind-Humbrecht, Maison Trimbach.

❸ **CALIFORNIA CHARDONNAY** has largely built its name on its big, barrel-aged flavors. There are unoaked and discreetly oaked versions, to be sure, but for this tasting you really need something full of toasty American flavor— and preferably a wine from a quite recent vintage, in which the oak character is still powerfully to the fore. **Seek out** Beringer, Au Bon Climat, Bell.

"As long as it doesn't unbalance the wine, oak-aging can add extra depth and complexity."

Oak aromas can be introduced into a wine either by fermenting the juice in **oak barrels** or by aging it in oak after fermentation, or both. Because so many winemakers do this to Chardonnay, many people **mistakenly believe** that all Chardonnay **tastes oaky**. If nothing else, this tasting proves that this is not the case!

The first wine in this tasting is an unoaked **AUSTRALIAN CHARDONNAY**. It was vinified in **stainless steel**, hence there is no oak involved. Notice its **pale**

yellow color with **green tinges**— a hint that there is no oak. It has fresh, **fairly discreet** but quite complex aromas of **ripe peaches**, with hints of **green apples and pears**, and on the palate it is clean and fresh, again with **ripe, exotic fruit** tones, including **pineapple** and a certain **creaminess** that is characteristic of Chardonnay.

The second wine to taste, a **GEWÜRZTRAMINER** from Alsace, is also unoaked. This grape variety has a **fatty, oily** character and is very **aromatic**, so that wine made from it has a certain **opulence and richness**, even though it has never seen the inside of a barrel. The wine has a very **dark, intense gold** color which—to the eye, at least— suggests oak-aging. It has a huge

nose, full of **ripe bananas and apricots**, and is rich and opulent on the palate with pronounced **fruit and white flower** flavors.

The **deep golden** color of the third wine—a **CALIFORNIA CHARDONNAY**—provides the first clue to oak-aging, and this is immediately confirmed when you take your first sniff. This wine has a huge nose, full of **nutty, warm bread** aromas, a result of its being aged for 30 months in French oak barrels. It is full of **ripe peaches** and **exotic fruit** on the palate, but on top of this there are flavors of **toasty, buttery brioche** added by the oak. The result is a **more complex** wine than either of the unoaked wines in this tasting, with a **richer, creamier** texture.

AUSTRALIA
MARSANNE

The Goulburn Valley in Victoria contains some of the oldest and largest plantings of Marsanne grapes in the world. The top producers are Mitchelton and Château Tahbilk, each with its own distinct style. Mitchelton is heavily oak-influenced, lemon-accented, oily, and rich, especially when aged. Tahbilk is unoaked and delicate in its youth, but develops a honeysuckle bouquet over time. Both are well worth trying.

COLOR An attractive deep gold with highlights of silver.

AROMA Exotic, full of character; lemon, smoke, minerals, hazelnut, quince, and fig.

TASTE Muscly, oily texture; medium acidity; complex, elegant, and long.

BUYING Look for the Mornington Peninsula or Goulburn districts. Note that the older the wine, the nuttier and oilier it will be—this is just how it ages.

ENJOYING This wine is perfect with white meat, meaty fish such as monkfish or tuna, and even charcuterie. Decant it to let some air enhance the flavors.

BRANCHING OUT Wines similar to Marsanne include fat, mature Hermitage or Châteauneuf-du-Pape Blanc from France, or perhaps Sémillon from Australia's Hunter Valley.

NEW ZEALAND
CHARDONNAY

New Zealand's climate varies widely across its wine regions, so there are many different styles of Chardonnay. My advice is first to try a few wines from the different regions. Once you have found your favorite area, focus on its wines to find your favorite producer.

MARSANNE
Château Tahbilk

Auckland and Northland, two warm parts of North Island, tend to make rich, ripe, broad-flavored Chardonnay. Wines from Gisborne in the east are soft and luscious, with ripe apricot and melon flavors. South of Gisborne lies Hawke's Bay—my favorite source of New Zealand Chardonnay. The wine is well balanced, complex, and concentrated, with peach and pineapple flavors. On South Island, the wines tend to show more citrus flavors. Marlborough, for example, produces zesty wines with good acidity—like the world-famous Sauvignon grown here. In Central Otago, the Chardonnay has a green-fruit and flint character.

COLOR Pale; straw yellow, with greenish tinges.

AROMA Very pronounced; ripe, exotic fruits, vanilla, brioche, and peach.

TASTE Rich and round; lemony acidity balanced with refreshing length.

BUYING Names to know for good New Zealand Chardonnay include Craggy Range, Kumeu River, Te Mata, Wither Hills, and Chard Farm.

ENJOYING The stylistic latitude of New Zealand Chardonnays means they go well with many foods. I enjoy them with grilled seafood and green salad.

BRANCHING OUT Compare the fruit and acidity of well-made South Island wines with Chardonnays from cooler corners of California and Australia.

Proof that New Zealand Chardonnays can beat the best

When you provide regular tastings for clients interested in learning more about wine, it often becomes quite competitive, as most people like to think they can identify wines. Over the years, I have discovered a few wines that I use in tastings because I know people will be convinced that they are one particular style, when they are actually something completely different. It all adds to the fun! One of these is New Zealand Chardonnay. Time after time people drink it and confidently decide that it's a Côte de Beaune, or even a Puligny-Montrachet! It is made from Chardonnay grapes, it's true, but even the best New Zealand Chardonnay will be only half the price of a Côte de Beaune.

GEWÜRZTRAMINER

The German word *gewürz* means "spiced," and wines made from the Gewürztraminer grape have a decidedly spicy character. The cool climate of New Zealand is well suited to cultivating this variety, as slow ripening permits the development of complex fruit flavors. Most of New Zealand's Gewürztraminer plantings are in Gisborne and Hawkes Bay, North Island. Others, in Marlborough on South Island, make less exuberant wines, but they have an attractive perfume.

COLOR Deep golden yellow to dark straw or light amber.

AROMA Exotic; minerals, flowers, lychee, pineapple, ginger, nuts, spice.

TASTE Rich and round; lemony acidity balanced with refreshing length.

BUYING Go for the youngest vintage available, preferably one from South Island for greater complexity and a fresher style. I enjoy wines from Villa Maria and Hunters.

ENJOYING Serve these wines with spicy Asian and Pacific Rim foods. Or drink them my favorite way—on their own as a summer aperitif.

BRANCHING OUT New Zealand Gewürztraminer is often compared to its Alsatian cousin, but the structure of the wines is actually quite different, because of the different levels of acidity. Try them and see for yourself.

SOUTH AFRICA
CHARDONNAY

I find that the most successful South African Chardonnays offer some of the weight and fruit intensity that is typical of the New World, combined with some of the complexity and minerality that is more typical of the Old. In general, South African Chardonnay offers great buys for all budgets. Explore and enjoy!

Districts such as Robertson—which is situated inland and is very hot and dry—produce bold, "Australian-style" wines; whereas cooler coastal regions, such as Constantia, make wines that are closer in style to those of Burgundy. Stellenbosch may have the climatic conditions to get the balance just right. This is South Africa's star wine-producing region, 30 miles (50 km) to the east of Cape Town. The mountains and sea that surround Stellenbosch bring cool breezes to the vineyards and balance the fruitiness of the grapes with racy acidity.

CHARDONNAY
Simonsig

Another up-and-coming area is the Overberg district, specifically the Elgin and Walker Bay areas. The temperate climate here (and a lot of hard work!) is resulting in Chardonnays of classic character.

COLOR Pale intensity; gold with a hint of green.

AROMA Rich, complex; honey, lemon, lime, baked apple, vanilla, and toasty oak.

TASTE Delicate and highly complex, with good acidity and a long finish.

BUYING Top producers of South African Chardonnay include Bouchard Finlayson, Hamilton Russell, Meerlust, Mulderbosch, Simonsig, and Thelema.

ENJOYING I relish these wines well chilled as a summer aperitif, but they also make excellent partners for delicate fish dishes.

BRANCHING OUT Compare the cool, sleek nature of well-made Chardonnay from coastal South Africa with wines from Burgundy's Côte de Beaune.

"Great-value wines. The best come from around Stellenbosch, and fall between the typical New World and Old World styles—fruity but still complex. Awesome!"

FULL, OPULENT WHITES

WORLD WINES

ROSÉ

Rosé has not always been taken seriously— mass-market wines of past decades have given the style a bad name. However, attitudes are changing and rosé is again finding its niche. And with increased demand has come dramatically improved  quality. Most fine rosé wines are not made from special rosé grape varieties, but from red grapes, such as Syrah, Grenache, and Pinot Noir. Even some of the most robust red varieties, such as Nebbiolo and Cabernet Sauvignon, can be made into fresh, strawberry-fruity rosés. Strongly associated with the vine-growing areas around the Mediterranean Sea—and more recently, with parts of the New World that boast a similar climate—these are wines to be enjoyed in the spirit of that region, in relaxed gatherings of friends on a summer day.

STYLE PROFILE ROSÉ

FROM PALEST BLUSH TO RUBY

Rosé is not, as some people assume, simply a mixture of red and white wine—and only rarely is it made from special "pink" grapes! Rather, the wine comes from red-skinned grapes that are vinified using a special technique known as *saignée* ("bleeding"). In it, the grapes are macerated with their skins very gently and for only a short time to bleed out a little color into the juice, which is then vinified as white wine. The longer the juice remains with the skins, the darker the pink color of the resulting wine. A good rosé wine should be bright, with a light to medium rose-petal color—almost a light ruby. Some rosés (particularly those known as "blush" wines) are extremely pale pink.

GROUND HEAT
The large, flat stones that litter the soil in the southern French appellation of Tavel absorb heat during the day and release it at night, allowing the grapes to ripen more fully; this gives Tavel rosés their deep, fruity complexity, and allows them to command relatively high prices for this style.

"Cheerful and welcoming, fruity and fresh, rosé wines add joie de vivre *to any summer picnic or garden party."*

REFRESHING RED BERRIES

Rosé wines are not matured in oak, so they should always have a refreshing texture. You should also find intense, well-defined, ripe red fruit, such as strawberries and raspberries, and the aromas should be zesty and subtle, with delicate hints of violet, and even some spice. Even though rosé is perceived as a lighter style, good examples should show complexity. The flavor overall should be fruity and fresh, with balanced lemony acidity and medium alcohol, and the finish should be pleasant, and medium to long.

Not all rosé wines are light in body. Fuller-bodied rosés come from southern France, particularly Tavel, Corbières, Bandol, and Côtes de Provence; Italy (where rosé is known as *rosato*); Spain (look for *rosado*); as well as from the New World, most notably from Australia, Chile, and, increasingly, Argentina. The lightest rosé tends to come from Sancerre in the Loire Valley—and from California, where it is called blush wine. The two, however, are very different: Sancerre rosé is dry

RED GRAPES, PINK WINE
Inside, "red" grapes have the same translucent flesh as white grapes. A brief period in contact with the dark skins allows just a little color to leach into the juice and only a few of the body-building tannins, keeping rosé wines light.

TASTE TRAIL

If you like the lightest, most easy-drinking styles of rosé, look to wines from the Loire Valley in France, such as **ROSÉ D'ANJOU**. Those from **SANCERRE** are also light-bodied, but are drier and more sophisticated. If you prefer fuller wines, try muscular, jewel-bright Garnachas from **NAVARRA**, Spain, fresh and fruity **CABERNET SAUVIGNON** rosés from Chile, or vibrant **GRENACHE** rosés from the Barossa Valley in Australia. At the top of the range are the wonderfully complex rosé wines from **TAVEL** in France.

SERVING Serve rosé well chilled, and if you are drinking it with a meal, try to keep the wine chilled throughout. These are summery wines, ideal for enjoying around a barbecue grill with friends; or perhaps they begin as aperitifs, only to become part of a light lunch. With its frivolous image, rosé is too often ignored as a good companion to food. However, the best rosé wines, such as Tavel, match perfectly with salads, pasta, and pizza, and even with curry and other spicy foods.

and delicate, with notes of red currant and flowers, and can be expensive, while "white" or blush Zinfandels are classic easy-drinking wines for those with a sweeter tooth—worthy rivals to Mateus and Lancers, those evergreen crowd-pleasers from Portugal.

DRINK OR STORE?

Rosé wines are meant for drinking young, often the younger the better. You should not store the wine for more than two or three years—age will turn the once bright pink wine an unappealing onion brown. Never be tempted to buy a rosé that is old—even if it looks like a bargain!

FRANCE
CÔTES DE PROVENCE

Pink wines from Provence are a splash of joy—they remind me of sunny summer days in one of the most beautiful parts of the world. Côtes de Provence is the largest appellation in this part of southern France, covering a wide area along the shores of the Mediterranean.

Local rosés are made primarily from the Grenache and Cinsault grapes, and they are mostly dry, light, and fresh. While best enjoyed straight from the vineyard, or at least in the local area, Côtes de Provence rosés are known worldwide, and rarely disappoint—even at bargain prices. For a better-quality rosé at only a little extra cost, try Provence's second-largest appellation, Coteaux d'Aix en Provence, which is a little inland and farther west. Also try Coteaux du Varois.

COLOR From light to salmon pink, and sometimes even light orange.

AROMA Varied, often herbs (thyme, dill), flowers, and red fruits.

TASTE Dry and fruity; very bright and refreshing.

BUYING Buy the most recent vintage. Try Clos St Magdeleine, Château de Pampelonne, and St Roch-les-Vignes.

ENJOYING Drink these wines well chilled with a traditional Provençal dish, such as tomatoes and peppers roasted in olive oil and garlic.

BRANCHING OUT Compare the lively fruit of these wines with other rosés from across southern France.

ROSÉ

WORLD WINES

BANDOL

This fine rosé from Provence is fairly full. Its deep color comes from the local Mourvèdre grape; adding Grenache and Cinsault to the blend brings fruit flavors and softens the tannins.

COLOR A delightful color that varies from deep pink to pale ruby.

AROMA Subtle; cherry, strawberry, dried herbs, and notes of spice.

TASTE Dense but elegant, with a fresh structure; long and complex finish.

BUYING Try the châteaux J. P. Gaussen and Pibarnon, and Domaine du Pey Neuf.

ENJOYING Bandol is ideal with seafood and Provençal fish soup. It's also great with spicy food and roasted vegetables.

BRANCHING OUT Compare this wine with a Bergerac rosé for its structure, or with a Chilean Cabernet Sauvignon rosé for its fruity intensity.

TAVEL / LIRAC

Tavel is a small appellation at the Mediterranean end of the Rhône Valley, not far from Châteauneuf-du-Pape. This part of the wine world is dominated by hearty reds, but the Tavel district makes only rosés. In fact, by the mid-20th century this was the most famous rosé-producing area in the world. Tavel's wines are still among the finest in France. A full body, deep fruit characters, and a persistent length combine with all the freshness expected from a good rosé to set Tavel apart from almost all other pink wines.

Made mainly from Grenache and Cinsault grapes, the wine is always very dry. Its aromas are simultaneously floral, fruity, spicy, and nutty. The vibrant color ranges from bright pink through ruby to even copper for older wines. The distinctive colors, the lively aromas, and the fruity flavors are all a result of carbonic maceration. This is a winemaking technique in which the grapes are crushed by their own weight (rather than by a conventional press), allowing each one to start its own fermentation—just like a tiny winery.

While Tavel is a great rosé, it is a little expensive. An alternative can be found just to the north of Tavel, in the appellation of Lirac. Here, too, the wine is relatively full-bodied for a rosé, offering a soft pink color with aromas of red fruit and almond. If you are trying Lirac rosé, also look for some of the district's robust reds. I think they offer great value relative to the more famous wines of the southern Rhône.

COLOR Light ruby, with subtle nuances of lilac; deepening to copper with age.

AROMA Fine and complex; flowers, honey, and bursting with fresh red fruits.

TASTE Well structured, supple, fresh, and dry, with a pleasant round finish.

BUYING Look for very young wines from Tavel and Lirac. Among producers of these wines, I recommend Château d'Aqueria, Domaine de la Mordorée, and Domaine Pélaquié.

ENJOYING I enjoy these rosés well chilled with Niçoise salad, or with grilled seafood kebabs.

BRANCHING OUT Compare the fruit and the weight or body of Tavel and Lirac wines with rosés from the Navarra region of Spain.

ROSÉ

WORLD WINES

A teenager in Tavel learning about climate, soil, and tradition

I already knew of Tavel's reputation when I first went there at age 14! The visit was organized as part of my wine training by the Confrèrie des Vins de Tavel. I remember noticing how dry and chalky the soil was, and how the vineyards were littered with large, flat stones, which absorb heat during the day and slowly release it at night, giving the wine its special character. At the end of the visit, I was invited to become a Confrère, and I attended a traditional ceremony in Avignon. This visit taught me the importance of soil and climate in influencing the style of wine, and also how important tradition is in keeping up the standard and the character of a wine—particularly a great wine like Tavel.

FRANCE
ANJOU

Anjou is in the western part of the Loire Valley, and it is home to two styles of rosé wine. The first of these, Rosé d'Anjou, is made using several grape varieties (including Gamay, Cabernet Franc, and Cabernet Sauvignon) and is light and fresh. The second, Cabernet d'Anjou, is also fresh, but deeper and more complex. Produced from a blend of Cabernet Franc and Cabernet Sauvignon, this well-balanced wine has a touch of sweetness about it.

COLOR Attractive pale to medium pink, with a silver rim.

AROMA Charming, aromatic; crushed berries, flowers, and gentle spice.

TASTE Fruity, elegant; refreshing acidity and a long, pleasant finish.

BUYING Make sure you look carefully at the label, as these two wines are very different. For me, the best examples are produced by Langlois Château, Domaine Ogereau, and Château de Fesles.

ENJOYING Anjou rosé is perfect for a barbecue or with any charcuterie. Try the drier style with seafood, salads, or smoked salmon.

BRANCHING OUT Anjou is similar in style to Côtes de Provence. Try it with some New World rosés, too; they tend to be much heavier.

SANCERRE

Sancerre is best known for its crisp whites made from the Sauvignon Blanc grape variety. However, Sancerre rosé is also highly regarded in France. It is made from Pinot Noir grapes, and is light and refreshing, with concentrated fruit flavors. Sancerre's fame can make the wines expensive. Check the label to ensure that you have chosen a good producer; little else on the bottle will signal quality.

COLOR Pale pink salmon, with delicate onionskin highlights.

AROMA Intense; delicate red berries, spice, and notes of vanilla and leather.

TASTE Fresh, delicate; harmony of fruit and alcohol; long, complex finish.

BUYING There are loads of producers here, so you have to be very careful—they don't all have the same high standards. I recommend J. M. Roger, Lucien Crochet, and Vincent Pinard.

ENJOYING Avoid any heavy foods. You will find that this wine is truly excellent with salads, grilled fish such as haddock, and even roast chicken.

BRANCHING OUT Sancerre is unlike most other French rosés, which are based on Grenache or Syrah: it has more in common with Pinot Noir reds. You could compare it with other Pinot Noir rosés from the Jura and also from Italy.

CORBIÈRES

This rosé is a fantastic buy! It is produced in a rugged corner of Languedoc-Roussillon (southern France), where consistently great weather ripens red grapes including Cinsault, Carignan, and Syrah. This large subregion is best known for robust reds—and these great-value wines are improving every year. But the fresh and fruity rosés should not be overlooked. They are summer in a glass!

CORBIÈRES
*Château du
Vieux Parc*

COLOR Bright, deep pink to light purple, with a silvery rim.

AROMA Young, aromatic; hints of strawberry, raspberry, and bilberry.

TASTE Clean, refreshing; medium weight and well-balanced acidity.

BUYING Don't work too hard to find anything "fine"—there are not many upmarket producers in this wild countryside. I like Château du Vieux Parc and Domaine de Fontsainte.

ENJOYING I love this wine with polenta. Also drink it with cold meats and black olive tapenade, or perhaps a few spicy sausages.

BRANCHING OUT Try Corbières wines alongside rosés from Côtes du Roussillon or Fitou, which have a similar character.

COTEAUX DU LANGUEDOC

This is the oldest vine-growing region in France, and currently the source of some very exciting reds. But this is also the place to find some lighter-style rosés that offer very good value. There are many subregions within this stretch of the Midi, but I particularly enjoy the delicate, floral Costières de Nîmes. Even the generic label, AOC Coteaux du Languedoc, rarely disappoints.

COLOR Dark pink, with nuances of red terra-cotta tiles.

AROMA Delicate; cherry, red berries, and hints of flowers.

TASTE Light, fresh, and pleasant, with a long, clean finish.

BUYING Coteaux du Languedoc is an up-and-coming appellation bursting with potential for amazing quality. Château Moujan and Château Creissan are two of the best producers, although the list is growing rapidly.

ENJOYING These rosés are light and vibrant. Drink them well chilled and young. They are perfect for picnics or pizza parties, as well as for stews and creamy dishes.

BRANCHING OUT If you like Coteaux du Languedoc rosé, stay within the neighboring appellations in the Languedoc and you won't go far wrong.

CÔTES DU ROUSSILLON

This region really delivers: almost every rosé from the Côtes du Roussillon is of excellent quality. At their best, the wines are intense, deeply colored, and highly perfumed—a gift of the Mediterranean sunshine. However, when you are buying rosé, take care not to pick up a bottle labeled Côtes du Roussillon Villages. This wine is very often worth trying, but it will be a red. A single word makes all the difference!

COLOR Bright; charming salmon pink, sometimes with onionskin tinges.

AROMA Elegant and fairly intense; ripe strawberry, raspberry, and cherry.

TASTE Well structured; refreshing acidity and intense fruit; very long finish.

BUYING Look for cooperatives. These wineries can be very dynamic and produce some of the most appealing wines. But I also recommend Château de Jau and Château de la Casenove.

ENJOYING Try these rosés with seafood or grilled fish. Their full structure means that they go well with red meat. In my opinion, they also work with spicy food!

BRANCHING OUT If you prefer the darker rosé style, try also a New World Cabernet Sauvignon or, from France, a Bandol or even Tavel.

ITALY
TUSCAN SANGIOVESE

The Sangiovese grape makes rosé with a good spine of lemony acidity. There are two main styles of this *rosato* from Tuscany, and both are dry. The first, made with a minimum of 85 percent Sangiovese, is perfectly represented by Cipresseto. This wine is refreshing, upfront, and light. The second, represented by the wines of Bolgheri on the coast, blends Sangiovese with Cabernet Sauvignon and Merlot, and is more serious and elegant in style.

**TUSCAN
SANGIOVESE**
Antinori

COLOR Bright, ranging from a light ruby red to deep pink.

AROMA Youthful; heaps of red berries, with sweet spice and notes of violet.

TASTE Dry and well structured; harmonious and pleasant; fruity finish.

BUYING The volume of production of these wines is high and, therefore, variable. It is important to find the right producer; I recommend Antinori, Avignonesi, and Guado al Tasso.

ENJOYING Both of these wines are great with light food. They complement pizza and pasta, too—particularly if the wines are well chilled.

BRANCHING OUT Try these alongside rosés from northern Italy or from Rioja in Spain—the fruit is just as intense. For more power, sample a New World Cabernet Sauvignon rosé.

ROSÉ

WORLD WINES

TASTE TEST: GRAPE VARIETY

How does the grape variety influence the taste of rosé wines?

❶ **SANCERRE** is, of course, a famous white wine from France's Loire Valley, but the appellation can also be applied to a very delicately colored and stylish rosé, made from the Pinot Noir grape. It's not easy to find, but from a good producer, is well worth the search. **Seek out** Jean-Max Roger, Vincent Pinard, Hippolyte Reverdy, Lucien Crochet, Henri Bourgeois.

❷ **CÔTES DE PROVENCE** from southern France, near Nice, produces a renowned and popular rosé, usually based on Grenache and Syrah grapes, and often sold in a distinctive, curvaceous bottle. Although my recommendations are not among the cheapest, it really is worth spending a little more on wine from a top producer to ensure that you get all the classic flavor of the appellation. **Seek out** Château Vignelaure, St Roch-les-Vignes, Domaines Ott, Château de Roquefort, Domaine Richeaume.

❸ **BANDOL**, also in the south of France, produces a fuller rosé from the robust Mourvèdre grape that can take a little age. **Seek out** Domaine de Terrebrune, Château de Pibarnon, Château Pradeaux, Domaine Tempier.

"It is the myriad different colors that first hit you when you begin to survey the rosé wine shelves."

There is **no simple correlation** between the color and the taste of a rosé wine. The winemaker **decides the color** of the wine, by choosing how long to macerate the grapes, but the flavors are down to the **grape variety**. Most of the **fruit flavors** are contained in the **grapes' skins**, as is the tannin and the color. To make rosé, red grapes are macerated for a much **shorter time** and at **cooler temperatures** than for red wine so that the color is **pink rather than red** and **no tannins** are extracted.

Our first wine in this tasting, the **SANCERRE**, is made with **Pinot Noir** grapes. It is a pale, **poached-salmon pink** color and it has very fresh aromas of **bilberries** and **raspberries**. There is lots of fresh, delicate **red-berry fruit** on the palate and, importantly, **no tannin**. This is essentially a **light, easy-going** but **classy** wine, with a **dry finish**.

The second wine, the **CÔTES DE PROVENCE**, is made with **Grenache** grapes, which are also used to make inky-black red wines. To make rosé, they are macerated at a **low temperature** so that just the right amount of **fruit character** is extracted before the fermentation begins. Grenache grapes give up their color very easily, producing a **much darker** rosé that is **raspberry pink** in color. In contrast to the Sancerre, the Grenache grapes give this wine **ripe, jammy strawberry** fruit on the nose, and very ripe flavors of strawberries with hints of **caramel toffee and vanilla**.

The third wine, the **BANDOL**, is made with **Mourvèdre** grapes, which are **very dark** in color and make some of the most muscular red wines in France. However, this rosé is **lighter in color** than the Côtes de Provence, indicating a shorter maceration time. It has aromas of **toffee** and **red fruit** and is light and fresh on the palate with **raspberries** and **overtones of herbs and pepper** that are characteristic of this grape variety.

GREECE
NEMEA

Most people would never think to choose a Greek rosé, but young Greek winemakers are creating fruit-driven wines of real quality. Produced in the mountains toward the north of the Peloponnese, Nemea has great potential for elegant and stylish rosé. The wines are made mainly from the Xynomavro and Agiorgitiko (St. George) grapes. The best examples are refreshing, light, and made for drinking when between six months and one year old.

COLOR Bright; medium intensity; light to darker salmon pink.

AROMA Aromatic; strawberry, pomegranate, and wild fruits of the forest.

TASTE Pleasant, well structured, and refreshing; clean acidity; long finish.

BUYING I suggest that you try Ktima Kosta Lazaridi, Strofilia, and Domaine Porto Carras.

ENJOYING These wines are great with feta cheese salad or, even better, sitting on a sunny terrace with a pizza!

BRANCHING OUT Try this wine alongside an Anjou rosé, a Sancerre rosé, or an Italian rosé, all of which have a similar weight—much lighter than a New World rosé.

SPAIN
NAVARRA

If you like Sangria, then I think you'll enjoy Navarra rosé. This wine is well structured and full of flavor. In this region, the Garnacha grape is fermented to yield a deep pink color and a fresh, dry style. Even though Navarra has to struggle for recognition in the shadow of its neighbor Rioja, the rosés are more intense, with slightly sweeter flavors and a higher alcohol content. Overall, I find that they offer much better value for money.

NAVARRA
Bodegas Ochoa

COLOR Deep pink ruby, with onionskin tinges.

AROMA Complex, ripe, and elegant; forest fruits, blackberry, herbs, and spice.

TASTE Full and rich, but refreshing; red berries and good acidity, with a very long finish.

BUYING From the leading producers, I can recommend the wines of Bodegas Ochoa, De Sarria, and Co-op San Roque.

ENJOYING These wines are perfect for a summer party—complementing tapas as an appetizer, followed by traditional paella. They also work well with fish such as mullet or Provençal brandade.

BRANCHING OUT Australian Grenache rosé and Chilean Cabernet rosé have plenty in common with Navarra, given their ripe fruit and gentle spiciness.

RIOJA

Rioja has long been Spain's leading wine region, but it is only recently that recognition of its achievements has spread around the world. Rioja *rosado* (rosé) is made primarily from the Garnacha grape variety, and the wines are rich, round, and fruity. Although they have a ripe texture, they manage to retain their underlying acidity for refreshment. If you stick with good producers, you will be assured of consistency in both style and quality.

COLOR Deep and distinctive rose-red, with a ruby rim.

AROMA Youthful and delicate; wild red fruits; strawberry and cherry.

TASTE Fresh, full flavor, with a slightly creamy texture; long, clean finish.

BUYING I recommend López de Heredia, Marqués de Cáceres, and Valdemar. A few of the best cooperatives are also worth considering.

ENJOYING These wines are superb out on the terrace with olives and chili peppers, and delicious with a feast of cured red meats, saucisson, or stew.

BRANCHING OUT Compare the delicate fruit of Rioja rosés with the more pungent and refreshing Loire Valley style typical of the wines of Chinon, Anjou, and even Sancerre.

PORTUGAL
PORTUGUESE ROSÉ

Portugal has two well-known rosé wines—Mateus and Lancers. Mateus rosé is produced in northern Portugal, primarily in the Douro and Bairrada regions. It is a slightly sparkling, semisweet wine made from a blend of grapes including Baga, Bastardo, and Touriga Nacional. Lancers rosé is produced in the same region, with a similar blend of grapes. It has lightly floral, red-fruit aromas, and is light bodied.

COLOR Very light pink (Mateus); deep pink with salmon hues (Lancers).

AROMA Limited; red fruits with a hint of flowers, vines, and peach.

TASTE Slightly fizzy; fruity, refreshing, and not too sweet; charming finish.

BUYING These wines grew to become global brands during the last century, and part of that success came from catering to regional tastes: they are made to different sweetness levels for different international markets.

ENJOYING Serve these wines as aperitifs, or with spicy Asian or Mexican cuisine. Grilled or barbecued meats are also a good match.

BRANCHING OUT Mass-market wines are a starting point from which to explore the world of rosé. If you like their lively fruitiness, try a Côtes de Provence from France.

PORTUGUESE ROSÉ
Mateus

UNITED STATES
SYRAH / GRENACHE

Syrah and Grenache are two Rhône Valley grape varieties that have taken root across the California winescape. Both of them are well suited to the state's generally warm and arid climate, yielding ripe and flavorful fruit. Much of the harvest is used to make the full-bodied reds that have gained such a huge following over the past decade. (Producers and consumers smitten by this style call themselves Rhône Rangers!) But these grape varieties also make charming, flavorful rosés, with intense colors and a wide range of jammy fruit flavors.

Like the reds, these rosés are full bodied and tend to be quite high in alcohol, and this makes them great with a range of foods, including roasted meats. Actually, I think they make an excellent, well-balanced alternative to many light reds. Despite this versatility, these wines are relatively niche compared to the popularity of sweet White Zinfandel (*see p.162*). Dry California rosés are still in their infancy, but they are making rapid progress and show great potential for creating a big noise in the wine world—so keep a close eye on them.

COLOR Elegant deep pink, with tinges of darker ruby red.

AROMA Intense and youthful; cherry, blackberry, and red summer berries.

TASTE Well structured and well balanced; rich flavors; good length.

BUYING Try the latest vintage from wineries such as Bonny Doon, Eberle, McDowell, and Dehlinger.

ENJOYING I think these rosés are great well chilled with spicy Asian dishes, or with barbecued sausages and a crisp, green salad.

BRANCHING OUT Taste these vibrant, full-flavored wines alongside young rosés from South America and Australia.

GRENACHE
McDowell

"Americans don't do things by halves, and their Syrah and Grenache rosés are no exception—these intense wines boast real power!"

ROSÉ

WORLD WINES

ROSÉ

WORLD WINES

UNITED STATES
WHITE ZINFANDEL

In the US, the red grape variety Zinfandel is used to make a rosé known as White Zinfandel, or "blush" wine, which became very popular during the 1980s. Sweet and slightly fizzy, this wine is aimed largely at the young-adult market. It is an uncomplicated wine, and not one for the connoisseur. However, when served well chilled, it is charming and friendly enough in its own way, and makes easy sipping for those with a sweet tooth.

COLOR Bright; extremely pale pink—only a "blush" of color.

AROMA Limited; peach, lemon, and red-fruit jam (raspberry, strawberry).

TASTE Slightly fizzy, with a touch of sweetness; long, lemony finish.

BUYING Very few producers have been prepared to base their reputation on this wine, but some of the leading names include Sutter Home, Buehler Vineyards, Beringer (Stone Cellars), and Cutler Creek.

ENJOYING This wine is difficult to match with food, as it is quite sweet. I would serve it with spicy food—though nothing too heavy or rich. It could work with a tuna salad, too.

BRANCHING OUT If you appreciate the sweetness of this wine, try Mateus rosé from Portugal, although I'd steer you more toward a Côtes de Provence.

ARGENTINA
ARGENTINIAN ROSÉ

Argentina's signature reds and whites—from Malbec and Torrontés, respectively—have proven great successes worldwide. But their triumph has, in turn, restricted the development of great rosés. Argentina's winemakers have generally held back on rosé production, other than for largely local consumption.

Of what is available in this wine style, Cabernet Sauvignon produces fresh rosés with crisp acidity and a host of ripe fruit flavors. However, as shown by Argentina's red wines, the Malbec grape variety may be the future for rosés in this country. Malbec rosés tend to be big rather than delicate, with fruity aromas of cherry and raspberry. They are rich, lush, and very full and satisfying. Argentinian winemakers are also experimenting with rosé made from Merlot, which has a slightly sweet edge. Who knows, pink may yet be popular!

COLOR Ranges from deep, rich pink to a pale ruby red.

AROMA Aromatic; cherry, raspberry, and spice.

TASTE Light to medium bodied; extremely smooth on the finish.

BUYING Drink these rosés as young as possible—ideally within a year of the harvest. Look for wines from producers such as Trapiche and Catena.

ENJOYING These are good wines for summer-evening sipping, but they are always welcome at a picnic.

ARGENTINIAN ROSÉ *Trapiche*

BRANCHING OUT Compare the vibrant, fruity aromas and flavors of these rosés with similar wines from neighboring Chile.

Great buys from Mendoza— the new kid on the block

The best wine-making region in Argentina is Mendoza. When you visit Mendoza, you see just how special it is, having a perfect balance between the heat of the flat plains and the cool of the Andes mountains, which rise up behind it. As recently as the mid-1990s, Argentina was largely unknown to wine lovers, but its great reds have proved themselves with quality and value for money. I visited some of the smaller vineyards in the Mendoza region, such as San Rafael and San Juan, and these producers are beginning to make full rosés from red grapes such as Cabernet Sauvignon and Merlot. I was happy to drink these wines when before I might have chosen a light red—for example, with a lunch of cold meats.

CHILE
CABERNET SAUVIGNON

The Chileans have succeeded in using Cabernet Sauvignon to create delicious, fresh, and fruity rosés. They offer both a lighter version and a fuller style, each with a host of fresh berry flavors. Sipping them is like drinking a glass of pure fruit juice! They are consistently good and excellent value for money.

COLOR Rich, deep pink, with ruby highlights; good intensity.

AROMA Pleasant and youthful; red berries and citrus fruits.

TASTE Ripe and round; fresh, harmonious, and cheerful, with a good length.

BUYING These are generally a safe buy. My favorites are Santa Rita, Undurraga, and Caliterra.

ENJOYING This is a fun choice for a relaxed lunch, or as a pick-me-up at the end of a hard day. It goes well with grilled or roasted meats and stewed fish.

BRANCHING OUT If you like the soft berry fruits in this rosé, try any other New World Cabernet Sauvignon.

AUSTRALIA
GRENACHE

Australia's hot climate is ideal for making fruity, vibrant, refreshing rosés. The best are made from Grenache grapes, and those from the Barossa Valley, South Australia, are the finest of all. These wines express a lively fruitiness on the nose; but what makes them so special is their perfect balance of acidity and alcohol.

GRENACHE
Geoff Merrill

COLOR Deep rose-petal pink, with tinges of silver.

AROMA Aromatic, with fresh strawberry, cherry, and herbs.

TASTE Fresh, fleshy, and intense, with crisp acidity and good length.

BUYING Try smaller names like Geoff Merrill, Turkey Flat, and Mount Hurtle.

ENJOYING Drink this refreshing wine on its own, or with broiled shrimp or barbecued steak. Delicious!

BRANCHING OUT Taste this wine alongside a Grenache from southern France: note the balance between fruit and alcohol in each.

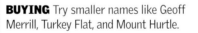

"A summer wine not to be missed! I like to enjoy a Grenache rosé in true Aussie style—around the barbecue."

NEBBIOLO

Nebbiolo is a variety associated with northwest Italy, where it produces the big and robust red wine Barolo *(see p.234)*. However, the climate of Australia presents superb growing conditions for this lighter expression—although the wine is still rich for a rosé. Australian Nebbiolo production has become very successful. It is more structured and meaty than many other pink wines, and it is especially good with food, thanks to its naturally high acidity.

COLOR Deeper pink than many rosés, with purplish tinges.

AROMA Young and fresh; bilberry, red berries, spice, and dried herbs.

TASTE Full, harmonious, and refreshing, with a crisp finish.

BUYING Production of this variety is still a niche pursuit, so you may need to search around a little. Top names include Garry Crittenden, Cobaw Ridge, and Parish Hill.

ENJOYING Try Nebbiolo with any tomato-, olive-, or garlic-based dish, such as penne Siciliana (penne pasta in a tomato and vegetable sauce) or bourride (a fish stew with a garlic sauce).

NEBBIOLO
Garry Crittenden

BRANCHING OUT The fine structure, fruitiness, and high acidity remind me very much of Syrah-based rosés from Tavel or Coteaux d'Aix-en-Provence.

ROSÉ

WORLD WINES

FRUITY, LIVELY REDS

Among the greatest and most enjoyable of all wines, fruity, lively reds are easy to drink and flexible—from once-in-a-lifetime aged Burgundy *crus* to lunchtime and barbecue wines, such as Valpolicella from Italy or raspberry-fruity Tarrango from  Australia. The Pinot Noir grape is the mainstay of this style of wine, giving complex but lively, fruity red wines. Other key varieties are Gamay—a vibrant grape, which most famously creates Burgundy's Beaujolais wines; Lambrusco, Barbera, and Dolcetto, which make some of the most famous Italian reds; Cabernet Franc, a variety planted in Chinon in France's Loire Valley and throughout the Bordeaux region, as well as in the New World; and South African Pinotage, a relative of Pinot Noir that makes light, juicy, Southern-Hemisphere reds.

STYLE PROFILE
FRUITY, LIVELY REDS

LIGHT AND JUICY

Keeping the tannins under control is the key to creating a fruity, lively red wine. This is why many of the grapes that go into making this style of wine have big berries and thin skins, which give maximum juice but minimum tannin. The wines also tend to be produced in cooler climates where the ripening period is relatively slow, giving the berries plenty of opportunities to develop their distinctive fruitiness. One last essential factor in keeping tannin levels down comes from the vinification process itself. Many light red wines are produced using a special technique called

"These are beautifully perfumed wines with loads of firm, crushed berry fruit and a silky-smooth finish."

carbonic maceration *(see pp.42–3)*, a process that keeps tannin levels to a minimum while allowing the best extraction of flavor from the grapes.

PINOT NOIR

The star grape variety of the fruity, lively reds has to be Pinot Noir, although it is notoriously difficult to grow. It also gives low yields, but this is essential if it is to produce wines of good quality. The grape is both typically and exceptionally well represented in the light, but complex, examples of French Burgundy (where Pinot Noir finds its most perfect growing conditions); it is also found in wines of California, Australia, South Africa, Chile, and New Zealand. Here, in the New World, the wines are much more "up-front" and voluptuous than their Old World counterparts, and they are, quite frankly, taking the wine world by storm.

Although generally all fruity, lively reds (regardless of their grape variety) have a bright ruby color, the best will be a slightly darker shade of ruby, and will have a full bouquet. The aromas of these wines are quite intense, and are generally

VINES IN THE VENETO
This cool, northern region is the home of Valpolicella, an Italian red whose reputation has been damaged by thin wines from overcropped vines growing on the plains. The *classico* vineyards on the steep, stony hillsides, however, produce wines of real depth and complexity.

GLOBETROTTING GRAPE
Elegant Pinot Noir makes its leanest and silkiest wines in cooler climates, and is grown in regions as far afield as Alsace in northeastern France, New Zealand's South Island, and British Columbia in Canada.

TASTE TRAIL

The Gamay grape makes the wonderfully fruity **BEAUJOLAIS**, a great place to start exploring fruity, lively reds. **CABERNET FRANC** wines from Chinon or Saumur in France and **PINOTAGE** from South Africa are also well worth investigating. But the classic variety for fruity, lively reds is **PINOT NOIR**. Try Pinots from Alsace and Sancerre for a classic light style, or from Australia, New Zealand, Carneros in California, and Oregon for amazing fruit intensity. Top of the Pinot Noir range, in both price and complexity, is **BURGUNDY**.

ENJOYING These summer wines are best served slightly chilled (at "cellar temperature")—ideally for 30 minutes in the refrigerator or ten minutes in ice water. The colder the wine, the more fruity and complex it will taste. These wines are great both on their own and served with light meats, charcuterie, salads, and spicy food. Spanish fruity, lively reds go well with tapas; German, with roast pork; New World, with barbecued meat or fish, and vegetarian foods.

dominated by the youthfulness and freshness of the red fruit. There may be notes of banana and a spiciness, too. The wine will feel lively on the palate, with tastes of fresh berries and peppers. There is no significant influence of new oak in fruity, lively red wines, and so the best examples should have a light, airy texture with a smooth, medium to long finish.

DRINK OR STORE?

Although these wines are light and not as dramatic as powerful reds, a great deal of care goes into their vinification, which can make them expensive. Most, however, should be drunk within two years, while they are fresh. The exception to this rule is good Pinot Noir, which may keep for up to 30 years.

FRANCE
CÔTE DE NUITS

Warning! These wines may steal your heart. I've certainly been under their spell for many years. The Burgundy region offers a wide range of wine styles. There is a vast number of appellations and classifications, and thousands of producers. From a single vineyard, half a dozen different domaines will give you very different wines with different qualities and prices. The key to success when choosing among these numerous and diverse wines is finding a producer that suits you—which means you need to taste and taste and taste! Pinot Noir is the grape behind all of the great reds here—a challenging variety for even the very top producers.

CÔTE DE NUITS
Confuron-Cotetidot

The best vintages offer elegance, delicacy, complex fruits, and silky tannins, while in poorer years this grape can produce wine that is acerbic, lacking fruit flavor, and dominated by herbaceous smells. The most famous and—in my opinion—the best Pinot Noir wines of Burgundy come from the Côte de Nuits district, at the northern end of the Côte d'Or (or the "golden slope"). These wines have the greatest depth and concentration of all red Burgundies. They improve with age for at least five years, and the best vintages can continue doing so for up to 35 years.

The Côte de Nuits contains a string of wine-making communes, and about two dozen *grand cru* (or "great growth") vineyards. Some of the most famous red Burgundy comes from the village of Gevrey-Chambertin. These wines tend to be very deep in color, and they develop a wild and earthy character over time. The wines from Morey-St-Denis and Chambolle-Musigny are lighter and particularly elegant, and full of finesse. Vougeot reds are floral when young, but develop an earthy and trufflelike character with age. Vosne-Romanée is regarded as producing some of the best (and most expensive) wines in the world. They are utterly intense, but also delicate, with tannins, fruit, and acidity that are perfectly balanced. Nuits-St-Georges, and the lesser-known Marsannay and Fixin, have no *grands crus*, but they still produce some excellent and world-class wines.

In my opinion, the finest vineyards are the following: Chambertin, Chapelle-Chambertin, Griottes-Chambertin, La Romanée-Conti, Romanée-St-Vivant, La Tâche, Échézeaux, Bonnes-Mares, Clos de Tart, Clos de la Roche, and Le Musigny. Look for these on the bottle—but don't tell your accountant!

COLOR Bright, dense ruby red to purple, with mauve tinges.

AROMA Cherry, blackberry, plum, spice, herbs, pepper, earth, leather, figs.

TASTE Powerful yet delicate; soft, silky, rich, fruity, and lively.

BUYING Nowhere in the world is it more important to buy according to producer name (over anything else) than in Burgundy. Since Pinot is so fussy and the weather is so fickle, good producers are your only refuge from disappointment. There are many good producers, so seek advice from your wine merchant. Briefly, I enjoy Sylvain Cathiard, Confuron-Cotetidot, Denis Mortet, Henri Gouges, Georges Roumier, and Armand Rousseau.

ENJOYING Good examples deserve to be enjoyed on their own. Try also serving a Côte de Nuits with a fillet of venison or a girolle mushroom casserole.

BRANCHING OUT Compare the weight and fragrance of good young red Burgundy against New World Pinot Noirs. Try wines from California's Russian River Valley or Oregon's Willamette Valley, or from Central Otago or Martinborough in New Zealand.

JURA POULSARD

Poulsard is an unusual red grape variety from the Jura region of eastern France. It is very thin-skinned, and so light in pigment that it can easily be used to make white wine. You might find this wine marketed as Arbois, where it is often blended with Pinot Noir or Trousseau. In Bugey, another region of eastern France, it is sometimes called Mescle.

SANCERRE ROUGE
Jean-Max Roger

COLOR Varies from a pale red to an orangey pink.

AROMA Very distinctive; cherry, raspberry, red currant, and vanilla.

TASTE Extremely delicate, fruity, and refreshing, with a long finish.

BUYING In my opinion, Jacques Puffeney and Domaine Rolet are the best producers, although you will find many good Poulsard winemakers throughout the whole region.

ENJOYING Poulsard reds (and rosés) are best served slightly chilled. This is a lovely wine to drink in summer with pâtés, a salad, or crudités. Poultry and Poulsard work well together, too.

BRANCHING OUT Use this wine to begin your own wine-tasting evening— it will be very popular! For comparisons, try it alongside a Pinot Noir from Alsace or even a Bandol rosé.

SANCERRE ROUGE

I'm rarely impressed by red wines from Sancerre, the Loire region famous for Sauvignon Blanc *(see p.106)*. However, some producers are beginning to take their reds as seriously as their whites, and making wines that match some of the lighter Burgundies for both charm and elegance. The fruity aromas of Pinot Noir are very similar, but Sancerre Rouge will rarely age well.

COLOR Distinctive pale ruby red, with an orange rim.

AROMA Delicately perfumed, with fresh red berries, earth, and spice.

TASTE Dry and pleasant; high acidity; balanced tannins; medium to long finish.

BUYING I recommend the wines of Jean-Max Roger and Domaine Henri Bourgeois. For any examples, make sure you drink them younger than two years.

ENJOYING A classic combination is slightly chilled Sancerre Rouge with charcuterie, but I also like these wines with spicy food and paella, because the wine is so refreshing.

BRANCHING OUT For an interesting comparison, try a Nuits-St-Georges or a Gevrey-Chambertin. Although these are made from the same grape variety, the contrast is incredible. When you taste them, you will see why Burgundy is world famous for its Pinot Noir!

FRUITY, LIVELY REDS

WORLD WINES

FRANCE
CÔTES DU FRONTONNAIS

This up-and-coming appellation of southwest France has truly caught my attention. There are two styles of production: the first is traditional—meaning full and tannic, and based to a significant extent on the Bordeaux grapes Cabernet Sauvignon, Cabernet Franc, and Malbec, along with Syrah; the second style is modern—meaning light and more fruit-driven, mainly using the local Negrette grape.

COLOR Bright ruby red, with vibrant pinkish tints.

AROMA Intense raspberry, cherry, lilac, fresh plum, spice, and licorice.

TASTE Subtle fruitiness and earthy flavors; medium length.

BUYING This may be one of the smallest appellations in France, but it is certainly well known by the locals for good value! Some of the best producers are Château Plaisance, Château le Roc, and Chateau Baudare.

ENJOYING Imagine you are in the mountains among friends, sharing a bottle of one of these wines with some lunch from the grill, and a soft, delicate Pyrenean cheese. It's heaven!

BRANCHING OUT If you like this style, expand your horizons with a Merlot from the Languedoc, a classic Fitou, a Bergerac Rouge, or a young Argentinian Malbec.

SAUMUR-CHAMPIGNY / CHINON

The neighboring regions of Anjou-Saumur and Touraine offer spectacular scenery of rolling vineyards surrounding ornate châteaux in the heart of the Loire Valley. At the border between these two regions, the wines of Saumur-Champigny and Chinon are the best local reds. This is the home of the Cabernet Franc grape, which thrives in the volcanic chalk soil known as tufa.

A typical Cabernet Franc wine combines sweet raspberry or red currant flavors with sweet pepper characters and crisp, refreshing acidity. Always seek out the best vintages, as the wines can be very herbaceous and leafy in poor years.

Of Saumur-Champigny and Chinon, I think Chinon is the more interesting. Although Saumur-Champigny's wines are very similar, in my view they are a little less structured. Both of these reds have similarities to Beaujolais, primarily because of their berry aromas. Their structure is light, but I think they have a concentration of fruit and spice flavors that really appeals.

CHINON
Charles Joguet

COLOR Profound deep ruby to crimson, with a purple rim.

AROMA Intense; raspberry, strawberry, dark fruits, and sweet spice.

TASTE Soft, delicate, aromatic, with a satisfying length.

BUYING Vintages vary greatly in the Loire, so ask your wine merchant for advice. I particularly enjoy the wines of producers Charles Joguet and Bernard Baudry.

ENJOYING A bottle of young Saumur-Champigny or Chinon is superb with a summer picnic or barbecue, or a fall meal of lighter roast meats.

BRANCHING OUT Compare the fruit flavors and structure of these reds with Beaujolais from Burgundy or with Valpolicella from Italy. Another wine with similar characteristics is Cabernet Franc grown on the US West Coast.

"These great red wines from the Loire Valley, made mainly from the Cabernet Franc grape, are light in structure, with a concentration of fruit, spices, and flowers."

BEAUJOLAIS

Richly flavored, light, and exuberant, Beaujolais is a classic of the wine world. Its easy-drinking nature reflects the character of the Gamay grape, and also a winemaking process called carbonic maceration, which considerably enhances the soft-fruit flavors.

Beaujolais is the southernmost extent of the Burgundy region, and the wine is sold according to a number of appellations. The most famous is Beaujolais Nouveau, which is ready to drink a few weeks after the harvest, but I prefer Beaujolais-Villages for its superior quality and relative finesse. The very best wines generally come from a few classified *crus* (communal appellations), each with their own distinct style. Juliénas and Moulin-à-Vent produce deep, intense, and complex wines that conjure up a mixture of violet, black currant, and strawberry, and can have a mineral edge. Fleurie wines are popular for their more delicate floral style, while Chénas wines have intense fruit and flower aromas. I have harvested the grapes in Morgon, and I still love the balance of juicy crushed berries with the dense and compact structure of that wine.

BEAUJOLAIS
Domaine de la Madone

COLOR Bright and light ruby red, sometimes crimson; darker for the *crus*.

AROMA Charming, vibrant; youthful red-berry fruits, pepper, violet, and banana.

TASTE Fruity and low in tannins, with a long, refreshing, succulent finish.

BUYING Top Beaujolais will age, but it's best to drink young *cru* wines. Domaine de la Madone, Château des Jacques, and Georges Duboeuf are reliable names.

ENJOYING Beaujolais works well with most vegetables and meats, but it's especially good with Christmas turkey. More concentrated wines, such as Juliénas and Moulin-à-Vent, are superb with game or red meat.

BRANCHING OUT These vibrant, fruity wines have clear similarities with Italian Valpolicella or Dolcetto. Try them also with some fun Australian Tarrango.

FRUITY, LIVELY REDS

WORLD WINES

TASTE TEST: FRUIT

Try these three reds to understand what is meant by "fruity" and "lively."

❶ ❷ ❸

❶ **CHINON** is a fairly large AOC in France's Loire Valley, making wines from the Cabernet Franc grape. Given its size, there is an inevitable variety in quality; if you can't find a Chinon from a good producer, a Bourgueil or Saumur-Champigny would work equally well here. **Seek out** Clos des Marronniers (Domaine du Roncée), Couly-Dutheil, Charles Joguet, Bernard Baudry. Vintage can be important with Loire reds; choose a young wine, or seek advice.

❷ **ST-LAURENT** is the Austrian version of the Burgundian Pinot Noir, and a truly top-class wine.

It can be hard to find outside its native Austria, but is always a safe buy, because at all levels of quality (and price) it offers wonderful fruit complexity. **Seek out** Pittnauer, Umathum, Johann Gisperg, Gesellmann.

❸ **DOLCETTO** is the sweeter, lighter little brother of the giants of Piedmont, Italy—Barolo and Barbaresco—and is the most structured of the three. As with the other wines in this tasting, light chilling enhances its fruit character. **Seek out** Prunotto, Marchesi di Grésy, Enzo Boglietti, Azienda Agricola Negro.

"These lively red wines are all about their fruit flavors, which burst unashamedly on to the palate."

The key to a well-made **fruit-driven** wine is that there is **minimal influence** on the flavors from any oak used to age the wines, and that the tannins are kept well **under control**. This allows the **true characteristics** of the fruit to come to the fore.

The basis of the **CHINON** wine is the Cabernet Franc grape, which is also used as part of the blend for red Bordeaux wines. If not fully ripe, Cabernet Franc can be quite **"green"**-tasting, making rather thin and watery wine. But when

ripened successfully, it can produce **smooth** wines with **lively, juicy fruit**. This particular wine is from one of a clutch of appellations in the Loire Valley in France that specialize in red wines rather than the more famous white wines of the region. It has a **lively, fresh** nose with **spice, blackberries, and leafy green peppers** on the palate, with hints of the hedgerow in its **sloe fruit**. It can be served slightly chilled without losing any of its character, and combines **fine fruit** with a **dry finish**.

The **ST-LAURENT**—a wine from Austria that many people may not be familiar with—is a very fruit-driven wine from a **cool climate**. It is made essentially in the Pinot Noir style, but with

softer tannins and distinct **berry fruits**. This wine has a lovely fresh, **red-berry** nose with lots of **soft fruit** and **berry flavors** on the palate, nicely **balanced tannins**, and a **clean finish**.

The third wine in this tasting is the **DOLCETTO**. Its name literally meaning **"little sweet one,"** this wine comes from Piedmont, and although this region lies in northern Italy, the days during the ripening season are **warm and sunny**. This wine has an amazing **dark cherry red** color and a wonderful nose of **sweet red fruits**. On the palate it carries through with ripe **black morello cherries, sweet fruits** that seem to burst open in your mouth, and a **soft, smooth texture**.

SPAIN
MENCÍA

The Mencía grape is grown mostly in Galicia, northwestern Spain, and in the neighboring Bierzo region. This underrated variety is capable of making fruity reds of great quality. Bierzo's wine is rich, aromatic, and very well structured. Valdeorras, just to the south of Bierzo in eastern Galicia, produces wine similar to Bierzo's, but cooling Atlantic breezes keep the alcohol content relatively low, while maintaining a good natural acidity.

COLOR Deep garnet with a purple rim; medium intensity.

AROMA Hints of oak and red fruits; prominent dark cherry.

TASTE Intense, with fragrant red fruits, chocolate, and minerals in the finish.

BUYING Don't look for old vintages—concentrate on finding younger examples of newer-style wines from producers such as Bodegas C. A. del Bierzo and Pérez Caramés.

ENJOYING This wine goes extremely well with tapas or grilled meats. One of my favorite pairings is Bierzo with goat pâté and goat cheese—a taste of the real Spain.

BRANCHING OUT Taste this wine alongside a lighter style Rioja *joven*, which is more fruit-driven, or with a soft, smooth Dolcetto from Italy.

VALDEPEÑAS

The Tempranillo grape, known locally as Cencibel, thrives in the roasting hot summers of high-altitude central Spain, giving wines from the Valdepeñas region a wonderful balance between fragrant, ripe fruit and a rich, soft texture.
What's more, aging in American oak barrels lends attractive notes of toast or vanilla to the grape's vibrant cherry fruit. This is a lovely, easy-to-drink wine.

VALDEPEÑAS
Bodegas Los Llanos

COLOR Medium crimson, with a pinkish rim and good intensity.

AROMA Fresh ripe berries, with notes of leather and vanilla.

TASTE Richly flavored, balanced, and refreshing, with a long finish.

BUYING This region has finally emerged from its grim fate during the Franco era, when it was a source of cheap wine for distilling. Today, there are several high-quality producers, including Felix Solis, Bodegas Los Llanos, and Viña Zara.

ENJOYING I enjoy good examples of these wines at summer barbecues. Their straightforward character makes them a good buy for casual parties.

BRANCHING OUT The sweet fruitiness of Valdepeñas is similar to a *crianza* Rioja or Navarra, or even an Italian Barbera. Surprisingly, you can even find similarities between the best Valdepeñas and a luscious Côte de Beaune.

SOMONTANO

Make a note now—I promise this region will be a really big winner for Spain. Somontano, meaning "under the mountains," is located at the foot of the Pyrenees, between Penedés and Navarra. The area produces wine largely from Moristel grapes, and they are often blended with Tempranillo. The result is soft and light, with velvety, rich, fruity flavors, and an authentic Spanish feel.

COLOR Deep, bright cherry red, sometimes with violet hints.

AROMA Ripe red and black fruits; notes of vanilla, chocolate, and spice.

TASTE Beaujolais-like velvety texture, light structure, fruit, and soft tannins.

BUYING In my opinion, this highly underrated region really deserves your consideration. Good producers are Enate and Viñas del Vero. I recommend that you find a young vintage and enjoy it right away.

ENJOYING Lightly chill this wine to reinforce its fruity character. Drink it on a warm evening with light meats, tapas, and barbecued foods. Why not try it with spicy merguez sausages?

BRANCHING OUT Compare a Somontano with a Beaujolais and a Rioja. If its flavors are most like the Beaujolais, it may be 100-percent Moristel; if it is more like the Rioja, there will be Tempranillo in the blend.

FRUITY, LIVELY REDS

WORLD WINES

GERMANY
SPÄTBURGUNDER

German red wines are often difficult to obtain outside Germany, but when you do come across them, the regions to look for on the label are Baden and Pfalz. These wines, made from the Spätburgunder grape (better known as Pinot Noir), can range from a light, rosé-style red through to a fuller version similar to a French Burgundy. Spätburgunder wines are generally fragrant, light, elegant, and velvety, with a very smooth finish.

COLOR Normally ruby red, but can be a very light pink.

AROMA Bright green and fresh, with cherry, vanilla, nuts, and pine.

TASTE Hints of blackberry, herbs, and minerals, with a gentle, smooth finish.

BUYING This wine could be a rising star, and among many good wineries, Bernhard Huber and Friedrich Becker are outstanding producers. Look for the classification QmP, or a reference to the grower's association VDP.

ENJOYING Match this wine with German food such as pork roast or bratwurst, although it also goes well with game and poultry in general. Its dry finish also suits blue cheeses.

BRANCHING OUT There is huge stylistic diversity in German Spätburgunder, but really good examples can be compared with a top red Burgundy and hold their heads up high!

AUSTRIA
ST-LAURENT

St-Laurent takes its name from Saint Laurentius Day, in the second week of August, when this grape normally begins to ripen. It is thought to be a relative of Pinot Noir, because of the way it develops in the vineyard and also because of its aromas and flavors. Consequently, producers usually make the wine as they might a Pinot, with a fruity, smooth, and pleasing result.

While the Pinot style is the typical form of St-Laurent, a few producers have started to experiment with a fuller, more robust approach, and the outcome is a rich and velvety wine, which I think could be the start of something great. St-Laurent already produces some of the finest Austrian reds, and there may be more to come!

ST-LAURENT
Umathum

COLOR Bright ruby red, with a medium intensity of color.

AROMA Pronounced and full aromas of fresh blackberry and strawberry.

TASTE Fleshy and fruity, with balanced acidity and polished tannins.

BUYING Look for recent vintages and enjoy them while they are young. Among producers, I recommend Umathum and Gesellmann.

ENJOYING I enjoy this wine lightly chilled for summer quaffing, but it is quite versatile and works with roasted lamb, game, and pasta dishes.

BRANCHING OUT Taste this wine with some other Austrian reds. In order of weight or structure, sample a St-Laurent followed by a Zweigelt, and then a Blaufränkisch.

A rare confession from an inward-looking Frenchman!

Before I first came to England, I didn't realize that countries like South Africa and New Zealand produced great wines—we are quite inward-looking in France when it comes to wine! I was even less knowledgeable about Austrian wine, but the first restaurant I worked in had St-Laurent on the list. I remember asking: "What is St-Laurent? Is it a producer? And what is the grape variety... and what is Austria doing making a red wine?" Today, this wine is one of my bestsellers, bought by people who like an unusual alternative to Burgundy. Admittedly, St-Laurent can be hard to find, but if you see it offered, it's well worth trying—very fruity and lively, and quite refreshing.

SWITZERLAND
SWISS LIGHT REDS

Few people think of Switzerland as a wine-producing country, but that's because virtually nothing is exported—the Swiss drink it all themselves! And when people do know of Swiss wines, it is usually whites with which they are familiar. But Switzerland does produce some refreshing light reds that are cheerful and fun—and that are rapidly gaining popularity with the Swiss wine-drinking public.

Most of Switzerland's wine-producing areas are at too high an altitude for the grapes to ripen easily, which restricts the amount of wine that this small Alpine nation can make. The majority of the grapes are grown in the extreme west, closer to France and around the great lakes. The microclimate of the lakes region has a big influence on the vines, since the light winds slow down the ripening process, allowing the grapes to develop more flavor and complexity.

The main wine regions are Valais, in the upper reaches of the Rhône River, and Vaud, to the northwest of Valais. Pinot Noir (also known as Klevner) thrives in Switzerland and is the leading red grape variety, followed by Gamay. Both of these varieties can be blended together, and the result is a wine called Dôle (in Valais) or Salvagnin (in Vaud).

Swiss Gamays are similar in many ways to young Beaujolais wines, being aromatic and smooth, with just a little hint of spice. However, Gamay wines sometimes lack the depth, body, and richness of the Burgundy wines. Syrah, as well as some unusual local grape varieties such as Humagne Rouge and Cornalin, may be added to the blends to give extra interest.

The Italian-speaking parts of Switzerland, around Ticino, produce a light style of Merlot that benefits from the climatic influence of the Italian lakes. It is well rounded and refreshing, especially since the experiments with new oak have calmed down.

SWISS LIGHT REDS
Simon Maye & Fils

COLOR Varies with the grape variety, but often very light.

AROMA Bright and lively, with raspberry, bilberry, and mint.

TASTE Generally very fruity and highly refreshing.

BUYING If you are able to find any Swiss light reds, they are likely to be from the cooperative Provins. (Try something from the Maître de Chais range.) Among the best producers are Marie-Thérèse Chappaz, Daniel Gantenbein, Jean-René Germanier, Simon Maye & Fils, and Luigi Zanini.

ENJOYING I really like Swiss light reds slightly chilled as summer aperitifs. Even better, drink them with fresh perch or any light fish dishes.

BRANCHING OUT Compare the light fresh style of a good Swiss Pinot Noir with similar wines from Canada and also from Germany (where Pinot Noir is known as Spätburgunder). I suggest that you also taste a Swiss Gamay alongside Beaujolais and note the differences.

ITALY
BARBERA

Barbera is a great wine for everyday drinking. It is known as the "people's wine" in the Piedmont region of northwest Italy, because it represents the greatest part of the normal daily wine consumption for the locals—and more than half of the area's total red wine production. Wines made from the Barbera grape variety come in a wide variety of styles, from intense reds to a sparkling version called Verbesco.

There are three dominant growing zones: Asti and Alba are the two most important, followed by Monferrato. The wines of Asti are a great bargain: charming and well made, with really appealing ripe fruit flavors. In fact, if Beaujolais *crus* stopped being sold tomorrow, I would turn straight to Barbera d'Asti!

Wine from neighboring Barbera d'Alba is well structured, with a ripe and chunky texture. If you like modern Barolo *(see p.234)*, you will find that this is not quite as full or gripping in the mouth, but you will still really enjoy it. Having said that, be patient with this wine—I recommend that you keep it for at least three or four years.

I love the amazing diversity of Barbera wines from Piedmont, with each having its own character based on its particular place of origin. As the quality of these wines continues to improve, I'm beginning to get really excited by their complexity and elegance, as well as enjoying their straightforward approach. They have a fleshy texture and ripe fruit flavors, and an acidity that gives them a special freshness.

COLOR Medium to deep garnet red, with a ruby rim.

AROMA Full and aromatic; blackberry, licorice, spice, and flowers.

TASTE Ripe fruity flavors, with bright acidity, supple tannins, and good length.

BUYING Most good Barbera has a spine of acidity that benefits from spending three or four years in the bottle, so don't be in a rush to open it. Among the best producers, I would recommend Braida, Pio Cesare, Aldo Conterno, and Vietti.

ENJOYING I like to drink Barbera at lunchtime, or just sitting outside on a warm summer evening. This wine is extremely versatile, and makes an excellent match for most Italian and Mediterranean dishes.

BRANCHING OUT Taste this wine alongside the other Piedmont favorite— Dolcetto. Before tasting, lightly chill both of these wines; 30 minutes in the refrigerator should do the trick.

"The greatest Barberas are simply the best chilled red wines to enjoy on the patio on a warm summer day with friends, around a barbecue sizzling with spicy sausages."

TASTE TEST: VINIFICATION

Discover how different techniques in the winery can affect taste.

❶ ❷ ❸

❶ **FLEURIE** is the most famous of the Beaujolais *crus*, and thus commands high prices. Make sure you choose a good producer. **Seek out** Fleuries from Georges Duboeuf—La Madone, Clos/Domaine de Quatre Vents, and the one labeled "Prestige"—are all delicious. Look also for wines by Château de Fleurie and Domaine Luce Chevalier.

❷ **NEW ZEALAND PINOT NOIR** from Central Otago to the south of South Island can claim quite a climatic affinity with Burgundy: this inland region, far from the moderating influence of the sea, has quite an extreme climate, with warm summers and cold winters. It is certainly Burgundy's newest competitor, but with its charming fruit character is perhaps even more appealing. **Seek out** Amisfield, Carrick, Felton Road, Chard Farm, Rippon Vineyard.

❸ **SPÄTBURGUNDER** is the German version of Pinot Noir—its name translates as "black grape of Burgundy"—and at its best (for example, from the Pfalz region), it really does taste like a cool, stylish Burgundy. **Seek out** Meyer-Näkel, A. Christmann, Dr Bürklin-Wolf, Knipser, Koehler-Ruprecht.

"The winemaker decides which vinification techniques to use based on the grape variety and the climate."

Each technique produces a different style of wine—fruit-driven, ripe but restrained, or cool and complex.

The first wine, **FLEURIE**, is made by **carbonic maceration**. Rather than being crushed, the grapes are put into the fermentation tank whole under a **blanket of carbon dioxide**. Fermentation takes place inside each individual grape, so the juice has **less contact with the skin**, resulting in a fruity wine with **no tannins**. Sample the aromas: there are **fresh, crushed red-berry fruits**, typical of wines made by carbonic maceration, and hints of **black currant**. The wine has a **fresh palate**, open and light, with notes of **red-berry fruit** and **violet flowers**.

The **NEW ZEALAND PINOT NOIR** is made using **cold fermentation**. In warm climates, the grapes are often **harvested at night**, when it is cooler, and fermented at **low temperatures**. This prolongs the fermentation process, allowing as much of the fruit to be extracted as possible without the wine tasting "cooked" or "burned." This wine is the color of **ripe red cherries** and has aromas of **black cherries** and **chocolate**, much **richer** than the Fleurie. On the palate, the alcohol is noticeably **restrained**, allowing lively **fresh cherry fruit and sweet pepper** flavors to come to the fore, with **soft tannins** that refresh the palate at the end.

Now try the **SPÄTBURGUNDER**, also made with Pinot Noir grapes, but vinified using the **traditional fermentation and skin contact** method. Grown in a cooler climate, these grapes need to macerate at a **higher temperature** for longer in order to extract the maximum fruit and tannins. The color of the wine is **lighter** than the Pinot Noir, and it has a complex set of aromas: **peppery red-berry fruit** with slightly **vegetal, farmyardy, and leathery** notes. This complexity is carried through on the palate, with the same **leathery red fruit** and **well-balanced tannins**.

ITALY
DOLCETTO

Dolcetto translates as "little sweet one." This refers to either the sweetness of the harvested grapes or the fact that the people of Piedmont perceive the wine as sweet relative to their other reds. (It is in fact dry.) Dolcetto is softer and fruitier than Barbera *(see pp.176–7)*, but it has much of the same invigorating acidity.

There are seven denominations, or DOCs, for this wine, all in the Piedmont region. The best known, and for me the finest, is Dolcetto d'Alba. Dolcetto di Dogliani and Dolcetto di Diano d'Alba complete a trio of leading districts. Dolcetto di Ovada and others produce mostly very simple and juicy wines, although some, termed *superiore*, are more potent. Dolcetto is important to the region's economy, so the style of the wine has been developed to make it broadly appealing. This winemaking work has greatly improved all Dolcetto in recent years.

COLOR Deep ruby red through to black cherry; good intensity.

AROMA Abundant licorice, crushed blackberry and raspberry, and almond.

TASTE Delicate and fruity; rich and full-flavored but light; good length.

BUYING Buy Dolcetto when it is young, and drink it while it is still fresh and fruity, even though the best examples may keep for five years or so. Marchesi di Grésy, Prunotto, and Enzo Boglietti are among my favorite producers.

ENJOYING Dolcetto is an excellent all-around red. It's a versatile and reliable standby for drinking with any Italian dish. I particularly like it with risotto, pizza, or even cold meats and pâté.

BRANCHING OUT Compare the exuberant fruit of these vibrant, fun reds with good Valpolicella from northeastern Italy, and also with Beaujolais from France. All are best lightly chilled.

TENUTE CISA ASINARI DEI MARCHESI DI GRESY

2003
MONTE ARIBALDO®

DOLCETTO D'ALBA
denominazione di origine controllata
vino ottenuto con uve provenienti dal vigneto Monte Aribaldo
in comune di Treiso d'Alba
messo in bottiglia dal viticoltore – estate bottled by
Tenute Cisa Asinari dei Marchesi di Grésy
Barbaresco – Italia

DOLCETTO
Marchesi di Grésy

"Think of this wine if you want a taste of Italy, and you will not be disappointed. Dolcetto was just made to drink with piping hot pizza straight from the oven."

BONARDA

Bonarda grapes are grown in scattered parts of the of Piedmont and Lombardy regions, but this Italian variety is actually grown more widely in Argentina. This is a shame, since I would love it if more people were able to enjoy one of my favorite wines from this grape, called Oltrepò Pavese. Bonarda wines are smooth and almost "too drinkable". They are just right when you want a fruity red.

COLOR Intense ruby red to purple, becoming lighter at the rim.

AROMA Very distinctive, with plum and black cherry.

TASTE Light and fruity, with cherry dominant; smooth texture.

BUYING The recent success of this grape variety is due to the care and importance that producers such as Alighieri and Loc Casa Ferrari give to producing this excellent wine.

ENJOYING You can drink these wines with light foods, such as charcuterie. But one of my favorite matches is pasta shells with sausage, mozzarella, ricotta, and tomatoes.

BRANCHING OUT If you are a fan of the meaty and spicy feel of this wine, try an Argentinian Malbec, a Rioja *crianza* from Spain, or a light Sangiovese from Tuscany.

LAMBRUSCO

How times change! Lambrusco was the world's best known and most widely consumed Italian wine in the 1970s. Now many people completely avoid it. There are plenty of poor examples around, but real Lambrusco can be wonderful. It has a vibrant red color, and its light, fresh profile goes really well with the rich sauces and meats of its home region of Emilia-Romagna in northeastern Italy.

LAMBRUSCO
Umberto Cavicchioli
& Figli

The first thing I look for in a good Lambrusco is the dominant aroma of violets. Then I look at the fizz, which boils up when the wine is poured but should disappear immediately to leave a faint ring of white around the edge of the glass. The best wines include Lambrusco di Sorbara, Lambrusco Salamino di Santa Croce, and Lambrusco Grasparossa di Castelvetro.

COLOR Bright ruby red, with a brief froth of bubbles when poured.

AROMA Fruity and jammy, with a distinct scent of violets.

TASTE Very light, vibrant, and fresh; intense berry flavors.

BUYING Grab the youngest wine available and drink it immediately! Look out for Umberto Cavicchioli & Figli, Giacobazzi, and Chiarli & Figli.

ENJOYING Serve Lambrusco lightly chilled, paired with basic Italian dishes like egg pasta, cold meats, or grilled sausages.

BRANCHING OUT This is a wine to put a smile on your face. If you like its cheeky character, try the fun and funky Tarrango of Australia.

The day I learned that you really can enjoy a chilled red wine

A few summers ago, I went with a friend of mine to visit his uncle in the Emilia-Romagna region of Italy. We traveled to his large house, out in the country, on a scorching-hot day. After the introductions, our host served us a Lambrusco; because of my bad experiences of the wine in France and England, I think I might have even winced a bit. However, my friend's uncle knew exactly what he was doing. He'd chosen a wine from a great local producer, and he'd chilled it just a little. The wine was awesome—very refreshing, with a slight sparkle and fresh berry fruit flavors. Try a Lambrusco (avoid the cheapest examples) chilled for about 30 minutes in the refrigerator before you sample it, and see what you think.

CANAIOLO

Canaiolo is a small but important part of the blend used for the famous Italian red Chianti *(see p.201)*. Some traditional Chianti can be quite "green," or lacking in fruit, but the Canaiolo grape softens the wine and brings out its charm. This variety is also grown outside Tuscany, in Umbria and the Marches, and more recently in Sardinia.

COLOR Delicate pale ruby, with bright highlights.

AROMA Very exuberant and aromatic; fresh raspberry and strawberry.

TASTE Soft and light, but with all elements in harmony; very pleasant.

BUYING Canaiolo is very rarely used on its own; it's almost always blended with other varieties, especially in Chianti. So single-variety wines may be impossible to find outside of Italy—you'll just have to save this for your next visit!

ENJOYING Drink these wines with light dishes; strong or spicy food will smother the flavors. They are best with herbed lamb, veal and cabbage, or pork loin with caramelized onions.

BRANCHING OUT If you can't find single-variety Canaiolo, other light and fruity reds with an Italian flavor include Barbera d'Asti and the softer Dolcetto d'Alba.

FRUITY, LIVELY REDS

WORLD WINES

ITALY
VALPOLICELLA

Valpolicella is located in northeastern Italy, in the Veneto region. It is a very popular wine produced in enormous quantities, but this volume includes some low-quality examples that have harmed Valpolicella's image. Wine snobs look down on it, and one wine critic even went as far as to call it "insipid industrial garbage." To be fair, very few recent examples have disappointed me; the quality really has improved.

Regular Valpolicella is light, fragrant, and fruity. It has a charming and easy-drinking feel, reflecting the character of the dominant Corvina grape. Styles vary, though, depending on how much of the slightly inferior Rondinella and Molinara grapes are in the blend. The best wines are generally those labeled *classico*, from the hilly heart of the region. If you see a wine labeled *classico superiore*, then go for it. You should expect a more structured and more complex wine, but still in the light and fruity style. Also look for *ripasso* wines, which make use of leftover grape pomace and lees from the potent Amarone della Valpolicella *(see p.235)* to yield maximum depth and character.

VALPOLICELLA
Serègo Alighieri

COLOR Bright, charming, ruby red, with good intensity.

AROMA Black and red berry fruits, with notes of dried herbs and flowers.

TASTE Fresh and subtle, with cherry and discreet tannins.

BUYING Buy young *classico* or *ripasso* wines. Good producers include Allegrini, Serègo Alighieri, and Tommasi.

ENJOYING I drink this wine with simple Italian foods—pasta, salads, pizza—or else just on its own, slightly chilled, on a hot summer day.

BRANCHING OUT You can have an enjoyable evening tasting Valpolicella with a range of light, fruity reds, including neighboring Bardolino, Piedmont's Dolcetto, a good Beaujolais from France, and even an Australian Tarrango.

"The quality and style of Valpolicella varies greatly—from light, fruity classico superiore *to rich* ripasso *wines—so make sure you pick one that suits your taste."*

BARDOLINO

This is a cheerful, easy-to-drink wine from the shores of Lake Garda in the Veneto region. Like neighboring Valpolicella, it is made in large quantities. Bardolino is a blend of three local grape varieties (Corvina, Molinara, and Rondinella), and its style is very much fruit-driven—like a bowl of ripe cherries! There is also a lively Beaujolais Nouveau-style of this wine, known as Bardolino Novello.

COLOR Bright ruby red, with medium to pale intensity.

AROMA Mainly berry fruits, with hints of almonds and spice.

TASTE Fruity, with balanced acidity and tannins.

BUYING Sadly, there are oceans of bland Bardolino out there, so I suggest that you stick with recommended producers to avoid disappointment. Two of my favorites are Guerrieri-Rizzardi and Lamberti.

ENJOYING Always drink the latest vintage, ideally within a year. This wine is best enjoyed at its own level with a simple dish such as a pizza—nothing fancy.

BRANCHING OUT If you enjoy Bardolino you won't be disappointed by a Valpolicella *classico*, or perhaps a soft Brouilly from Beaujolais in France. Also try it alongside a South African Pinotage. Fun guaranteed!

SAGRANTINO DI MONTEFALCO

The superstar grape of Umbria is Sagrantino di Montefalco, which is grown around the small hilltop town southeast of Perugia. The area is more famous for its sweet wine, which is called Sagrantino Passito, but the dry wines are on the up. They typically show lots of heady black fruit aromas and soft flavors. Montefalco Rosso is another wine from the same region, but it is less distinguished, being based on the Sangiovese grape.

PINOT NOIR
Château des Charmes

COLOR Deep ruby red, with medium to pale intensity.

AROMA Mainly berry fruits, with hints of almonds and spice.

TASTE Dry, round, and fruity, with balanced tannins; medium length.

BUYING You are unlikely to see more than one of these wines on a retail or restaurant list. But if you have a choice, I recommend Fratelli Adanti, Antonelli, or Domenico Benincasa.

ENJOYING I like to drink the dry version of Sagrantino di Montefalco with light meats and, in the winter, with roasted meats. Excellent!

BRANCHING OUT It's worth tasting this exceptional wine alongside a firm Chianti Classico and a soft Dolcetto d'Alba. Sagrantino is rather like a blend of the two.

CANADA
PINOT NOIR

Most people are surprised when I recommend Canadian reds, but these come from the lush, green Niagara Peninsula of Ontario or the semidesert climate of the Okanagan Valley in British Columbia—not the Canadian Arctic! Overall, the wines are light and refreshing, with fragrant red fruits and a lively texture. While more famous for sweet ice wines *(see p.293)*, Canada offers dry whites and reds well worth sampling.

COLOR Attractive ruby to cherry red; quite pale.

AROMA Elegant, with fresh red fruits, earth, and spice.

TASTE Vibrant and fruity, with balanced acidity and subtle tannins.

BUYING For the best-quality wines, look out for the VQA classification symbol on the label. My three favorite producers are Château des Charmes, Inniskillin, and Mission Hill.

ENJOYING Try these wines with light meats, or with meaty fish, such as sea bass. Never serve them with anything too flavorsome or powerful—go for delicate dishes.

BRANCHING OUT You should note that, although this is a New World wine, it is very much in the European style. Compare it with an Alsatian red or a Pinot Nero from Italy.

UNITED STATES
PINOT NOIR

Oregon just buzzes over Pinot Noir. This is one of the best places in the world outside France for this wine, and good Oregonian examples offer the concentrated fruit character of California's Carneros district with the earthy, mineral touch of Burgundy. The northern Willamette Valley is the center of production, where very small producers craft top-quality wines. The prices are relatively high, but the wines are worth every penny.

COLOR Intense, deep ruby color, with a light ruby rim.

AROMA Well defined; cherry, jammy strawberry, fresh herbs, spice, vanilla.

TASTE Fleshy, balanced acidity; bags of fruit; silky tannins; good length.

BUYING A few wineries are flying the flag for this amazing corner of American wine country. Domaine Drouhin, Argyle, Adelsheim, and Elk Cove are some personal favorites.

ENJOYING Serve these wines with lamb casserole or with venison. Alternatively, follow the example of Oregonians, and drink them with grilled salmon and seasonal vegetables.

BRANCHING OUT In my view, these wines are a rival to the best of French Burgundy. Try them alongside a Vosne-Romanée or Chambolle-Musigny from the Côte de Nuits, and see if you agree!

FRUITY, LIVELY REDS

WORLD WINES

❶ GEVREY-CHAMBERTIN is one of the most famous names of the Côte de Nuits in Burgundy; go for a fine producer to really do it justice. **Seek out** Domaine Trapet Père & Fils, Armand Rousseau, Denis Mortet, Domaine Harmand-Geoffroy, Bernard Dugat-Py, Dominique Laurent.

❷ OREGON PINOT NOIR rarely disappoints, which is just as well, since its quality has earned it some quite hefty prices. Look especially for wines from the Willamette Valley region. **Seek out** Domaine Drouhin, Adelsheim, King Estate, Patricia Green Cellars, Brick House.

❸ NORTH COAST PINOT NOIR from California is among the most refreshing of Pinots, packed with fruit. Look for the Carneros and Russian River Valley regions; to the south, coastal Santa Barbara can produce wines in a similar style. **Seek out** Ramsay, Sanford, Au Bon Climat, ZD Wines.

TASTE TEST: CLIMATE

Explore the effect of climate in three Pinot Noirs from around the world.

Vineyards of Clos de Vougeot on the Côte de Nuits

"Warm sunshine allows grapes to shrug off their inhibitions and reveal their fruity exuberance."

The wines in this tasting are all made from the same grape variety— Pinot Noir—and come from three regions with slightly different climates that make some of the finest wines from this grape in the world.

As a general rule, the key to a great red wine is the **balance** between **fruit, acidity, tannin, and alcohol**. The very best wines have a **perfect balance** of these four characteristics. While the **complexity and depth** of Pinot Noir wines come from a **slow ripening** of this variety in **cooler climates**, the grapes still need **plenty of sunshine** to bring out their **fruitiness**.

The first wine is the **GEVREY-CHAMBERTIN** Pinot Noir from the Côte de Nuits. The grapes for this wine are grown in the **most northerly** part of the Côte de Nuits, where the climate is **cool year-round**. It has a spicy nose with **green peppers** and some **stalkiness**. On the palate it has **red-berry fruit**, but it also has an **earthy character** with quite firm tannins and a **dry finish**. The fruit is ripe but **not luscious** and it is held in by the **firmness of the tannins**.

Taste the **OREGON PINOT NOIR** next. Like the Côte de Nuits, Oregon has a temperate climate— perfect for Pinot Noir grapes—but is **warmer**, with a fine balance between **sunshine** and **cool breezes**. The wine has a **huge nose** full of **sweet cherries** and **strawberries** and on the palate, these fruits come through, perhaps

in a **more delicate** way than in the Côte de Nuits. This is a very **classy** wine; it doesn't give everything away at the first taste. It is the **most rounded** style of the three wines in this tasting, with **great depth** and **complexity**.

Finally, try the **NORTH COAST PINOT NOIR** from California. The climate here is more **predictable** than that of the Côte de Nuits; there is a **cool ocean breeze** but **more hours of sunshine**. Can you smell that sunshine on the nose of this wine? It is certainly much more **open** than the first wine, with aromas of ripe **red and black berry fruit**. Its nose is not as big as the Oregon wine, however, reflecting its slightly more temperate climate. This wine is **exuberant** on the palate with **sweet black cherries**, hints of **vanilla** (from the oak) together with **strawberries and raspberries**.

UNITED STATES
CALIFORNIA PINOT NOIR

California shows an amazing capacity for Pinot Noir, with complex flavors and superb, well-balanced, juicy textures. Unlike the historic and confusing patchwork of Burgundy, you need remember only four districts: the Russian River Valley and Carneros in the north, and the Santa Ynez Valley and the Santa Maria Valley in the south.

All four districts rely on the cooling influence of maritime fog to extend the growing season. This allows the grapes to mature more slowly, giving wines of wonderful character and great balance. Ironically, growers once avoided such places because the fog prevented the kind of heat that Californians embraced for ultraripe grapes. But when more European elegance and balance were required, that cooling fog became a blessing. I like the consistent quality of good California Pinot Noir—save these wines for special occasions.

COLOR Bright deep ruby to cherry red; fairly solid.

AROMA Intense; berries, cherry, leather, sweet spice, vanilla.

TASTE Big, rich, and voluptuous, with great balance.

BUYING I prefer established names like Saintsbury, Rochioli, Kistler, Sanford, Williams-Selyem, and Kendall-Jackson.

ENJOYING These rich wines are a great match for roast beef and game. Their upfront fruit also makes them a pleasure to drink on their own.

CALIFORNIA
PINOT NOIR
Kendall-Jackson

"*Ripe black cherries, with sweet, spicy oak. Voluptuous, with a great balance between fruit, acidity, and tannins. At their best, these California wines are a real rival to the French!*"

BRANCHING OUT

Compare the fruit and weight of California Pinot Noirs with their New World cousins from New Zealand. You can also contrast their structure with that of good red Burgundy.

NEW ZEALAND
PINOT NOIR

People (especially French people) often ask me about the difference between Australian and New Zealand wines, and which of them is better. My answer is that both countries produce fantastic wines. Broadly speaking, Australia has a warmer and drier climate, so the wine tends to be full of big, brash, "in-your-face" fruit. The climate of New Zealand is generally cooler and wetter, and this produces more restrained, and perhaps more refined, fruit flavors. They are both great, but they are very different.

PINOT NOIR *Wither Hills*

New Zealand's rise to fame in the wine world began in Marlborough, on the South Island, where the perfect combination of fine soil, sunshine, and cooling sea breezes makes for brilliant Sauvignon Blanc. But this area also grows particularly fresh Pinot Noir, with a fruitiness that just explodes in your mouth. This is definitely my kind of wine! It is still relatively new on the market, but it could be a real rival to French Burgundy.

The Central Otago region, in the southern part of South Island, is the most southerly vineyard in the world, but it is also the fastest-growing wine area in the country. There is such a buzz about this place among Pinot-philes. The cool climate makes for a long growing season—a key element in the production of the best Pinot Noir.

Some great Pinot is also produced in the Martinborough region of Wairarapa, at the southern end of the North Island. This area has good soil, lower rainfall, and long spells of sunshine, producing fruity and distinctive wines. In fact, Martinborough was the original home of New Zealand Pinot. It is still an area to watch.

COLOR Dark ruby—darker than most European Pinot Noirs.

AROMA Raspberry, cherry, plum, savory herbs, and spicy oak.

TASTE Red berries, with toasty oak and vanilla; ripe, round, and sexy!

BUYING There are so many great wines to try. Look for Ata Rangi, Wither Hills, Craggy Range, Palliser Estate, Isabel Estate, Felton Road, Peregrine— I could go on and on!

ENJOYING The fresh flavors of New Zealand Pinot Noir are best enjoyed when the wine is young. I like this vibrant wine on its own as an aperitif, but it also makes a fine accompaniment to delicately flavored dishes, such as mushroom risotto.

BRANCHING OUT New Zealand Pinot Noir and good examples from Oregon display the same depth and fruity appeal. For the same reasons, compare these wines with a Pinot Noir from Australia's Yarra Valley.

FRUITY, LIVELY REDS

WORLD WINES

SOUTH AFRICA
LIGHT REDS

The wine world is showering praise on South African Sauvignon Blanc *(see p.127)* and full-bodied examples of Shiraz *(see p.252)* right now. But the story doesn't end with these popular grape varieties. The lesser-known red Cinsault (or Cinsaut) came to South Africa from Languedoc in southern France, and it produces lively, aromatic wines.

Another French import is Pinot Noir, but success has been far more limited here than in New Zealand or even Oregon. The conditions in South Africa are generally too warm for great Pinot, but there are some exceptional wines being crafted along the south-central coast at Walker Bay and the Hemel-en-Aarde Valley, close to the whale-watching town of Hermanus.

   The combination of Cinsault and Pinot Noir—quite literally crossing the two vines to create something new—resulted in South Africa's very own

SOUTH AFRICAN LIGHT RED
Backsberg

Pinotage. Some people say you either love or hate this red, but I don't think it's as simple as that. The styles vary tremendously, and this can make understanding these wines pretty difficult. In general, they have a light and juicy feel.

COLOR Deep red to purple, with a ruby to tile-red rim.

AROMA Raspberry, cherry, plum, savory herbs, spicy oak.

TASTE Balanced and smooth; high acidity; long, fruity finish.

BUYING There are many great producers. Try Bouchard Finlayson, Hamilton Russell, Boekenhoutskloof, Charles Back, Meerlust, and Backsberg.

ENJOYING I think Pinotage is great alongside fresh salmon or trout, and the boldest versions go very well with barbecued meats and spicy dishes.

BRANCHING OUT If you like Pinotage, try spicy, red-fruited wines of the Languedoc-Roussillon region of France—such as good Vins de Pays and the appellations Fitou and Corbières.

"Although style and quality vary greatly, Pinotage is the flagship of South African reds. It offers a wide range of fruit flavors, with hints of meat and chocolate."

AUSTRALIA
PINOT NOIR

Much of Australia is too hot for the production of great Pinot Noir. However, certain pockets of this vast landscape have tremendous potential, and there is no shortage of Australian winemakers who are avid Pinot Noir fans and eager to find sites where their beloved grape can work its bewitching magic. The most established regions for Pinot Noir in Australia are the Yarra Valley, a small area in Victoria to the northeast of Melbourne, and the island state of Tasmania, off the coast of New South Wales. Other exciting places include the Mornington Peninsula and Geelong, both in Victoria, and the Adelaide Hills of South Australia.

The Yarra Valley has a moderately cool climate and good rainfall, and this helps to make it one of the most suitable regions yet discovered for Australian Pinot Noir. If you like Pinot that bursts with immediate, fresh, and tasty fruit, then I'm sure you will enjoy these wines.

   Tasmania was known for many years as the "Apple Isle," a reference to the cold climate that made it more suitable for growing apples than for heat-loving orchard fruits, such as peaches and oranges, which are grown elsewhere in Australia. But the recent search for a cool climate to make both elegant Pinot Noir and superior sparkling wines in a Champagne style has placed Tasmania firmly on the map.

   Tasmania has many new vineyards and wineries, but they tend to be tiny, and the wine they produce is relatively expensive. The Tasmanian climate is actually quite close to that of Champagne and Burgundy, so the wines produced here have a refreshingly light-to-medium body. They are not as rich as you would expect from wines from mainland Australia, but can display a more complex subtlety. They often show a hint of herb and spice in their aromas, in addition to the cherry and plum flavors found in Yarra Valley wines.

If you are looking for a New World Pinot Noir that is both ripe and yet restrained, try some from Tasmania. And while you're at it, I also think you should sample some of this island's excellent sparkling wines *(see p.269).*

COLOR Intense and attractive; cherry-plum.

AROMA Black cherry and plum, with hints of French oak.

TASTE Fresh, youthful, gamey, spicy, and savory, with a good balance.

BUYING I suggest buying recent vintages of these wines, so that you can enjoy their vibrant character. Among producers, I recommend Dromana Estate, Coldstream Hills, Scotchman's Hill, Stonier, Bannockburn, and Pipers Brook.

ENJOYING I often drink Yarra Valley or Mornington Peninsula Pinot Noir on its own, but it also complements a lovely plate of cold meats or cheese on a base of lettuce. Perfect!

BRANCHING OUT Try some of these great Australian Pinots alongside vibrant, fruity examples from New Zealand. Also try comparing them with US Pinot Noirs from the Russian River Valley in California. It makes a fascinating evening of tasting!

TARRANGO

There are some wines that I can't take completely seriously, but I still enjoy them for being fun, funky, and full of life. Drinking Tarrango is like eating fresh raspberries! It is light, lively, uncomplicated and very refreshing—characteristics it shares with Beaujolais from France. I think it is easy drinking personified—I love to chill a bottle, and then chill out with friends.

The Tarrango grape took its name from the town in Victoria, Australia, where it was developed in 1965. The variety is a cross between Touriga Nacional—a port grape—and the rich white Sultana. The breeders' aim was to produce a variety that grew perfectly in the Australian climate, and would make light, fun red wines. They certainly succeeded!

TARRANGO
Brown Brothers

COLOR Light cherry red, with a medium intensity.

AROMA Loads of fresh, crushed red fruits; pleasant and youthful.

TASTE Juicy, charming, and refreshing texture; fruity, with good length.

BUYING You should buy Tarrango as young as possible, because its light structure is not intended to last. Also, don't bother looking for a range of producers—Brown Brothers is really the only one worth trying.

ENJOYING Tarrango is perfect for summer evenings around the barbecue grill, and also goes well with light dishes and cold meats.

BRANCHING OUT The light, juicy style of Tarrango is similar to a Gamay from one of the *cru* villages of Beaujolais in France—those from Fleurie or Brouilly are particularly good.

FRUITY, LIVELY REDS

WORLD WINES

The time I was Tarrangoed at a wine-tasting!

If you are a wine professional, people like to test you by making you taste a wine and tell them what it is. Some grape varieties are easy to identify, but there will always be a few that stump you. A few years ago, I was at the Brown Brothers winery in Australia, tasting classic styles such as Cabernet Sauvignon and Chardonnay. Then someone gave me a glass of light-red wine with aromas of crushed red fruits. Possibly a Beaujolais style, I thought, but are they growing Gamay grapes here in Victoria? It was juicy and refreshing, with lots of raspberry fruit and good length, but it wasn't Gamay. The grins on the faces of my hosts grew wider with each wrong suggestion I made—they knew I'd been Tarrangoed!

RIPE, SMOOTH REDS

Perhaps the largest and most diverse of all the wine categories, the ripe, smooth reds include everyday drinking wines, such as cherry-ripe Chilean Merlots, through to prestigious classics, such the *grands crus classés* of St-Émilion—also made from the  Merlot grape. Other varieties for special attention are Sangiovese, the key grape in the blend that makes Italian Chianti; and Tempranillo, which Spanish bodegas use in the wines of Rioja and Navarra. While this group includes some of the most special and expensive wines in the world, there are ripe, smooth reds for any occasion, throughout the year—and for any time after noon! They match beautifully with nearly all kinds of food—but don't let that stop you from picking up a glass just for the pure enjoyment of its delicious fruit and silky texture.

STYLE PROFILE
RIPE, SMOOTH REDS

SUPPLE, VERSATILE WINES

This category provides a fascinating cross-section through world production. In the past, many of the wines described here would have been considered full bodied, but in recent years the emergence of intensely rich and heavy New World wines has shifted perceptions, and many are now considered to be "medium" reds. These wines are inevitably characterized by their grape variety, as well as the climate in which the vines grow. Overall, they are riper and more structured than light reds, and tend to be darker in color with more licorice and spicy flavors. Many are aged in oak barrels—not necessarily new ones—giving them a savory essence. They are fleshy, but not harsh, and will almost certainly entice you to drink some more!

RIOJA COUNTRY
Arguably Spain's greatest grape variety, Tempranillo is grown in several regions, but most famously contributes its distinctive, intense flavors and dark color to Rioja.

"The most popular wines in the world—their harmonious personalities mean there's something here for almost everyone."

An inexpensive ripe, smooth red wine should have a luscious, fresh, fruity bouquet, without too much depth or complexity. Although the emphasis of the wine's taste is on fruit, the palate should be balanced, as should its texture; the tannins should be discreet. An expensive ripe, smooth red will offer complexity, finesse, and subtlety with a fleshy body and perfectly balanced structure. Flavor rather than weight will dominate the wine, and it will have polished, round tannins.

ROUNDED, FULL FRUIT FLAVORS

The ripe, smooth red category offers an enormous range of wines, all the way from full bodied to light, but overall they should be smooth and round in texture, with complex aromas and full flavors. Expect to find garnet through to dark cherry at the core of these wines, although the rim may be lighter—ruby to tile red. As the wines age, they generally become lighter in color. Aromas vary according to country of origin and grape, but are generally intense, with black fruits, dried herbs, sweet spices, and leather. These wines should

MERLOT ON THE VINE
Most notably associated with some of the finest, most expensive Bordeaux wines, Merlot produces less exalted but hugely seductive, velvet-soft wines elsewhere in southern and southwestern France.

TASTE TRAIL

New World **MERLOTS** are smooth, fruity, reliable wines that make an excellent jumping-off point for this style. And while **ST-ÉMILION**, **CHIANTI**, and **RIOJA** are the big European names and classic flavors here, seek out some of the underrated but stylish wines that live in the shadow of their famous neighbors: elegant **BORDEAUX** appellations, such as Côtes de Blaye and Canon-Fronsac; new-style, claretty **NAVARRA** wines from Spain; and sweet, juicy **VINO NOBILE DE MONTEPULCIANO** or lingering, black-cherry-and-spice **TORGIANO** from Italy.

ENJOYING As a general rule, serve these wines at room temperature, although some, such as Zinfandel, can be served cool. There is no need to decant ripe, smooth reds, nor to allow them to "breathe." You can drink these versatile wines with a huge array of foods, such as pasta and pizza (try a Chianti or Cannonau); light meats (try Montepulciano with pork or poultry); most vegetarian foods; and even fish (try Dornfelder).

exude a harmony of ripe fruit and tannins, with a good balance of alcohol. Expect a long, satisfying finish, lasting some six to eight seconds.

DRINK OR STORE?

Chilean Merlots and wines such as Rioja will make reliable standbys in your wine store, suitable for everyday drinking in summer or winter; although, of course, you might want to keep some Merlots, most notably St-Émilion *grands crus*, for special occasions—and who can blame you? Only the best wines, and wines from certain vintages, are suitable for aging, so if you are looking for ripe, smooth reds to lay down, seek advice from your wine retailer. Most versions from the New World are intended for drinking while young—within three to five years.

FRANCE
ST-ÉMILION / POMEROL

St-Émilion and Pomerol are two dynamic Bordeaux wine districts. Each has its own identity, but the key to the success of both is the Merlot grape, with Cabernet Franc its junior partner. Merlot grown here produces a deeply colored wine with aromas of ripe black fruit. The winemaking technique adds layers of smoke, cedar, and vanilla. Powerful, yet smooth and rounded, these wines have elegance and finesse. They can be drunk when young, but are best after five to ten years in the bottle—so be patient!

St-Émilion wines are divided into three classifications: *grand cru*, *grand cru classé*, and *premier grand cru classé*. The *grand cru* wines are smooth and pleasant, with vibrant fruit. St-Émilion *grand cru classé* wines are richer and more complex, and usually the best buys—relatively speaking,

"The Merlot grape thrives in St-Émilion and Pomerol, making some truly exquisite wines. Keep an eye out for bargains from the satellite appellations!"

in this pricey region of the wine world. The highest category, *premier grand cru classé*, is divided into levels A and B. Level A contains only the world-famous châteaux of Cheval Blanc and Ausone.

Beyond these three classifications, there are also a number of "satellite" appellations that are permitted to use St-Émilion in their name: Montagne St-Émilion, Puisseguin St-Émilion, Lussac St-Émilion, and St-Georges St-Émilion. These wines have the classic Merlot style, with a medium body and a spicy finish. They also offer good value.

The smaller Pomerol district has no classification system—but the wine speaks for itself. It is rich and lush, with a tremendous fruit concentration.

COLOR Deep ruby-red, becoming black cherry with age; great intensity.

AROMA Intense fruits and spice; over time, cedar, smoke, spice, and leather.

TASTE Perfectly structured; rich, round, velvety, and smooth, yet dense and full.

BUYING Vintages vary in this corner of Bordeaux, so seek advice from your wine merchant. Leading lights include Belair, Figeac, L'Eglise-Clinet, Pétrus, and Vieux-Château-Certan. Also look out for Haut Gravet.

ENJOYING These wines work well with lamb and spring vegetables, traditional roast beef and potatoes, or even hearty stews. Give them the benefit of a large glass to project their fabulous aromas.

BRANCHING OUT The fruit and structure of St-Émilion and Pomerol wines are quite similar to good examples from neighboring Côtes de Castillon—but the prices of the latter are a lot more appealing.

CÔTES DE CASTILLON

Côtes de Castillon is an exciting corner of the Bordeaux region. For many years this district suffered from underinvestment, but now it's just bustling with activity. Like St-Émilion, the dominant grape is Merlot. Côtes de Castillon wines are great buys, and charming and elegant when still young. They also have depth and complexity, and should be high on your shopping list.

COLOR Dark black cherry, with a ruby rim.

AROMA Overripe dark fruits, with dried forest herbs, leather, and bitter chocolate.

TASTE Dense and ripe, with well-integrated tannins; smooth, long finish.

BUYING I just love these wines, especially since the 2000 vintage. So many of the smaller châteaux stand out. Some of my favorites are Château Brisson, Château la Grande Maye, Château Arthus, and Château d'Yott.

ENJOYING This wine is very flexible. Serve it with leg of lamb and roast potatoes, or try it with any white meat. Drink at any point within five years of the harvest.

BRANCHING OUT Compare Côtes de Castillon with Côtes de Bourg or the "satellite" appellations of St-Émilion. They have rustic charm, and juicy black fruits like a Pomerol.

CÔTES DE BOURG

Côtes de Bourg is a small hilly district at the confluence of the Dordogne river and the Gironde estuary. Originally planted by the Romans, it is the most productive of the Bordeaux *côtes* (hillside) appellations, and it has recently improved in quality. The wines are made mainly from Merlot grapes, and they are particularly fruity. They are also good value.

COLOR Medium-deep ruby red, with a pink rim.

AROMA Fruit-driven, subtle; red berries, flowers, minerals.

TASTE Round, velvety, and gentle, with ripe tannins.

BUYING A small group of châteaux here are really amazing, including Château Falfas and Château Roc de Cambes. But there are still more to come! The latest vintages are showing huge improvements, too.

ENJOYING You can get the most from this wine's fruity texture with a dish of roast chicken and fresh tagliatelle—very satisfying. Or try it with a nice leg of lamb and roast potatoes.

BRANCHING OUT Try this wine alongside one from neighboring Bergerac, or a Carmenère from Chile. It's also great fun to compare it to other Bordeaux Merlot-based wines— Côtes de Castillon, Fronsac, St-Émilion, and more.

CÔTES DE BOURG
Château Falfas

FRANCE
PREMIÈRES CÔTES DE BLAYE

Premières Côtes de Blaye lies to the north of Côtes de Bourg. The wines are made mainly by cooperatives, but some individual producers are crafting high-quality examples. Blaye actually specializes in white wine, so finding those may be easier; but it is worth searching out the excellent reds. They can be beautifully structured and elegant, and offer great value.

COLOR Lively and bright ruby red, with medium intensity.

AROMA Cherry and other red fruits, with hints of tobacco, spice, and vanilla.

TASTE Elegant; round and fresh, with supple tannins and a medium length.

BUYING The word "Premières" on the label is crucial, since the appellation Côtes de Blaye is for whites only. Château les Bruelles and Château Charron are truly excellent individual producers.

ENJOYING Serve this red at a slightly cool ("cellar") temperature. It's brilliant with red meat, roast chicken, or rich pasta dishes. It also works with stir-fries.

BRANCHING OUT If you like this wine, you should also try Côtes de Castillon, which is similar in structure.

FRONSAC / CANON-FRONSAC

Fronsac, on the right bank of the Gironde, is one of the most exciting Bordeaux districts. If you like the delicacy of St-Émilion and the velvety character of Pomerol, then this wine is for you. It has complexity, intensity, and subtlety of flavor, but without too much weight. Canon-Fronsac is the best part of the district, and now is the time to get some—before the world catches on and prices rise.

COLOR Garnet red, with a ruby rim and good intensity.

AROMA Delicate; fresh red fruits with notes of herbs, toast, and vanilla.

TASTE Finesse and elegance, with suaveness and a concentration of flavors.

BUYING Go with younger wines, up to five years old. Wine from almost any château will be tasty, but try Château de la Dauphine and Château Fontenil.

ENJOYING After 30 minutes in a decanter, serve with Châteaubriand, gratin potatoes, and fresh green beans.

BRANCHING OUT Compare this with a Haut-Médoc wine, such as a *cru bourgeois* from a good year. This will show you the differences between the so-called Left and Right Bank wines.

MONDEUSE

Mondeuse is a grape variety from Savoie in eastern France, and it is usually sold as Vin de Savoie. For me, this wine is a real winner after a long day's skiing. I would place it somewhere between a Fleurie from the Beaujolais region, because of its freshness and weight, and a Crozes-Hermitage from the Rhône Valley, because of its fruity and spicy aromas.

COLOR A deep-colored red, with an opaque texture.

AROMA Intense and complex; violets, pepper, spice, red fruits, licorice.

TASTE Well structured and juicy; refreshing acidity; long, clean finish.

BUYING Among producers, I can recommend Domaine Tardy and Domaine Quénard. Although Vin de Savoie has moderate aging potential, I would suggest that you drink this wine no more than two or three years after the vintage.

ENJOYING I adore Vin de Savoie served with calves' liver and mashed potatoes—never anything too spicy, as that would clash with the wine. Serve it at a cool ("cellar") temperature to reinforce its fruit intensity.

BRANCHING OUT Try Vin de Savoie alongside a Beaujolais and a Crozes-Hermitage, and notice how it really sits somewhere between the two. Taste it with an Austrian Blaufränkisch, for an interesting contrast.

"The modern Bordeaux; rarely disappointing and constant in quality— without draining your wallet!"

CORBIÈRES

You can find some great red wines from Corbières, the leading appellation of the vast Languedoc-Roussillon region. Exciting new winemakers and plenty of outside investment are generating richer and more complex wines than ever before. Increasing quantities of Syrah grapes in these blends (at the expense of less-inspiring local varieties) make the best of them smooth, full of character, and great value for money.

COLOR Dark ruby to garnet, with a pinkish rim.

AROMA Mediterranean sunshine feel; blackberry, cherry, spice, dried herbs.

TASTE Complex flavors; rich and dense, but with a long, smooth finish.

BUYING These wines will rarely disappoint, unless you expect something highly complex and intense at a very low price! Look for Château Auris and Château la Voulte-Gasparets.

ENJOYING These wines are for early drinking. They are great with grilled chicken and green peas, or with any meat or vegetarian dish that is not too strongly flavored.

BRANCHING OUT Compare Corbières with a good Merlot. Although Merlot is not a part of the blend permitted in this appellation, the wines are—to my taste—similar in character.

FITOU

Fitou is a wild, hilly landscape where the Languedoc and Roussillon come together in southern France. Fitou has been recognized with its own appellation for almost 60 years and is well known in France, but only fairly recently has it gained a wider reputation. At one point, producers here made the mistake of concentrating on volume at the expense of quality, but the region is now rebuilding its identity.

Within the Fitou appellation, there are two very different areas. The inland mountain zone produces dark, herbal wines. These contrast with wines from the coastal zone, where cooling sea breezes lighten the flavors. Total production is controlled by four big cooperatives, and while Carignan used to be the dominant grape, new blends are incorporating Grenache, Mourvèdre, and Syrah. These wines are certainly showing much more fruit and balance. I think the overall quality has greatly improved in recent years, but there is still work to do. Watch this space!

COLOR An intense ruby red, with tile-red nuances.

AROMA Red berries, pepper, plum, toast, chocolate, and vanilla.

TASTE Rich and fleshy; balanced tannins, and a full-flavored finish.

BUYING Look for young wines from Bertrand Bergé, or top blends from the Mont Tauch cooperative, such as Les Douze and L'Exception.

ENJOYING Try good Fitou with pork stew or charcuterie. It also works very well with roasted vegetable pasta dishes.

BRANCHING OUT Compare the spicy fruit characters of good young Fitou with reds from the surrounding Corbières appellation and from the Minervois region farther north.

The invasion of the Australian winemakers

So there I was, in a remote farming community in Languedoc, southwestern France, sitting in a café talking in English on the phone to my family back in the UK. Two men came over and greeted me with a loud "G'day mate!" These guys were among a number of Australians who have set up in the region to make wine using state-of-the-art production and quality control methods. The Aussies have not only improved the reputation of wine in Languedoc-Roussillon, but also spurred the locals into making better and more consistent wines themselves. The big cooperatives that make most Fitou are now concentrating on quality rather than quantity, and making an impact beyond France, especially through supermarkets.

RIPE, SMOOTH REDS

WORLD WINES

TASTE TEST: BODY

Discover exactly what makes a red wine light or full bodied.

❶ ❷ ❸

❶ CALIFORNIA PINOT NOIR at its absolute best can be as good as French Burgundy, matching its delicate complexity and well-balanced juicy texture. **Seek out** Ramsay North Coast (Kent Rasmussen), Sebastiani Sonoma Coast, The Ojai Vineyard, Sanford, Saintsbury, David Bruce Chalone Vineyard.

❷ MINERVOIS from the south of France is made from Grenache, Syrah, and Mourvèdre grapes— similar to a good Rhône, but at half the price. It used to be considered a good cheap bottle, but today—as this tasting

reveals—the wines can be really sophisticated. **Seek out** Château du Donjon, Septombres, Château Gibalaux Bonnet.

❸ BAROLO is a ripe, powerful, noble, slow-maturing wine from a small region in the Italian Piedmont. Leave it until last in this tasting because it has firm tannins that will knock out your palate. **Seek out** Prunotto, Brezza, Massolino, Rocche Costamagna Rocche dell'Annunziata. Vintage is important with these wines, but a run of great years for Barolo means that anything from 1995 to 2001 is a safe bet.

"The majority of ripe, smooth reds can be described as 'medium-bodied'—but what exactly does that mean?"

Body is a critical factor when choosing a red wine. When you consider the body, you are thinking about **how the wine feels** in the mouth—is it **light and thin** or **substantial and thick**? In this tasting, you will try a light-, a medium-, and a full-bodied wine.

You can normally tell quite a lot about the body (or density) of a wine from its **color**. Typically, the darker the color, the **fuller the wine**. But, as with most things, there are exceptions, as our first wine, the **CALIFORNIA PINOT**

NOIR, proves. This dark-colored wine has a **light body** but an intensely fruity nose and a **ripe fruit** texture, **silky tannins**, and great acidity. The aroma has **hints of vegetable** and **farmyard**, but on the palate the fruit is dominant—lots of ripe **berry and cherry** flavors with **hints of spice** and **leathery** overtones. The alcohol balances the fruit, and is actually **quite strong**, but it is not at all apparent. The tannins are **well-balanced** with the fruit.

The second wine in this tasting, the **MINERVOIS**, comes from Languedoc-Roussillon and is a blend of Syrah with Carignan and other grapes. Its character is distinctly **peppery**, with **ripe, black fruits** and **undertones of vanilla** that

come from the oak-aging. It has a **fuller body** than the Pinot Noir, with good length, **velvety tannins**, and a rich, ripe palate. It is very **meaty**, and you can almost feel you are "eating" the wine.

The **BAROLO**, from the cool northeast of Italy, is made from the Nebbiolo grape, and has a much **firmer texture** than the first two wines. It has **firm tannins** that dry the mouth without being acerbic. This wine has a **heavy, dry** taste, with **wood and spice** to the fore. The fruit is not pronounced on the nose, and the length is not over-long. This is a very **sophisticated** wine; not as approachable as the Minervois, but **long-lasting** and **complex**, and very definitely **full bodied**.

FRANCE
ST-CHINIAN

I have never really thought of St-Chinian as part of the Languedoc—even though this district sits right in the middle of it. St-Chinian wines remind me more of the style of the Rhône Valley. Their concentration and meaty structure are perfect, especially with their wonderful underlying ripe fruit character. Buy St-Chinian for good value, but also keep an eye on it for great things in the future.

COLOR Distinctive deep crimson, with ruby or orange nuances.

AROMA Rich and powerful; black fruits and pepper, together with notes of tar and leather.

TASTE Dense, round, ripe tannins; good structure, long and complex.

BUYING More than one specialty wine merchant I know says this region is really on the move. Look for examples from Château Viranel and Domaine Canet-Valette.

ENJOYING These wines will make a fine companion for any red meat, but my favorite match is game with black lentils and baby onions, or a rack of lamb with rosemary and roast potatoes.

BRANCHING OUT St-Chinian is one of the firmer wines of the region; its structure is more similar to that of a Bergerac, and it has some of the spicy character of a Côtes du Rhône Villages.

MINERVOIS

Minervois is like a vast, south-facing amphitheater in the hills of the western Languedoc. This hot and sunny landscape produces well-structured wines that are full of character. Local cooperatives and small growers have greatly improved quality recently by reducing yields at harvest and upgrading their wineries. Some wines even spend a short spell in oak barrels. The result is round and dense, and a great buy.

FAUGÈRES
Domaine du Météore

COLOR Intense garnet red, with ruby to orange nuances.

AROMA Rich and complex; blackberry, quince, almond, and cinnamon.

TASTE Dense and ample, but with finesse; long, fruity finish.

BUYING While most Minervois wines should be drunk early, those from the best châteaux can be kept for a few years. I would include La Livinière, Château du Donjon, and Château Fabas in that category.

ENJOYING I like to serve this wine at a picnic with cold meats or pâté. It also works well with a winter casserole in a red wine stock.

BRANCHING OUT The flavor of this wine reminds me of the sweet fruitiness you find in Merlot—perhaps from Chile—but compare it also with a wine from its neighbor, Faugères.

FAUGÈRES

Imagine a wild, beautifully rugged, Mediterranean landscape. This is Faugères, and its wine is a hearty blend from old Carignan and Cinsault vines, bolstered by more weighty Mourvèdre and Syrah grapes. Faugères wines have a well-defined personality, and the *terroir* lends a meaty character to their "serious" dark fruit flavors. Previously underrated, this up-and-coming wine region is brim-full of potential.

COLOR Really dark black cherry, with a deep ruby rim.

AROMA Overripe dark fruits, with dried forest herbs, leather, and bitter chocolate.

TASTE Dense; well structured, with ripe flavors and well-integrated tannins.

BUYING Like St-Chinian, this region is creating a buzz with specialty wine merchants. Among producers, I particularly like Domaine du Météore and Domaine Deshenrys.

ENJOYING This wine is tasty and suave—never overtly powerful. It goes very well with stews, poultry, loin of pork, barbecued sausages, or even a roast chicken salad.

BRANCHING OUT Contrast this wine with a Gigondas from the Rhône Valley. They are made from essentially the same grape blend, but their characters are strikingly different.

ITALY
CHIANTI

The traditional image of Chianti is a straw-covered bottle set on a red checkered tablecloth in the corner of a rustic *taverna*. Such romantic scenes reflect Chianti's enduring popularity, but due to overproduction it no longer has a reputation for real quality. Of course, some producers still make superbly concentrated and well-balanced basic Chianti, but most of the finest examples come from the *classico* zone, the area between Siena and Florence. I think Chianti Classico is the only version worth consideration.

Sangiovese is the key grape in this blend, and it gives brilliant, vivacious fruit flavors. In good *classico* wines, these combine with oak-aging to offer complexity and real personality. Of the other, smaller Chianti zones, I would recommend Rufina as an alternative to Classico. When well made, these wines can represent better value, too. A step up from Chianti Classico is the fantastic Chianti Classico Riserva, which has slightly more body than regular Chianti Classico and longer aging before it is released for sale.

COLOR Lively, brilliant ruby red, tending to garnet with aging.

AROMA Violet, cherry, dark berries, plum, and spice, especially cloves.

TASTE Medium bodied; tannic when young; soft and velvety after aging.

BUYING Quality varies widely, so look for well-known names such as Antinori, Felsina, Fonterutoli, Fontodi, and Volpaia.

ENJOYING Beyond conventional Italian fare, these wines go very well with roast pork and many vegetable dishes.

BRANCHING OUT
The weight, fruit characters, and length of good Chianti is quite similar to wines from Montepulciano (Vino Nobile) and Montalcino (Brunello).

"The star of Tuscany! A blend of Sangiovese and other grapes, Chianti is soft and velvety, with aromas of violet, plum, cherry, and spice."

ITALY
VINO NOBILE DI MONTEPULCIANO

This wine lives in the shadow of its famous neighbors, Chianti and Brunello di Montalcino. All three are made from the same grape variety—Sangiovese—but they have very different styles. Vino Nobile is somewhere between Chianti and Brunello; it is fuller and fruitier than the former, but not as rich and dense as the latter.

Montepulciano is a small town in the hills of Tuscany, near Siena. The wines here fall into three broad categories—Rosso, Vino Nobile, and Vino Nobile Riserva. The Rosso, the lightest, is meant for drinking young. The medium-bodied, well-structured Vino Nobile ages quite well, thanks to its acidity and tannins. The Riserva, a little higher in alcohol, is aged for longer. Despite being less popular than its two

VINO NOBILE DI MONTEPULCIANO
Poliziano

rivals, Vino Nobile was one of the first wines to be granted Italy's highest wine classification, DOCG.

COLOR Distinctively deep ruby-red, with hints of purple.

AROMA Strong cherry; minerals, spice, wood, earth, and game.

TASTE Rich and full, but smooth; firm tannins and good acidity.

BUYING Poorly made Vino Nobile is thin and tart, so buy top names such as Avignonesi, Contucci, and Poliziano. Don't confuse it with Montepulciano d'Abruzzo from southern Italy.

ENJOYING This wine is a treat with beef ravioli, risotto, and even Irish stew!

BRANCHING OUT Taste the full spectrum—from Rosso to Riserva—from a single producer. The only things that separate them are the different harvest yields and aging requirements.

Pasta, poached egg, and red wine: a perfect breakfast combination!

I love Italy, especially in fall, during the truffle season. I will never forget one meal I ate in Italy on a wine-tasting trip. We had been working hard all day, traveling from one winery to another, tasting the wines and visiting the cellars. At 11 pm, we at last made it to a bustling little restaurant for dinner. Plates of *antipasti* and fine wines appeared as if by magic. We chatted long into the night, until our hosts announced that it was time for breakfast. A plate arrived with a single ravioli, about 4 in (10 cm) across, in a light cheese sauce and covered with grated truffle. Inside the pocket of pasta was the most perfectly poached egg. The combination of the flavors and the silky smooth Italian wine was delicious. I was in heaven!

ALEATICO

I love the floral aromas of the relatively rare Aleatico grape variety. It's a tremendous shame that it is so little known. Seek out the rich, sweet Aleatico wines from Tuscany, where these wines are at their finest. They are also produced as Aleatico di Gradoli in Latium, near Rome, and as Aleatico di Puglia in the deep south. All of these wines have the same aromatic, smooth, and warming qualities.

COLOR Rich, deep, and intense vermilion, with a ruby rim.

AROMA Very pronounced and refined; sweet spice, black fruits, and violets.

TASTE Rich, strong, velvety; medium acidity, balanced tannins, good length.

BUYING These wines are generally difficult to find outside Italy, but two of my favorite producers are Francesco Candido and Felice Botta. You should also be aware that the wines from Latium and Puglia may be fortified, and thus will be considerably sweeter than their Tuscan counterparts.

ENJOYING I enjoy this wine for a refreshing change. Try it with a lunch of cured meats or even at a barbecue.

BRANCHING OUT Compare the richness of Aleatico wines with fuller Amarone della Valpolicella wines of the Veneto region (see p.235).

CANNONAU

I am a great believer in the potential of Sardinia to produce high-quality wines. Cannonau is the island's best-known red grape, and is generally accepted to be the same variety as Grenache in France. But the sea breezes and the warm temperatures on Sardinia create ideal growing conditions, and older bush vines offer berries ripened to their fullest. These are very distinctive reds.

CANNONAU
Argiolas

COLOR Quite a dense ruby red, with a bright pink rim.

AROMA Crushed fresh cranberries; elegant, smoky, peppery.

TASTE Round, fleshy, fruity; medium acidity, integrated tannins, long finish.

BUYING Only a limited amount of Sardinian wine reaches the international market, but two names to look for are Argiolas and Sella & Mosca.

ENJOYING Try Cannonau with rabbit casserole or roast chicken. It also works with slightly stronger dishes, including venison or other game, and even a very mature cheese.

BRANCHING OUT Contrast Cannonau with the structure and austerity of a Nebbiolo-based wine from northern Italy. For similarities, try a Garnacha from Navarra in Spain.

TORGIANO

This is a fantastic wine—much like a well-structured Dolcetto *(see p.180)*. Torgiano is a small town in the central Italian region of Umbria, and named after the castle at its center: Torre di Giano. The wine has a growing reputation, and it's a real rival to Chianti. The same grape—Sangiovese—comes into its own here to yield density and delicacy, with a rich and smooth finish.

COLOR Bright ruby red to garnet, with good intensity.

AROMA Complex; black cherry, almond, spice, "animal," and oak.

TASTE Rich and round; refreshing acidity, excellent balance, long finish.

BUYING Most of this wine is drunk locally, but it's one not to miss, so buy it when you can. I recommend the producers Lungarotti and Consorzio Vitivinicola Perugia.

ENJOYING Torgiano's potential for aging makes it worth keeping for four to five years. It's great with lamb meatballs and penne, or similar pasta dishes.

BRANCHING OUT Compare this red with Tuscan wines, such as Vino Nobile di Montepulciano or Brunello di Montalcino. They are similar in style, but Torgiano is often better value.

NERO D'AVOLA

Nero d'Avola—also called Calabrese—is the most widely planted variety of red grape in Sicily, where it thrives and really shows the island's potential for quality. It's one of Italy's finest indigenous grapes, and is a superb asset to blending thanks to its firm structure and an ability to age. Together with Merlot it makes a very fine, elegant, and complex wine.

COLOR Deep black-cherry, with a purple rim.

AROMA Complex; ripe black fruits, plum, chocolate, and spice.

TASTE Rich and round, with lemony acidity and good tannins.

BUYING This grape variety is only rarely used on its own, and the best value wines are blends. Some of my favorite examples are from Santa Anastasia and Gulfi Vineyards.

ENJOYING I enjoy this wine with barbecued or grilled sausages and chops. It's also fabulous with roast beef or a juicy loin of lamb with dried herbs. Pizza works well with it, too!

BRANCHING OUT At the cheaper end, these wines are very fruit-driven and rather like a Beaujolais-Villages from France—not too sophisticated, but nevertheless very pleasant.

NERO D'AVOLA
Santa Anastasia

RIPE, SMOOTH REDS

WORLD WINES

TASTE TEST: FRUIT QUALITY

Exactly what is meant by "fruit quality" in a wine?

❶ RIOJA RESERVA from the famous Spanish region works well in this tasting, but you could substitute a Navarra Reserva or a Ribero del Duero Reserva. **Seek out** Conde de Valdemar, Marqués de Griñón, Artadi, Marqués de Murietta, CVNE.

❷ CHIANTI CLASSICO RISERVA is the finest rank of Chianti and well worth the slightly higher price. **Seek out** Villa di Geggiano (Bandinelli), Antinori, Frescobaldi, Castello di Fonterutoli, Fontodi.

❸ NAPA VALLEY CABERNET SAUVIGNON is high in alcohol, but don't be put off—its structure is big enough to take it! **Seek out** Frog's Leap, Stags' Leap Winery, Beringer, Duckhorn, Spottswoode, Joseph Phelps.

❹ ST-ÉMILION makes some of the best Merlot in the world. There are so many châteaux that it can be hard to choose; look for *grands crus*. **Seek out** Château Haut Gravet, Château Lalande de Gravet, Château Canon, Château de Pontbel.

❶ ❷ ❸ ❹

"The fruit quality of a red wine can range from ripe and round, to leafy and fresh, to rich and jammy."

"Fruit quality" is the summation of the aromas and flavors of fruit in a wine; these can derive from the grape and the vinification method, but are also influenced by aging in oak, and can develop with bottle age.

The **RIOJA RESERVA** has been aged for two years in oak and one year in the bottle. It has **leathery** aromas at first, closely followed by **cherries, chocolate, and sweet spice**. The fruit comes to the fore on the palate with **ripe cherry** and hints of **chocolate and coffee**, none overpowered by the oak.

The **CHIANTI CLASSICO RISERVA** has been aged for three years in oak barrels. It has very different aromas—**spice, smoky oak**, and hints of **menthol and pine**. These have melded with the **fresh, leafy, plum and cherry** fruit to give great **complexity**, with a **steely structure** provided by the wine's **high acidity**.

Like the Rioja, the **NAPA CABERNET SAUVIGNON** has been aged for two years in oak barrels. It has complex aromas that include **ripe, jammy black currants and blackberries**, with **sweet spice, tar, and licorice** that give it a sort of mountain freshness. On the palate it is **ripe and smooth** with lots of juicy, **jammy black fruit**, which points

to the fact that it comes from a warmer climate. Despite being aged in American oak, the fruit is **firmly to the fore**.

The last wine in the tasting is the Merlot from **ST-ÉMILION** in Bordeaux, also aged for two years in oak. The denseness of color reveals its **fruit quality**; very **concentrated**, tightly packed aromas of **black fruits**, together with the **toasty caramel** hints supplied by the oak-aging. On the palate it is **round and smooth** with loads of **black-fruit flavors**. Produced in a cooler climate than the Cabernet, this wine has a much **firmer structure**, but there is no aggressiveness from acidity or tannins; everything is **in balance** to let the fruit quality shine through.

ITALY
ROSSESE

If you like delicately flavored and fragrant wines, then this is certainly one to try. Rossese offers very appealing aromas of red berries, and is full of character. It is sold as Rossese di Dolceacqua, from a small DOC district in Liguria—the Italian Riviera. This region is best known for its white wines, which are based on the Vermentino grape variety, but this red is worth seeking out.

COLOR Ruby, with purple or dark orange reflections; garnet with age.

AROMA Fragrant, fruity, and slightly spicy; intense rose when aged.

TASTE Dry and tasty, with a round, smooth structure; bitter almond finish.

BUYING Rossese is a fantastic variety! However, only the best wines can be left to age for more than a couple of years. There are many small producers tucked away in the hills here, but my favorites are Cane and Lupi.

ENJOYING This wine is generally at its best during the first three years after harvest. It is superb with rich, full-tasting dishes such as rabbit with herbs, stuffed pigeon, or guinea fowl.

BRANCHING OUT Try this wine alongside a Cannonau or Teroldego. Notice the Rossese's fruitier flesh and livelier finish.

TEROLDEGO ROTALIANO

Teroldego grapes are at home on the Rotaliano plain to the north of Trento in northeastern Italy. Here they produce fruity, elegant, easy-drinking wines very similar to good *cru* wines from Beaujolais, France—just right for summer! However, individual wines from this region have their own distinct personalities, and they show why Italy is such a treasure trove of fascinating wine.

COLOR Elegant, deep ruby-red, with a pinkish rim.

AROMA Charming; juicy berries, violets, dried fruits, and tar.

TASTE Flattering and balanced, with soft ripe fruits and low tannins.

BUYING The younger the vintage, the better and fresher this wine will be. Also, look out for *Riserva Classico* on the label—it's the finest! Among producers, I particularly recommend Mezzacorona.

ENJOYING Drink Teroldego slightly chilled. It works very well with homemade lasagna, and it's a real treat at family barbecues or Sunday picnics. It's very unpretentious, and very good.

BRANCHING OUT Compare this wine with Fleurie from Beaujolais, France, or with an upmarket California Pinot Noir. The lively fruit and juicy textures are very similar.

TEROLDEGO
ROTALIANO
Mezzacorona

SANTA MADDALENA

In my opinion, this is one of the best wines from the Alto Adige region, in the foothills of the Italian Alps. It's made from a local variety called Schiava, which is blended with other grapes. The climate here swings dramatically between freezing winters and boiling-hot summers, and these extremes heighten the flavors and aromas of these wines. Santa Maddalenas are greatly appreciated in Italy, Austria, and Germany—but everyone should be entitled to share in the pleasure!

COLOR Deep ruby, with tile red developing over time.

AROMA Fresh cherry and black currant; smoke, almond, and walnut.

TASTE Fleshy, rounded, and very well balanced, with a medium-length and slightly bitter finish.

BUYING There are relatively few producers of this wine, which is sold mainly locally. Kettmeir and Roner are two of the best.

ENJOYING Drink this wine within three years of the harvest, and enjoy it with cured meats, charcuterie, barbecues, meaty fish such as tuna or sea bass, or even lasagna.

BRANCHING OUT If you like this style of wine, try Cannonau and Nero d'Avola. For a contrast, try a more powerful Cabernet Sauvignon, also from here in the Alto Adige region.

ROSSO PICENO / ROSSO CONERO

These two wines, from the Marches region of east-central Italy, have fabulous potential. The main difference between the two is the grape varieties: Piceno is mostly Sangiovese, like Chianti, and is the fuller wine. It is also the dominant denomination in terms of quantity. The smaller Conero is mainly Montepulciano, and is a "serious" wine—although still very drinkable.

COLOR Typically an elegant ruby red to garnet.

AROMA Fresh and fruity, with hints of almond.

TASTE Well-balanced fruit and acidity; medium texture and good depth.

BUYING These two cousins are from the same region and clearly have a similar name, so take care when buying because the styles are quite different. I can recommend the producers Monte Schiavo and Cocci Grifoni.

ENJOYING The refreshing styles of these wines cut through creamy sauces, such as carbonara. They are also a great success with hearty stews or game, including rabbit and venison.

BRANCHING OUT Try these wines alongside a rich Brunello, or even a velvety Cabernet Sauvignon from the Haut-Médoc of France. The comparison will show Conero and Piceno as fabulous wines and very good buys.

LAGO DI CALDARO

Another star from the Alto Adige region, this wine is made mainly from the Schiava grape (also called Vernatsch). Its high quality is a result of the favorable climate around the lake from which the wine takes its name. Look out for Lago di Caldaro—it's destined for success.

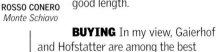

ROSSO CONERO
Monte Schiavo

COLOR Typically an elegant ruby red to garnet.

AROMA Fresh and fruity, with hints of almond.

TASTE Well-balanced fruit and acidity; medium texture and good length.

BUYING In my view, Gaierhof and Hofstatter are among the best producers of Lago di Caldaro.

ENJOYING Serve this wine, ideally when it is two or three years old, with meat dishes such as loin of pork or chicken chasseur.

BRANCHING OUT Try Lago di Caldaro with Santa Maddalena, its nearest neighbor, or with a Merlot of the same region. Note the subtle differences.

AUSTRIA
MEDIUM REDS

Blaufränkisch and Zweigelt are two interesting Austrian reds. Blaufränkisch is the country's most planted grape variety, and it makes wines like fuller, denser Beaujolais, with high acidity and intense fruit flavors. Zweigelt is a cross between Blaufränkisch, which adds flesh and flavor, and St-Laurent, which gives structure. It has an elegant Pinot Noir style, but with more body and weight.

COLOR Garnet for Blaufränkisch; a deeper, ruby red for Zweigelt.

AROMA Intense wild berries, spice, and violets in both wines.

TASTE Both have excellent balance, though Zweigelt is less acidic.

BUYING I recommend Lenz Moser, Umathum, and Gisperg.

ENJOYING Blaufränkisch is good with white meats or roast lamb; Zweigelt with a summer barbecue, charcuterie, or even chicken and fries.

BRANCHING OUT The texture of these wines is similar to Fleurie or St Amour from Beaujolais, France, or to a New Zealand Pinot Noir.

RIPE, SMOOTH REDS

WORLD WINES

"Little known and certainly worthy of more fame, these fruity, ruby-red Lago di Caldaro wines really are something you should try."

GERMANY
DORNFELDER

Germany has a relatively cool, damp climate, so red wines make up a small fraction of total production, and dark, full-flavored reds are even more unusual. Dornfelder is a local grape variety that produces deeply colored red wine with an intense aroma and a palate that is harmonious and well structured.

I think the best examples of this wine offer more pleasure than most German Spätburgunders (Pinot Noirs). And I'm not alone—the juicy, red-berried flavors of Dornfelder are a great success in Germany, and more and more of this variety is being planted. It even has the ability to cope with oak-aging, which adds further complexity to its range of flavors. Give it a few more years, and I am sure this wine will start to show favorably alongside many Merlots and Cabernets. Of course, German reds can be hard to find outside the country—a reflection of the national appetite for red wine—but good Dornfelder is worth seeking out.

COLOR Very intense dark garnet, with a ruby rim.

AROMA Attractive red berries and sweet forest fruits.

TASTE Very fruity; soft, velvety finish, with a slight hint of tannins.

BUYING Most Dornfelder is grown in the Rheinhessen and Pfalz. Among producers, look for Lingenfelder and Leiningerhof. Buy and drink it young.

ENJOYING Dornfelder goes well with roast beef, barbecued ribs, and meatballs. Roquefort is a good cheese match. Serve this wine slightly chilled.

BRANCHING OUT The fruit and weight of these wines is similar to a good Zweigelt from Austria; it's worth tasting it alongside a slightly fuller St-Laurent from either Austria or Germany.

Me? Drinking German red wine? Sacré bleu!

Taking a river cruise along the Rhine is one of the greatest tourist experiences in Europe, especially if you're a wine-lover, because you can expect to sample some excellent German whites. I was on a Rhine cruise once, just passing the famous Lorelei cliff. To my horror, the steward served a German red, not a white (a sacrilege for a Frenchman!), with some strong bratwurst. There was no escape, however, so I gave it a try. The wine was Dornfelder: dark and full-flavored, with excellent balance—and it made me eat my words as well as my sausage! It put me in mind of a French Merlot, with slightly different but very satisfying aromas. Most Dornfelder is drunk within Germany, so if you are there, you must try this fine red.

SPAIN
RIOJA

When people think of Spanish red wine, they automatically think of Rioja. It is a name known throughout the world. That name actually comes from the Rio Oja, a little stream that flows into the larger Ebro River, which itself cuts through most of northeastern Spain. The wines of Rioja are made mainly from the Tempranillo grape, which is native to Spain. It produces deep colors and rich flavors, and has great potential for aging. These wines have amazingly complex aromas, and over time they develop leathery, spicy characters.

Generally speaking, Spanish wine is defined by age, so the main label terms *crianza*, *reserva*, and *gran reserva* refer to the amount of time that the wines have been matured in oak barrels, and then in bottles, before being sold. At one end of the quality scale are wines labeled *joven* (meaning "young"), which have little or no oak-aging. The *jóvenes* are all about vibrant fruit. The *crianzas*, which have spent a year in the barrel and another in the bottle, offer great complexity but are still dominated by fruit characters. The *reservas* offer more vanilla, spice, and leathery notes due to an extra year in oak. Finally, the *gran reservas* are the finest and greatest wines. These are produced only in the best years and spend at least two years in the barrel and three more in the bottle before sale. As a result, they have an intense bouquet. Of course, their character is completely Spanish, but their complexity reminds me of good red Burgundy from France, and their depth brings to mind the great wines of Piedmont, Italy.

You might also see one of the different districts of Rioja on the label. There are three, and each has a slightly different terrain and climate: Rioja Alta, Rioja Alavesa, and Rioja Baja.

Rioja Alta in the northwest makes big, assertive wines that need time to soften. When mature, they are the finest and most delicate wines in the region. Rioja Alavesa, also in the northwest, accounts for a small part of the total Rioja vineyard area, and makes soft, rich, fruity wines. The Rioja Baja district is in the southeast, and the flat valley floor here is too fertile for good-quality grapes. The result is a more ordinary wine based largely on the Garnacha (Grenache) grape variety.

With all that said, the estates of Rioja are free to buy and blend fruit from all three regions, so the name of the producer most defines what you are getting in the bottle.

COLOR Deep, intense garnet, with a ruby to terra-cotta rim after aging.

AROMA Raisins, dried plums, figs, dark cherries, tobacco, spice, vanilla, and leather.

TASTE Rich, round, fresh, fruit-driven, and classy; soft tannins; very good length.

BUYING Wow! There are so many names that I could recommend. I suggest that you start with the wines of Marqués de Cáceres, Marqués de Griñón, Marqués de Murrieta, Marqués de Riscal, Muga, Palacios Remondo, and the fabulous Roda.

ENJOYING These wines are quite versatile, so don't limit them to Spanish-themed meals. Try Rioja with lamb or veal dishes. Match younger *joven* and *crianza* wines with bolder flavors, and save older (*reserva* and *gran reserva*) wines for more delicate dishes.

BRANCHING OUT Rioja varies from being bold and fruity to delicate and savory. In a tasting, it's fun to contrast its overtly Spanish character with the more international-style wines produced in the neighboring regions of Navarra and Somontano.

"Rioja is available in such a variety of styles that there is one to suit any palate. This famous and hugely popular red wine is truly world-class."

SPAIN
NAVARRA

Most of the world knows about Navarra because of the summer festival of San Fermin—the running of the bulls in Pamplona. And when it comes to wine, this region in northeastern Spain is known almost solely for its *rosado* (rosé)—but all that may soon change. Wine production in Navarra is actually dominated by reds, and recent improvements in these wines are beginning to pull the entire region out of the enormous shadow cast by neighboring Rioja.

There are five different growing districts in Navarra, and each has its own terrain and climate: Tierra de Estella, Valdizarbe, Baja Montaña, Ribera Baja, and Ribera Alta. In terms of quality, the first is probably the most interesting, even if the last three produce most of the wine.

Traditionally, the wines of Navarra were made from Garnacha grapes blended with Tempranillo and other Spanish varieties. The result was a slightly dull version of Rioja. But new investment, new techniques, and the introduction of new grape varieties, such as Cabernet Sauvignon and Merlot, have moved the style of Navarra's wines in a new direction—away from Rioja and toward Bordeaux.

Even Navarra's white wines have tended to drift across the French border (stylistically speaking), resulting in fine, barrel-fermented Chardonnays of great

NAVARRA
Señorío de Sarria

character. And we must not forget the *rosados*, which I also enjoy immensely. They are some of the best in the world.

Any of these wines could wave the flag for Navarra in the world wine market. But if forced to choose, I'd wave the red flag. Just watch out for the bulls!

COLOR Black cherry, with a ruby to brick-red rim.

AROMA Jammy blackberry, sweet spice, coffee, undergrowth, vanilla, and almond.

TASTE Smooth, fleshy, and pleasant, with good acidity; rounded by American oak.

BUYING For proof that Navarra means more than *rosado*, you need look no further than the wines of producers such as Chivite (especially the Colección 125), Bodegas Ochoa, Palacio de la Vega, and Señorío de Sarria.

ENJOYING These smooth, balanced wines are an excellent match for lighter roast meats, such as lamb. But they also work well with zestier fare—from chorizo sausage to spiced vegetable couscous.

BRANCHING OUT The use of international grape varieties, such as Cabernet Sauvignon and Merlot, and the French training of many winemakers working here, makes it interesting to compare the fruit and structure of these wines with examples from St-Émilion in Bordeaux—which is not that far north of Navarra.

PORTUGAL
DOURO

Long famous for the fortified wine, port, the Douro region has more recently started producing some amazing unfortified wines. The coolest parts of the region have the perfect conditions to achieve great complexity and intensity with the popular Touriga Nacional grape. Also, these wines are benefiting from the introduction of new production technology and much-improved quality control. Great things are coming!

COLOR Dark and inky, with a purple to ruby rim; good intensity.

AROMA Complex, rich; tar, licorice, dark chocolate, and black fruits.

TASTE Big, ripe, and smooth; refreshing acidity and a very long, clean finish.

DOURO
Casa Ferreirinha

BUYING Make sure the label does not say "port"—which is a sweet, fortified wine—and that it specifies the denomination (DO) as Douro. I recommend the producers Casa Ferreirinha, Ramos Pinto, and Quinta de la Rosa.

ENJOYING These wines age well—up to about five years— and they are hard to beat with a meal like roast rack of lamb.

BRANCHING OUT Fans of Douro wines should try a big French Cahors or a Malbec from Argentina, as they have similar structures and fruit characters. They are intense and rich, but still approachable when young.

GREECE
RAPSANI

A famous wine in Greece, Rapsani comes from the eastern coast of the country, in the foothills of Mount Olympus. According to myth, this is the original source of nectar, the divine drink of the ancient gods of Olympus. The key grape variety is Xynomavro *(see p.246)*, which here makes a rounded wine with ripe black fruits and mellow tannins. Rapsani is aged in oak casks to give a hint of stimulating spice.

COLOR Bright deep ruby, with pink or orange tips.

AROMA Elegant and subtle, with sweet spice and dried fruits.

TASTE Round and velvety; juicy, with refreshing acidity and good tannins.

BUYING You can enjoy the best of these wines when they are young, but also for up to five years from harvest. Evangelos Tsantalis, Biblia Chora, and Ktima Mercouri are all very good producers of Rapsani.

ENJOYING I love to drink this wine with moussaka or herby, spicy, Greek mutton or lamb chops. It's also a treat at a barbecue party on the beach!

BRANCHING OUT If you've sampled Rapsani on vacation and want to try a similar style, you'll get close with a soft Merlot. Also try Rapsani alongside a Tempranillo from Rioja, especially one aged in oak, such as a *crianza*.

CHILE
CARMENÈRE

This wine is really grabbing my attention right now. It is a relatively new discovery, but it's proving to be a great success and the Chileans are adopting it as their flagship wine. Carmenère is Chile's very own grape variety, and you can think of it as playing the same role as Zinfandel in California, or Pinotage in South Africa. Carmenère has a truly individual character, and the wines are an excellent buy.

Carmenère is not actually "new"; it was widely cultivated in Bordeaux in the 18th century. It was transplanted from France to Chile in the late-19th century, and while it flourished in South America, it became a fading memory in Europe. But the true identity of this variety disappeared in Chile, because it was confused with Merlot for a long time. It was only during the 1990s that much of Chile's rich "Merlot" was discovered to be Carmenère. The "lost grape of Bordeaux" then started to be

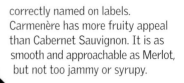

CARMENÈRE
Santa Rita

correctly named on labels. Carmenère has more fruity appeal than Cabernet Sauvignon. It is as smooth and approachable as Merlot, but not too jammy or syrupy.

COLOR Rich and distinctive dark cherry or garnet, with a ruby rim.

AROMA Intense figs, plums, cherries, black fruits, sweet spice, and chocolate.

TASTE Round, harmonious, and beautifully structured, with bags of flavor.

BUYING Drink this wine in its fruity youth. Leading producers include Errazuriz, Concha y Toro, Santa Carolina, and Santa Rita.

ENJOYING These wines make great social sipping, but they also complement duck breast and venison, and work well with smoked mackerel.

BRANCHING OUT Carmenère is a Chilean specialty, but its fruit profile and soft texture are similar to a US Merlot from California or, especially, from Washington State.

"Carmenère is Chile's own unique variety—and I just can't get enough of it! This wine has tremendous fruitiness, but is well structured, smooth, and consistent."

RIPE, SMOOTH REDS

WORLD WINES

❶ RIOJA JOVEN in the traditional style is often tactfully described as "rustic," but in the more modern style (the label is often a clue), it should be full of vibrant fruit. **Seek out** Esencia (Conde de Valdemar), Carta de Oro (Berberana), Marqués de Cáceres, and CVNE, makers of Cune, Viña Real, and Contino wines.

❷ RIOJA CRIANZA is one step up from Joven, having received a minimum of two years of aging, and is well worth its slightly higher price. **Seek out** Vallobera, Marqués de Griñón, Marqués de Riscal, Marqués de Cáceres, Berberana.

❸ RIOJA GRAN RESERVA is the highest-quality Rioja and is produced only in the best vintages. **Seek out** Viña Tondonia (López de Heredia), Artadi, Viña Ardanza, Marqués de Murrieta, CVNE.

TASTE TEST: OAK-AGING

How does oak affect the flavors in red wines?

Rioja aging in barrels, Bodegas Campillo

"The levels of Rioja classification perfectly demonstrate how oak-aging can affect a wine's flavor."

All red Rioja—Spain's flagship red wine—is made with a blend of grape varieties, but at least 70 percent must come from the **Tempranillo** grape. Differences in style are achieved by **aging** the wine in **oak barrels** for different lengths of time; some wines have **no oak-aging**, while others—the Gran Reservas, made only in the **best years**—have at least **five years'** aging in both barrel and bottle before they are released for sale.

The first wine in this tasting is the **RIOJA JOVEN**. This is a classic Tempranillo-based wine that has had no oak-aging at all. Young and fresh in the modern style, it is **straightforward, easy-going** drinking with lots of **ripe red fruit**. While the Rioja character supplied by the Tempranillo grape is there, this is **not a complex wine** to brood over. But it's great for barbecues on the deck!

The second wine in the tasting is the **RIOJA CRIANZA**. Again made with Tempranillo grapes, the designation *crianza* means that this wine has been **aged for a year in barrels** that are usually made from American oak, and then kept by the winery for another year after bottling in order to make sure that the wine is ready to drink as soon as it is bought. It has a **more complex** set of aromas and flavours than the Joven, with **blackberry fruit**, hints of **cherries and sweet spice**, and a very definite undertone of **vanilla** that comes from the oak.

Vanilla may be the first aroma that hits you with the third wine in this tasting, the **RIOJA GRAN RESERVA**. This wine is only made with the **best-quality grapes** picked from the **oldest vines**, and has been aged for a minimum of **five years** before being released, with at least two spent in **oak barrels**. The aromas and flavors are **amazingly complex**, with **chocolate, prunes, coffee, and dried fruit**, and hints of **tobacco and licorice**, along with the telltale **vanilla**.

So many people, in Europe at least, have memories of Rioja as easy, enjoyable **"vacation drinking"** that Rioja Gran Reservas remain undervalued. The result is that these **consistently good**, finely crafted, **carefully nurtured**, deep, and **complex** wines represent **excellent value for money**.

CHILE
MERLOT

Chilean Merlot has lost some of its impact on the world of wine owing to changing fashions, and also to the rise of Carmenère. But its quality is still consistent and it can sometimes be exceptional. The wine is at its best in the Maipo and Maule valleys. Here, Merlot has a rich, dense character, but it is less brassy than many Australian wines—closer, perhaps, to the style of St-Émilion *(see p.194).*

COLOR Profound, with good intensity; rich black cherry.

AROMA Delicate and powerful; ripe black fruits; cherry, spice, and prune.

TASTE Rich, round, and smooth; great balance, harmonious tannins, and a clean finish.

BUYING What do you do when there are so many different wines? Here are a couple of safe bets: Viña Alamosa and Casa Lapostolle. Also look out for wines from Errazuriz and Santa Rita, which are generally superior to wines from the Central Valley.

ENJOYING I enjoy these good-value wines over a lunch of grilled steak and salad, or even on their own, since they are not overpowering on the palate.

BRANCHING OUT These appealing wines compare closely with their cousin Carmenère, also from Chile, as well as with South African Merlot and "satellite" appellations of St-Émilion, too.

AUSTRALIA
MERLOT

Australian Merlot is used mainly in blends with Cabernet Sauvignon or Shiraz; but in recent years single-variety Merlot has taken off, too. These tend to be big wines with soft, chunky fruit. Beyond typical berry and plum aromas, the best examples have a more complex range of scents, including mint, violet, lavender, and pepper. These wines are always approachable and easy to drink.

COLOR Deep garnet, with a ruby rim and good intensity.

AROMA Mulberry, plum, blackberry; hints of spicy oak and cigar box.

TASTE Smooth, velvety, concentrated; refreshing, with charm and delicacy.

AUSTRALIAN MERLOT *Yalumba*

BUYING There are hundreds of producers of Australian Merlot, but I think the most approachable are Yalumba, Fermoy Estate, and Evans & Tate. Look for wines from Australia's more temperate regions.

ENJOYING I recommend serving these wines with grilled meats, or any type of hearty stew or casserole. They also go well with cheeses, and, of course, just on their own.

BRANCHING OUT This wine is juicy and straightforward, so it reminds me of its Chilean counterpart. As a contrast, try the better St-Émilion wines, which will demonstrate its simplicity.

NEW ZEALAND
MERLOT

Merlot from New Zealand is a recent phenomenon, and the Hawke's Bay region on North Island is the center of its development. The warm and sunny climate of Hawke's Bay— the driest in the country— allows Merlot to achieve lively and juicy flavors. Many of the best wines from this region are blended with other grapes, particularly Cabernet Sauvignon; and while they are not yet fully available on the world market, they are showing great potential.

COLOR Elegant and intense dark garnet, with a ruby rim.

AROMA Big and juicy, with notes of forest fruits, ripe plum, toffee, leather, earth, and spice.

TASTE Smooth, complex; exceptional balance; full flavors; lingering finish.

BUYING Don't look for the famous Marlborough region on the label, because that's on South Island; North Island is best for Merlot. Top wineries include Te Awa Farm Winery, Esk Valley, and Morton Estate.

ENJOYING These wines go well with lighter meats, such as poultry, pork, and lamb. Alternatively, you can enjoy them on their own.

BRANCHING OUT For this wine, the best comparison is with Merlot from South Africa or Washington State. New Zealand Merlot does not really have the depth of good wines from St-Émilion.

UNITED STATES
CALIFORNIA MERLOT

Some people are categorically critical of Merlot, in the same way that others adopt an "ABC" (Anything But Chardonnay) attitude to whites. This is ridiculous. Good Merlot offers tremendous pleasure, and California produces some great examples—perhaps the New World's finest.

Merlot arrived in the US in the 1860s, but it was only 30 years ago that winemakers along the North Coast started to transform what had long been a harsh and tannic wine into something soft and flattering. As a result, American Merlot became a simple, fun drink—perhaps "too easy" to enjoy for a credible or serious reputation. But well-crafted California Merlot offers real depth and complexity without losing its fruitiness and smooth personality. The best examples probably come from the Napa Valley, but producer names mean more than anything when it comes to finding great wines.

MERLOT *Newton*

COLOR Distinctive, intense dark garnet, with a ruby rim.

AROMA Juicy black forest fruits, ripe plum, toffee, leather, earth, and spice.

TASTE Smooth, balanced; full flavors, and a lingering finish.

BUYING Aged wines show grace, but it's best to drink these wines fairly young. Look for Beringer, Newton, Stags' Leap, and Duckhorn.

ENJOYING California Merlots go well with hearty dishes, such as côte de boeuf, or lamb shank with garlic and potatoes.

BRANCHING OUT Compare the ripe fruit and fine texture of good California Merlot with the structured wines of Canon-Fronsac or St-Émilion in France.

Beating the language barrier in the Napa Valley

After I won Sommelier of the Year, my boss kindly sent me on a week's trip to California wine country. It got off to a great start when, on landing, I realized I wasn't going to be needing the scarf and gloves I set off in. But it soon became apparent that, although I'd spent a year in England, I was completely baffled by the American accent—I couldn't understand a word! Fortunately, the vineyards, the wineries, and the stunning wines all spoke for themselves—of technology and investment, but also knowledge and passion. A week experiencing these world-class wines, capped by a glorious balloon flight that gave us a perfect view of the Napa Valley, convinced me that God didn't just give France the best vines and the best winemakers!

WASHINGTON LEMBERGER

Lemberger is a grape that I fell in love with after the very first sip. It makes wine with finely balanced tannins and wonderful cherry flavors. Lemberger is very successful in cool climates, because its low natural acidity helps it to ripen well in difficult conditions. Washington State is one of the few places where the grape is established, although it is actually the same variety as Austria's Blaufränkisch (see p.207). Unfortunately, Washington Lemberger is not produced in great quantities, so it can be a little hard to find—but it's worth seeking out.

COLOR Ranges from light to dark red; lighter wines are normally sweeter.

AROMA Black cherry, with just a hint of spiciness and chocolate.

TASTE Light to medium in body, and very lively and versatile.

BUYING This undiscovered wine may have unlimited potential. Some of the star winemakers are Kiona Vineyards, Thurston Wolfe, and Latah Creek.

ENJOYING This is not a wine for aging. Rather, enjoy its youthful charm and complex flavors over a plate of cheese or charcuterie. You'll fall in love with it!

BRANCHING OUT Compare this wine with a structured Syrah like Crozes-Hermitage on the one hand, and a lush New Zealand Pinot Noir on the other. See where it falls on this spectrum.

RIPE, SMOOTH REDS

WORLD WINES

RICH, DENSE REDS

Big wines with big names, the rich, dense reds are filled with the aromas of forest fruits and feel like liquid velvet on the palate. They are powerful, complex, sophisticated wines, and perfect to enjoy with warming food on winter evenings.  The king of grapes for this wine style is Cabernet Sauvignon, the variety of the great Bordeaux Médoc wines and also of some of the best red wines from California and Australia. Syrah (or Shiraz) from the Rhône Valley in France creates elegant, complex wines, not only in the Rhône, but notably in Australia and California, too. Nebbiolo, key to the great Italian reds of Barolo and Barbaresco, is another classic; and there are many other rich, intense grape varieties making superb wines—Mourvèdre, which makes Bandol and Australian Mataro, being just one.

STYLE PROFILE
RICH, DENSE REDS

CONCENTRATED FLAVOR

These big red wines are typically made from grapes with small berries and thick skins—the classic example being Cabernet Sauvignon. Although these grapes give lower yields of juice, they are rich in color and also in tannin (which gives the wine structure and longevity). These grape varieties need warm climates to ripen fully, otherwise the wine they make is harsh and acerbic. This is why they are most successful in the more southerly parts of Europe and in the New World. Wherever the grapes are grown, good soil drainage is key to producing superior fruit for full-bodied

"With loads of dark, wild fruits and spice, these wines reveal layer upon layer of depth and complexity."

reds. When the soil is well drained, the vine's roots have to grow downward in order to find water and nutrients deep underground. As they do so, they pick up minerals and trace elements, which then emerge as rich flavors in the grapes themselves.

DARK FRUITS AND SPICE

Wines made from grapes grown in warmer climates (as in the New World) generally have more fruit and "jammy" character, and generally this style benefits less from bottle-aging. Many New World wines are aged in new oak barrels before bottling. This gives the wines softer, buttery flavors, such as vanilla, and allows producers to release them on to the market within five years, as the wine is ready to drink sooner. In the Old World, particularly in the Bordeaux and Rhône wines of France and those of Piedmont in Italy, the deep, complex, dry flavors often take years to reach their peak. As the wine ages, the tannins soften, becoming more integrated into the body of the wine, which ultimately achieves a perfect balance of ripe tannin, fresh acidity, and rich fruit.

AT HOME DOWN UNDER
Grapes destined to make rich, full reds need a climate with plenty of sun to concentrate their flavors, but not so hot that they scorch. Australia's Barossa Valley, northwest of Adelaide, has the perfect conditions.

STEEPED IN HISTORY

In the New World, the Syrah grape takes on the name of Shiraz, the mighty desert city of ancient Persia, where some say this variety originated. Fittingly, the wines it makes have rich, warm, and enduring flavors.

TASTE TRAIL

CABERNET SAUVIGNON is the king of the rich, dense reds. Look for this grape on labels of excellent wines from Chile, South Africa, Australia, and the US, and dominating the blend in the great, complex Bordeaux of the Médoc. Try also **SHIRAZ** from Australia's Barossa and Hunter valleys, **SYRAH** from the Rhône, **NEBBIOLO** from Italy, Argentina, and California, **BRUNELLO** from Italy, and **ZINFANDEL** from California. Or be adventurous, and try the lesser-known **MOURVÈDRE** from France, or **TANNAT** from France and Argentina.

ENJOYING Serve these wines at room temperature; they will feel alcoholic if too warm, and overly tannic if too cold. Decant the wine 30 minutes to two hours before drinking—the air will release the complex aromas, and any sediment will stay in the bottle. These wines complement roast meat, or heavy vegetarian main courses with fleshy vegetables, such as eggplant. Gattinara and Barbaresco match well with veal and game, Shiraz and Zinfandel with spicy foods.

When you swirl a rich, dense red, the wine should leave a gloss (its "legs") on the inside of the glass, especially when young; these are more viscous wines than other styles of red. Color should be a deep, inky black cherry, with nuances of purple in youth and of warmer red tiles with age. Aromas should be intense and "jammy," with licorice, figs, prunes, coffee, chocolate, tobacco (and cigar box), spice, leather, and notes of vanilla. The tannins should balance the structure of complex flavors, and the finish should be fresh and very long.

DRINK OR STORE?

The best of these wines are expensive, as they will have spent 18 to 24 months in oak barrels—adding to the cost of caring for the wine before bottling. They should then be bottle-aged for more than five years to reach their full potential.

FRANCE
PAUILLAC

Pauillac is the heart of the Médoc peninsula, which in turn is the epicenter of the Bordeaux region of France. I suppose you could argue that Pauillac is at the center of the wine world—but it's rather academic. The wines of this commune have always been among my favorites. They are rich and complex, full of character and concentration, and they show superb finesse. If you think such a string of adjectives is a little over the top, you need to try these velvety wines.

The maritime climate and deep gravel soils of this district combine with old vines of mainly Cabernet Sauvignon to yield something truly special. Pauillac includes three of the five top estates in Bordeaux—the *premiers crus*, as designated by the official classification system in force here since 1855. They are probably the most famous names in the entire wine world: Château Latour, Château Lafite-Rothschild, and Château Mouton-Rothschild. Other celebrated producers in the official classification here include Château Pichon-Longueville-Comtesse de Lalande, Château Pichon-Longueville-Baron, and Château Lynch-Bages.

These wines are archetypal Cabernet Sauvignon—dark, maybe even opaque, garnet-red in color with intense aromas that become even more complex and varied with aging. They are full and powerful, with a perfect balance of structure and elegance. They also evolve

"Pauillac—Bordeaux's 'Velvet Heart'! These wines are built on Cabernet Sauvignon, making elegant wines that are full bodied, intense, and fantastic."

and soften to their best only gradually over time; this can take 15 years—and much longer for the greatest examples.

Along with the wines of the St-Estèphe commune to the north, these are the most firmly structured Bordeaux wines. But Pauillacs also show plenty of rich, fleshy fruit on that firm framework. And underneath that flesh beats the heart of Bordeaux.

COLOR The classic Bordeaux coloring of deep garnet, with a ruby rim.

AROMA Complex; delicate black fruits, chocolate, leather, tar, tobacco.

TASTE Dense, concentrated, round and balanced, with unforgettable length.

BUYING From a plethora of great names, I suggest you start with Château d'Armailhac, Château Batailley, Château Clerc-Milon, and Château Lynch-Bages.

ENJOYING Pauillacs are perfect partners for classic roasted meat and game dishes. Make the most of their amazing aromas by decanting them a couple of hours before drinking—and then serve them in large glasses.

BRANCHING OUT The profound structure and body of these wines set the benchmark for Cabernets and Cabernet blends around the world. Compare good Pauillac with the best reds of the Napa Valley, and with top Cabernets from the Coonawarra and Margaret River districts of Australia. Pauillacs show their best with some age—often in excess of a decade—while New World Cabernets are generally produced for early pleasure. Consequently, make your comparison with wines aged between these two ideals—at, say, six to eight years old.

MARGAUX

Margaux wines remind me of silk. They are deep, mellow, and fragrant, but they feel more supple and smooth than anything else in Bordeaux. As with the neighboring commune of Pauillac, the wines of Margaux are made primarily from Cabernet Sauvignon grapes, supported by varying amounts of varieties such as Merlot, Cabernet Franc, and Petit Verdot. The result is a world-famous combination of depth, complexity, elegance, and finesse.

MARGAUX *Château Palmer*

These wines are rich, rounded, and polished—a profile that places many of this commune's producers in the famous, 150-year-old classification of Bordeaux's finest wines.

At the top is Château Margaux, one of the most sought-after names in the wine world. However, its well-deserved fame is also cause for confusion. You need to note that Château Margaux is located within the commune of Margaux—but they are not one and the same. When you see Margaux on the label, make sure you know what you are buying—and what you are paying for.

Although Château Margaux is the only *premier cru* (First Growth) in the Margaux commune, this district is certainly not short of other fine wines. It is possible to find Second, Third, Fourth, and Fifth Growths that taste truly amazing. The Second Growths include classic wines such as Château

Brane-Cantenac, and the many great Third Growths include Château Kirwan.

You also should be aware that some estates produce second-tier wines from barrels that are not quite good enough for their top-of-the-range blends. For example, the second label of Château Margaux is Pavillon Rouge de Château Margaux, which has a high reputation and is simply excellent. At all levels, Margaux is the last word in wine for rich, smooth elegance.

COLOR Classic and elegant; bright, deep garnet, with a ruby rim.

AROMA Ripe red and black fruits, cinnamon, earth, and coffee.

TASTE Complex, smooth, rich; full-flavored, with a savory finish.

BUYING This is the largest commune in the Médoc, so the quality of the wine varies more widely than elsewhere. It is best to stick with leading names, such as Château Giscours, Château Lascombes, Château Rauzan-Ségla, Château Margaux, and Château Palmer.

ENJOYING Despite their ability to cope with very long aging, these wines are lovely after only five years. They sit beautifully alongside meat dishes such as pan-fried calves' liver, or rare sirloin or rump steak.

BRANCHING OUT Compare the rich fruit and silky texture of good Margaux with the finest Cabernet-based wines from anywhere in the world.

RICH, DENSE REDS

WORLD WINES

FRANCE
ST-JULIEN

St-Julien stands in the shadow of Pauillac and Margaux, its neighbors to the north and south along Bordeaux's Médoc peninsula. St-Julien is the smallest of the main communal appellations on the so-called Left Bank, but its Cabernet Sauvignon–based wines represent the most consistent quality in the entire region, and some perform well above their official status.

St-Julien has relatively few châteaux in the official 1855 classification. It has no *premiers crus* (First Growths), but its Second Growths sit comfortably among the best of Bordeaux. Some are known informally as "Super Seconds," and they are indeed super. There are also excellent unclassified properties

ST-JULIEN
Château Léoville-Barton

producing remarkable wines, such as Château Gloria. In general, St-Julien is reliably complex and full of character.

COLOR Deep, dark garnet, with a purple to ruby rim.

AROMA Complex. Myrtle, violet, black fruits, chocolate, vanilla, and earth.

TASTE Savory and elegant, with depth and concentration.

BUYING The following châteaux all produce great wines: Léoville-Barton, Léoville Las Cases, and Gruaud-Larose.

ENJOYING The firm structure and deep flavors of these wines show best with simply prepared meats like roast lamb or grilled steak.

BRANCHING OUT Compare the texture of a good St-Julien with an austere St-Estèphe, a muscular Pauillac, and a silky Margaux.

The day I fell in love with a beautiful, and mature, woman

St-Julien is one of the great wines of the Médoc peninsula, and when you are a young man in France with not much money, this is one of those wines that you see but can never afford to drink!
The first time I ever tried St-Julien was during my apprenticeship in Paris. It was a Château Branaire 1982—how lucky was I? It was love at first taste! This commune is generally known for the "feminine" style of its wines—meaning that they are not too robust or overpowering. St-Julien wines certainly live up to that description. They age elegantly and gracefully, like a beautiful woman, and they have the strength and finesse to grow ever more appealing as the years pass by!

ST-ESTÈPHE

St-Estèphe produces the most austere wines of the Bordeaux region. This is because of its clay subsoil and a climate that is particularly cool. The resulting wines have high acidity, firm tannins, and less fruitiness than those of more southerly subregions. But this is still a truly great wine, and I believe that in a warm year St-Estèphe can be the best of Bordeaux.

COLOR Intense; deep garnet to rich crimson red.

AROMA Black cherry mingling with violets, wood, and spice.

TASTE Robust, with marked acidity and tannins; balanced and well structured.

BUYING Château Montrose and Château Cos d'Estournel are top names, but try Château Phélan-Ségur as well.

ENJOYING The best red meat, simply cooked, melds wonderfully with the tannins and richly complex flavors of St-Estèphe. These are classic wines and extremely long-lived. You may need to wait a long time to really enjoy them—sometimes up to 20 years.

BRANCHING OUT There is something about these wines that reminds me of a spicy Côte Rôtie. For an interesting tasting, contrast a good, structured St-Estèphe with a more silky "satellite" appellation of St-Émilion.

LISTRAC

This tiny appellation is marketed as either Listrac or Listrac-Médoc. It has no prestigious classified châteaux, although certain well-funded estates have developed reputations among wine connoisseurs as being good-value options in what is generally a high-priced corner of the wine world.

Listrac's inland location and heavy clay soils make for a solid rather than a fragrant style of wine. I find their character is closer to St-Estèphe than to nearby Margaux. They are made from a typical blend of Cabernet Sauvignon with Merlot and Petit Verdot, but the results are somewhat austere. However, Listrac's producers have begun to introduce more Merlot into the blend, and this makes great sense. The Merlot grape is more suited to the soils here, so a greater proportion of this fleshy variety should make the wines more rounded and appealing. The established success of a few leading estates in this commune shows that greater things are possible, but we will have to wait and see what happens—the appellation has not yet achieved its full potential.

COLOR Very dark black cherry, with purplish tinges.

AROMA Dark fruits, spice, and leather, with hints of vanilla from oak-aging.

TASTE Well structured; firm and refreshing; exceptional length.

BUYING The best examples of Listrac come from châteaux with a *cru bourgeois* rating. My favorites among these are Château Clarke, Château Fonréaud, and Château Fourcas-Hosten.

ENJOYING Good young Listrac is really great with lamb chops or a rich beef casserole and roast potatoes.

BRANCHING OUT Compare the firm structure of Listrac with the wines of neighboring Moulis. The differences are a reflection of the soils—clay and limestone versus gravel.

LISTRAC
Château Fourcas-Hosten

"The 'quiet man' of the Médoc! Listrac is very austere and robust, with dark fruit flavors, pepper, and licorice notes. It ages very well, up to about 20 years."

MOULIS

Moulis is one of the best-kept secrets of Bordeaux. It's the smallest of the communal Médoc appellations, but I usually describe the wines in bigger terms. They are "baby St-Estèphes" because of their austerity, but they shed their tannins faster than St-Estèphe wines and find an ideal balance much sooner. Moulis wines are sometimes regarded as "lesser" wines, but they are real winners—and the lower prices are great news for buyers!

COLOR Deep black cherry, with a few hints of garnet red.

AROMA Dark forest fruits, undergrowth, licorice, tar, pepper, toast, smoke.

TASTE Perfect harmony; balanced and well structured; long and pleasant finish.

BUYING These wines are ready just a few years after harvest, so don't bother to keep them for a long time. Among the best producers of Moulis are Château Chasse-Spleen, Château Baudan, and Château Poujeaux.

ENJOYING Like most traditional French wine, Moulis is meant for food. I enjoy it with a good cut of beef, roasted lamb, or any hearty stew or casserole.

BRANCHING OUT Compare the fruit and structure of these wines with the so-called "second wine" of one of the great *grand cru classé* châteaux.

RICH, DENSE REDS

WORLD WINES

TASTE TEST: BODY

Just what do we mean by "rich and dense" when we talk about red wines?

❶ ❷ ❸

❶ CALIFORNIA PINOT NOIR is our fruity, lively red, the lightest wine here. With their great climate and cutting-edge technology, Californians make some great Pinot Noirs, especially those that come from the Carneros or Santa Barbara regions. **Seek out** Au Bon Climat, Sanford, Andrew Murray Vineyards, Cuvaison, Byron.

❷ CARMENÈRE, the new Chilean flagship red, is the middleweight for our purposes here. Full of textured fruit, it's like a rich, smooth Merlot, but with more structure and personality. Like many wines from Chile, it's also a great buy. **Seek out** Santa Rita, Casa Donoso, Caliterra.

❸ AUSTRALIAN SHIRAZ from the Barossa and Hunter valleys proclaim even by their appearance that they are going to be the big hitters in this tasting. You could substitute a South African Shiraz from the Stellenbosch region or a voluptuous California Syrah—but don't choose one with Petite Syrah/Sirah on the label: it will be a lighter wine. **Seek out** Glaetzer, Rockford Basket Press, Geoff Merrill, Grant Burge, Tower Estate, Jim Barry.

"Body is about more than just intensity of flavor— it has to do with the weight and structure of a wine."

For this tasting, I've chosen two wines that are among the **most flavorsome** within the Fruity, Lively Reds category and the Ripe, Smooth Reds group, and pitted them against a **heavyweight Shiraz**, so that we can discover just what makes a Rich, Dense Red.

The styles of red wines as categorized in this book refer to their **weight and structure**. Acidity and tannins give a wine its **backbone**—the framework that supports the wine's flavors and other taste components. That backbone is then **"fleshed out"** by the **fruit quality**. Light reds have **little or no tannin** with **fresh, ripe** but **light fruit** aromas; medium-bodied or "round" reds have **some tannin**, with **ripe but not heavy fruit**, and full-bodied reds have **lots of everything**!

Taste the **CALIFORNIA PINOT NOIR** first. You will see from its color that this is a **lighter style** of wine. It has subtle, **floral** aromas and **refreshing red-berry** fruit. You can taste lots of **juicy, ripe red fruit** on the palate, but it still feels **light and subtle** and **elegant** in structure.

Now try the **CARMENÈRE** from Chile. The color is **darker** than the Pinot Noir—**dark cherry** with a **lighter, ruby** rim. It has aromas of **vanilla, smoke, and petroleum** over **plum, cherry, and black fruits**. The fruit is **ripe and round** on the palate but **not too heavy**, still holding something back.

Now taste the third wine, the **AUSTRALIAN SHIRAZ**. This is a very dense, dark, **opaque inky-red** color. There are aromas of **black fruits, spice, tar**, hints of **stewed brambles**—and, fittingly considering that it comes from Australia—**eucalyptus**. The alcohol is high but is in **perfect balance** with the fruit, and the wine feels **thick in the mouth** but is in no way syrupy. It is **big and powerful** but everything is in the right balance. All in all, the perfect example of a rich, dense red wine.

"Red Pessac-Léognan wines have elegance and class, and are truly great wines—voluptuous and deep, with wonderfully rich, ripe fruit."

FRANCE
GRAVES / PESSAC-LÉOGNAN

Although many people know Graves for its excellent whites, some of the world's best reds also come from this subregion of southern Bordeaux. Many of these Cabernet Sauvignon–based wines are rich and powerful, with great structure.

The best reds generally come from a special district called Pessac-Léognan. This area includes top estates, such as the First Growth Château Haut-Brion—the only property in Graves to feature in the famous 1855 Bordeaux classification.

As a whole, the Graves appellation has a good reputation and maintains a high standard. This may be a reflection of its own classification system, whereby each château is reviewed every ten years, and either upgraded or declassified. It's a great incentive to maintain quality.

COLOR Deep garnet red, with a characteristic purple rim.

AROMA Classic and very delicate; black fruits, violets, baked bread, leather.

TASTE Rich, round, powerful; coffee, minerals; great tannins; long finish.

BUYING I recommend Domaine de Chevalier, Château Haut-Brion, Château La Louvière, and Château Pape Clément.

ENJOYING Red Graves is a fine match for roast venison or game terrine. Large glasses will exploit its nuanced aromas.

BRANCHING OUT If you like Cabernet Sauvignon, the wine world is your oyster: good examples from Chile, Napa Valley, or New Zealand will never disappoint.

CAHORS

A blockbuster from southwestern France, Cahors is a dense wine based on the Malbec variety, which is known locally as Côt or Auxerrois. The wine is made in the Bordeaux style, but the fruit is more concentrated, since the Cahors region is farther inland and has a warmer climate. A top Cahors is muscular and perfectly suited for aging. Over time it becomes more refined and velvety, with marked finesse and a very long, almost "infinite" finish. It's a true classic, and one set to emerge into the spotlight.

COLOR Particularly dark and deep cherry red, with a ruby rim.

AROMA Black fruits, spice, dried herbs, chocolate, truffles, leather.

TASTE Rich and powerful, with firm tannins, concentration, and finesse.

BUYING This is the flagship wine of the southwestern hinterland of France. Top producers include Château la Coustarelle and Château du Cèdre. But beware lesser examples, which can be "green" (unripe) and stalky.

ENJOYING Don't drink these wines too young; they repay a few years' patience. Serve them with roast beef or, best of all, with a cassoulet de Castelnaudary, a traditional French stew.

BRANCHING OUT If Cahors is to your taste, you're bound to appreciate another dark horse, Malbec from Argentina, made from the same grape, but richer and even more intense.

MADIRAN

Madiran is a remote corner of southwestern France that produces red wine from a very hardy local grape variety called Tannat. It used to be that the harsh tannins meant keeping the wine for ten years or more before you could consider opening it. But a younger generation is now pursuing a more accessible fruity style. Madiran is still not very well known, but I think it deserves to be. So my advice is to give it a try—you will not be disappointed.

COLOR Opaque and dark, inky red, with a purple rim.

AROMA Intense; jammy black and red fruits, sweet spice, tobacco, licorice.

TASTE Savory, velvety, dense, well-structured, and complex; long finish.

BUYING Château Bouscassé, Domaine Capmartin, and Château d'Aydie are the leading names. Whichever you choose, don't open the wine young—and when you do, let it air in a decanter for a couple of hours.

ENJOYING Drink these wines with a rich cassoulet de canard from Toulouse—you can't beat this combination. Alternatively, try them with a confit of duck with spicy lentils.

BRANCHING OUT If you like this wine, you will probably also enjoy the fruitiness and intensity of the Italian classic red Barolo.

RICH, DENSE REDS

WORLD WINES

FRANCE
HERMITAGE / CROZES-HERMITAGE

Hermitage is an iconic French wine. It comes from a tiny district, but it has long been the most famous name in the northern Rhône Valley, and one that resonates throughout the entire wine world. This appellation is home to the Syrah grape—a very distinctive variety that makes deeply colored, aromatically expressive, and very full-bodied wines. Syrah is now very popular worldwide, but there is a great difference between the New World style—often called Shiraz—and that of the French original. Whereas Shiraz from Australia has a soft texture and is rich with jammy fruit flavors from the moment it's bottled,

CROZES-HERMITAGE
Gilles Robin

Syrah from the Rhône is fairly tannic and peppery when young; it needs time to reveal its dramatic appeal.

Hermitage is located at the southern end of the northern Rhône Valley wine region, not far from Valence. The vines are planted on steep hills and terraces along the river to gain the maximum exposure to the sun. A small amount of the white varieties Roussanne and Marsanne may be blended with the Syrah to enhance the wine's floral complexity, but it remains a dark, highly concentrated red with potential for long aging—as much as 20 years.

With age, the aromas and flavors of smoke, earth, prunes, and even olives emerge, and then those firm tannins mellow. In the end, Hermitage achieves an exceptional balance between robust power on the one hand and smooth elegance on the other.

The little brother of this iconic wine is neighboring Crozes-Hermitage. These wines are also an expression of Syrah, but while Hermitage comes from a very small patch of steep hillside vines facing the sun, Crozes-Hermitage comes from larger, flatter plateau vineyards. The result is a slightly lighter style that is more approachable when young. There is inevitably some variability in quality, but there are excellent wines and they generally offer good value for money.

COLOR Deep and rich; inky black with a garnet rim.

AROMA Classic; spice, violets, black currant, smoke, and truffle.

TASTE Robust, with savory flavors; firm but ripe tannins; good length.

BUYING As a general rule, Hermitage is for special occasions and investment, Crozes for enjoyment. I particularly enjoy the wines of Michel Chapoutier, Jean-Louis Chave, Alain Graillot, Paul Jaboulet Aîné, and Gilles Robin.

ENJOYING Both Hermitage and Crozes-Hermitage are classic partners for hearty dishes, including beef bourguignon, meaty casseroles, roast lamb, and game such as pheasant.

BRANCHING OUT Here's an interesting experiment: taste a Crozes-Hermitage from leading estate Chapoutier alongside a wine made by the same producer and from the same grape variety—but in Australia! Domaine Tournon, in the cool Mount Benson district of South Australia, is a Chapoutier project and a truly Rhône-style Shiraz.

Bravely defending my country in the vineyards of the Rhône Valley!

During my National Service in the French army, I made lots of trips to vineyards, to see where the great wines are made. On the day I visited the Rhône Valley, famous for its intense heat, it snowed! It was very cold, but very beautiful. The drive down the Rhône Valley from Côte-Rôtie to Hermitage reminded me of Hollywood, because there were huge signs on the hillsides advertising the particular vines that produce these fabulous wines. (Like a real tourist, I had my photograph taken in front of one of these enormous signs!) The terraces rising from the valley of the Tain River produce Hermitage, but the plateau at the top is devoted to Crozes-Hermitage, which is slightly lighter in style and a little less intense.

CÔTE-RÔTIE

Côte-Rôtie is probably the finest red wine of the northern Rhône Valley. I call it the ultimate expression of Syrah: deep, dark, rich, and elegant. But part of this wine's elegance is the result of the white grape Viognier, which is permitted to constitute 20 percent of this blend. It adds both complexity and a flowery aroma. Côte-Rôtie wines age well, but production is limited, so they can be expensive.

COLOR Very deep garnet red, almost black; more orange-tinted with age.

AROMA Dark fruits, undergrowth, leather, chocolate, spice, flowers, oak.

TASTE Very rich; deep and full bodied, with firm tannins.

BUYING There are many producers in this little district, and quality varies. I recommend producers such as Guigal, Gerin, and Bonnefond. Also look for the vineyard names La Turque, La Landonne, or La Mouline on the label.

ENJOYING This wine is a superb match for game, strong cheeses, and full-flavored grilled vegetables. Serve at room temperature after letting it air in a decanter for an hour.

BRANCHING OUT The structure and power, as well as the finesse, are very similar to a Hermitage or a Cornas—all Syrahs from the northern Rhône.

ST-JOSEPH

St-Joseph represents a lighter style of Syrah, at least in comparison with other northern Rhône appellations. These are elegant wines, without dominant tannins. They have rich fruit, and a smooth, harmonious, and velvety texture. St-Joseph wines can age for up to six years, and they can be very good buys—but it's best to stick with recommended producers.

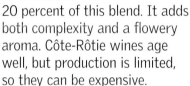

ST-JOSEPH
Domaine Chèze

COLOR Garnet, with a ruby rim; intense and fairly rich and opaque.

AROMA Complex; pepper, black currant, violet, woody undergrowth.

TASTE Smooth and delicate, with a firm structure balanced by ripe fruit.

BUYING There are two real styles here: a rustic one, which is firmly structured, and the softer style, where fruit flavors are dominant. Among producers, I recommend Domaine Chèze, Pierre Gaillard, and Chapoutier.

ENJOYING These wines make ideal partners for lamb, stews, and barbecues. They're also great fun with a lunch of cold meats, cheese, and bread.

BRANCHING OUT Petite Sirah, from California, is lighter than the true Syrah grape, making wine comparable to this lighter Rhône. Carmenère from Chile or a Washington State Lemberger should also suit your palate.

CORNAS

A tiny appellation, Cornas makes deep, dark, complex Syrah that is a real rival to the neighboring Hermitage. The Cornas district is composed of awkward little terraces along the west side of the Rhône, to the north of Valence. Production from such a tough terrain is very limited, so grab a bottle whenever you can. Cornas needs quite a few years to soften and reveal its amazing complexity.

COLOR Very dark, deep cherry red, with a heavy intensity.

AROMA Intense; pepper, black currant, blackberry, plum, spice, undergrowth.

TASTE Strong, dense, and tannic when young; very well balanced.

BUYING These are powerful wines—don't be surprised to see 14.5% ABV on the label. Among producers, Auguste Clape and Jean-Luc Colombo are the two names to know.

ENJOYING Cornas wines are great with classic French meat dishes. Actually, I find they can be like a stew in that, after opening, they're always better on the following day.

BRANCHING OUT The rich and velvety fruit of these wines is similar to a Pauillac or a very good Cahors. Also, contrast their full, dense structure with a lighter Pinot Noir or even a Gamay.

RICH, DENSE REDS

WORLD WINES

FRANCE
CHÂTEAUNEUF-DU-PAPE

The top wines of the southern Rhône Valley are named after the summer residence of the Roman Catholic popes during their exile to Avignon in the 14th century, something commemorated by the papal crossed keys embossed on all Châteauneuf bottles.

The structure and personality of these wines are unique, owing to the unusual blend of grapes and the special soil found here. Thirteen different varieties are allowed in the blend, several of them white, which is very rare for a single appellation.

In reality, most Châteauneuf wines are based on Grenache, and the other grapes are used as a kind of "seasoning" to add complexity. The area's soil is made up of large pebbles (*galets*) that soak up heat by day and gently release it at night, ensuring full

CHÂTEAUNEUF-DU-PAPE
Château de Beaucastel

ripeness of the grapes. And it is this combination of vine and stone that makes such spicy, juicy, heady wines.

COLOR Classic and intense; deep garnet, with a ruby rim.

AROMA Wild black fruits, sweet cherry, tobacco, leather, smoke, coffee, and spice.

TASTE Voluptuous, round; firm tannins when young; harmonious; long finish.

BUYING Try Château de Beaucastel, Château Rayas, and Château la Nerthe.

ENJOYING Châteauneuf is ideal with barbecued sausages, venison steaks, or beef casserole.

BRANCHING OUT Neighboring Gigondas and Vacqueyras can give most Châteauneufs a run for their money. Try Grenache-based Barossa Valley Australian wines, too.

How picnicking tourists can affect the vintage

One of the most unusual, and probably most romantic, places I have ever picnicked is Châteauneuf-du-Pape. There is a tumbledown old tower there, built on a little hill of the region's famous stony soil, that looks out over an amazing panorama of vineyards. Sitting there one summer with friends, we decided that our simple lunch of bread, cheese, and *saucisson* needed a little extra something, so we picked one or two of the grapes growing nearby. Although they weren't ripe, I will never forget the amazing flavors that were already apparent in those grapes. I'm afraid to say that we did eat quite a few—the vintage must have been smaller that year!

GIGONDAS

Gigondas is a close relative of Châteauneuf-du-Pape in style and power. Although it does not have the same potential for aging, it is more charming and pleasant when young. Gigondas is also a much better buy than its more famous counterpart. Trust me, at a time when we are all looking for alternatives to the big names, this underrated southern Rhône appellation is definitely one to go for.

COLOR Intense, deep black cherry, with a ruby rim.

AROMA Concentrated forest fruits, with pepper, smoke, tar, and licorice.

TASTE Rich and round; elegant, ripe tannins; refreshing acidity.

BUYING Recent vintages are some of the best ever. Here are five of my favorite producers: Ste Cosme, Jaboulet, Chapoutier, Domaine de Font-Sane, and Domaine Amadieu.

ENJOYING Share this wine with friends over some roast beef or game—an unforgettable combination. I also love it with tender roast leg of lamb or creamy cheeses.

BRANCHING OUT South African Shiraz is another rich, dark, and exuberant wine that drinks fantastically well when young, and is more European in style than other New World Syrahs.

VACQUEYRAS

Watch for Vacqueyras—it's buzzing with dynamism, quality, and passion, and gets better each year. Made from the same grapes as those used in Gigondas and Châteauneuf-du-Pape, it is rich and solid, but remains fresh and elegant. The wonderful balance between fruit and tannin allows it to age well for about five years.

COLOR Garnet, with a ruby rim; it looks powerful and rich, but also delicate.

AROMA Red and black fruits; older wine has spice, smoke, figs, and game.

TASTE Dark and deeply rich, dry flavors, full of black fruits.

BUYING Archimbaud-Vache and Domaine des Amouriers are the top names. Also try older vintages sold as "Côtes du Rhône Villages Vacqueyras."

ENJOYING Serve this wine at room temperature in a really big glass, and after 30 minutes in a decanter. It goes beautifully with grilled meats and stews.

BRANCHING OUT If you've cottoned on to this up-and-coming appellation, tune in to other rising stars Priorat from Spain, and Australian Mataro.

LIRAC

Lirac may lack the structure and depth of other wines from the southern Rhône Valley—such as Châteauneuf-du-Pape—but it is still full, elegant, and rich in red fruits. While its youthful vigor is great, it can be kept for three to five years, during which time it will soften and develop some "animal"-like characteristics.

COLOR Classic deep ruby red to dark garnet.

AROMA Red berries, and black pepper; with aging, leather, earth, and licorice.

TASTE Medium-bodied, but with full, very fruity flavors.

BUYING I love this wine when it is a couple of years old. Château de Ségriès and Château d'Aquéria are my favorite producers.

ENJOYING Serve Lirac with a coq au vin, or with a steak with pepper sauce and roasted root vegetables.

BRANCHING OUT If you like this, try Bandol from Provence, or New World wines made from the Mourvèdre grape.

BANDOL

This is the king of Provence wines! I like the way it combines power and richness with depth, elegance, and complexity of flavors, without being aggressive. This is owing to a clever blend of grapes, and also to long aging in oak barrels. The powerful Mourvèdre is the key variety, with Grenache and Cinsault providing softer flavors. Mourvèdre thrives in this part of the world, especially in Bandol—a natural amphitheater facing the Mediterranean Sea.

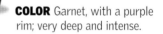

BANDOL
Domaine Tempier

COLOR Garnet, with a purple rim; very deep and intense.

AROMA Jammy black fruits; earthy, "meaty," spicy, with dried herbs.

TASTE Velvety, polished, structured; ripe tannins; long, aromatic finish.

BUYING The producers that stand out are Domaine Tempier, Château de Pibarnon, and Mas de la Louvière.

ENJOYING Bandol can be enjoyed young, after a short time in a decanter to let it breathe, but it also has the potential to be kept for more than ten years. It makes an excellent partner for beef or spicy sausage.

BRANCHING OUT The richness of Bandol compares well with a Margaux, while its sweet fruit intensity reminds me of Brunello. Try them and see!

RICH, DENSE REDS

WORLD WINES

"Based on Syrah and Mourvèdre grapes, Lirac combines power with elegance, depth, richness, and complex flavors. Wine for a winter day!"

❶ MARGAUX is the largest of the Médoc's communal appellations, producing—dare I say it—the most "feminine" of Médoc wines in style, ripe and with delicate weight. **Seek out** Château Brane-Cantenac, Château Cantenac Brown, Château Palmer, Château Rauzan-Ségla.

❷ PESSAC-LÉOGNAN is possibly Bordeaux's oldest viticultural district, part of the Graves appellation. Its stony soils produce well-structured, richly textured wines. **Seek out** Château Pape-Clément, Château Larrivet-Haut-Brion, Château la Mission-Haut-Brion, Domaine de Chevalier, Château Malartic-Lagravière.

❸ ST-ESTÈPHE is the most northerly of the four classic communes of the Médoc region of Bordeaux; its wines are said to have a more austere and "silky" feel, with a natural longevity. **Seek out** Château Cos d'Estournel, Château Montrose, Château Calon-Ségur, Château Phélan-Ségur.

TASTE TEST: *TERROIR*

Can terroir *really affect taste in wines made from the same grape?*

Cabernet Sauvignon vines on the gravel-and-limestone soil of St-Estèphe

"Is it really true that terroir *can influence the taste and texture of a wine? Try these three wines and find out!"*

The wines in this tasting are all from one geographically defined **wine region**—Bordeaux in France—and from **the same vintage**—2001—but from different subregions, each with its own specific *terroir*—the combination of **climate and soil** in a particular area. By the way, I've recommended some **magnificent** (and, as a result, quite expensive) wines, from **eminent Bordeaux properties**; you may need to consult a specialty merchant to track down my choices.

The first wine to taste is the **MARGAUX**. The Margaux area has a **gravel soil** that is ideal for producing Cabernet Sauvignon with a **delicate weight**, fragrant aroma, and fine **tannic structure**. This particular wine has a **mellow, velvety texture**, and is **rich, intense**, and **very round**. The ripe tannins are just sufficient to balance the texture, leaving the wine **just dry enough**.

The second wine is from **PESSAC-LÉOGNAN** in the Graves region of Bordeaux, farther to the south. This area has **large stones** in the soil, rather like Châteauneuf-du-Pape in the Rhône Valley, that heat up during sunny days and **hold their heat** through the cooler nights, helping to **keep the vines warm**. Because of this, the wines tend to be **richer** and **more intense**. This wine also has a **smoky nose** that is reminiscent of many wines from this area, with a **hint of sawdust**. Its character reflects the *terroir*—it is a **"monster,"** but is ripe and **not too powerful**.

Finally, the **ST-ESTÈPHE**. This subregion is **closest to the sea** within the Médoc. It is on quite high ground, and the climate is **tempered** by both the river and the sea. There are areas of **limestone soil** here, known as *calcaire de St-Estèphe*. This type of soil is **cooler than gravel** and produces Cabernet Sauvignon with a slightly **more austere** character than elsewhere in Bordeaux. The wine has a very **dark red-black** color. It has **abundant fruit**, great tannins, and **fantastic length**, but with a very **firm structure** that should soften up with more bottle age. My advice is—come back in ten years!

This tasting should demonstrate without a doubt that, with masterly winemaking, subtle differences in **climate and soil** can allow different facets of the **personality** of a grape variety to shine through.

ITALY
BAROLO / BARBARESCO

The hills of Piedmont are home
to Italy's finest red wines. Barolo
and Barbaresco boast power,
depth, and real character. They
are high in alcohol, high in tannin,
and high in acidity—and not for
the timid! Nebbiolo is the grape
variety used to craft both wines.
It is named after the mists—
the *nebbia*—that settle over the
vineyards on cool mornings of
Piedmont's harvest season.

Barolo is the bigger and bolder of
the two wines, and it has an amazing
capacity to age. Standard Barolo
must be aged for two years in oak or
chestnut barrels and one more year in
the bottle before being sold. The *riserva*
wines must be matured for a total of
five years in barrel and bottle. Even
then, both versions generally need
several more years in the cellar before
being opened. For some modern-minded
producers, this is too much, so they are
making a more approachable style with

*"Barolo is rich, dark,
concentrated, and
well structured, with
layer upon layer of
flavor; and one of
the best wines in the
world for aging."*

more supple fruit and rounder tannins when still relatively young. Whether traditional or modern, the quality of these wines continues to rise.

Barbaresco, an equally stunning wine, is not as big as its neighbor, but it can have more elegance and finesse in its early life. This is the regional "queen" to Barolo's "king." Good Barbaresco is more obviously charming and fruitier than Barolo, often with better balance and more integrated tannins. However, I think both Barolo and Barbaresco are what might be called "enthusiasts' wines," as merchants or consumers may need to cellar them for more than a decade. With such long aging, I save them for very special occasions.

COLOR Deep garnet, with a purple rim; tile-red after aging.

AROMA Tight; ripe, wild black fruits, plum, licorice, tar, truffles, spicy oak.

TASTE Unique; firm, high acidity; solid, marked tannins; elegant, infinite length.

BUYING Vintages vary, so ask a good merchant for advice. Among producers, try Giacomo Conterno, Bruno Giacosa, Azienda Agricola Negro, and Prunotto.

ENJOYING Good Barolo and Barbaresco suggest the scent of black truffles, so dishes using these luxurious fungi are often a fabulous match. These wines also work very well with roast meats, especially roast pork. Finally, I like them with chicken cacciatore.

BRANCHING OUT If you enjoy Barolo's broad-shouldered textures and dark fruit characters, you are likely to be a fan of other Italian heavyweights, too, such as Brunello from central Italy, and Aglianico from the south.

GATTINARA

This is a baby Barolo! Gattinara is made from the same Nebbiolo grape used to produce Piedmont's leading wine, but here it is called Spanna. Like Barolo, Gattinara is matured in barrels before being bottled, and it has the same ability to improve with age. But these wines offer more pronounced fruit characters and softer tannins, even if they lack Barolo's depth and class. They are also a much better buy.

COLOR Dark cherry, with ruby to orange tinges.

AROMA Ripe and intense; red and black fruits, smoke, and coffee.

TASTE Well balanced, charming, and refreshing, with round tannins.

BUYING Try wines from Mario Antoniolo, Travaglini, and Le Collineare. They can be difficult to find, so you may need to contact a specialty merchant.

ENJOYING Gattinara is great with all roasted meats, game, or poultry, and also with risottos. However, my favorite match is pan-fried calves' liver, mashed potatoes, and crispy bacon.

BRANCHING OUT Compare this wine's wide range of similarities—color, aroma, flavor, texture (but not price!)—with a Barbaresco or a Nebbiolo d'Alba.

AMARONE DELLA VALPOLICELLA

Amarone della Valpolicella, or simply Amarone, is a uniquely Italian creation. Harvested grape clusters are dried on straw mats for at least three months before fermentation. This concentrates their sugars and produces a rich, jammy flavor. It's a very intense red—and potent, with up to 17 percent alcohol. It also has a distinctive bitter finish, which gives real freshness. Amarone can be drunk young, but it improves with age.

AMARONE DELLA
VALPOLICELLA
Masi

COLOR Deep garnet, with rich nuances of dark, portlike purple.

AROMA Black cherry, plum, figs, tobacco, leather, earth, bitter almond.

TASTE Complex, powerful, strong; smooth, full flavors; very long.

BUYING Look for *classico superiore* on the label. Also, note that *recioto* means it's a sweet wine. Masi, Serègo Alighieri, and Allegrini are excellent producers.

ENJOYING I enjoy a young Amarone with steak, braised meat, game, or pasta with pesto; older examples of the wine are great with strong cheese.

BRANCHING OUT Amarone is truly unique—but for something that approaches this interesting wine, try the sweet red wines of the south of France, especially *grand cru* Banyuls.

ITALY
AGLIANICO

I am a great fan of these wines, and I still remember the first time I tried them. What I particularly enjoy is their determination—they have such well-defined character. Their significant power and body is supported by so much ripe fruit flavor that they really make your mouth water.

Aglianico is a red grape variety that was brought to Italy by the Greeks more than 2,000 years ago. In fact, the name Aglianico is a corruption of the Italian word *ellenico*, meaning "Greek" ("Hellenic"). After two millennia, it is probably safe to call it an indigenous variety—it was cultivated by the ancient Romans to produce one of their favorite wines, the legendary Falerno.

Today, Aglianico makes its home in the mountainous landscape east of Naples, where it thrives in volcanic soils and gives its best results at higher altitudes. Production focuses on two places: Basilicata and the Taurasi district of Campania.

Aglianico del Vulture is the star denomination of the Basilicata region. The name comes from the extinct volcano Vulture, which dominates the expanse of surrounding vineyards. The wines have a certain rustic austerity in their youth, but their warmth and concentrated fruit flavors evolve over five to ten years to show silky finesse.

Taurasi, in neighboring Campania, is the hero of southern Italy. This Aglianico-based wine is named after one of the 17 villages that make up its growing district, which gained DOCG status—Italy's highest wine classification—in 1993. I have heard this wine called "the Barolo of the

South," because it shares the power and intensity of the top wine of the Piedmont region. I agree with this comparison. Taurasi is an underrated wine of the highest quality, and like Aglianico del Vulture, it shows its best after some time in the bottle.

Aglianico itself is just beginning a well-deserved renaissance in wine circles, so it should be high on your list of new wines to taste – if you can call a 2,000-year-old wine "new"!

AGLIANICO
Mala Terra

COLOR Deep garnet red, with attractive ruby to orange reflections.

AROMA Dark berries, violets, woody undergrowth, herbs, prunes, chocolate.

TASTE Great harmony, with marked acidity and concentrated fruit flavors.

BUYING From the Aglianico del Vulture denomination of Basilicata, try the wines of Fratelli d'Angelo, Mala Terra, and Paternoster. From the Taurasi denomination of Campania, look for Antonio Caggiano and Mastroberardino.

ENJOYING I always think of Aglianico as a winter wine, so I like to match it with robust dishes—beef casserole or roast pheasant, for example—or with aged, sharp cheeses such as Gouda, Asiago, or Provolone.

BRANCHING OUT Compare the structure and fruit of a good Aglianico with similarly big, bold wines from farther north in Italy—Barolo, Brunello, and Barbaresco—and with Nebbiolo wines from the New World.

BRUNELLO

Brunello di Montalcino is one of the driving forces behind the global success of top Tuscan wines. Its classic quality is on a par with the great reds of Piedmont—Barolo and Barbaresco—as well as with the leading appellations of Bordeaux. It very deservedly was one of the first wines in Italy to be awarded the elite classification DOCG.

The name Brunello is the local term for the Sangiovese Grosso variety, the strain of Tuscany's dominant red grape that seems to thrive around the town of Montalcino. Actually, the Italian word *bruno* means "dark," and Brunello is so called because of its dark skin.

The Brunello grape is similar to the Sangiovese of Chianti, but the wines are quite different. The key to those differences is the climate in which the grapes are grown. It is hotter and drier near Montalcino than in other parts of Tuscany, and this gives Brunello its especially deep, ripe character. That same depth makes young Brunello impossible to drink—it is just too big, tannic, and firm, even though it's balanced with bags of fruit flavors. It needs to be tempered by time, so all Brunello is aged in barrels for at least 24 months, and it cannot be released until its fifth year. In practice, it is normally kept in wood for three to five years to soften the tannins and allow development of the sought-after aromas of leather, truffles, spice, and woody undergrowth. Even then, these wines are often best no sooner than a decade after the harvest.

You might also come across the younger sibling of this wine, Rosso di Montalcino, which is made from the same grapes but is not aged for as long. This is also a great red, but expect it to have more vibrant fruit flavors and less tannin, allowing for earlier drinking.

At its finest, I think Brunello di Montalcino is one of the world's best wines. If you are lucky enough to have a very old Brunello, you might want to save it for a special occasion.

BRUNELLO
Silvio Nardi

COLOR Opaque black cherry, with a purple rim; tile-red with aging.

AROMA Intense; dark fruits, plum, leather, forest fruits, spice, and earth.

TASTE Wonderful complexity; rich, firm structure; round tannins after aging.

BUYING These sought-after wines do not come cheap, but this level of quality rarely does. Among producers, I suggest you try the wines of Biondi-Santi, Costanti, and Silvio Nardi.

ENJOYING Like Aglianico, Brunello feels like a winter wine to me. I always pour Brunello at Christmas or New Year's dinner. It is perfect with traditional roasted meats and mixed grills. Its mature, savory aromas work extremely well with pheasant, too. Serve it in place of a Bordeaux to surprise your guests!

BRANCHING OUT If Brunello is to your taste, you needn't be afraid to tackle big, firm, southern European wines with less hefty price tags, such as Portuguese Dão and Greek Xynomavro.

RICH, DENSE REDS

WORLD WINES

RICH, DENSE REDS

WORLD WINES

ITALY
CARMIGNANO

If you like good Chianti, I think you'll really enjoy its neighbor, Carmignano. This tiny district has been firmly on the map since 1716, when Grand Duke Cosimo III marked out some of Europe's first quality wine-producing zones by official decree. The vineyards are set on low hillsides to the west of Florence, where they enjoy reliably warm daytime temperatures. This means that the grapes can be harvested earlier than in surrounding areas, and well before the fall rains.

The resulting wines are consistently good from year to year—part of the reason for their coveted DOCG status. Relatively lower acidity and firmer tannins make these wines more refined than many Chiantis. Part of that distinctive character comes from the addition of about 10 percent Cabernet Sauvignon grapes to the traditional Chianti mix of Sangiovese and Canaiolo. Barco Reale, an alternate version of Carmignano, is lighter-bodied, has brighter acidity, and is a little smokier than standard Carmignano. The flavors also show a charred, bitter streak that complements the wine's fat, rounded, fruity texture. Both versions of Carmignano are best after five to six years of aging. And with just seven fiercely proud producers, they match great value with high quality.

COLOR Intense ruby red to purple; lightens with age.

AROMA Blackberry, plum, and licorice; hints of white pepper.

TASTE Full-bodied and fruity, with chalk and lime undertones.

BUYING With only a few producers, it's hard to go wrong. Try Fattoria di Ambra, Fattoria di Bacchereto, and Villa di Capezzana.

ENJOYING I think Carmignano pairs very well with cheesy pasta dishes, such as spinach and ricotta cannelloni or mushroom and parmesan ravioli.

BRANCHING OUT Compare the structure and texture of Carmignano with its similar but fuller-bodied Tuscan neighbor Chianti Classico.

"I love this wine as an alternative to Chianti. Carmignano is made in the warm Tuscan foothills, and is deliciously fruity and full-bodied, with a slight chalky feel."

SPAIN
RIBERA DEL DUERO

Often overshadowed by the dominance of Rioja, this full red wine is a personal favorite of mine, and it has a growing following around the world. Ribera del Duero is a beauty, so don't miss it!

The name Ribera del Duero comes from the Duero River, halfway between Madrid and the Bay of Biscay, which becomes the Douro of port fame as it flows west into Portugal. The climatic conditions in this valley are quite extreme. It is an arid place with hot days and cold nights during the summer, and quite brutal winters. These conditions create a higher acidity in the Tempranillo grape (grown here under the local name Tinto Fino) than is found in Rioja. The resulting wine has great intensity, a solid structure, and a luscious texture. It is a sure sign of success that more of these vines are being planted along the Duero each year.

RIBERA DEL DUERO
Bodega Matarromera

COLOR Deep garnet, with a purple rim; great intensity of color.

AROMA Black currant and spice; full, but freshly perfumed.

TASTE Complex, elegant fruit; thick but rounded.

BUYING The top names here include Vega Sicilia and Pesquera, but I can also recommend Aalto, Hacienda Monasterio, and Bodega Matarromera. They are all stars in the Spanish firmament!

ENJOYING Ribera del Duero makes a fine partner for hearty dishes, such as sausage and mashed potatoes, braised rack of lamb, or tournedos Rossini. Fantastic!

BRANCHING OUT The dense fruit of Ribera del Duero wines can be found in other Spanish heavyweights, so if you enjoy them, try Priorat and the up-and-coming Toro, too. It's also well worth seeking out a Malbec from Argentina.

RICH, DENSE REDS

WORLD WINES

A mountain journey to find the perfect vine-growing conditions

Along with a group of London sommeliers, I once visited the vineyards of the Ribera Association. We took the bus for an hour from the airport at Madrid, then began to climb into the mountains along narrow roads through the passes. After a while, we were all terrified, not daring to look down into the chasms below. Finally, we came across the vineyards, stretched out along the hillsides. Here, conditions are ideal for perfectly balanced wine: full exposure to the sun balanced by the cool air of high altitude. The result is a longer ripening season, producing wine of great density and complexity. Ribera is comparable with the Bordeaux style, especially Pauillac *grand cru classé*—so if you like that, you should try this!

TASTE TEST: ALCOHOL LEVEL

Discover the influence of alcohol on the taste of a wine.

❶ **BROUILLY** is the most fruit-driven Beaujolais wine, but a Fleurie would work just as well in this tasting. **Seek out** Georges Duboeuf, Domaine Cheysson, Domaine Combillaty, Mommessin.

❷ **CHILEAN CABERNET SAUVIGNON** is an easy-drinking red and a great buy. Look for wines from the Rapel Valley—these have the most complexity. **Seek out** Leyenda (Las Casas del Toqui), Santa Rita, Casa Lapostolle, Cousiño-Macul, Los Vascos.

❸ **CALIFORNIA ZINFANDEL** is a flagship wine of this sun-kissed state, and at its best is a unique and unbeatable wine. **Seek out** Ridge, Nalle, Beringer, Kenwood, Mondavi.

❹ **AUSTRALIAN SHIRAZ** is big, bold, and powerful. For this tasting, choose a Shiraz from the Barossa Valley, since this has the perfect climate for producing well-balanced wines. **Seek out** O'Leary Walker, Glaetzer, Grant Burge, Geoff Merrill, Rosemount Estate.

"Whether the alcohol level is low or high is not what makes a good wine—it's all about the balance."

Alcohol level can vary widely between wines, although as a general rule it is **higher** in wines from **hotter, sunnier climates** where the grapes contain **more sugar** when harvested. Alcohol is not noticeable on the nose of a wine, but is recognizable as a warm, sometimes even a burning sensation at the back of the throat when you taste the wine. In a good wine, the alcohol should **not dominate** the senses, but should be in **perfect balance** with the fruit, acidity, and tannins.

The first wine in the tasting is the **BROUILLY**. This is a **lightweight, fruit-driven** wine. It has aromas of **crushed fresh berries**, with a **refreshing style**. The wine is vinified using the carbonic maceration process *(see pp.42–3)*, and has both **low tannins** and **low alcohol**. It has flavors of **ripe strawberries**, and is **pleasant and easy-going**, its **light fruit** balanced by the low level of alcohol.

Now turn to the **CHILEAN CABERNET SAUVIGNON**. This has aromas of **raspberries and black fruits**, and also **nettles** and hints of **undergrowth**. It is **very dry**, and the alcohol is quite **dominant**. The tannins are **firm**, but the **acidity is high** and the fruit is not quite ripe enough for perfect balance.

Now try the **CALIFORNIA ZINFANDEL**. This wine is **heavy and full** but **not too sweet**. It has distinctive and **complex aromas**, which include **plums and green pepper**. There is a **good balance** between fruit and alcohol, and the relatively **high alcohol level** serves to **soften the tannins**.

The final wine in the tasting is the **AUSTRALIAN SHIRAZ** from the Barossa Valley. This is a strong wine, but does not taste **too alcoholic** because it is balanced by the **rich, ripe, dense fruit** qualities. This is a very **bold** wine: lots of straightforward but **powerful ripe fruit**, with firm tannins, good acidity, and **high alcohol**—all in **excellent balance** with one another.

SPAIN
TORO

It is no surprise that the boiling summer heat and the lack of rainfall at the heart of Spain produce solid, powerful, "black" wines. The Tempranillo grape variety is well established here, but it produces wines that are darker and more tannic than those of Rioja, and that may prove to have greater aging potential. Toro is still on a learning curve, but this is certainly a region to watch.

COLOR Distinctive deep, inky red-black, with a purple rim.

AROMA Ripe dark fruits; blackberry, cherry, smoke, coffee, minerals.

TASTE Strong, solid, concentrated, and powerful; jammy fruits; good length.

BUYING Among producers, I recommend Bodegas Frutos Villar and Piedra.

ENJOYING This wine is really good with cured meats, paëlla, and barbecues. Serve it at room temperature; if it is any cooler, the tannins will be accentuated too much.

BRANCHING OUT Try these wines alongside Rioja—while they are certainly more powerful than Spain's most famous red, they share its characteristics of oak-aging and the buttery finish that this imparts. For the same reason, you should also relish a well-oaked South African Cabernet Sauvignon.

CONCA DE BARBERÁ

In the Catalan language, a *conca* is a basin-shaped valley gouged out of the mountains, and it's often a fantastic place for ripening grapes. Red Conca de Barberá wine is made from a blend of Tempranillo, Garnacha, and Cabernet Sauvignon grapes. It is an intense and complex wine, with plenty of warmth and ripe fruit. This wine can be difficult to obtain, but it is well worth making the effort.

COLOR Dark, deep, black cherry, with a ruby rim.

AROMA Intense, complex; blackberry, chocolate, smoke, licorice, and spice.

TASTE Firm, with elegance and depth; polished tannins; good length.

BUYING With barely more than a dozen wineries, this district has a very limited output. But look for wines from Josep Foraster and from Torres—especially the Reserve!

ENJOYING I particularly enjoy this wine as an accompaniment to homemade sausages with mashed potatoes, or to complement a confit of duck breast with black lentils.

BRANCHING OUT Many of these rich, dense wines remind me of Gigondas or Crozes-Hermitage, because of their sweet fruit and spicy characters.

TORO
Bodegas Frutos Villar

TERRA ALTA

Terra Alta may be the least-known wine in Catalonia, northeastern Spain, but this small DO near the more famous Priorat denomination is slowly improving in quality. The area's high altitude yields wines that are concentrated and rich in fruit, but the acidity is fairly pronounced thanks to the mountains and the cooling sea breezes. There is amazing potential here. Watch for it.

COLOR Garnet red, with a ruby rim; medium to deep intensity.

AROMA Red berries, with spice, smoke, herbs, and woody undergrowth.

TASTE Refreshing acidity, with ripe flavors; balanced tannins; good length.

BUYING After years of relative inactivity, the local cooperatives are really experimenting and developing what they offer. However, among individual producers I recommend Bàrbara Forés and Pedro Rovira.

ENJOYING This is a perfect wine for lunchtime charcuterie or weekend barbecues. It's also great with midweek steak and fries. It's not complex or "deep," but it is very tasty.

BRANCHING OUT I think there's an interesting comparison to be made between the tannins and acidity of these wines and Nebbiolo-based wines from northern Italy.

PRIORAT

There is a real excitement about Spanish wine right now, and if there's one place that can lay claim to kicking it off, it is Priorat. This region produces world-class wine that everyone is treating very seriously—not least because of its hefty prices.

Priorat is an isolated corner of Tarragona province, southwest of Barcelona. The region's ancient Garnacha and Carignan vines have spent nearly a century working their roots deep into the stony soil, and they give only tiny harvests of highly concentrated fruit. The vines were rediscovered by a group of well-funded wine pioneers in the mid-1980s, and the wines they make are big and powerful, with smooth tannins and perfectly balanced acidity. They are almost magical and capable of long aging, but they tempt you from the moment they enter your hands.

PRIORAT
Álvaro Palacios

COLOR Very opaque; inky, with a purple rim.

AROMA Black fruits, figs, tobacco, herbs, dried fruit, and spice.

TASTE Dense, structured, and solid, but with a round, ripe texture.

BUYING New investment is flooding into Priorat, but my favorites are the regional pioneers Álvaro Palacios, Clos Mogador, Costers del Siurana, and Mas Martinet.

ENJOYING Full-on wine calls for full-on food, such as spit-roasted boar or lamb roasted with rosemary and garlic. Large glasses amplify Priorat's superb aromas.

BRANCHING OUT The weight and power of Priorat compare well with the "biggest" wines from around the world. Try them alongside good Barossa Shiraz from Australia.

A master class in wines from northeastern Spain

A few years ago, I took part in a Spanish wine tasting in London with René Barbier, proprietor of Clos Mogador. He showed me the different vintages and explained the subtle differences in the various Priorat wines. It was a real master class! Priorat is an up-and-coming wine-producing area, situated in the "amphitheater" of hills surrounding the great city of Barcelona. The wines are made from the same grape varieties as Châteauneuf-du-Pape, but have the same exposure to the sun as Portuguese Douro wines. As I discovered, the result is a fantastic intensity and depth, and real consistency in quality. I would recommend them as an alternative to French wines, or even as a first choice!

TARRAGONA

I am convinced that this corner of northern Spain will make its mark very soon. Most of the production is everyday whites from the same grapes used in Cava, and the region is also known for its sweet wines. But Tarragona's red wines have good fruit and appealing structure. They don't yet rival their neighbors in Priorat and Conca de Barberá, but they are still harmonious and extremely enjoyable early-drinking wines.

COLOR Quite an opaque wine; silky red with a ruby rim.

AROMA Intense; a cocktail of black fruits and black pepper.

TASTE Great balance; harmonious, elegant, well structured; long finish.

BUYING Tarragona is a very small denomination, and it may be difficult to find one of its reds. Talk to a specialty merchant, and look for wines from Cellers Scala Dei and Torres.

ENJOYING Serve this red with some crusty bread and saucisson, or with some tapas. I think this is a wine for drinking while soaking up the sun on a mountainside overlooking the sea, and talking with friends.

BRANCHING OUT Try these wines with *crianza* Riojas and Navarras, also from Spain. They will give you the same smooth, sunny, slightly peppery drinking as Tarragona. Corbières and Faugéres from the south of France will repay exploration too.

RICH, DENSE REDS

WORLD WINES

PORTUGAL
BAIRRADA

The mention of Portuguese wine generally brings to mind port, or perhaps lighter and more recent creations such as Mateus rosé. People often forget, or perhaps do not realize, that Portugal has been making dry table reds for many centuries, at least since Roman times. The coastal region of Bairrada is dominated by these wines. At their best, Bairrada reds have an intense fruitiness and plenty of vigor—and they are also fabulous buys.

During the 19th century, Bairrada was Portugal's leading source of basic drinking reds, and also home to the country's first professional viticulture school. Today, almost all of Bairrada's reds come from mature vineyards planted with the local Baga grape. When well crafted, Baga has wonderful brambly fruit flavors and a structure that gives it a great capacity to age. However, most local production is in the hands of thousands of small growers who sell their fruit to cooperative wineries, and both groups currently seem more focused on quantity rather than quality. (A lot of the region's crop goes into Mateus rosé.)

Fortunately, several dedicated private estates are now exploiting the potential of Baga, and they are creating some truly inspiring wines. In a wine world of growing uniformity, Bairrada provides a welcome splash of diversity.

COLOR Intense black cherry, slightly fading at the edges.

AROMA Tar, herbs, black cherry, black currant, tobacco, and pepper.

TASTE Big, voluptuous; firm, balanced acidity; rich fruit.

BUYING Try Casa de Saima, José Maria da Fonseca, and Luis Pato.

ENJOYING These are ideal barbecue wines. Their peppery vigor makes them great with spicy sausages.

BRANCHING OUT Good Bairrada is similar to wines from Dão, and also to Touriga Nacional–based reds from the Douro region.

DÃO

For many years, Dão was marketed as Portugal's best red-wine region. Sadly, it was controlled by cooperatives that often produced hard, tannic wines that lacked fruit. But a number of younger growers have realized the potential of this region, and they have begun making wines in a fruitier style with better balance. Touriga Nacional, Portugal's finest red grape, grows particularly well here, and it plays a key role in the spicy, peppery Dão blend.

COLOR Deep and intense ruby, and quite opaque.

AROMA Pronounced and fairly dry, with black currant, spice, and herbs.

TASTE Dry, firm tannins, with sufficient fruit flavors; good length.

BUYING For the moment, there are very few producers of any commercial significance here, except the giant Sogrape and Dão Sul.

ENJOYING Serve Dão reds with heavier, meaty dishes, such as slow-cooked stews. They can also work well with bouillabaisse.

BRANCHING OUT You must try Dão alongside Tarrango! You won't believe that this boisterous Australian grape variety has the grape used to make Dão—Touriga Nacional—as one of its parents.

DÃO Sogrape
Duque de Viseu

RIBATEJO

Ribatejo is the agricultural heartland of Portugal, tracing the banks of the Tejo River, northeast of Lisbon. It is home to some of Portugal's largest wine estates. Much of the production is white wine, but the reds are the real attraction here. There are plantings of international varieties, such as Cabernet Sauvignon and Merlot, but seek out wines made with the local Trincadeira or Touriga Nacional varieties.

COLOR Inky but bright; purple to ruby rim and good viscosity.

AROMA Very pronounced, with black fruits and hints of licorice and leather.

TASTE Well structured, backed up by ripe black fruits and good acidity.

BUYING Check the label to avoid confusing the Ribatejo denomination with the regional appellation Ribatejano. Among producers, D. F. J. Vinhos is the name to know.

ENJOYING These big wines need bold food. Try them with game, or hearty beef or lamb stews.

BRANCHING OUT Many of these wines are blends of local grapes, such as Trincadeira, with global ones, such as Cabernet Sauvignon. Try them alongside straightforward Chilean Cabernet to appreciate how the native Portuguese varieties work within these wines.

GREECE
AGIORGITIKO

Greece has been producing wine for thousands of years, but very little of it has reached what might be called a world standard. One possibility is Agiorgitiko (St George), the grape variety of Nemea in the Peloponnese. Known locally as the "Blood of Hercules," it is rich, intense, and smooth—similar to Merlot, but firmer. To my mind, drinking Greek wine is really about the "Greek experience," rather than trying to replicate, say, a Bordeaux.

COLOR Deep garnet red, with ruby at the edges.

AROMA Very fruity, with blackberry and hints of black cherry.

TASTE Full, with medium fruit, low acidity, and a long finish.

BUYING I honestly think the best way to find good Greek wine is to go on vacation there. But among more widely available producers, I recommend Boutari and Tsantali.

ENJOYING Get into the spirit and serve this wine with Greek-style grilled lamb, feta cheese, and a crisp salad.

BRANCHING OUT Compare the fruit and structure of this wine against a St-Émilion "satellite" from Bordeaux, or a Carmenère from Chile. They are not far off!

AGIORGITIKO
Boutari

RICH, DENSE REDS

WORLD WINES

GREECE
XYNOMAVRO

Xynomavro is the dominant grape variety of northern Greece, where it is used to make wines in the Naoussa, Amindeo, and Goumenissa districts. It has a deep color and prominent acidity. (Its name means "acid black.") The tannins can be harsh, but the best wines age well and develop a complexity like a fine Barolo. In warm years, they are deliciously soft, even when young.

COLOR Deep garnet red, fading to ruby at the rim.

AROMA Intense and fresh; pleasant ripe fruits; citrus and mineral hints.

TASTE Full and firm, with pronounced acidity and complex fruit flavors.

BUYING Something at least eight years old should have a good balance. Among Xynomavro producers, give Aidarinis and Castanioti a try.

ENJOYING I recommend that you drink this wine only with food, especially slightly spicy meats.

BRANCHING OUT Fans of Xynomavro wines will also enjoy Nebbiolo-based reds from northern Italy.

LIMNIO

The Limnio grape, native to the island of Limnos, is mainly grown in the Rapsani district of northern Greece. Its wines are well structured and high in alcohol, with considerable body. Some wines need aging for a year or more in barrels. The best may be blended with Cabernet Sauvignon or Cabernet Franc.

KADARKA *Takler*

COLOR Attractive, dark black cherry, with a pinkish rim.

AROMA Dried herbs, cherry, plum, jammy black currant, and white pepper.

TASTE Full, velvety texture; fruit-driven, with warmth and good length.

BUYING Go for the most recent vintages. Papaïoannou and the Samos Co-op are my favorite producers.

ENJOYING Limnio is great with grilled lamb, and an ideal wine for barbecues.

BRANCHING OUT Limnio is similar in structure to a French Chinon, and in texture to an Argentinian Malbec.

"Xynomavro and Limnio are deep and full, but also quite acidic. I liken them to Barolo, and the best can challenge the Italians!"

HUNGARY
KADARKA

Kadarka is the leading red grape variety of Hungary, and the most important variety in the famous Hungarian wine Egri Bikavér (Bull's Blood). Sadly, the mass-production techniques of the Communist era led to a cheap, sour drink that ruined the image of this famous wine. But a modern generation is now producing Bikavér to suit global tastes. This full-bodied red can be very aromatic and spicy.

COLOR Medium to deep ruby red, with orange tinges.

AROMA Very fruity, with strong hints of spice and wild flowers.

TASTE Full bodied, strong, powerful, and well structured, with a long finish.

BUYING Tibor Gál's wines are the stars of modern Hungary. The classy Bikavér uses a lot of Cabernet Franc and Merlot, but is just great. Other top producers include Takler and Blue Danube.

ENJOYING It's best to drink this wine when it's young, although a wine that has been aged in wood for three or four years is excellent with a sirloin steak. My own personal favorite is Bull's Blood and lamb chops—after which I can take on the world!

BRANCHING OUT This fleshy, spicy red puts me in mind of a pure Syrah like Cornas from France.

BULGARIA
MELNIK / MAVRUD

Melnik and Mavrud are the most interesting of Bulgaria's indigenous grape varieties. Melnik is the main city of the southwestern region, along the Greek border, and it gives its name to this local grape variety. The wines are weighty, tannic, and truly Balkan (and rather Greek-like) in style. The southern region is home to the Mavrud variety, which produces hearty, plummy wines that benefit from a period of oak-aging.

COLOR Dark garnet with ruby to brick- or tile-red nuances.

AROMA Not too obvious; forest fruits, vanilla, and spicy oak.

TASTE Firm tannins, solid, heavy; moderate acidity and fruit; good length.

BUYING These may be wines to cellar for eight years or so to really get the best out of them. Among producers, Santa Sarah Privat and Vinzavod Assenovgrad are truly good.

ENJOYING Drink Melnik with locally inspired savory stuffed peppers or mutton. With Mavrud, I recommend you stick with some of the recent vintages, and drink it with something quite hearty or even spicy.

BRANCHING OUT These wines remind me of a mature Châteauneuf-du-Pape, but you could also compare them to a Greek Agiorgitiko or Xynomavro— they are like close cousins.

SERBIA AND MONTENEGRO
VRANAC

The quality of wine from the Balkans has been variable over the years, but the best Vranacs have been compared to the wines of Bordeaux, which I know might surprise some people! The Vranac grape variety is native to the mountainous region of Montenegro. It makes a dry red wine with a rich character and robust structure, and it typically shows a pronounced bitterness.

COLOR Deep ruby red; intense but fading at the rim.

AROMA Full of character; cherry, prune, green pepper, and hints of green walnut.

TASTE Robust and full, with firm tannins, a slight bitterness, and rich fruit.

BUYING Despite the full structure of this wine, it doesn't improve with age— so buy recent vintages. Among producers, I recommend Snova and A. D. Plantaze.

ENJOYING Serve this wine in its youth with food that is rich in flavor, or maybe with a creamy cheese. In the summer, Vranac can be great served slightly chilled.

BRANCHING OUT The mineral bitterness of Vranac wines is not to be considered a fault. In fact, for wines with a similar characteristic, try comparing them to a *cru bourgeois* from the Haut-Médoc of Bordeaux, or to an Italian Nebbiolo.

CROATIA
PLAVAC MALI

Much of Croatia produces white wine, but the Dalmatian coast has become a successful red-wine region. Plavac Mali is a native grape, and it is used to make deeply colored, intense wine that is naturally high in alcohol. There seems little doubt that this variety is related to Zinfandel *(see p.250)*, so if you enjoy California's signature wine, you should give its European counterpart a try.

COLOR Good, well-balanced coloring of dark garnet, with a ruby rim.

AROMA Fairly simple black fruits; intense, peppery, plummy.

TASTE Strong; medium acidity, generous alcohol, and rich texture; medium finish.

BUYING Production of this wine is quite limited, but it's worth pursuing something from Dalmacijavino (Plavac Marjan) or Grgich. Also, enjoy the wine while it's young.

ENJOYING Serve this wine slightly cool to reinforce its fruity intensity and balance out the alcoholic strength. I always drink Plavac Mali with food, maybe with chops or something from the barbecue grill.

BRANCHING OUT Plavac Mali's rich texture is similar to that of a Californian Zinfandel or a good-quality Italian Primitivo, while the flavor reminds me of a Spanish Tempranillo wine, such as a Reserva Rioja.

PLAVAC MALI
Dalmacijavino

RICH, DENSE REDS

WORLD WINES

TASTE TEST: TANNIN

Learn to identify and taste the effect of tannins in red wine.

❶ NEW ZEALAND PINOT NOIR is a refined, fresh, and above all fruity red wine. The best regions for growing Pinot are Marlborough and Central Otago, both on New Zealand's South Island. **Seek out** Alana Estate, Carrick, Morton Estate, Cloudy Bay, or any other producer from South Island.

❷ RED BORDEAUX from the Haut-Médoc on the so-called "Left Bank" of this famous winemaking region in France is wonderfully rich, dense, Cabernet Sauvignon-based wine. It really improves with age—for this tasting, choose a wine with six years or more of bottle aging.

Seek out Château Larose Perganson, Château Cissac, Château La Lagune, Château Cantemerle, Château Monbrison.

❸ BARBARESCO from the northwest of Italy is a true heavyweight, with a price tag to match. Its Italian neighbor Barolo will also work well in this tasting. **Seek out** Azienda Agricola Negro, Bruno Giacosa, Angelo Gaja, La Spinetta. It is important to choose a wine with some age for this tasting, but avoid examples from 2002, which was not a good year for this wine. Any year from 1995 to 2001 is a safe bet.

"Tannins play an essential role in creating the structure of all red wines, however light-bodied the style."

Tannins are astringent substances that are present in the **skins and seeds** of grapes (these are considered **"good" tannins**), as well as the **stalks** (considered **"bad" tannins**, because they often contribute green and bitter flavors), and they give a framework or structure to a red wine. Tannins also leach into wine from the **wood of oak barrels** used for aging. You can identify tannins in a wine by reflecting on the feel left in your mouth when you have taken a mouthful of a **crisp, green apple**,

or of **strong black tea**. The **drying effect** these have on your gums is a result of the tannins. In general, the **higher the tannins** in a wine, the **more fruit** it needs to balance them, and therefore the **more weighty** the wine.

Try first the **NEW ZEALAND PINOT NOIR**. This wine has very **low tannins** and any it does have are kept well under control by the **juicy fruit**. **Refreshing tannins** are present—you can feel their effect in your mouth—but they **do not dominate** the wine.

The tannins are very noticeable in the **RED BORDEAUX**, but they are **firm, ripe, and polished** rather than harsh and bitter and serve to give a **refreshing feel** to the wine rather than making it too

drying—perfect characteristics for a wine that will **age well**. In fact, this wine should improve with age for another **ten years**. Be sure to decant the wine two hours before serving, to bring out the **flavors and complexity**.

The third wine in the tasting, the Italian **BARBARESCO**, has the most **pronounced tannins**, distinctive when you first taste the wine but **classy, ripe, and well balanced** by the fruit, as well as the **acidity**, which is characteristically high in the Nebbiolo grape variety from which this wine is made. So this wine has **high tannins, high acidity, and high alcohol**, but all are **well integrated** with each other to give a **delicious** wine.

UNITED STATES
ZINFANDEL

Zinfandel is rooted in the history of the American west; it was originally planted to make wine for pioneering gold miners. Sadly, it has also been cultivated in unsuitable locations and pushed for high yields with poor results. More recent, high-quality examples are complex, dense, rich, and full of flavor. This wine also responds quite well to maturing in oak barrels, which gives it great balance.

COLOR Garnet red, with ruby to orange tinges; variable intensity.

AROMA Distinctive and complex, with plum and green pepper.

TASTE Rich, round, and heavy, but with refreshing acidity; very long.

BUYING The best Zinfandels can age for decades. However, it can be so good when young that it is difficult to keep for any length of time. Among producers, I like Nalle and Ridge.

ENJOYING Zinfandel can be enjoyed on its own as a fruity aperitif, but I like it best with barbecued steaks and sausages. Serve it in large glasses to get the most of its heady aromas.

BRANCHING OUT Compare Zinfandel with a very young and powerful New World Pinot Noir for a similar explosion of pure fruit flavors. Zinfandel's rich structure also has much in common with that of St-Émilion Merlot.

CABERNET SAUVIGNON

Modern California wine was born in the 1970s when a Napa Valley Cabernet Sauvignon defeated Bordeaux's best in a blind tasting now known as "The Judgment of Paris." Thirty years later, the finest of these red wines remain world-class, showing finesse, complexity, and lovely ripe black fruit, with well-balanced texture. Most are oak-aged, but in a more classical and delicate way than in the recent past, when they were far too woody for my taste.

Without doubt, the finest California Cabernets come from the Napa Valley. Almost every spare plot of land here is planted with vines, but Cabernet performs best in the Rutherford, Stags' Leap, St. Helena, and Oakville districts.
　In terms of character, Rutherford wines show amazing longevity and depth, while Stags' Leap wines possess stylish elegance. And beyond pure Cabernets, there are excellent Bordeaux-style blends of Cabernet Sauvignon with Merlot, Malbec, Cabernet Franc, and Petit Verdot. These are locally known as "Meritage,"

and you may see this term on the label. Of course, such consistently great performance has made Napa the most prized agricultural land in America, so almost all of these wines are relatively expensive. But if you feel like splurging, there is no questioning their quality.

COLOR Deep, dark garnet red, with a purple to ruby rim.

AROMA Cherry, blackberry, leather, smoke, warm bread, coffee beans.

TASTE Robust, but delicate and classy; perfect balance.

BUYING Look for the Napa Valley—the epicenter of great American Cabernet Sauvignon. Try Beringer, Dominus, Duckhorn, and Stags' Leap Winery.

ENJOYING Drink these wines with full-bodied food—grilled steak or roast lamb. California Cabernets are so rich in fruit that they are great on their own, too.

BRANCHING OUT If you like these wines, you should also be able to invest with confidence in a fine Pauillac from Bordeaux, or a top Cabernet from Washington State—especially from the Red Mountain and Walla Walla districts.

"At its best, the unique, intense character and velvety feel of a Napa Valley Cabernet Sauvignon can challenge French Bordeaux. I consider it a real treat."

SYRAH

The state of California enjoys a Mediterranean climate, so it is a wonderful place to cultivate Rhône Valley grape varieties, such as Syrah. While Syrah wines display obvious elements of their European ancestry, they also tend to be more voluptuous and richer in style than the Rhône Valley reds. The best examples of Syrah wines have truly excellent depth, and just enough tannins to enhance their structure and complexity. They really are sexy, satisfying stuff!

COLOR Dark and inky, with a purple to ruby-red rim.

AROMA Elegant, stylish, pronounced; blackberry, spice, cedar, herbs, mint.

TASTE Voluptuous, smooth, big; complex texture, with a long and impressive finish.

BUYING The popularity of Rhône varieties in California means that large quantities are produced, and the quality is variable. I look for wines from Alban, Araujo, Bonny Doon, and Joseph Phelps.

ENJOYING My favorite matches for California Syrah are roast duck and black olives, or a very simple filet mignon. Of course, a glass of Syrah on its own is also a treat.

BRANCHING OUT Go global! Gather some friends and compare these rich wines with good Syrahs/Shirazes from Chile, South Africa, the Barossa Valley of Australia, and the Cornas district of the Rhône Valley in France.

RICH, DENSE REDS

WORLD WINES

ARGENTINA
MALBEC

Argentina adopted the Malbec grape variety from Cahors, southwest France *(see p.227)* in the 19th century. However, the Argentinian wines made with this grape are richer and much more fruity and intense than their French equivalents. In Mendoza, the Andean climate helps to produce a wine that combines the New World style—ripe and up-front—with more European-like acidity and firmer tannins. This makes it perfect for food matching.

COLOR Intense and very dark, inky red, with a ruby rim.

AROMA Distinctive; blackberry, plum, coffee, game, spice, and oak.

TASTE Rich, fleshy, refreshing acidity; balanced tannins; good length.

BUYING Go for younger vintages. I don't think these wines are improved by cellaring. Among producers, I recommend that you try Bodega Norton, Dona Paula, and Catena Alta.

ENJOYING Malbec can reveal fabulous qualities with many types of meat, but my favorite companion is roast rack of lamb cooked with herbs. Just fantastic!

BRANCHING OUT I think this wine can be described as halfway between a Carmenère from Chile and a Cabernet Sauvignon from South Africa. These are all very vibrant, rich, appealing wines.

MALBEC
Bodega Norton

CHILE
CABERNET SAUVIGNON

I'm a big fan of Chile, especially when I want an easy-to-drink red wine—nothing too intense, but very well made. These reds generally represent great value and are best for early drinking. Cabernet Sauvignon is the most widely grown variety, and the wine is fruity, clean, and concentrated. The dominant region is the Central Valley, but my own favorite is the Rapel Valley, where a cooler climate permits a slightly sleeker wine.

COLOR Garnet red, with a ruby rim and deep intensity.

AROMA Black currant, chocolate, sweet spice, hints of mint; ripe but elegant.

TASTE Charming, delicate, well flavored, with perfect balance.

BUYING Check the label for the Cachapoal and Colchagua districts—the top vineyard zones. Leading producers include Santa Rita, Los Vascos, and Casa Lapostolle.

ENJOYING These versatile wines can be enjoyed on their own, or with hearty foods—chops, steak, sausages, or tuna.

BRANCHING OUT New Zealand and South Africa offer similarly good value, if slightly stalkier, Cabernets to Chile. If you prefer smoother, fruitier wines, try New World Merlots.

SOUTH AFRICA
SHIRAZ

South African Shiraz has a smoother, cooler-climate feel to it than the full, fruit-driven wines of Australia. It's often closer to the French style—and some producers even prefer to call it Syrah. Even so, it still has the exuberance typical of Shiraz, and it represents a combination of very good value and excellent quality. You may see it in a blend with Cabernet Sauvignon, as this has been a great success here.

SHIRAZ
Backsberg

COLOR Deep plum, typical of the Shiraz style.

AROMA Rich black fruits; smoke, chocolate, and black pepper.

TASTE Exuberant and rich, with great depth and complexity.

BUYING Although most Shiraz wines improve with age, I can't recall tasting a mature one from South Africa. They are so delicious when young, who would bother to wait? Try wines by the producers Backsberg and Meerlust.

ENJOYING This complements steaks or spicy stir-fries very well, and it seems almost perfectly designed for barbecues.

BRANCHING OUT Try one of these wines alongside a Crozes-Hermitage from the Rhône and a Barossa Valley Shiraz. It seems to share many characteristics with both. Wonderful!

CABERNET SAUVIGNON

South African Cabernets combine vibrant black fruit flavors with a firm, more traditional structure. In this way, their style is somewhere between the New World and the Old. This combination has not only great depth, but also real balance and finesse.

These wines are usually aged in French oak, which gives them more class than exuberance—and some European polish. Their purity and complexity make them my favorite Southern Hemisphere Cabernet. You should also look out for blends of Cabernet with Merlot and other Bordeaux varieties, which emulate the classic French model. Some of the more adventurous blends employ a proportion of Pinotage, South Africa's signature grape variety, or Shiraz.

CABERNET SAUVIGNON
Rustenburg

COLOR Dark inky red to black, with purple nuances.

AROMA Black currant, plum, chocolate, hints of spice.

TASTE Rich and velvety, with perfect balance and great character.

BUYING Try wines from the Stellenbosch district. I recommend De Trafford, Rustenberg, and Rust en Vrede.

ENJOYING These Cabernets are fantastic with a steak, but they also give great pleasure on their own.

BRANCHING OUT The fruit and texture of these wines compare well with good Cabernets from Western Australia and the Rapel or Aconcagua regions of Chile.

"These are some of my favorite Cabernet Sauvignons—halfway between the jammy Australian style and the drier, tighter wines of Bordeaux."

AUSTRALIA
SHIRAZ

Australian Shiraz is the definition of bold and spicy wine. Although powerful, it is very approachable and easy to drink, even when young. This profile has done much to transform the Australian wine industry into a world leader during the past two decades.

Some of the best Shiraz wines come from the Barossa and Hunter valleys, two of the country's oldest wine regions. The Barossa, northwest of Adelaide in South Australia, may offer the ultimate expression of Australian Shiraz. Local creations, such as Penfolds Grange and Henschke Hill of Grace, are icons of the wine world. The Hunter Valley is north of Sydney in New South Wales, and its Shiraz tends to be more tannic and age-worthy. However, rainfall here makes vintages more variable. Most Australian Shirazes are broadly appealing, and you don't have to fork out too much for a bottle—which just adds to their charm.

COLOR A rich, dark purple to inky red, with a ruby rim.

AROMA Black fruits, spice, dried plum, tar, smoke, and eucalyptus.

TASTE Rich, profound, velvety, with refreshing tannins; very long finish.

BUYING This is Australia's signature wine, so I could write an enormous list of great producers. Among my favorites are Brokenwood, Clonakilla, D'Arenberg, Glaetzer, Henschke, and Penfolds.

ENJOYING Aussie Shiraz is made for barbecues, but I enjoy it with boldly flavored foods. Try it with game casserole. Also, use large glasses to maximize those amazing aromas.

BRANCHING OUT If you enjoy the immense fruit and weight of these wines, you will also like gutsy Shiraz (or Syrah) from South Africa, Chile, California, and the northern Rhône Valley of France, especially the Cornas district.

Another airline meal, another movie—all in the quest for wine

I remember well my first (and only, so far) trip to Australia. After 19 or 20 hours in the air, imagine my relief when the captain told us we were crossing the Australian coastline. I was desperate, by then, to get my feet back on the ground. Poor, innocent me. It took another five hours to reach Sydney! That's how long it takes to fly across Australia. It's so vast that the Barossa Valley is just as unique a vinegrowing area to Australia as Rioja is to the whole of Europe—and that's what makes it so difficult to generalize about "Aussie Cabernet" and "Aussie Shiraz." If I drove from Champagne to Chianti, I'd hardly expect to be met with the same wines—yet that's the distance that separates the Barossa and Hunter valleys.

CABERNET SAUVIGNON

Australia produces ripe, exuberant, and very attractive Cabernets that are winning fans worldwide. My two favorite sources are Coonawarra in South Australia and Margaret River in Western Australia. Coonawarra wines have really intense fruit, but with layers of complexity. Margaret River wines offer beautiful balance, fresh berry fruit, and fine tannins. They are more about class than weight, and can age very well.

CABERNET SAUVIGNON
D'Arenberg

COLOR Deep, inky dark cherry to garnet, with a ruby rim.

AROMA Obvious; dark cherry, cedar, tobacco, black currant, and chocolate.

TASTE Round and rich, but elegant and complex; firm tannins; good length.

BUYING Look for D'Arenberg, Katnook, and Wynn's Coonawarra Estate in South Australia, and try Cape Mentelle and Moss Wood from Western Australia.

ENJOYING Australian Cabernets are a dream with roast lamb and mint sauce, but I enjoy them at summer barbecues with kebabs, ribs, and sausages.

BRANCHING OUT Try these intense, juicy wines with similar, good-quality Cabernets from the Rapel Valley of Chile or South Africa's Stellenbosch district.

MATARO

This wine hasn't yet reached many store shelves, but it could be on the verge of huge success. Mourvèdre, known in Australia as Mataro, is generally used as part of a blend, where it brings structure and complexity to the finished wine. However, on its own it is amazing—very individual, firm, and solid, with marked tannins plus lots of wild, dark fruit.

COLOR Intense garnet red, with a purple rim.

AROMA Jammy black fruits; earthy, "meaty," and spicy, with dried herbs.

TASTE Velvety, full of character, and well structured, with ripe tannins.

BUYING This grape variety is rarely used on its own, but at least the Australians put it on the label. Try wines from Turkey Flat and Best's—both are great producers.

ENJOYING You definitely need a strongly flavored meat dish to go with this wine. I also like it with zesty pastas and most strong cheeses.

BRANCHING OUT Mataro is the deep voice in several harmonious blends—look for it on the label. If you can find a wine that is 100 percent Mataro, you will discover that its big structure is reminiscent of that of powerful reds from the Old World, such as Bandol.

RICH, DENSE REDS

WORLD WINES

SPARKLING

Traditionally the wine of celebration the world over, sparkling wine is an instant mood-lifter, and, whatever the quality, the first glass always tastes great. These wines are a feast for the eyes, too, the streams of bubbles rising through crystal-clear colors, from pale straw to golden yellow, or the most delicate of pinks to ruby red, all crowned with a silver rim. You will know a really good sparkling wine by the way its tiny, refreshing bubbles caress your palate, tantalizingly inviting you to take another sip. Light and dry, sparkling wines should leave your mouth feeling refreshed, and have discreet but fresh aromas of pear, apple, citrus, and floral tones. I defy anyone to drink a glass of sparkling wine without smiling—it really does induce a sense of *joie de vivre*!

STYLE PROFILE SPARKLING

A WORLD OF BUBBLES

The term "Champagne" is reserved for sparkling wines made in one particular area of northern France. However, Champagne now accounts for a mere 1 in 12 bottles of sparkling wine sold. Other parts of the world and other regions of France offer some excellent alternatives, notably *crémant* wines from France, Cava from Spain, and Asti from Italy. Australia, New Zealand, and California are making some good fizzies, too.

The single most important grape variety in sparkling wine is Chardonnay, but these wines are typically made from blends. The classic Champagne

"Joy and celebration, elegance and charm— sparkling wines have to be the quintessential party drinks."

CHAMPAGNE CELLARS
In the *méthode traditionnelle*, a sugar-and-yeast mixture is added to still, fermented wine, which then begins to ferment again within its tightly stoppered bottle.

blend is Pinot Meunier and Pinot Noir (both red grapes) and Chardonnay, each of which adds something different to the wine. Spanish Cava uses local grapes such as Macabeo and an ever-increasing amount of Chardonnay. Local grape varieties tend to be used in Italy and Germany, while in the New World, Chardonnay and Pinot Noir dominate.

IT'S ALL IN THE SPARKLE

The bubbles that give these wines their sparkle are achieved through a process known as secondary fermentation. In traditional methods (those used in Champagne or in wines labeled *méthode traditionnelle* or *méthode champenoise*), secondary fermentation is set off in the bottle itself, and a special stopper (later replaced by a cork) prevents the gas from escaping. More modern techniques are the tank method and carbonation. In the tank method, secondary fermentation occurs in a sealed tank. These wines can be good, but tend not to be as subtle as those made by the *méthode traditionnelle*. In carbonation, no secondary fermentation occurs at all. Gas is injected into the wine from a cylinder,

COOL CLIMATE CHARDONNAY
When Chardonnay grapes are harvested in the cool, northerly vineyards of Champagne, they are often only just ripe. This means they have high acidity, which in turn gives a good balance of fruit and alcohol in the resulting wine.

TASTE TRAIL

Sparkling wines made just with Chardonnay should be fresh and light. In sparkling wines that are blends, aromas should be clean but not specifically reminiscent of any particular grape variety. At the cheaper end is the light and refreshing **PROSECCO** from Italy or **CAVA** from Spain, made with Chardonnay and Macabeo. The classic blend of Chardonnay, Pinot Meunier, and Pinot Noir is used for the greatest of sparkling wines, **CHAMPAGNE**, but also for many excellent sparklers from California, New Zealand, and Australia.

ENJOYING Chill sparkling wine for about 30 minutes in the freezer or two hours in the refrigerator. To preserve the bubbles, don't "pop" the cork: hold it and twist the bottle, which should release the cork with a quiet sigh. Serve the wine in tulip-shaped glasses or flutes, which enhance the flow of bubbles; avoid coupe (saucer) glasses. Seafood (particularly oysters) and other very light dishes go well with dry sparkling wines. Match sweeter examples, such as Asti or Sekt, with cakes and desserts.

resulting in large, short-lived bubbles—and wines of unreliable quality. A good sparkling wine will display a phenomenon called the *cheminée*—a chimney of bubbles, rising from the bottom of the flute to the center of the liquid's surface; the bubbles then move out to form a circle around the inside of the glass. Cheaper sparkling wines may seem slightly metallic on the nose. If there is a hint of mushroom, the wine is "tired": drink it right away, as it will not improve.

DRINK OR STORE?

You don't have to buy big brands to get great sparkling wine: as all sparkling wines are blended, lesser brands can be just as good. But however much you spend, sparkling wines are not intended for aging; most Champagne is best drunk within ten years of the vintage.

FRANCE
CHAMPAGNE

Champagne is more than a sparkling wine—it is a catalyst for celebration, and a symbol of success. The very "pop" of its cork will enliven the mood of an entire room. Champagne also suggests romance, not least because of the romantic story of its origin. Legend has it that Dom Pérignon, a monk and the cellar-master at the Abbey of Hautvillers in north-central France during the 1690s, inadvertently started a "secondary fermentation" of the abbey's wines after they were bottled. The result was a more palatable drink with refreshing bubbles—Champagne!

Although the original techniques for making this sparkling wine are now much refined, the process is still long and difficult. Three grape varieties can be blended to produce Champagne, each of which grows best in one of Champagne's three primary sub-regions. Pinot Meunier thrives in the Vallée de la Marne, which stretches along the banks of the Marne River. This is a robust grape, providing fruitiness in the wine. It makes up the base for all but some of the finest Champagnes. Pinot Noir grows best in the Montagne de Reims subregion, just to the south of the city of Reims. This grape provides structure, depth of fruit, and longevity. Chardonnay succeeds in the Côte des Blancs area, south of the town of Epernay. This grape adds finesse and elegance.

Most Champagne "houses," the colloquial term for the major producers, buy their grapes from the region's thousands of small growers, and then blend them to create their house style. If you see the words *grand cru* or *premier cru* on the label, it means that the house has blended the wine using grapes from one or more of Champagne's specially classified villages, where local conditions mean that the grapes are of a higher quality than elsewhere in the region.

Apart from the blending, a Champagne's style is affected by the *dosage*—a process in which a mixture of still wine and sugar (known as *liqueur d'expedition*) is added to the just-completed Champagne. The amount of sugar added during *dosage* dictates the sweetness of the Champagne. Champagnes with no added sugar are labeled *Ultra Brut*, *Extra Brut*, or *Brut Zero* and are extremely dry. Moving along the stylistic scale: *Brut* indicates a very dry wine; *Extra-Sec*, dry; *Sec*, medium-dry; *Demi-Sec*, sweet; and *Doux*, very sweet.

Most Champagne is nonvintage (NV), meaning that it is a blend of wines from several years—a technique that ensures consistency of style. However, exceptional harvests result in the creation of vintage Champagne, which is a wine made using grapes from that year alone. Only in vintage years do houses deviate from the normal blend of their house style, and then only so they can make wine with even greater depth and finesse.

Another clue to quality is a set of initials often found at the bottom of the wine label. In descending order of quality these are: NM (*Négociant Manipulant*), which indicates that the producer has bought the grapes from one or more of the region's growers. Most of the Champagne houses are *négociants manipulants*. RM (*Recoltant Manipulant*) indicates that the grower himself has made the wine from his own grapes. CM (*Co-operative Manipulant*) indicates that the wine has been produced by a cooperative of grower-producers. Finally, be wary

CHAMPAGNE
Pol Roger

My voyage of discovery to the home of Champagne

I will never forget my very first trip to Champagne! I visited a small Champagne house just at the time of *assemblage*, when the winemaker creates the "base" of the Champagne—a carefully crafted blend of still, dry white wines. This is a crucial time, because it is the exact blend, or *cuvée*, that defines a house's individual style. I was given a glass of the still wine to try—ouch! It was so dry and sharp I could hardly drink it. It was hard to imagine that this harsh liquid could become the beautiful sparkling wine I love, but I knew that it is precisely because of the *cuvée's* high acidity that the finished Champagne—after secondary fermentation, when the wine gets its famous bubbles—is so crisp and refreshing!

of MA (*Marque Auxiliare*). While cheaper, it is usually Champagne of lower quality that has been created for restaurants or supermarkets.

COLOR Pale to medium gold, with silver tinges; fine, steady bubbles.

AROMA Elegant; fresh apple and citrus fruit; biscuit; flowers; mineral hints.

TASTE Complex, refreshing; creamy texture; delicate bubbles; long finish.

BUYING Among standard *cuvées* from the major producers, I recommend Bollinger, Deutz, Laurent-Perrier, Louis Roederer, Pol Roger, and (for deeper pockets) Krug. For truly special events, there is nothing like prestige wines such as La Grande Dame from Veuve Clicquot, Cristal from Louis Roederer, or Dom Pérignon from Moët & Chandon. Among the smaller, independent growers, look for Philipponnat.

ENJOYING Champagne is the ultimate aperitif. It transforms any gathering into a special occasion. Be sure to use tall glasses (flutes) to enhance the streams of bubbles. This wine works well with oysters or smoked salmon, and it's great with many Chinese dishes!

BRANCHING OUT
The aromas, texture, and finesse of nonvintage Champagne compare well with good sparkling wines from Sonoma or Mendocino counties in California, or from the Marlborough region of New Zealand.

CHAMPAGNE
Laurent-Perrier

SPARKLING

WORLD WINES

FRANCE
LIMOUX

Nestled in the foothills of the French Pyrenees, the town of Limoux produces two styles of sparkling wine. Blanquette de Limoux is this region's traditional fizz, which its producers claim predates Champagne. The second, "new" wine is the classy and elegant Crémant de Limoux, which was given appellation status in 1990.

Blanquette de Limoux must be at least 90-percent Mauzac—a local grape variety that is also known as Blanquette—with the rest made up of Chardonnay and Chenin Blanc. It has a light, bubbly structure and appley flavors, and is competitively priced. However, Crémant de Limoux is now the flagship wine of the region. It contains a maximum of 10-percent Mauzac, so the majority is Chardonnay and Chenin Blanc. The result is zesty, refreshing, and quite delicate.

LIMOUX
Château Rives-Blanques

COLOR Bright, pale to medium straw yellow, with silver tinges.

AROMA Youthful, aromatic; pear, peach, apricot; bread, biscuit.

TASTE Round and creamy, with lemony acidity; good length.

BUYING You are most likely to find wines from the Sieur d'Arques cooperative, but also look for Château Rives-Blanques and Domaine de Flassian (Antech). Buy the youngest wines available.

ENJOYING Blanquette de Limoux and Crémant de Limoux are both excellent "spur-of-the-moment" wines. You just need to chill them, pour, and smile!

BRANCHING OUT If you have the opportunity, try a Blanquette and a Crémant from the same producer side by side. The character of the Mauzac variety makes a significant difference.

Buying wine in Limoux—by the barrel, not the bottle!

In Limoux, down in Languedoc, there is a wonderful event called *Toques et Clocher*—literally "chef's hat and church." It originated with the church giving alms to the community. Nowadays it's more of a festival, with music in the street and a great deal of wine-tasting! You can try the wine and, if you like it, buy a barrel at auction there and then. After they have finished maturing, the bottles of wine are sent on to you. This is a great way to find out about this very promising region, which is especially well-known for its Chardonnay-based whites. A dynamic AOC, with fine quality and great consistency, it has recently focused its efforts into producing great sparkling and red wines. Limoux is one to watch!

LOIRE

The Loire Valley does not spring to mind as a region that makes top-class sparkling wines—but it is! Its climate and *terroir* are very similar to those of Champagne, and some of the Champagne houses themselves have set up subsidiary wineries in the Loire. Producers here use the traditional method to make sparkling wine *(see p.258)*, and the leading grape variety is the region's own Chenin Blanc.

COLOR Pale lemon to straw yellow, with silver tinges.

AROMA Fresh, elegant; green apple, citrus fruits, pear; mineral hints.

TASTE Charming and delicate; fine bubbles; balanced, clean finish.

BUYING The best Loire sparkling wines come from the town of Saumur—look for it on the label. Winemakers to note include Baumard, Les Vignerons de la Noëlle, and Bouvais Ladubay.

ENJOYING I think this wine is a great alternative to Champagne. It makes an ideal aperitif. Try it also with smoked salmon, or with seafood, such as oysters.

BRANCHING OUT A fresh South African sparkling wine made from Chenin Blanc will compare well with Loire, as do the *crémant* wines of Alsace, which are similarly light, appley, and refreshing.

DIE

Clairette de Die and Crémant de Die are two significant sparkling wines from the Rhône Valley. The Clairette, made from golden Muscat and Clairette grapes, is produced by the local *méthode dioise*, in which the bubble-making second fermentation is natural. The result is a gently sparkling, sweet wine. Crémant de Die is made exclusively from Clairette grapes, and secondary fermentation is by the traditional method, as it is with Champagne.

COLOR Pale golden yellow, with tinges of green.

AROMA Fresh, elegant; apple, pear, white peach, and minerals.

TASTE Delicate, with light, fine bubbles; clean, beautifully balanced finish.

BUYING This is a subtle wine, so don't mix it with crème de cassis to make a Kir cocktail—you will destroy its sparkle. Top producers include Jean-Claude Raspail, Cave Monge-Granon, and Domaine Achard.

ENJOYING These wines are an ideal aperitif. But drink them within three years of bottling to ensure that you get the most of their subtle texture, fine aromas, and complexity.

BRANCHING OUT You'll find that same, slight sweetness and scented quality in Asti from Italy or a Blanquette de Limoux from France.

CRÉMANT DE DIE
Jean-Claude Raspail

BURGUNDY

Crémant de Bourgogne can be an exceptional sparkling wine. Made in the traditional method using Chardonnay grapes, it easily matches some good Champagnes in finesse, if not depth. But because the wine cannot be sold under the label "Champagne," it is a much better buy. The best wines are from the region's cooler parts, including Chablis and Mâconnais.

COLOR Bright straw yellow, with green tinges.

AROMA Complex; baked apple, citrus fruit, pineapple, pear, nuts, and toast.

TASTE Smooth and round, with fine, fresh bubbles; long, flavorsome finish.

BUYING Many large cooperatives make this wine as part of their portfolio, but there are many good small producers, too. You will need to look around to find the best. I can recommend Caves de Bailly and Bernollin as good producers.

ENJOYING This wine works best as an aperitif with a few nibbles, but it's also great with crab, lobster, or any good seafood.

BRANCHING OUT If you enjoy this, try a fine New World sparkling Chardonnay, such as Green Point from Australia or Graham Beck from South Africa.

ALSACE

Crémant (sparkling wine) from the Alsace region of northeastern France is fresh and complex, with lots of personality. The wines are often blends built on Pinot Blanc grapes. I tend to prefer those based on Pinot Gris, as they seem to be richer and have better acidity. I suggest that you also try the sparkling rosés from Alsace, which are based on Pinot Noir. They often have finer aromas and flavors than pink Champagne.

ALSACE
Dopff au Moulin

COLOR Pale to medium straw yellow, with silver tinges.

AROMA Young and elegant; apple, citrus, flowers.

TASTE Clean, pure, and light, with well-integrated bubbles.

BUYING These wines are very popular in Alsace, so they are widely produced by the better cooperatives. I can recommend producers such as Dopff au Moulin and Gustave Lorentz.

ENJOYING Serve Crémant d'Alsace well chilled to enhance its citrus flavors. It's a great summer aperitif, and a lovely, subtle alternative to many Champagnes.

BRANCHING OUT Why not try Crémant d'Alsace with sparklers from Tasmania and Canada. They will provide a similar crisp style—and quite a talking point, especially if you have French guests!

SPARKLING

WORLD WINES

SPAIN
CAVA

The Catalan town of Sant Sadurni d'Anoia is home to the world's favorite sparkling wine. Yes, you heard correctly—Cava is more popular than Champagne! Recent sales have surged to such an extent that Cava now outsells all other sparkling wines.

There are two reasons for Cava's sensational boom: first, it is a high-quality wine produced by the same traditional method used to make Champagne; and second, it is an extremely good buy. But don't consider Cava a "discount" or second-class Champagne—it has its own very distinct character.

The traditional wine is a blend of three native grape varieties: Parellada for creamy texture and weight, Xarel-lo for complexity, and Macabeo for crisp acidity. In addition, the use of Chardonnay is gaining popularity for its delicate elegance. However, this practice is also stirring up a bit of a storm in the region, with claims that it is eroding the wine's authenticity and identity.

Cava is usually bone-dry, with gentle fruit flavors. Cava Gran Reserva, which is matured in winery cellars for about three years, has an even greater aromatic complexity.

CAVA
Freixenet

COLOR Medium lemon yellow, with green tinges.

AROMA Intense and youthful; pear, citrus fruits, and notes of exotic fruits.

TASTE Refreshing and clean; good, harmonious balance; lemony finish.

BUYING The twin titans of Cava are Codorníu and Freixenet. Also look for the wines of Marqués de Monistrol, Raventós i Blanc, and Agustí Torelló's Kripta.

ENJOYING I drink these wines as aperitifs, but if you like food with your fizz, match them with simply prepared seafood or other light and delicately flavored meals.

BRANCHING OUT If you like your sparkling wine to have some character—like traditional Cava—you are likely to also enjoy Blanquette de Limoux or Crémant de Die from France, and also good Rieslingsekt from Germany.

"Cava is often sold at a quarter of the price of Champagne, and the best is light and well balanced, and ideal for party receptions!"

ITALY
PROSECCO

The cool climate of the Veneto, in northeast Italy, is perfect for cultivating the Prosecco grape variety. Some of the crop is made into still wine, but Prosecco's flagship wines are its refreshing *spumantes*, which are made using the tank method *(see p.258)*. Prosecco is very slightly sweeter than many other sparkling wines, and it can be easily identified by the hint of bitter almond flavor at its finish. I think it's delicious.

COLOR Bright; pale yellow, with greenish tinges.

AROMA Clean, with citrus, green apple, flowers, and bitter almond.

TASTE Subtle and well balanced, with a nutty and ripe, exotic-fruit finish.

BUYING There are hundreds of producers, all making wines at different levels of quality. Carpenè Malvolti and Adriano Adami are two good names, but try to find a vintage-dated bottle—it will be well worth it!

ENJOYING Drink Prosecco as the Italians do—as an aperitif. I enjoy it as a refreshing accompaniment to lunch on the terrace, but it's also a perfect partner for a light summer dessert.

BRANCHING OUT Prosecco is a lightly fizzy sparkler, a characteristic it shares with Clairette de Die from France. If you find that the more aggressively bubbly styles of sparkling wine are not to your taste, look also for wines labelled *pétillant*, or perhaps try a bone-dry, *frizzante* Vinho Verde.

FRANCIACORTA

Franciacorta's dry, sparkling wine is the new star of Italy. It's produced in eastern Lombardy, where the alpine climate offers cool nights and warm days to maintain a high level of acidity in the grapes—important for the freshness of the resulting wine. Most sparkling Franciacorta is made using the Pinot Bianco grape variety, which gives fresh and fruity wines. If you prefer your sparkling wine to be creamier, try the fantastic Riserva.

COLOR Bright; pale straw yellow, with silver tinges.

AROMA Finesse, intensity; pineapple and hints of other exotic fruit; almonds.

TASTE Elegant, delicate; complex texture with balanced acidity; very long.

BUYING These are so delicious! Try one from Fratelli Berlucchi, Bellavista, or Antinori. For a little more money you can buy one of their Riserva Bruts.

ENJOYING These wines are the perfect accompaniment to roast chicken or any type of simply prepared fish. They also work well with seafood linguine, and are a pleasure to drink just on their own.

BRANCHING OUT I'd compare this with a Crémant de Loire from France. Both wines display the same freshness, weight, and bubbly feel.

ASTI

In the region of Piedmont, in northwest Italy, the town of Asti produces two sparkling wines—Asti and Moscato d'Asti. In the past, inferior-quality mass production undermined their potential (and reputation), but many small estates are now taking these wines more seriously. Of the two, Moscato d'Asti is the more sophisticated, with gentler bubbles. Asti is quite sweet, and very easy to drink. Fabulous fun.

ASTI
Gancia

COLOR Bright, pale lemony yellow, with greenish tinges.

AROMA Aromatic; peach, apricot; flowers; a touch of the exotic.

TASTE Light, with a lemony acidity and sweetness on the finish.

BUYING Gancia and Rotari (Mezzacorona) are two recommended producers. Drink these wines young. You can enjoy a number of glasses, since they're light and quite low in alcohol.

ENJOYING I love these wines as an aperitif, perhaps with a bowl of nuts. They are also perfect with apple tart or peach mousse. Just make sure you chill them well—the colder the better!

BRANCHING OUT If you enjoy Moscato d'Asti and Asti, expand your sparkling wine experience by also trying Prosecco, Clairette de Die, or Blanquette de Limoux—all light and aromatic sparkling wines.

SPARKLING

WORLD WINES

❶ PROSECCO is Italy's flagship sparkler. Look for "Valdobbiadene"—this is the best. **Seek out** Azienda Vinicola Col de' Salici, Carpenè Malvolti, Adriano Adami, Bisol. Make sure you choose a dry version (labeled Brut).

❷ CAVA from Spain can be truly excellent, and a great buy! It's worth paying a little extra for the higher quality of a *reserva* or vintage Cava. **Seek out** Marqués de Monistrol, Freixenet, Codorníu, Augustí Torelló Kripta.

❸ CHAMPAGNE is the greatest of the world's sparkling wines. You really get what you pay for: the more expensive the Champagne, the higher its quality. **Seek out** Ruinart (Brut rosé), Deutz, Veuve Clicquot, Pol Roger, Louis Roederer.

TASTE TEST: VINIFICATION

Does the traditional method really produce better-quality bubbles?

Champagne vineyard near Reims

"The quality of the bubbles in a sparkling wine gives you a good indication of the quality of the wine itself."

The three wines in this tasting have been made using different techniques to **produce the bubbles** in the wine. As always, use your eyes first—look at the **size and number of bubbles** in each of these sparkling wines. This will go some way toward telling you something about the characteristics of the wine and how it was made.

First, try the **PROSECCO**. This wine has **big bubbles** that rise slowly up the glass. Its nose is **light and airy**, with hints of **green apples and flowers**. There is **little density** and the palate is light, unchallenging, and pleasant. The bubbles are **short-lived**, which points to the fact that Prosecco is

made using the **tank method**: the wine undergoes its second fermentation in a large tank and is then filtered and bottled under pressure. As a result it **lacks depth**. Even if labeled "Extra Dry," it certainly isn't—but it does make a great base for a Bellini cocktail!

Next, try the **CAVA** from Spain. This wine has a **more distinct nose** than the Prosecco, more **smoky**, with aromas of **peaches and apricots**. Cava producers have been under pressure to use more Chardonnay grapes in their sparkling wines, thus emulating the producers of Champagne. Many have resisted that pressure, preferring to persevere with the **traditional indigenous Cava grapes**—Macabeo, Parellada, and Xarel-lo. More and more producers do, however, use the *méthode traditionnelle* or traditional method of production, where the

second fermentation takes place **inside the bottle**. Look at your glass: there are not too many bubbles but they **last longer** than those in the Prosecco, traveling slowly to the surface. The texture is **slightly oily** and the wine is quite **dry on the palate** with hints of **grapefruit** and a slightly **bitter finish** typical of Cava.

Finally, turn to the **CHAMPAGNE**. Pink Champagne is the only rosé wine that may be made with a mixture of **both white and red grapes**, and the basis of this wine is Pinot Noir. This wine has **numerous small bubbles** and a good *cheminée* (the bubbles rise up the center of the glass, and move toward the outside edge to form a ring). The wine is **fresh and crisp** on the nose, with **multiple layers** of **peach and strawberry** fruits and aromas that are carried through onto the palate.

GERMANY
SEKT

Sekt is fruitier, sweeter, and lower in alcohol than Champagne and many other sparkling wines. Cheap Sekt uses base wines from France or Italy, and the blend is merely made to sparkle in Germany, using the tank method *(see p.258)*. However, Deutscher Sekt denotes a wine made in Germany using German grapes, such as Riesling or Müller-Thurgau. Single-variety Sekts, such as Rieslingsekt, are the best examples of this style.

COLOR Clear; delicate pale yellow, with silver tinges.

AROMA Youthful and freshly aromatic; citrus, green fruit, and pear.

TASTE Refreshing textures; integrated fizziness and a medium finish.

BUYING This wine is popular across Germany, so it's easy to find—but it's hard to find the best! Heymann-Lowenstein is a personal favorite, and I also enjoy Kupferberg.

ENJOYING This wine should be enjoyed on its own, as cold as possible. Alternatively, drink it after dinner with a strudel or a similar dessert.

BRANCHING OUT If you have been disappointed by poor-quality Sekt in the past, don't give up! And give Asti a try, too—both wines have really been reinvented in recent years.

SEKT
Kupferberg

UNITED STATES
CALIFORNIA SPARKLING WINES

California produces some of my favorite sparkling wines, with wonderful balance and incredible complexity. Good examples also seem less austere than sparkling wines from many other parts of the world, a character courtesy of that same fruity exuberance associated with most of California's still wines.

The ability of the region to produce superb wines led some of the biggest names in Champagne and even Cava to establish their own estates in California from the 1980s onward. After a frothy start, the local sparkling wine industry has settled down over the past decade, focusing on the cooler zones near the ocean. Chardonnay and Pinot Noir grown here ripen very slowly, equating to low sugar content and high acidity at harvest. Although that may not sound good, it is in fact crucial to producing fine sparkling wine.

When choosing Californian sparklers, look for the following appellations from the North Coast region, just north of San Francisco: the Anderson Valley area of Mendocino County; the Green Valley and Russian River Valley of Sonoma County; and Carneros, which straddles the south end of both Sonoma and Napa counties. In addition, there are a few areas that produce fruit for good-quality sparkling wine in the Central Coast region to the south of San Francisco.

CALIFORNIAN SPARKLING
Domaine Carneros

In general, you will not go wrong by choosing something with Sonoma or Mendocino counties on the label. Provenance apart, there is no question that California's sparkling wines are a good buy—often priced about one-third less than equivalent Champagnes. When it comes to style, dry wines are generally labeled Brut, and this is California's most popular fizz. For a bit more weight and texture, look for Blanc de Noir—a white sparkling wine made entirely from Pinot Noir grapes.

COLOR Bright, pale straw yellow, with green tinges.

AROMA Intense, complex; green apple, citrus, pineapple, pear, and brioche.

TASTE Elegant and refreshing, but full of flavor, with good length.

BUYING I recommend that you try wines from Domaine Carneros, Domaine Chandon, Gloria Ferrer, Iron Horse, Mumm Napa, Piper Sonoma, Scharffenberger Cellars, Roederer Estate, and Schramsberg Vineyards.

ENJOYING I recommend Californian sparkling wine as an aperitif to accompany canapés. It can also be served with monkfish or other delicate seafood. Truly excellent!

BRANCHING OUT The fruit character and the texture of Californian sparkling wines is comparable with good sparklers from the state of Victoria in Australia. Why not give both a try?

CANADA
SPARKLING WINES

A cool climate is the key to producing good sparkling wine, which makes Canada a potential hot spot. The wine industry is anchored by Ontario in the east and British Columbia in the west. While Ontario is by far the most significant, British Columbia has a more consistent climate, and so it may be a safer bet. Even so, Ontario offers a real treat in sparkling ice wine—even reds! Amazing.

COLOR Ranging from light gold to bright pale straw yellow.

AROMA Fruity (nectarine, apricot), and a hint of nuts, honey, and exotic juices.

TASTE Delicate but bright and lively, balanced by a natural lemony acidity.

BUYING You are most likely to find the brands Jackson-Triggs and Inniskillin, and both are top producers. Other leading names are Blue Mountain and Château des Charmes.

ENJOYING Serve these wines well chilled with a delicate fish dish, such as sea bass. They make great partners for smoked salmon and cream cheese, as well as other light appetizers.

BRANCHING OUT If you enjoy the crisp flavors of these wines, then you will probably also like *crémant* from Saumur or Alsace in France, or Franciacorta from Italy.

AUSTRALIA
SPARKLING WINES

It's a well-known fact that Australia offers a phenomenal range of great red and white still wines, so it should be no surprise to hear that its sparkling wines are brilliant, too. Most of them are made by the traditional method developed in Champagne, and nearly all of these wines use the classic Champagne grape varieties, Pinot Noir and Chardonnay. However, Australian producers also employ their own world-famous expertise and cutting-edge technology to make high-quality sparkling wines that are second to none.

With regard to regions, cool climates are always home to the finest sparkling wines. So Victoria, which lies in the far southeast of the country, has traditionally been the most successful. Many vineyards here benefit from the cooling influence of the ocean, while others benefit from cool mountain air—most notably those in the Great Western district, where the producer Seppelt does amazing work.

Another of the best zones is the Yarra Valley, where leading producer Green Point (Domaine Chandon) was established by the French Champagne house Moët & Chandon in the mid-1980s. The vineyards here are planted with all the traditional Champagne grape varieties—Chardonnay, Pinot Noir, and Pinot Meunier—and support a range of great vintage and nonvintage styles.

AUSTRALIAN SPARKLING
Seaview

If you are seeking a real discovery, look no further than the up-and-coming region of Tasmania. As an island, and as the most southerly part of the country (meaning nearest to Antarctica), the cool ocean breezes are even more influential. In fact, they can be a real challenge to good still-wine production, but they are ideal for the crisp acidity and low sugar levels desired for sparkling wine. While the output is small, Tasmania's potential is well recognized in the wine world.

One final Australian sparkling wine deserves mention, and it's the local specialty: sparkling red Shiraz. It's pure fun in a bottle—try it!

COLOR Pale straw yellow, with silver tinges; good, steady bubbles.

AROMA Youthful and complex; apple, pear, white peach, and a hint of bread.

TASTE Harmonious and delicate; good, refreshing acidity, and good length.

BUYING These wines are built for immediate pleasure; don't cellar them away. Reliable producers include Green Point (Domaine Chandon), Seaview, and Seppelt.

ENJOYING Aussie fizz is priced for regular drinking—not just special occasions. It's a great way to start the weekend or enhance Sunday lunch.

BRANCHING OUT Here's an interesting experiment: why not compare wine from an Australian producer founded by a Champagne house with a French wine made by the parent company? For example, try Green Point or Domaine Chandon alongside Moët & Chandon.

SPARKLING

WORLD WINES

NEW ZEALAND
SPARKLING WINES

New Zealand sparkling wines are beautifully balanced, combining fresh flavors with a high level of complexity. New Zealand's great advantage over other New World wine producers is that it has a primarily cool climate. This enables the grapes to ripen slowly and retain the acidity that is crucial to the wine's sophisticated texture.

Marlborough, at the north end of New Zealand's South Island, is often cited as the best area for sparkling wines, including such fine examples as Cloudy Bay Pelorus. On the North Island, Morton Estate produces a fine Brut Methode Traditionnelle. Most of these wines are made by the traditional method from Chardonnay and Pinot Noir grapes, and they generally offer finesse similar to the best basic Champagne *cuvées*—but at a fraction of the price. I often choose these sparkling wines as alternatives to Champagne.

NEW ZEALAND SPARKLING
Morton Estate

Some of my clients can tell the difference, but many cannot. Either way, we all agree that these are truly remarkable wines.

COLOR Bright, pale straw yellow, with silver tinges; fine bubbles.

AROMA Delicate; green apple, peach, flowers, and hints of warm bread.

TASTE Fresh and elegant; creamy and subtle bubbles; long, lemony finish.

BUYING Cloudy Bay (Pelorus) and Montana (Deutz and Lindauer) are the big names, but try Hunter's and Morton Estate, too.

ENJOYING These wines match very well with seafood, such as crayfish, crab, scallops, and caviar.

BRANCHING OUT For similar elegance and complexity, try good-quality Crémant de Limoux and Crémant de Bourgogne—all are wines I would choose over quite a few Champagnes.

"New Zealand sparkling wines are beautifully balanced, with complexity, freshness, and class. I think they strongly rival the best of France. Try one—you'll see what I mean!"

SOUTH AFRICA
CAP CLASSIQUE

Méthode cap classique is the South African term for wine that has been made in the traditional method developed for French Champagne. Cap Classique wines also use the traditional Champagne grape varieties Chardonnay and Pinot Noir. The local variety Pinotage, as well as Sauvignon Blanc, Chenin Blanc, Riesling, and Muscat, may also be used, usually just in lower-quality carbonated wines. While South Africa's still wines have impressed wine-lovers around the world with their rapid rise to excellence, its sparkling wines have generally not yet reached the highest standards. But South African winemakers are determined to rank among the best, so this industry is one to watch.

CAP CLASSIQUE
Villiera

As with all sparkling wines, climate is the key, and the climatic differences across South Africa can be quite extreme. Look for the cooler areas: wines from Constantia and Paarl are among my favorites.

Constantia lies in the Coastal Region and is tempered by breezes from the Atlantic Ocean and False Bay. The Paarl district, particularly Franschhoek ward, is moderated by the rivers and hills that lie within its boundaries. Some of the best Franschhoek sparkling wines are produced by Graham Beck—in fact, they are so good that they were chosen to toast Nelson Mandela at his presidential inauguration.

Although, in general, I believe that there is room for improvement in South African sparkling wines—the bubbles are often a little too big and detract from the finesse—they are certainly on their way up in the wine world.

COLOR Bright; pale straw yellow, with green tinges.

AROMA Medium intensity; fresh fruit, including pear and apricot.

TASTE Elegant, delicate; well-integrated bubbles; refreshing finish.

BUYING Among wine regions, I generally look for Paarl. Among producers, I recommend Boschendal, Cabrière, Graham Beck, J. C. Le Roux, Simonsig, and Villiera.

ENJOYING Jumbo shrimp, oysters, and caviar are even more delicious alongside rich South African Cap Classique wines.

BRANCHING OUT The fruit and texture of high-quality Cap Classique compares well with good sparkling wines from Sonoma, California, and Victoria, Australia.

SWEET AND FORTIFIED

In the days when dinner ended with a rich dessert, sweet wines were a normal part of a meal. But even though these wines have lost favor, they continue to provide some of the best tasting experiences in the world. Most—even the great classics  like Barsac and Sauternes—are blends of grapes. Sémillon is the most important variety, but Riesling, Chenin Blanc, and Muscat are also used. Fortified wines are also usually blends, with spirit added to increase strength and stop the fermentation. The key grape varieties in sherry are Palomino, for delicacy; Pedro Ximénez, for a fuller type of sherry; and Moscatel, for sweetness. While the dark, figgy, red dessert wines of southern France are made largely from Grenache, an astonishing number of varieties are used—some 85 different grapes—to create port.

STYLE PROFILE
SWEET AND FORTIFIED

AIDS TO CONCENTRATION

In most cases, sweet and fortified wines are created when grapes stop fermenting before all their sugar has turned to alcohol. This "residual" sugar is what makes them taste sweet. In the case of sweet wines, such as Sauternes and Tokaji, fermentation either ceases naturally or is stopped by the addition of sulfur dioxide. In fortified wine, such as sherry and port, the producers add alcohol to kill off the yeast and thus halt fermentation. The best sweet and fortified wines are made from berries that have a super-concentration of sugar. Concentration is achieved in three main ways. First, the grapes may be dried in the sun. Second, they may be left in the

"Voluptuous, with a deep intensity, rich bouquet, and a silky structure, the best sweet wines have huge aging potential."

frost, creating so-called "ice wines." Finally, the grapes may be subjected to a benign disease, "noble rot," caused by the fungus *Botrytis cinerea*.

CONCENTRATED FLAVORS

Producers of dry wines fear botrytis because it can discolor grapes and give their wine undesirable flavors. But for the makers of such great sweet wines as Sauternes, Barsac, and Monbazillac from France, Trockenbeerenauslese from Germany, and Tokaji from Hungary, the noble rot is an ally, growing over the ripened grapes as they hang on the vines, shrinking and dehydrating them without breaking their skins. This concentrates not only the grapes' sugars, but their acid and flavors too, producing wines that are sweet but not cloying: a certain amount of acidity is vital in sweet wines to keep freshness and balance.

At their best, these wines are full and rich, luscious and subtle, with lemony acidity underlying the sweetness and a clean, fresh, and persistent finish. Whites should be bright, the color of pale gold or straw, with silver-green nuances turning

FREEZE-DRIED GRAPES
To make Eiswein, or "ice wine," grapes are left long after the harvest period in the hope that a hard frost will strike, freezing the water in the berries and so leaving a higher concentration of sugar in the juice.

THE NOBLE ROT
Since noble rot does not grow uniformly over the grapes, several pickings (by hand) are needed. This and other factors make production of these wines expensive—but the cost is well worth it.

TASTE TRAIL

Sweet wines may often seem expensive, but don't forget, you will probably drink only one small glass. **RIESLINGS** from Germany and from Alsace in France have quite high acidity, while **MUSCAT** makes the vibrant, exotic sweet flavors of Beaumes de Venise and Madeira, and **SÉMILLON** is the key grape for the great, honeyed wines of Sauternes. **SHERRIES** range from dry and salty to caramel-sweet and nutty, while **PORT** has the darkest flavors of all.

ENJOYING Serve most sweet and fortified wines "colder than cold." This will bring out the wines' acidity, which is the key to their freshness, balancing their sugars and preventing them from tasting sickly. If they are served too warm, the wines will feel heavy and sticky. If serving with dessert, the wine should be sweeter than the dessert, or the wine will taste bland. However, don't limit sweet wines to the dessert course. They can make great partners for some blue cheeses, or try the classic combination of Sauternes with foie gras.

to hints of gold. Port should be intensely opaque. All should have high viscosity, with extremely long "legs" in the glass *(see pp.76–7)*. The aromas change if the wine is botrytized—becoming concentrated, even mushroomy. These are complex wines, with intense, delicate aromas. Look for fig, marmalade, honey, pineapple, dried apricot, grapefruit, spice, chocolate, and licorice.

DRINK OR STORE?

These wines have excellent potential for aging, sometimes for up to 50 years. They can be costly, either because they have been aged and therefore stored by the winemaker or the retailer for many years, or because of the risk involved in successfully making them—leaving grapes on the vine long after the normal harvest in the hope that they will attract botrytis or will be frozen on the vine.

FRANCE
SAUTERNES / BARSAC

This is nectar! Sauternes is a small district located in the southernmost corner of Bordeaux, and it produces the most famous dessert wines in the world. These wines are a complex and luscious blend of Sémillon with a little Sauvignon Blanc to balance acidity and maintain freshness, and perhaps a small amount of Muscadelle for extra flavor.

The district of Sauternes surrounds the confluence of the Ciron and Garonne rivers, where the misty mornings and warm afternoons are perfect for the development of *Botrytis cinerea*. This seemingly magic fungus is known as "noble rot," and it is the key to producing the shriveled grapes necessary for these opulent wines.

Wines labeled as Sauternes are produced not only in the commune of Sauternes itself, but also in neighboring Bommes, Fargues, Preignac, and Barsac. However, Barsac has its own appellation, and its wines may be labeled as either Barsac or Sauternes. (Most high-quality producers seem to choose the former.)

Barsacs are somewhat lighter and not quite as rich as wines from other parts of Sauternes, but they are very sweet and aromatic. As with all Sauternes, they improve with age for at least more than a decade; the greatest wines thrive beyond 50 years.

Vintages vary in Sauternes, because the ripening of the grapes and the development of noble rot is a delicate

balance. As a result, top châteaux may forgo production in some years. Such scrutiny makes for remarkable wines, but it also means that they are rather expensive. Even so, Sauternes is a "must-try" among dessert wines.

COLOR Deep gold to bright straw yellow, with silver tinges.

AROMA Intense, complex; honey, dried apricot, pineapple, marmalade, acacia.

TASTE Oily, but balanced by a marked acidity; rich with a long, clean finish.

BUYING Among many great producers, I recommend Château Climens, Château Rayne-Vigneau, Château Rieussec, Château Suduiraut, and Château d'Yquem. That final name is a wine icon, and so makes for a rock-solid investment.

ENJOYING Sumptuous Sauternes is a classic match for foie gras or blue cheese. It also pairs very nicely with crème brûlée or apple tart.

BRANCHING OUT If you're bitten by the botrytis bug, head also for unctuous Hungarian Tokaji *aszú* and New World wines labeled "botrytized Sémillon"—or, for a lighter texture and bright acidity, try Bonnezeaux or Quarts de Chaume from the Loire Valley, or New World botrytized Riesling.

"The champion dessert wine, Sauternes delights the senses with its unique flavors and aromas. A real treat for any wine-lover!"

COTEAUX DU LAYON

These wines come from the heart of the Loire Valley, in the Anjou district. During the fall months, the Layon River brings morning mists that encourage the growth of noble rot in the vineyards, essential for sweet wine production here. Coteaux du Layon wines are based on Chenin Blanc, and I feel they are lighter, more upfront, and easier to enjoy young than Sauternes.

COLOR Beautiful golden yellow; intense and bright.

AROMA Complex, expressive; marzipan, peach, apricot, quince, and cinnamon.

TASTE Suave, oily, rich; balanced with marked acidity; full; very long finish.

BUYING Please try the wines of Château de Fesles and Château Pierre Bise. They're brilliant! Also, within Layon are two unofficial *crus*— Bonnezeaux and Quarts de Chaume. These sweet wines are quite expensive, but they are without doubt among the very best in the world.

ENJOYING These wines are always best when served as cold as possible. Try them with caramelized tarte tatin and vanilla ice cream. Gorgeous!

BRANCHING OUT Compare Coteaux du Layon wines with a fine *Beerenauslese* Riesling from Austria— they are similarly impressive, although the fruit characters might differ slightly.

ALSACE

Prime locations on the sun-soaked slopes of the Vosges Mountains in Alsace are well suited to ripening grapes for sweet wines. The best examples fall into two classifications based on the sugar content of the final wine. The lighter style is *vendange tardive*, while *sélection de grains nobles* is fuller and even syrupy. The wines are made from four different varieties: upfront, fruity Muscat; complex, pearlike Pinot Gris; spicy, floral Gewürztraminer; and sticky, lemony Riesling.

ALSACE
Rolly Gassmann

COLOR Pale straw to golden yellow, with green tinges; bright and pleasant.

AROMA Intense, elegant; ripe, exotic fruit; citrus; flowers.

TASTE Delicate, fruit-driven; long, harmonious finish.

BUYING The variety of styles is overwhelming, so it comes down to finding a good producer. I suggest Rolly Gassmann, Zind-Humbrecht, and Deiss.

ENJOYING The Rieslings are amazing with Bleu d'Auvergne cheese, while the Muscats are superb with peach mousse.

BRANCHING OUT Explore all the possibilities here: compare the same grape made as a *vendange tardive* and a *sélection de grains nobles*, or different grapes vinified in the same style.

SWEET AND FORTIFIED

WORLD WINES

FRANCE
MUSCAT DE BEAUMES-DE-VENISE

This wine from the southern Rhône Valley is made from a variety called Muscat à Petits Grains, and is classified as a Vin Doux Naturel (or VDN, literally meaning "natural sweet wine"). VDNs are made in the same way as port. This means that they are sweet and have a high level of alcohol (about 15% ABV). Even so, these are delicate wines with an appealing fruit structure. I think they're almost good enough to eat!

COLOR Bright straw to lemon yellow, with silver tinges.

AROMA Vibrant; very aromatic; exotic fruits; flowers, honey, and spice.

TASTE Rich and strong, with a delicate texture and long, fruity finish.

BUYING Many producers have this wine as part of their portfolio, but good examples from Domaine de Durban, Chapoutier, and Domaine de La Pigeade are particularly delicious.

ENJOYING Drink this wine while it is still young, and serve it well chilled. The locals tend to drink it as an aperitif, but it goes extremely well with light desserts or alongside a fruit salad.

BRANCHING OUT Try an Alsace Muscat *vendange tardive*, or a New Zealand Gewürztraminer. They all have similarly subtle aromas and weight.

RIVESALTES

Rivesaltes in southern France is home to two Vins Doux Naturels (VDNs)—Rivesaltes and Muscat de Rivesaltes. The fortified wines of the Rivesaltes appellation can be split into two categories, white and amber, depending on the blend of grapes (including Grenache, Macabeo, and others). White Rivesaltes has a strong, rich texture, while amber Rivesaltes is more like a fruity Tawny port. Muscat de Rivesaltes is made from two varieties of Muscat. Best drunk when it's young, it is a delicate, aromatic wine with a rich texture.

BANYULS
Domaine du Mas Blanc

COLOR Bright; deep gold to amber, with a silver rim.

AROMA Intense but elegant; quince, fig, apricot, almond, exotic fruits.

TASTE Rich, oily, and structured, but well balanced with a long, clean finish.

BUYING Domaine Cazes, Domaine la Casenove, and Domaine Lerys are all great producers.

ENJOYING These wines were my grandmother's favorite, and I'm a big fan of them, too. They are a good buy and delicious with chocolate tart.

BRANCHING OUT Try Rivesaltes with Muscat de Frontignan and Beaumes-de-Venise. Rivesaltes will be the stickiest.

BANYULS

Banyuls is produced on gravelly soil terraces around the town of Collioure, along the Mediterranean French coast near the Spanish border. High standards among a few dedicated producers result in Grenache-based fortified wines with huge complexity and finesse. For more subdued fruit, but more chocolate and spice flavors, try wine with the *grand cru* designation. I think it's more like a Châteauneuf-du-Pape than a fortified wine!

COLOR Opaque; dark garnet, with a ruby to tile-red rim.

AROMA Intense, delicate; fig, quince, prune, chocolate, licorice, and spice.

TASTE Full, rich; round, smooth texture, balanced by tannins and a fresh acidity.

BUYING This is a wine you can enjoy for decades. Look for the vintage-dated bottlings—they are out of this world. Domaine du Mas Blanc and Castell des Hospices are excellent producers.

ENJOYING I love these wines so much I would choose them over port to end a meal. They are delicious slightly chilled with cheese or a chocolate dessert.

BRANCHING OUT Taste this wine alongside a Tawny or LBV port. You'll find that Banyuls has more fruit flavors and is less alcoholic.

MUSCAT DE FRONTIGNAN

Frontignan is a small appellation of the Languedoc region, right on the Mediterranean coast near Sète. Muscat de Frontignan is produced using the delicate Muscat à Petits Grains grape variety, and it's one of the world's finest fortified wines. Its combination of depth and elegance is really down to the *terroir* of this tiny district— including the sea breezes that maintain Frontignan's refreshing acidity and balance.

COLOR Pale gold to straw yellow, with green tinges.

AROMA Youthful, intense, complex; pineapple, passion fruit; flowers.

TASTE Intense, delicate, and subtle, with a great concentration of flavors.

BUYING If the label indicates VDL (or *vin de liqueur*), it means that the bottle contains spirit mixed with grape juice. This is not the same as Vin Doux Naturel, and should probably be avoided. Among producers, Château de Stony and Château de Six Terres are very good indeed.

ENJOYING Serve this wine well chilled as an aperitif. It also works very nicely with any summer fruit tart.

BRANCHING OUT Wines that taste precisely of sweet, ripe, but fresh dessert grapes are surprisingly rare! If you love them, choose lightly fizzy Muscato d'Asti from northwest Italy for an aperitif with the same flavor, and keep the Frontignan for dessert.

MAURY

This sweet, fortified wine from Roussillon is made mostly from Grenache Noir. Despite its light texture, it's more complex than Banyuls. Vines are grown on hilly, stony schist soils far from the sea. This harsh environment gives nutty-raisiny fruit characters.

COLOR Bright dark cherry, with a ruby rim. Good depth.

AROMA Powerful and rich; spice, fig, cocoa, blackberry, and prune.

TASTE Ample, rich, vinous, and suave; fresh, balanced by mellow tannins.

BUYING Domaine Maurydore and Mas Amiel are among the best producers.

ENJOYING Serve this wine slightly chilled with chocolate tart.

BRANCHING OUT If you like this, you must try Banyuls, or a Tawny port.

RASTEAU

Rasteau, a little-known Vin Doux Naturel (VDN) of southern Rhône, is made from Grenache, the same variety used in Côtes du Rhône. The lighter style is a fine aperitif; the heavier Rasteau Rancio style is a true dessert wine.

COLOR Deep garnet, with a purple and orange rim.

AROMA Complex; dried fig, walnut, prune, spice, black currant, dried herbs.

TASTE Dense, well structured, and powerful, but harmonious; good length.

BUYING I recommend Domaine la Soumade and Domaine de Beaurenard.

ENJOYING Drink this wine with a rich Black Forest cake.

BRANCHING OUT This compares well to the two other sweet reds from southern France—Banyuls and Maury.

A cold, red, dessert wine? Absolutely!

I find that red fortified wines are hard to sell, and it's often hard to convince someone that they can be really delicious. People tend to be more comfortable with a white Sauternes or Barsac. I recall serving Maury to a customer who exclaimed, "But it's red, and it's being served really cold!" Then he tried it with a fig dessert, and he's never looked back. While the rule about white wines being served cold and red wines at room temperature generally holds true, there are times when it just isn't appropriate. Light reds like Beaujolais, for example, are great after 30 minutes in the refrigerator, and a full, rich white Côte de Beaune is wonderful at cellar temperature—not too cold. In the end, it's all about enjoyment!

SWEET AND FORTIFIED

WORLD WINES

SPAIN
SHERRY

The fortified wines produced around the town of Jerez in the Andalucía region of southern Spain are the oldest in Europe. Exports date back at least 700 years, and these wines were a global favorite during the late 19th century. Sadly, their popularity has plummeted over the past few decades—but they are worthy of a renaissance.

Most sherry is made from two grape varieties, individually or in combination. The first is Palomino, which accounts for 90 percent of production and makes a delicate, dry wine. The second variety is Pedro Ximénez (PX), which is dried in the sun after harvesting, to concentrate its sugars and so make a full, rich, dark wine.

Every bottle of sherry that you find will fall into one of two basic categories: *fino* or *oloroso*. The dividing line between the two is a yeast called flor. If a "blanket" of flor develops on the surface of the wine as it ferments—protecting the wine from oxidation and contributing a distinctive, delicate taste—it's a *fino*. If that flor never develops, the sherry becomes a deeper, nuttier-flavored *oloroso*.

Once the fermentation has finished, the wine is fortified according to whether it is a *fino* or *oloroso*. Pure grape spirit is added to raise the alcohol level to around 15.5% for a *fino*, a level at which flor will flourish during maturation, or to 18% for *oloroso* sherries, which prevents flor from forming during maturation. The wines are then matured using a complex system of fractional blending called the *solera* system.

There are several styles of *fino* sherry. Standard Fino is light and dry, while Manzanilla is delicate and pungent, with almond flavors. A darker, nuttier Manzanilla that has been bottled after the flor has disappeared is known as a Manzanilla Pasada. The equivalent for

SHERRY
Delgado Zuleta

Standard Fino is the amber, nutty Fino Amontillado. A simple "Amontillado" is a *fino*-style wine that is even darker and softer than Fino Amontillado, while "Pale Cream" sherry is just sweetened *fino*, and is of limited quality.

Oloroso sherries are "flor-less," intentionally oxidized wines with a deep brown color and a rich, nutty flavor. Most Spanish *oloroso* sherries are dry, but "Cream" sherries and Amorosos tend to be sweetened, lower-grade versions.

Finally, there is the rare, aged Palo Cortado. This begins as a *fino*, but then evolves as an *oloroso*, developing a rich nuttiness and a darker color.

COLOR Pale lemon to deep gold and dark, russet brown.

AROMA Intense, classy; nuts, citrus fruit, flowers, and a hint of caramel.

TASTE Round and complex; low acidity, balanced alcohol, long finish.

BUYING Among producers, I can recommend Argüeso, Delgado Zuleta, Emilio Hidalgo, Emilio Lustau, Gonzalez-Byass, and Hidalgo (La Gitana). If buying *finos*, always try to get the youngest wine available.

ENJOYING Serve dry sherry chilled as an aperitif or with tapas. Sweet sherry is best at room temperature with a cheese course at the end of a meal.

BRANCHING OUT If you can get hold of them, compare the full range of styles, from Standard Fino or Manzanilla, through to Amontillado, *oloroso* sherry, and Palo Cortado.

Sampling sherry in Jerez—a bar crawl with a difference!

The town of Jerez—the center of Spain's sherry district—is baking hot in the middle of a summer day. It is still too hot to eat large, heavy meals in the evening, which is why snack-sized plates of food called tapas are so popular. After 9 pm the tapas bars are full to the brim. Old men sit together as they have done for the last 60 years, young couples grab a bite to eat before a party, and suited professionals stand at the bar for a quick glass of sherry and a snack before going home. These locals obviously have their favorite bar, but as a tourist it is hard to resist visiting several in one evening. Every bar has its own food specialty, so you can eat a different course in each—and try a different style of sherry, too.

FINA
LOS 2
MANZANIL
LAS MEDAL
ARGÜ
Herederos de Argüeso
SANLÚCAR DE BARRAMEDA
ESPAÑA
N.º 132-CA
D.O. MANZANILLA SANLÚCAR

❶ FINO SHERRY is best drunk as soon as possible after bottling—so if you can find a wine merchant who looks to have a good turnover rate where sherry is concerned, you won't risk its having hung around for too long. **Seek out** Emilio Lustau, Gonzalez Byass, Bodegas Hidalgo La Gitana.

❷ MANZANILLA SHERRY is produced solely in the coastal town of Sanlúcar de Barrameda, where the sea air encourages a particularly thick blanket of flor yeasts and, in some wines, a distinct salty tang. **Seek out** Emilio Lustau, Delgado Zuleta "La Goya".

❸ AMONTILLADO SHERRY is in a more mature and softer style, its age rubbing the edges off the zingy dryness of Fino and adding more body and a nutty character. **Seek out** Emilio Lustau, Bodegas Gutierrez, Bodegas Delgado Zuleta.

TASTE TEST: AGING IN SHERRY

Explore the effects of aging in three different types of fino *sherry.*

Sherry aging in the *solera* barrel system

"The complicated solera *system for aging sherry produces some intriguing and delicious wines."*

The wines in this tasting are all types of *fino* sherry, which is made when a type of yeast (flor) begins to develop on the surface of the wine as it ferments. This **reduces** the wine's **acidity** by forming a **"blanket"** over the wine, preventing it from coming into contact with air and oxidizing. This results in a **more delicate** taste to the sherry than the *oloroso* styles, which **lack flor**.

Once fermentation is finished, the wine is **fortified**, and then aged using the **solera barrel system**, which ensures that the sherry's character remains **consistent** from year to year. The barrels are stacked, and the **youngest wine**, in the **top row** of barrels, is mixed with the **next oldest** sherry in the **row below**, which is then mixed with the still older wine in the row below, and so on, in a **blending "cascade."** The sherry is bottled from the **bottom row**, or *solera*.

Each row or stage in the *solera* system is known as a *criadera*, or **nursery**, and the different *fino* styles—standard Fino, Manzanilla, and Amontillado—spend **varying amounts of time** in the system.

Try the standard **FINO SHERRY** first. This should be the **youngest** of the three sherries in this tasting, and this is reflected in its **pale lemon yellow** color and **fresh, citrusy** aromas. On the palate, it is **light, dry, and delicate**, with hints of **saltiness and nuts**.

MANZANILLA SHERRY

traditionally passes through more *criadera* stages than Fino, but, like Fino, it is best drunk when **freshly bottled**. Compare its color with the Fino: you may be able to see that this **more developed** style has taken on a slightly **deeper colour**, although it is still a **pale yellow**. It still has the same **light body** and **delicate aromas**, but there is definitely **more depth** and complexity here.

Finally, sniff and taste the **AMONTILLADO SHERRY**. This is what *fino* sherry turns into with at least eight years' aging in the *solera*. The flor has died off, and the wine has therefore come into contact with the air, allowing it to oxidize. This gives the sherry a **golden amber brown** color, with a very complex range of aromas that include **chocolate, raisins, prunes, orange peel**, and **nutty hints**. This wine has a **higher alcohol** content than the other two and will last better in the bottle, and the texture in the mouth is slightly more **syrupy**.

SPAIN
MONTILLA

Montilla wines come from south of Córdoba in the Andalucía region. They are high in alcohol, but they generally are not fortified. Produced mainly from Pedro Ximénez grapes, they are similar in style to some sherries. Many supermarkets will classify them as dry, medium, or sweet (cream). The dry version is similar to *fino* sherry—having been aged under flor (a veil of yeast).

COLOR Bright; ranging from pale lemon to yellow to gold.

AROMA Fresh; citrus, spice, walnut, pear, flowers.

TASTE Clean, rich, round; balanced acidity and alcohol.

BUYING Until early in the 20th century, these wines were blended into sherry. Two producers who are excellent at demonstrating Montilla's own unique style are Pérez Barquero and Alvear.

ENJOYING Drink the dry version as an aperitif with salted nuts or smoked salmon. The medium or sweet styles work with many desserts—try pouring them over vanilla ice cream!

BRANCHING OUT There are obvious similarities between the dry style of Montilla and any *fino* sherry, perhaps Manzanilla, while the sweeter style is similar to a Cream sherry.

MÁLAGA

This fortified wine comes from the town of the same name in Andalucía. It is made from either Pedro Ximénez or Moscatel grapes, both of which make it very sweet. The harvested fruit is allowed to dry and concentrate in the sun before being pressed. As in port production, the makers of Málaga usually stop the fermentation to obtain the style they are seeking by adding neutral grape spirit. The wine may also be colored by *arrope*—a concentrated grape juice.

MONTILLA
Pérez Barquero

COLOR Dark chocolate brown, with orange nuances.

AROMA Powerful; tobacco, spice, coffee, licorice, prune, and walnut.

TASTE Rich and heady; strong but well balanced; full of flavors and character.

BUYING With appropriate storage, this sticky dessert wine can be kept for years. The older it gets, the better. The wines of Lopez Hermanos and Larios are especially delicious.

ENJOYING Málaga is a winter wine to drink with rich desserts; it's also great with mature Cheddar. I enjoy it with dark chocolate fondants.

BRANCHING OUT If you enjoy the sweetness and richness of Málaga, then you will probably also like sweet sherry and Setúbal from Portugal.

PORTUGAL
SETÚBAL

Setúbal is a fortified Portuguese wine from the Atlantic coast near Lisbon. It is made from the Moscatel (Muscat) grape variety. The production method is similar to that used for port: grape spirit is added to stop the fermentation and retain natural sweetness. The wine is then left in contact with the grape skins for several months, before being aged in casks for between five and 25 or even 50 years.

COLOR Distinctive tawny brown, with highlights of orange.

AROMA Pronounced and spicy; raisins, dried fig, and baked fruits.

TASTE Rich and heavy, but harmonious; syrupy, with intense, complex flavors.

BUYING The five- or six-year-old styles are fresher and have a more fruity character, while 20- or 25-year-old wines are more nutty and caramel-like. Among producers, Fonseca and Caves Velhas are reliable names.

ENJOYING Setúbal is a great partner with a variety of desserts. It works well with prune flan, chocolate tart, and rich Christmas fruitcake.

BRANCHING OUT While the Vin Doux Naturel (VDN) Muscats from France have some of the flavor of aged Setúbal, they lack its power. Try instead a 20-year-old Tawny port, a Jerepigo from South Africa, or even a red Banyuls Rancio.

MADEIRA

Madeira wines take their names from four local varieties. Sercial makes tangy, dry wines, while Verdelho wines are soft, medium-dry, and nutty. Wines made from Bual are rich and medium-sweet, with smoky complexity. Malmsey produces sweet wines with coffee-and-caramel characters.

Most Madeira is a blend of these grapes; to carry the name of a specific variety, the wine must be at least 85 percent that grape. Styles marketed as "Island Dry" or "Rainwater" are blends of the lesser Tinta Negra Mole grape.

After fermentation, Madeiras spend at least three months exposed to heat. This process, *estufagem*, caramelizes the sugars and oxidizes the wines, defining their character and enabling them to age for up to 200 years!

COLOR Dark brown, with gold to tile-red nuances.

AROMA Intense and delicate; plum, toffee, raisins, quince, and hazelnut.

TASTE Rounded; perfectly balanced; great depth and elegance.

BUYING Try Henriques & Henriques, Blandy's, Barbeito, and Cossart Gordon.

ENJOYING Dry Madeira is great with salted nuts. Bual and Malmsey work with Christmas fruitcake!

BRANCHING OUT The dark fruit flavors and the weight of a Bual Madeira can be found in LBV port, but you will notice that the "burned" (oxidized) Madeira character is missing.

MADEIRA
Cossart Gordon

"Often underrated, Madeira is an amazing fortified wine; its nose is brimming with delicious aromas, from nuts to chocolate, prunes, and apricots."

PORTUGAL
PORT

Oporto is the largest city in northern Portugal, and the namesake of the world's most famous fortified wine. Actually, the wine we call port is aged and shipped from the town of Vila Nova de Gaia, directly opposite Oporto on the estuary of the Douro River. But the vineyards and wineries that create port are located in the stark granite landscape 60 miles (100 km) up the river valley, centered on the town of Pinhão. The steep, terraced vineyards of this region are a wonder to behold—in fact, they are a World Heritage Site.

The Pinhão port-producing region is divided into three districts. Baixo Corgo is a small, relatively wet zone responsible for many inexpensive wines, while Douro Superior is the driest and most easterly zone. The greatest ports, however, are made in the central zone of Cima Corgo.

The vines themselves are a mix of local varieties, including Touriga Franca, Tinta Roriz, Tinta Barroca, and Tinto Cão. Each brings different attributes to the final wine, but the finest variety is Touriga Nacional. This grape is also being used for what I think are some fabulous table (meaning dry, unfortified) wines.

Traditionally, the grapes harvested for port are crushed by foot in large stone troughs called *lagares*. These are still in use for a few high-quality, limited-edition wines, but most producers now use mechanical crushers. During fermentation, when about half the sugar has turned to alcohol, the wine is run off into barrels containing (traditionally) one part brandy to four parts wine. The addition of spirit deactivates the yeasts, preventing further fermentation and leaving very sweet wines. The raw, young wines are then shipped downriver for aging and blending at Vila Nova de Gaia.

PORT
Quinta do Portal

When finished, port wines come in a range of styles. The basic wine is called Ruby. This is an appealing, fruity, nonvintage wine for everyday drinking. Smoother and more concentrated Ruby wines are labeled *reserva*. Tawny ports are smooth, complex, nutty-flavored, nonvintage wines that undergo long cask-aging. Look for age statements, such as "10 years old" or "20 years old" on the label. I think these wines are excellent served chilled as aperitifs. Late Bottled Vintage (LBV) port is wine from a single year that is aged in the cask over four to six years before bottling. This style has much more concentration and depth than Ruby wines, so LBVs are enormously popular.

The finest and most expensive port of all is Vintage, which comes from a single, exceptional harvest. After two years of cask-aging, the wine is bottled and should be matured for at least 15 years before drinking. In its youth, Vintage port can be nothing short of impenetrable, so I really recommend you don't open one before its 20th birthday. I suppose it's one of the few wines you can buy as a gift for someone on the day of their birth! Be aware that Vintage port is an unfiltered wine, so it accumulates quite a bit of sediment over time; it's all that deep coloring and tannin slowly settling out. As a result, this wine requires decanting, so you should stand the bottle upright for at least 24 hours—although two days is better—to allow the sediment to settle on the bottom before opening.

For the adventurous, one relatively rare style of port to try is Colheita. These single-vintage wines are aged in cask for a minimum of seven years, but

Brandy, folk music, and a barefoot party in a bathtub full of wine

Some port houses in Portugal's Douro Valley employ temporary staff to harvest the grapes and tread the wine. I say "tread" because that is exactly what they do—I know, because I've done it! The grapes are tipped into huge concrete or stone troughs called *lagares*. Wearing shorts and no shoes, I stepped through an antiseptic foot bath and into the *lagare*, which contained a rough mix of juice, seeds, stalks, and grape skins. The brandy flowed, and a folk band helped create a party atmosphere. Arm in arm, my fellow treaders and I stomped across the *lagare*, bringing our knees high up to our chests to push the skins down into the liquid. It was pleasure and pain combined. My feet and legs were stained purple for many days after!

some are allowed to age for 30 years. The wines have a complex, silky texture, and are a real treat.

All port producers have established house styles, so be willing to experiment and discover the perfect one for you.

COLOR Deep or opaque purple, with a brown rim.

AROMA Intense; dried fruit, spice, licorice, coffee, and almond.

TASTE Suave; vinous with a smooth texture; very well balanced.

BUYING I recommend a range of Tawny, LBV, and Vintage wines from Dow's, Quinta do Noval, Quinta do Portal, Taylor's, and Warre's.

ENJOYING This is an after-dinner drink, traditionally drunk with cheese. But I love to savor good port—especially if well-aged—with a bar of dark chocolate and a small cigar.

BRANCHING OUT Gather a group of friends and spend an evening comparing the spectrum of flavors and textures from a selection of styles—perhaps Dow's Ruby, Warre's Otima Tawny, an LBV from Taylor's, and an aged Vintage wine from Quinta do Noval. A wonderful way to pass the time!

SWEET AND FORTIFIED

WORLD WINES

ITALY
VIN SANTO

Vin Santo (meaning "holy wine") is an unforgettable treat from Tuscany. Production begins when harvested Trebbiano and Malvasia grapes are laid out to dry. Wineries then crush the raisined fruit at some point during the winter months—the longer it's left, the sweeter the resulting wine. The juice is fermented and then matured for three to six years in oak casks, which gives the wine its complexity and amber color.

COLOR Amber to deep gold, with a silver rim.

AROMA Elegant; jammy apricot; pineapple, honey, and almond.

TASTE Round, delicate; good acidity; good length.

BUYING This wine is often forgotten, but it makes a fantastic alternative to Sauternes. Antinori and Le Filigare are two top producers.

ENJOYING Try this wine with Italian biscotti or a nougat glacé, either of which will reinforce its slightly oxidized almond and vanilla notes. I also love it with caramelized apricot tart. Serve it well chilled.

BRANCHING OUT Strohwein (straw wine) from Austria has the same nutty finish, and Canadian ice wine has some of the sweet, tropical fruit flavors.

VIN SANTO
Antinori

MARSALA

Marsala has been made in Sicily since the late 18th century. Its production is similar to that of sherry, where fully fermented wine is fortified and then sweetened. The wines are labeled according to the amount of aging they have had—from *fine* (aged for one year), through *superiore*, *superiore riserva*, and *vergine* to *vergine stravecchio* (aged for more than 10 years).

MARSALA
Pellegrino

COLOR Deep amber to ruby, with orange nuances.

AROMA Full of character; dried fruit through to herbs and spice.

TASTE A powerful, opulent, and dry texture; intense, with a long finish.

BUYING Note the following style indications: *secco* (dry), *semi-secco* (medium), and *dolce* (sweet). I advise that you stay away from flavored versions. Pellegrino and de Bartoli are good producers.

ENJOYING Try good Marsala with creamy blue cheese, or even pecan tart. You can serve it chilled or at room temperature. Personally, I like it chilled.

BRANCHING OUT The texture and sweetness of these wines is reminiscent of Recioto della Valpolicella, as well as sweet sherry and Málaga from Spain.

MUSCATO

I am a great fan of these vibrant, light-hearted wines from the Asti district of Piedmont. They have a delicate sweetness that simply makes my mouth water! I think of Muscato d'Asti as a baby version of Muscat de Beaumes-de-Venise from France *(see p.278)*, because it has a lighter structure and a slight fizziness that enhances its fruity freshness. Perfect on a summer afternoon!

COLOR Limpid; pale straw to lemon yellow; bright, with green tinges.

AROMA Subtle and charming; mango, lychee, papaya, citrus, and melon.

TASTE Light, refreshing; pleasant hints of fizz and a clean, fruity finish.

BUYING There is also a still version, which can be difficult to obtain, and a sparkling style (*spumante*). In both cases, the wine is low in alcohol and doesn't improve with age. Among producers, I recommend Banfi.

ENJOYING Drink this wine as young as possible—it will be both fresher and more fun. Serve it well chilled as a superb aperitif or to complement a peach mousse.

BRANCHING OUT Muscat de Frontignan from France is the closest match—but don't forget that sweet, sparkling Moscato d'Astis have the same grapey flavor.

HUNGARY
TOKAJI

This wine is a Hungarian national treasure. Its fame stretches across both history and the globe: Louis XIV once declared it to be "the wine of kings and the king of wines." Historically, the village of Tokaj, located along the Tisza River in the northeast corner of Hungary, produced dry white wines. However, a threatened attack by the Turks during the 17th century postponed the harvest, leaving the local Harslevelu, Furmint, and Muscat grapes to shrivel on the vines. When this overripe fruit was eventually pressed, it produced the exceptional dessert wine that we know today.

The Tokaj region is well suited to producing sweet wines—warm weather and mists from the Tisza River and its tributaries provide perfect conditions for the growth of *Botrytis cinerea*, the benevolent fungus that causes "noble rot."

Tokaji is made in three categories: *szamorodni*, *aszú*, and *aszú eszencia*. *Szamorodni* is made with all the grapes that are left over at the end of the harvest—ripe, overripe, botrytized (affected by noble rot), and even rotten! The resulting table wine is dark yellow, sometimes sweet and sometimes dry, but always strong and less refined than the other Tokajis.

In my view, Tokaji *aszú* wines are the best. These are made using ultraripe, late-harvested, botrytized grapes. After the juice has been squeezed and fermented, the grapes themselves are crushed into a pulp, which is added to the wine to create the desired level of sweetness—something traditionally measured in "*puttonyos*"—before being matured. Each bottle of Tokaji *aszú* lists this *puttonyos* rating, ranging from three (least sweet) to six (most sweet).

Finally, *eszencia* is an *aszú* made using the best botrytized grapes from the best vineyards. These grapes exude little juice, but it is especially sweet and complex. The resulting wine is thick, and yet refreshing rather than cloying. *Eszencia* takes decades to mature and is incredibly rare and expensive. The best Tokaji wines can age for centuries in the bottle!

COLOR Deep golden yellow, with straw to orange tinges.

AROMA Intense; dried apricot, honey, walnut, raisin, prune, and sweet spice.

TASTE Voluminous and rich; good intensity and complexity.

BUYING Try the five- or six-*puttonyos* wines of producers such as Crown Estates, Disznókö, Oremus, Royal Tokaji, and the great István Szepsy.

TOKAJI
Crown Estates

ENJOYING Unctuous Tokaji *aszú* pairs well with foie gras and creamy blue cheeses. It's also a treat with apple tart.

BRANCHING OUT The only comparison can be with Sauternes—although some of the botrytized Sémillons from the New World are starting to challenge these two European aristocrats.

AUSTRIA
SWEET WINES

The finest sweet wines of Austria are produced around the Neusiedler See, a lake near the border with Hungary. Lots of sunshine and the high humidity caused by the lake promote the development of noble rot, which concentrates the grape sugars. In order of increasing sweetness, the labels indicate *Auslese*, *Beerenauslese*, and *Trockenbeerenauslese*. Also look for Ausbruch, which is a rare, complex dessert wine produced in the town of Rust.

COLOR Beautiful deep straw yellow, with golden highlights.

AROMA Concentrated and delicate; apricot, pineapple, flowers, and peach.

TASTE Perfectly balanced and structured; ripe flavors; great length.

BUYING Look for "Neusiedlersee" on the label of the finest wines; they are worth cellaring for up to a decade. Be aware that the three ascending degrees of sweetness correspond to rising prices, too. Nikolaihof, Knoll, and Willi Opitz are top producers.

ENJOYING One of my favorite memories of wine and food matching is an Austrian *Trockenbeerenauslese* with a creamy blue cheese—I can still taste it 10 years later!

BRANCHING OUT The weight and spectrum of flavors of a *Beerenauslese* compare well to an Alsatian *vendange tardive* Riesling or a botrytized Riesling from the New World.

SWEET AND FORTIFIED

WORLD WINES

TASTE TEST: VINIFICATION IN DESSERT WINES

Compare four sweet dessert wines made using different techniques.

❶ ❷ ❸ ❹

❶ ICE WINE is a fruity and intense style made from frozen grapes in Canada and Germany. **Seek out** From Canada, Faldo Estates, Inniskillin, Peller Estates, Château des Charmes.

❷ BOTRYTIZED WINE is made from grapes desiccated by *Botrytis cinerea*, the "noble rot." **Seek out** Elderton (Sémillon), Heggies Vineyard Estate (Riesling), Casa del Toqui (Sémillon), Château Suduiraut (Sauternes), Yalumba (Riesling).

❸ FORTIFIED MUSCAT retains much of the Muscat grape's sweetness, because fermentation is halted in the winery, stopping all the sugar from turning to alcohol. **Seek out** Château de Stony, Château de la Peyrade, M. Chapoutier, Domaine D'Arain.

❹ VIN SANTO is an Italian specialty from the Tuscany region, a dessert wine made from sun-dried grapes and aged for several years in the barrel. **Seek out** Antinori, Filigare, Avignonesi.

"The secret to the complexity of the best sweet wines lies in the painstaking, almost magical nature of their vinification."

Dessert wines are sweet because they have **residual sugar**. This means that their fermentation was **stopped** before all the sugar in the grapes **turned to alcohol**. Winemakers can therefore control the **sweetness** of their wine by deciding at which point of **ripeness** they harvest the grapes and at which point to **arrest the fermentation**. There are also several different techniques used to achieve a **high concentration of sugar** in the grapes either before or after they have been picked.

First try the **ICE WINE**. The grapes used to make this wine are **left on the vine** long into fall in the hope that they will **freeze** on the vine, and so will have a more **concentrated juice** when pressed. The wine has a set of aromas that are **sweet, ripe, and unctuous** at the same time as being **delicate and floral**. The **acidity is high** because the grapes have been grown in a cool climate, and this keeps the wine tasting **fresh** as well as sweet.

The complexity of aromas that is achieved in **BOTRYTIZED WINES**, made with grapes affected by the coveted botrytis mold, is amazing; layer after layer of aromas include **dried apricots, caramelized orange, spice**, and sometimes hints of **mushroom**.

In the mouth the wine is **intensely rich** but with enough acidity to **lift the weight** and balance the wine.

Fortified **MUSCAT** is vinified in a much more down-to-earth way: **grape spirit** is added to the wine to kill the yeast and **stop the fermentation**. This wine has a pleasant but **not particularly complex** set of aromas—**grapey**, with hints of **apricot and peach**.

The final wine is the **VIN SANTO** from Italy, made using grapes that are **left to dry out** on straw mats after picking. The dehydrated grapes are pressed and fermented, and the wine is **aged in oak** for three to six years. This gives the wine its **dark amber** colour and complex aromas of **apricot jam, pineapple, honey, and almond**.

AUSTRIA
EISWEIN

In my view, Austria makes the best ice wines in the world, offering complex flavors and zippy, lemony acidity. As elsewhere, the grapes are left on the vines until the onset of winter freezes the water within them, concentrating the sugars into a syrupy nectar.

COLOR Distinctive bright gold, with nuances of green.

AROMA Complex; ranging from citrus to crystallized exotic fruit and flowers.

TASTE Subtle and syrupy; persistent, concentrated, clean finish.

BUYING These wines are among the longest-lived dessert wines. Try the work of Willi Opitz and Salomon Undhof.

ENJOYING Serve well chilled with blue cheese or tarte tatin.

BRANCHING OUT Try Canadian ice wines made from Riesling, which are also sweet and complex.

STROHWEIN

Strohwein means "straw wine"—the grapes used in this wine are left out to dry on straw mats, usually in the wineries' lofts. This concentrates sugars as well as elements of the aroma and flavor. Strohwein is both complex and amazingly delicious.

COLOR Bright; deep gold, with straw to silver highlights.

AROMA Amazingly intense! Maple syrup, honey, ripe fruits, toffee apple.

TASTE Rich and ample; syrupy, but well structured and perfectly balanced.

BUYING I am especially excited by the wines of producers such as Willi Opitz and Helmut.

ENJOYING Try this wine well chilled with pear tart and roasted almonds, or even pistachio ice cream.

BRANCHING OUT Sample this alongside Italian Vin Santo. Both have a nutty finish, even though the production processes differ.

EISWEIN
Willi Opitz

GERMANY
SWEET WINES

German sweet wines are some of the best I have ever tried. They have excellent acidity to balance their sweet richness with a clean, fresh finish. Wines labelled *Auslese* will be sweet, but fairly light. *Beerenauslese* and *Trockenbeerenauslese* wines are sweeter, but more complex because they are made with riper fruit. *Trockenbeerenauslese* wines have also been affected by the fungal disease known as noble rot, which gives them an almost magical appeal. German Eiswein is also fantastic—very sweet, but never cloying, and with excellent balance.

COLOR Deep straw to golden yellow, with silver tinges.

AROMA Intense, elegant; fresh; dried apricot; citrus and exotic fruit; smoke.

TASTE Rich and opulent, underlined by a pronounced, balancing acidity; complex.

BUYING Germany gives more attention to this wine style than any other country, so there are many fine producers, such as Gunderloch and Selbach-Oster.

ENJOYING When well chilled, these wines are absolutely magical with foie gras. They also work extremely well with most fruit-based desserts.

BRANCHING OUT Sauternes and Barsac from Bordeaux have the rich but clean sweetness of a *Beerenauslese*, while the sweet wines of the Loire have even zingier acidity.

"Unique and special, Eiswein is truly an experience not to be missed! It has an intense sweetness and complexity, perfectly balanced by a wonderful lemony acidity."

CANADA
ICE WINE

This is the flagship of Canadian wine. It's made using Vidal or Riesling grapes, which are left on the vines until very late in the season. In the bitter cold conditions, the water inside them freezes, concentrating their sugars and flavors. Ontario's Niagara Peninsula has a perfect climate for producing this kind of wine, but look also for ice wines from British Columbia.

COLOR Lively, bright straw yellow, with green tinges.

AROMA Elegant; pineapple, peach, apricot, caramelized apple, and citrus.

TASTE Rich, opulent, and complex; exceptional lemony acidity; long finish.

BUYING Canada is the world's largest and most consistent producer of ice wines. I think they are delicious, and my favorite names include Inniskillin, Peller, and Château des Charmes.

ENJOYING These wines are especially rich and complex, and great with crème brûlée or caramelized pears. They also work well with sticky-toffee pudding or crêpes Suzette.

BRANCHING OUT Contrast Canadian ice wine with the more syrupy *sélection de grains nobles* Riesling from Alsace.

AUSTRALIA
MUSCAT LIQUEUR

The Australian Muscat grape has dark skin, so it's known locally as "Brown Muscat" or sometimes "Tokay." The wine is produced by an unusual mix of techniques. Overripe grapes are partly fermented and then fortified with spirit (like port). The wine is then matured using a *solera* system (like sherry) under a sun-heated roof (like Madeira). The result is a wonderfully rich wine. Why not taste it and see for yourself?

MUSCAT LIQUEUR
Brown Brothers

COLOR Opaque; dark brown, with a toffee rim.

AROMA Intense, pronounced; chocolate, toffee, almond, licorice, and vanilla.

TASTE Rich and heavy; balanced by a fine freshness and a long, complex finish.

BUYING These wines are part of the foundation of the Australian industry. The leading producer is Brown Brothers, but I also like the wines of Mick Morris.

ENJOYING Serve these wines well chilled. I think they're best at the end of a meal—perhaps with a chocolate dessert.

BRANCHING OUT Moscatel de Setúbal from Portugal and Pedro Ximénez (PX) sherries are similarly sticky treats with dark, complex flavors.

SOUTH AFRICA
JEREPIGO

Jerepigo is one of South Africa's specialties: a quality dessert wine made principally from Muscat à Petits Grains grapes. Unlike other wines, Jerepigo is fortified before, not during, fermentation. As a result, the alcohol level is quite high, but it is balanced by the wine's high level of residual sugar. Jerepigo's aromas are fresh and youthful, with distinctive notes of dried fig and exotic fruits—the signature of a Muscat.

COLOR Deep gold to straw yellow, with greenish tinges.

AROMA Elegant and powerful; dried fig, pineapple, mirabelle plum, flowers.

TASTE Strong, opulent, oily, and rich; great intensity; flavorsome finish.

BUYING Drink these wines young—they do not benefit from aging. Du Toitskloof Cellar and KWV are recommended producers.

ENJOYING This wine is consumed mostly within South Africa, and can be hard to locate elsewhere; but if you do come across some, try it with a fig tart.

BRANCHING OUT If you like Jerepigo, try Muscat de Rivesaltes from France—it has a similar sweet stickiness.

JEREPIGO
Du Toitskloof Cellar

PART 3
WINE:
A USER'S GUIDE

HOME AND AWAY

ENJOYING WINE AT HOME

I hope that this book helps you broaden your wine horizons, and demonstrates that there is a wine to match every occasion, however grand or humble. Wine doesn't have to be expensive in order to make an occasion memorable; while you may well choose a vintage Champagne to celebrate the marriage of your daughter with friends and family, a less expensive Cava will certainly make a summer cookout go with a swing. Fine wines that need to be decanted in advance may be your choice for that special dinner party, but if friends drop in unexpectedly, then you need a wine that will taste great as soon as the cork is pulled.

My brother-in-law still remembers the day he dropped in one Saturday morning to borrow a lawnmower. It was early spring and the sun was shining for what seemed like the first time in months. The children were playing in the yard, so we sat outside to chat. I opened a bottle of California Viognier and we sipped it as we talked. That wine was the perfect bottle for the moment— no special occasion, no ceremony, just friends, sunshine, and delicious wine!

WINE IN RESTAURANTS

Choosing wine in a restaurant is a potential minefield! Faced with a wine list full of names you have never heard of, and a table full of fussy diners who have all chosen different dishes from the menu, how can you make the right choice? My advice is simple; keep to what you know. You don't need to know the names of producers, or even vintages. You know now which grape varieties deliver which wine styles, depending on where they grow, and, armed with the ten golden rules

FAMILY GET-TOGETHER
Even the most spontaneous celebration can be turned into a memorable event with a well-chosen wine that captures the spirit of the occasion.

NEGOTIATING A WINE LIST
Choose from the menu first, and keep a budget for your wine in mind. Every list contains "safe," reliable choices—but a good wine waiter will enjoy helping you choose something new.

AT A FORMAL TASTING
A tasting organized by a wine merchant *(facing page)* will typically offer half a dozen wines for you to compare and discuss.

of food and wine matching on pages 320 to 333, you should be able to make an educated choice. Of course, you should welcome any help from a knowledgeable wine waiter—this is where good sommeliers come into their own. If they do their job well, they can turn a pleasant evening into a truly memorable one. They will listen carefully to what you say you enjoy drinking, bearing in mind what you have ordered to eat, and will be sensitive and respectful of your budget. Hopefully they will guide you toward wines from the restaurant's list that will perfectly complement your meal.

COURSES AND TASTINGS

Most people I know in the wine trade will admit that the more they learn about wine, the more they realize how much there is to learn! The world of wine is always expanding and is changing faster than ever. If you want to learn more, try some of the suggested Taste Tests in this book with like-minded friends—once you become unselfconscious about discussing aromas and styles, then attending a more formal tasting organized by a local wine merchant, or even joining a wine appreciation group or a tasting course at a community college, will be an exciting rather than a daunting prospect. There are also many specialty travel agents who arrange wine vacations and tasting trips to wine regions around the world: this is a great way to meet new friends and taste some of the world's best wines *in situ*.

GRAND VIN DE BORDEAUX

...EAU PAPE CLÉ...

...AND CRU CLASSÉ DE GRA...

...PPELLATION PESSAC-LÉOGNAN CONT...

PESSAC - LÉOGNAN

1998

...U PAPE CLÉMENT, PROPRIÉTAIRE A PESSA...

...N BOUTEILLE AU C...

PRODUCE OF FRANCE

BUYING AND STORING WINE

A little knowledge about wine styles makes a trip to your wine seller much more fun and exciting—even if you buy from your local supermarket. If you are looking for wine for a specific occasion, then you will probably have an idea of the style you want and why, and how much you want to spend. A knowledgeable  and friendly wine retailer will be able to guide your choice. If you are investing in wines for the future, then I cannot recommend too strongly that you seek the advice of a specialty wine merchant, who can prevent you from making costly mistakes. If you are buying to broaden your knowledge, then again, a specialist, or perhaps a wine club, may be the route for you. But if you are buying simply for fun, then the world of wine is before you on the shelves; experiment and enjoy!

BUYING WINE

FROM SUPERMARKET TO SPECIALIST

Most people buy their wine from a supermarket along with the groceries, or from liquor stores. Price alone is not always a guide to quality, and a little knowledge about how wines are labeled *(see pp.62–9)* will pay rich rewards. Sometimes a helpful store clerk can provide some educated guidance, and many wine retailers now have a selection of bottles open in the store for customers to try. A number of them also have tastings in the evenings where either the manager of the store or a visiting wine expert will take you through an array of wines.

A growing number of people buy their wine from wine clubs by mail order. You have to buy wines by the case, or mixed case, from these clubs, but the advantage is that they have their own buyers who source the wines direct from the

"When I taste a wine, I give it a rating out often based on its value for money—for me, it's got to deliver quality at the right price."

producers. As long as you are prepared to experiment with new wines and different styles, finding a club or a mail order retailer that reliably supplies wines that you enjoy can be an excellent way of exploring the world of wine.

Buying wine on the Internet is, of course, another relatively new avenue. There are many "virtual" wine companies on the net, but you will also find that some of the best wine merchants around the country offer their wines online. As with a club, you will probably have to buy by the case.

Buying wine at auction is not for the faint-hearted! There is always a tasting before the auction, which can give you some idea of what you are buying, but it is very important to also check on the history of previous ownership of the wine, because how it has been cellared up to this point can have a major effect on its quality.

HOW MUCH TO BUY?

When buying wine for a dinner or cocktail party, I always assume that one bottle is enough for four generous glasses. I allow two glasses of red wine and one-and-a-half to two of white per person. When serving Champagne, I allow six glasses per bottle, and plan for two glasses per person.

WINE AUCTION
If you buy at auction, do your homework and make sure the wine has been kept well. You should know exactly what it is you are bidding for and set a realistic price limit.

COMPARING NOTES
When I buy wines for my clients and customers *(facing page)*, I must put my personal tastes aside and bear in mind their needs and preferences. It's not too arduous a job!

STORING AND CELLARING

THE CASE FOR DRINKING UP

There are people who steadfastly believe that if you buy a cheap wine and then keep it for ten years in a dark cupboard, it will magically transform itself into something much better—and be worth considerably more. Would that this were so! The disappointing fact is that in nearly every case, the wine that was tucked away so carefully and kept guard over for so many years will have become sour and undrinkable. The best that you can usually hope for—and this is generally from only the very sturdiest red wines—is that they will more or less have remained the same while taking up valuable storage space. Lower-priced or even mid-priced wines bought at the supermarket or liquor store should, as a general rule, be drunk within one or (at most) two years of purchase.

STORAGE MONITOR
A combination thermometer and hygrometer allows you to check the temperature and humidity levels of your wine store.

SHORT-TERM SOLUTIONS
Even wines you will drink within a few months benefit from being stored lying down in a simple wine rack *(facing page)*.

WHERE TO KEEP EVERYDAY WINES

In the short term, most people do, however, generally have a small collection of bottles of wine that they store in a convenient place at home. We've all loaded our carts with them—a few supper favorites, something "a bit better" for Sunday lunch, something to open if friends drop in unexpectedly, or a bottle of fizz in case that good news arrives. Even the less expensive, everyday drinking wines should be stored on their side in a dark, dry, and cool place, such as a basement, or at least in an underused room on a north-facing wall. Unless your kitchen has a built-in temperature-controlled unit, storing wine in the kitchen where the temperature will rise, especially if the oven is on, or in a room constantly heated to a temperature that is comfortable for us, will not do the wine any good and may even spoil it before you are ready to pull the cork.

LYING DOWN IN THE DARK

The reason for storing wine bottles on their sides is that it keeps the wine in constant contact with the cork; the cork thus does not dry out and let in air. The reason for keeping them in the dark is that ultraviolet light can damage wine—that's why wine traditionally comes in green or brown bottles. There are certainly many more clear-glass wine bottles around these days, due to a combination of factors: first, many modern consumers prefer to see the color of the wine they are buying; second, wine generally moves much faster off the store shelves these days than previously, so it is at less risk of damage from store lighting; and third, wine retailers have generally learned to keep their wine in more favorable conditions. If, when buying wine, you come across a bottle that looks as if it

has been sitting for some time at the front of a shelf under uncomfortably hot lights, take my advice and give it a wide berth.

STORING WINES FOR KEEPING

For those who wish to go a stage further and buy wines to "lay down" for future drinking, a cellar is a necessity, either one that already exists in the basement of the house or one that is specially built. The ideal wine cellar is dark and free from vibrations, and has a humidity level of around 70 percent—essential to keep the cork moist and, of course, airtight—and the temperature should be constant at 54–64°F (12–18°C). Higher temperatures increase the rate of oxidation, and so the wine will age more quickly in warmer conditions. Wherever you plan to keep your fine wines, ideally they should not be kept in an area that will be used for any other type of storage if it means the wine is going to be disturbed on a regular basis. Also, if

you live in a low-lying area or flood plain, it is essential to make sure that your cellar is safe from flooding. There is nothing more heartbreaking than coming down to a flooded cellar—the bottles may all still be safely in their places but the labels could well be floating away, leaving you with no idea which wine is inside which bottle!

Unfortunately, most of us do not have the luxury of an existing wine cellar in our basement. But there are a number of easily achievable alternatives, including large refrigerators designed specifically for wine with temperature and humidity control. Another popular alternative that does not require a huge amount of extra room is a Spiral Cellar, which is excavated in your backyard using a kind of giant corkscrew. A spiral staircase or ladder is installed into the hole, with bottles stored in the walls around it. A Spiral Cellar is well worth the investment, especially for fine wines, which need perfect environmental conditions to age properly.

BUILDING UP A CELLAR

When choosing wines to keep, you need to do some serious research or get expert advice, and select only the best wines from the best vintages—it is another myth that all expensive wines get better with age. I think that the best principle is to buy a little at a time, and take your time. One of the great pleasures of having a wine cellar is to enjoy seeing it grow over the years. Aim for a balanced mix of white and red wines (almost no rosé wines keep). Port is, of course, the traditional drink to lay down for comings-of-age and suchlike, although it has fallen out of favor in recent years.

Many people concentrate on cellaring wines from one or two specific regions—Bordeaux or Burgundy, say—while others are more cosmopolitan. Whatever you decide to do, ask an expert for advice on the better producers from a region and the best vintages before you make any purchases. Great wine is made by the best producers every year, but even they would admit that some years are greater than others, and some wines need to be laid down for longer than others.

"So many people leave their wines too long before drinking. Wines are living products, and even the finest have a 'drink-by' date."

BOARDING YOUR WINE

If you have no room at home but are really serious about collecting fine wine, you should find a professional wine-cellaring company. There are several such companies, sometimes run as part of a fine wine retailer, who can offer you a wine buying and cellaring service in one. If you are purchasing wine *en primeur*—that is, reserving wine that is still in barrels at the winery—then obviously it will stay with the producer until it has been bottled. It can then be shipped to you and kept in bond in a wine cellar. ("In bond" means that the import duties have not been paid on the wine, and it must stay in a customs warehouse until the tax has been paid and it is legally imported.)

Once you have bought your wines, keep careful records of quantities, producers, and vintages. A good cellar should have an inventory that is updated as you add to your collection or withdraw and drink the wine. You can add comments about how the wine tasted, as well—if you open a wine that is not ready to drink yet, then make a note to wait before you open any more of it. Conversely, you may open a wine and realize that it is ready to be drunk and should not be kept for much longer; in this case it is useful to know how many more bottles you have of that wine.

These are the principles that any good cellaring service will apply to its precious charges, and if you follow them, you could enjoy your wine at its best, and make money on your investment!

WAREHOUSED WINES
Wines "in bond" are stored in a kind of limbo, reserved for their buyer in secured warehouses; only when all import duties and taxes have been paid is the wine delivered to the buyer.

VENERABLE CELLAR
However high our aspirations, few of us can hope to emulate the riches of the Louis Jadot cellars in Burgundy *(facing page)*, where 1959 Beaunes rub shoulders with a Richebourg from 1877.

SERVING WINE

After you have chosen and bought the right wine for an occasion, it makes perfect sense to serve it in the best way possible. You don't need lots of expensive equipment, but preparing and opening the bottle properly, sniffing the cork, pouring the wine, and tasting the wine and approving it before pouring for  your guests, are all part of a ritual that transforms the simple act of drinking into an exciting event for everybody present. Of course, you might want to cut down on the ceremony for a quiet supper at home—but, still, you'll never catch me sloshing unchilled white wine into tumblers! It would be an insult to my taste buds, as well as to the grower that made it. Properly chilled and served in a gleaming, thin-walled glass, the wine will transform even a simple omelet into "dinner for two."

SERVING TEMPERATURES

GETTING IT RIGHT

Temperature has a huge impact on the taste of a wine. Each style of wine has an optimum serving temperature at which it releases its aromas and flavors to best effect *(see box, below)*. But remember that there are exceptions to the guidelines given here; for example, you can serve cheap wines cooler than indicated to hide their imperfections.

Serving wine at the right temperature takes a little forward planning; begin by measuring the temperature of the liquid with a wine thermometer—an inexpensive but very useful accessory. If the wine needs to be cooled to its ideal serving temperature, simply place it in the refrigerator, where it will cool by about 4°F (2°C) every ten minutes; conversely, the wine will warm up at about the same rate when removed from the refrigerator and left at room temperature. If you need to chill wine quickly, 30 minutes in the freezer

"You can chill some light red wines, but don't overchill them—cool them gently down to 'cellar temperature' to bring out their fruit character."

(don't forget it, whatever you do!), or in an ice bucket, will be ample. Make sure that you don't overchill the wine, as this will kill its flavor and aromas. It will also make the cork difficult to pull, because the wax on the cork will harden and stick to the inside of the bottle. One of the best ways to keep a white wine perfectly chilled throughout a meal (although perhaps not the most attractive) is to use an insulated rapid-chill sleeve that slides over the bottle. Keep one of these in your freezer so that it is ready to use whenever you need it.

FEELING THE HEAT

Never warm red wine on a hot stove or in the microwave; over-warm wine tastes like cough medicine. And if a wine reaches body temperature, you won't taste it at all! If your chosen wine is too cool, warm it gently in an ice bucket filled with tepid water. Remember, though, that some light, young reds, such as Pinot Noir, Beaujolais, Valpolicella, or Loire Valley wines, are best served slightly chilled—place the bottle in the refrigerator 30 minutes before serving.

IDEAL SERVING TEMPERATURES
The table below gives the ideal temperatures at which to serve wines in each of my style categories. In general, the fuller the style, the warmer the wine should be—although all sparkling wines benefit from being served well chilled.

Light, crisp whites	39–43°F (4–6°C)
Juicy, aromatic whites	43–46°F (6–8°C)
Full, opulent whites	50–54°F (10–12°C)
Rosé	39–43°F (4–6°C)
Fruity, lively reds	54–57°F (12–14°C)
Ripe, smooth reds	61–64°F (16–18°C)
Rich, dense reds	64–68°F (18–20°C)
Sparkling	43–46°F (6–8°C)
Sweet and fortified	43–46°F (6–8°C)

CHILLED WHITE WINE
Foil chill sleeves are practical, but
an ice bucket always looks stylish
as well as bringing out the best
in a crisp, white wine.

OPENING AND SERVING

WHAT DO YOU NEED?

Serving wine correctly adds something to any occasion. You don't have to spend a fortune on fancy equipment, but it is worth investing in a good corkscrew that will not fragment corks—I favor designs that use a smooth metal spiral, rather than a sharp-edged "screw." Many corkscrews incorporate a sharp blade for cutting the capsule over the cork, but a short, sharp kitchen knife will do just as well. You could buy some good-quality white linen napkins and use these to wipe the bottle and clean up any spills—they add a real air of professionalism.

Glassware should be plain and unfussy, to allow the color of the wine to shine through, and thin-walled—a chunky glass psychologically prepares you for a coarse wine. Wine glasses should always

"Crystal decanters add sparkle to a dinner party, but for lunch on the deck, use a clear glass pitcher or carafe. Drape a napkin over it to keep out the bugs!"

have a stem—if you drink from a tumbler-style glass, the heat from your hands will warm the wine. And always, when you taste or drink a wine, hold the glass by its stem. Even if the bowl looks big enough to sit comfortably in the palm of your hand as you swirl the wine, resist the temptation.

You can buy a different glass for just about every style of wine, but you really need only four: a large-bowled glass that allows "big" reds to breathe; a smaller, tulip-shaped glass for white wines—the smaller volume means that the wines have less time to warm up; a tall, slender Champagne flute, which reduces the surface area of the drink that is open to the air, and so preserves the bubbles longer; and a shorter, stemmed glass for dessert wines, port, and sherry.

PREPARING TO SERVE RED WINE

A day or so before you plan to serve a fine red wine, stand the bottle upright to allow any sediment to settle to the bottom. When serving the wine, hold the bottle at the shoulder or the base—never by the neck—and do not agitate the bottle, as this will stir up the sediment. Many people open a bottle of wine a couple of hours before serving to let it "breathe." This is not particularly effective

REMOVING THE CAPSULE
A "foil cutter" removes only the top part of the capsule, but to pour cleanly, I prefer to remove the whole thing, using a sharp pocket knife with care.

GIVE IT A SWIRL
To "open up" a young red that is shy to release its aromas and flavors, I decant it and give it a quick swirl *(facing page)* to bring the wine in contact with the air.

because so little of the wine is in contact with the air; instead, simply serve the wine in a generously sized glass and swirl for a few moments. This will help to release the wine's aromas and flavors, and may soften the harsh tannins present in some young reds. Pouring the wine into a decanter will also bring the liquid in contact with the air, but the main reason to transfer the wine is to separate the liquid from any sediment that is in the bottle. You only absolutely need to decant wines that "throw" (or deposit) a large amount of sediment—notably some full-bodied reds that are more than ten years old, and port.

TO OPEN A BOTTLE

Using a sharp knife, cut the capsule at the top of the bottle and remove it carefully. Screw the corkscrew into the cork, then pull steadily and

A COOL RECEPTION
What better icebreaker could there be than a welcoming glass of perfectly chilled white wine, moisture beading on the glass?

PORT AHOY
Port needs decanting *(facing page)*, as it throws a heavy sediment. Don't serve it in a thimble—its rich, dark complexity of flavors needs room to expand.

gently, keeping the corkscrew straight so that it draws the cork vertically. Don't tug at the cork—let the corkscrew do the work! Clean the neck of the bottle with a white napkin to remove any deposits that have built up under the capsule, then pour a little of the wine into a tasting glass. Smell the wine to check that it is not corked *(see* Diagnosing Wine Faults, *pp.316–17)*; a corked wine will smell like dirty wet socks, and should be discarded.

If you are pouring straight into your guests' glasses rather than decanting, pour up to only about one third of the volume of the glass. If you are decanting the wine, pour all the wine from your tasting glass into the glass decanter and swirl it around in the base of the decanter; this will clean the decanter of any residual flavors. Pour the wine back into your tasting glass and taste it again, just to make sure there is nothing untoward in the decanter that may taint the wine. If the wine meets with your approval, you are ready to begin decanting.

Slowly pour the wine from the bottle in a steady stream down the side of the decanter. Position the bottle about 4 in (10 cm) above a lighted candle; this will allow you to see when the sediment arrives in the "shoulder" of the bottle (that is, where the curve is below the neck). At this point, stop pouring; you will inevitably have to sacrifice a little of the wine to avoid sediment in the decanter. You can now pour the wine from the decanter into your guests' glasses.

SERVING ETIQUETTE

The etiquette of serving wine can seem like a minefield, but this is not an area where you should get too bogged down. The fact that you have chosen a wine especially for your guests' enjoyment and served it with care, in spotless glasses, will put everyone at ease. And if a guest brings a gift of wine that will clash with the wines or the menu you have prepared, it is not necessarily bad manners to simply put it to one side, with thanks. After all,

you have put some thought into selecting just the right wines for the occasion, and making sure that they are at the correct temperature for serving.

It's always courteous to refill your guests' glasses for them; try (like a good sommelier!) to do this smoothly and discreetly, or you could make people feel uncomfortable. You should offer to refill just before the glass becomes empty, neither leaving a guest with an empty glass for too long, nor hurrying them to "drink up." To control drips when refilling a glass, twist the bottle slightly as you tilt it back to an upright position.

KEEPING OPENED WINE

Once a bottle of wine is opened, it quickly begins to oxidize and will last for three days at most. To slow down the rate of spoilage, push the cork firmly into the bottle, and keep the wine, even if it is red, in the refrigerator (don't forget to raise a red to the right temperature before serving again). Specialist "wine-saving" devices are available that inject gas (or create a vacuum) in the bottle to preserve opened wine, but I'm not sure that they do a much better job than simply replacing the cork and putting the wine in the refrigerator.

Some of the newer, composite corks are, I admit, very hard to get back in the bottle. That's because they're formed not from a single chunk of corkwood, which has some give in it, but from a compacted mixture of cork granules and adhesive. They keep wine perfectly well—but, once out, they are pretty unyielding. A synthetic cork can be hard to get a grip on, too. There is a huge range of bottle stoppers that come in handy if you can't replace the cork, but you don't necessarily need a "designer" model or one topped with a pewter ornament. The rather utilitarian-looking type with a little lever that creates a tight seal will do

the job just as well. And in the unlikely event that you have half a bottle of sparkling wine left over, there are special stoppers designed to fit the chunky necks of Champagne-style bottles.

OPENING AND SERVING CHAMPAGNE

For safety's sake here, I need to draw an analogy that rather detracts from the romance of sparkling wine. Champagne is bottled to the pressure of a car tire, and thus needs to be opened with care. Don't "pop" the cork unless you've just won the Daytona 500—it is dangerous and wastes precious liquid. Carefully cut the foil below the level of the cork, and gently remove it from the bottle. Keeping your thumb pressed on the cork, free the cage by turning the wire ring six times, and open the cage wide and remove it. Remove the cork by gripping it tightly and twisting the base of the bottle rather than the cork itself. Clean the neck of the bottle

and pour steadily into a flute, inclining the glass to control the fizz. Pouring Champagne is more difficult than pouring still wine because of the bubbles. Do you hold the guest's glass when you serve so that you can incline it, or leave it on the table and pour a little, wait a little? Personally, I feel in better control of the steady flow if I hold the glass as I pour, tilting it to reduce the amount of "mousse"—the foamy head of bubbles. I also like to pour all the glasses first and then hand them around—I feel that it is absolutely essential to a festive occasion for everyone to raise a full glass at the same time.

UNCORKING CHAMPAGNE
"Hold the cork and twist the bottle" *(facing page)* is the golden rule. Some people like to hold a clean napkin over the cork for extra grip and to act as a "safety net."

POUR GENTLY AND ENJOY
To pour Champagne without creating a frothing volcano, let the wine run gently down one side of the glass. Don't try to fill it right to the top.

DIAGNOSING FAULTS

CORK COMPLICATIONS

Wine continues to change after it has been bottled and shipped—even while it sits on your wine merchant's shelves. Wine that left the producer in good condition can occasionally spoil before it reaches your glass. One of the most common problems is contamination of wine by the chemical trichloroanisole (TCA), produced mainly by fungal growth on the cork. Such a "corked" wine smells musty and earthy—a bit like wet, dirty socks. It tastes dusty and bitter, and its fruit aromas vanish, leaving the wine with no character.

Some people estimate that as many as one in ten bottles is corked, but degrees of spoilage vary. If you suspect that the wine you've bought is corked, send it back (if in a restaurant)—you

"An oxidized wine is a step toward vinegar— its color becomes a deep golden brown and its flavors lose their freshness and fruitiness."

should get a refund or a replacement bottle. Part of the reason corked wine is common is that, as global production of wine has increased, good-quality cork has become hard to find. A good cork should look and feel tight and solid, while a poor-quality one will feel spongy and have flaws and even holes in it. Many producers of quality wine have turned to synthetic closures and even screw tops rather than risk using second-rate corks that may taint their wines. Since the role of the cork is to keep air out of the bottle, there seems to be no rational reason to believe that these new closures are inferior to cork.

OXIDATION

Another problem can be oxidation. If too much air has been allowed to get into the bottle, its contact with the wine will result in a flat and tired taste and a loss of fruitiness. Extreme oxidation makes the wine taste like nutty sherry. In order to prevent oxidation, producers add a preservative—sulfur dioxide—to their wines. However, heavy-handed use of this chemical can cause its own problems, giving the wine a "rough" feel, which is most obvious at the back of the throat, or may even make the wine smell or taste like bad eggs.

IS IT CORKED?
A key characteristic of corking is that it gets much worse with contact with air. If you are not sure at first, give the wine a swirl and a couple of minutes—there will then be no doubt.

CLASSY CORK
A good-quality cork *(facing page)*, firm and tight-grained, is still the closure of choice for fine wines, but cork shortages mean that more producers are turning to composite and synthetic corks.

EARLY WARNING
A sniff of the cork can alert you to a corked wine—while some people think it looks pretentious, I'll take that risk instead of a mouthful of spoiled wine any day.

WINE WITH FOOD

When it comes to matching wine with food, there are no rights and wrongs, just opinions and suggestions. Many of the old "rules" are being eroded by the spread of world cuisine and "fusion" cooking. And wine styles, too, are evolving: big, oaky New World Chardonnays, for example, go just as well with roast chicken  as the traditional choice of a light red wine. Of course, you can enjoy a delicious bottle of any wine that may not have anything in common with the food you are eating. But, believe me, it is one of life's greatest pleasures to enjoy a meal where the wine is in perfect harmony with the food. I knew from my earliest years that the right wine could turn the simplest family meal into an occasion—and ever since, I've been on a quest to match good food with perfect wine to create unforgettable meals.

MATCHING WINE STYLES WITH FOOD

DISPELLING THE MYTHS

There are no strict rules that say you cannot eat what you like with whichever style of wine you choose. The long-established myth that white wine should be drunk with fish and red wine with meat is just that—a myth! It may have held some truth 200 years ago when meat was roasted and fish was poached. And it is certainly true that tannin in red wine reacts poorly with fish. But these days we are blessed with a much wider range of meat and fish from all over the world, as well as a greater variety of wines. There are light, lively reds that make a fantastic match for "meaty" fish such as fresh tuna, and heavier, oak-aged whites that go superbly well with chicken.

"Finding wine and food that complement each other absolutely perfectly is one of my greatest pleasures in life."

EQUAL PARTNERS

The first factor to consider when looking for a perfect wine and food match is the relationship between the density of the food and the body of the wine. If the food is heavy, such as a stew or casserole, then you need to match it with a ripe and full wine, probably a red such as a Merlot or Shiraz. The strength of flavor of a dish, as a general rule, should be matched by the intensity of flavor in the wine that accompanies it. Chinese and Asian dishes, for example, which use a wide array of spices to create complex and intense flavors, need to be matched with wines that are also flavor-intensive; whites such as Gewürztraminer or Riesling make a far better match than soft, oaky Chardonnays.

The acidity in the food is another important factor to consider. Dishes that include lemon, apple, or vinaigrette need to be matched with wines with high acidity. Fatty or oily dishes – smoked salmon or fish served in a beurre blanc sauce, for example – also require wines with a higher level of acidity, to cut through the oiliness of the food and add an extra taste dimension.

SANCERRE AND GOAT CHEESE
Both the wine and this mild but refreshing cheese come from the Loire Valley. They match perfectly.

Some foods are notoriously difficult to match with wine: chili peppers, asparagus, eggs, and soup. The general rule would be to opt for a fairly neutral wine with not too much acidity. The problem with chili peppers is that often you taste very little else, so don't choose too expensive a wine! The flavor of asparagus is quite intense and needs a fairly intense wine to match, such as an oaked Chardonnay. It is best to avoid trying to match red wines with eggs, but there are so many different egg dishes that experimentation is a must. A good starting point, however, would be an unoaked Chardonnay or white Burgundy. With soups, obviously the best wine match will depend on the soup's flavor. In general, though, I usually recommend wines with high acidity to cut through creamy soups, or perhaps a fuller red wine with its strong tannins.

The cheese course can be a tricky one; not all cheese goes well with red wine. Generally, the harder the cheese, the better it is with reds; soft cheeses such as Camembert and Brie match well with white wines and, of course, there is the famous marriage (made in heaven, in my view!) between goat cheese and Sauvignon Blanc.

SAVING THE BEST FOR LAST

One of my favorite wine styles is dessert wine, and it is a shame that so many people choose a white wine with their starter, a red for the main course, and then go straight to coffee with dessert. They are really missing out, as some of the best wines in the world fall into the dessert category—Barsac, Sauternes, and Monbazillac, to name but a few. Delicious! The basic rule to follow is that the wine should be as sweet or even sweeter than the dessert it is paired with; if not, it will taste pallid.

My "ten golden rules" on the following pages give further ideas on how to successfully match food and wine styles, while the table opposite is a useful at-a-glance guide.

CHAMPAGNE AND OYSTERS
If you've pushed the boat out and ordered oysters *(left)*, then why not splurge on Champagne, too? These two strong characters are true soul mates.

MATCHING CHOCOLATE
Chocolate tart is one of my favorite dishes, and the sweet red wines of southern France, such as Rasteau, stand up well to its deep, rich flavors.

MATCHING FOOD AND WINE

The table below and the "golden rules" on the following pages are merely sets of suggestions, based on my experience as a sommelier, but if you like your lemon sole with a full, tannic red, go ahead and enjoy, with my blessing!

| ★★★ | avoid | ★★ | good match |
| ★★★ | acceptable | ★★★ | perfect match |

FOOD STYLE	LIGHT, CRISP WHITES	JUICY, AROMATIC WHITES	FULL, OPULENT WHITES	FRUITY, LIVELY REDS	RIPE, SMOOTH REDS	RICH, DENSE REDS
Smoked	★★★	★★★	★★★	★★★	★★★	★★★
Spicy	★★★	★★★	★★★	★★★	★★★	★★★
Salty	★★★	★★★	★★★	★★★	★★★	★★★
Rich and creamy	★★★	★★★	★★★	★★★	★★★	★★★
Light fish and shellfish	★★★	★★★	★★★	★★★	★★★	★★★
Meaty fish	★★★	★★★	★★★	★★★	★★★	★★★
Poultry	★★★	★★★	★★★	★★★	★★★	★★★
Game	★★★	★★★	★★★	★★★	★★★	★★★
Red meat	★★★	★★★	★★★	★★★	★★★	★★★
Stews and casseroles	★★★	★★★	★★★	★★★	★★★	★★★
Hard cheese	★★★	★★★	★★★	★★★	★★★	★★★
Blue cheese	★★★	★★★	★★★	★★★	★★★	★★★
Soft and creamy cheese	★★★	★★★	★★★	★★★	★★★	★★★
Grilled fish	★★★	★★★	★★★	★★★	★★★	★★★
Grilled meat	★★★	★★★	★★★	★★★	★★★	★★★
Cold meat and charcuterie	★★★	★★★	★★★	★★★	★★★	★★★
Soup	★★★	★★★	★★★	★★★	★★★	★★★
Vegetable dishes	★★★	★★★	★★★	★★★	★★★	★★★
Pasta and pizza	★★★	★★★	★★★	★★★	★★★	★★★
Egg dishes	★★★	★★★	★★★	★★★	★★★	★★★

TEN GOLDEN RULES FOR MATCHING FOOD WITH WINE

1 **SALTY DISHES NEED WINES WITH NATURALLY HIGH ACIDITY**

It is no coincidence that tangy Fino sherry goes so well with tapas—salted almonds, salted fish, and spicy, salty chorizo sausages, for example—because this combination of appetizer and aperitif evolved together in the same part of the world. Salt in food has the effect of neutralizing acidity in the wine and allowing the underlying fruit flavors to come to the fore—just as salt brings out the flavors in food. It is therefore best to choose wines that are naturally high in acidity to match salty dishes. With a salty cheese, such as Roquefort, always choose dessert wines with really zingy acidity, such as those from the Loire.

TRY Fresh anchovies or anchovy dishes, such as bagna cauda or pissaladière *(below)*, with Australian Riesling from the Clare Valley; moules marinières with Muscadet or Sancerre; feta cheese salad with Assyrtiko from Greece; Thai fish soup with well-chilled Pinot Grigio.

2 MEATY FISH DISHES CAN TAKE A LIGHT RED

Whoever had it laid down on tablets of stone that white wines are for fish and red wines are for meat should be put on bread and water rations for ever and a day. While it is true that tannins in red wine can create a nasty metallic taste when drunk with fish, there is fish and there is fish! Light, fruity reds with low tannins can match very well with fish with a dense, "meaty" texture, such as fresh tuna, salmon, and swordfish, especially if the wine is served slightly chilled. White fish, by contrast, tend to be light in texture and served with light sauces. These do need to be partnered with delicate white wines or, if the flavors are more intense, more juicy, aromatic whites.

TRY Tuna steak tartare and a spicy salsa with a Spätburgunder; roasted salmon fillet *(above)* with a Chinon; grilled or barbecued swordfish steak with a Carneros Pinot Noir from California; pan-fried monkfish wrapped in Parma ham with a chilled Dolcetto from Piedmont in Italy.

3 OILY FOODS NEED ACIDITY OR TANNIN

Some food-and-wine rules are about pairing like for like—sweet wines with desserts, for example—but others are about matching opposites, and this is certainly the case when choosing wines to complement oily foods. If dishes are oily, they are likely also to be fairly rich, sometimes creamy, but certainly with a degree of cloying opulence that needs to be tempered by the wine you choose to drink with them. If you are selecting a white wine, make sure it has a high degree of acidity, to cut through the fattiness or oiliness of the dish and leave a clean feeling on your palate. Tannin can do the same job; if you are choosing a red wine to match an oily dish—cheese fondue, for example—it will need to be fairly tannic to avoid tasting flabby.

TRY Smoked salmon *(facing page)* with a Sauvignon Blanc; scallops Mornay with a Chablis; cassoulet with chunky Barossa Shiraz; chicken Kiev with a California Roussanne; roast shoulder of lamb with an Italian Barolo or Barbaresco; roast goose with a Cabernet–Merlot blend.

4 SMOKY DISHES CLASH WITH OAKY WINES

Oak and smoke, in my opinion, is just too much of a good thing to make a good match. If you try to pair an oaked wine with a smoked meat or fish dish, you are in danger of overpowering your taste buds with too many very similar smoky, oaky flavors, and they will not be able to recognize anything else. Also, smoky dishes, by definition, have a strong flavor, and strong flavors in food need to be matched with a crisply fruity wine that refreshes the palate. Oaked wines have an oiliness and opulence that do not help to do so. White grapes to look out for that should guarantee an oak-free zone include Sauvignon Blanc, Riesling, Chenin Blanc, and the Pinots Blanc and Gris (Pinot Grigio in Italy). For smoked meats, choose from my Lively, Fruity Reds category: any more tannin, however soft, may join forces with the smoked flavors to create a "hard," woody taste.

TRY Smoked mackerel pâté with a Clare Valley Riesling from Australia; smoked salmon with a tangy French Sauvignon Blanc or, for a more festive occasion, a Pinot Meunier-based sparkling wine; smoked chicken salad with chilled Fleurie; smoked ham with Italian Barbera d'Asti.

5 **MATCH RICH, DENSE FLAVORS WITH SIMILAR WINES**

If your chosen dish is rich because it is creamy, try a crisp white wine to cut through the richness and refresh the palate. But rich dishes with greater weight and intensity of flavor normally require wines whose flavors and body pack a similar punch. If the wine is too light, it can be overpowered by the flavors and textures in the food. There are some classic extravagant pairings of food with white wine in this vein—foie gras and Sauternes and, less often served these days, lobster Thermidor with a Corton Charlemagne white Burgundy. But for the most part, we are talking rich, dense reds to partner hearty meat dishes here, especially those based on game or variety meats where you need a wine with good complexity of flavor to compete on equal terms.

> **TRY** Pan-fried chicken livers with Monbazillac; roasted haunch of venison with a Pauillac; game casserole with a Châteauneuf-du-Pape; seafood risotto with a Meursault or New Zealand Chardonnay; cottage pie or sausage and mashed potatoes with a Napa Valley Cabernet Sauvignon.

6 **SPICY DISHES NEED REFRESHING WINES**

Some people find that spicy dishes can overwhelm lighter styles of wine and prefer to match them with richer or even sweeter wines. I find that Chinese dishes generally work well with aromatic whites, such as German Riesling or Alsace Gewürztraminer, while more spicy Eastern cuisine benefits from being partnered with quite simple, crisp, dry whites, such as New Zealand Sauvignon Blanc or—the best choices in my view—a Pinot Grigio or a Chablis. These wines help to refresh the palate. Curry is not easy to match with wine. There are some good white partners for the lighter, more fragrant curries, but beware of ordering reds: most curries tend to knock back the fruit in a red wine, so the tannins become dominant. If the food is extremely spicy, it may be better to—just this once—forget the wine and stick to water or beer.

> **TRY** Chicken and beef with green peppers and black bean sauce with a Chablis; chicken with cashew nuts with a Spanish Albariño; Szechuan pork or Thai stir-fry *(facing page)* with a German Riesling; Thai red curry with a Gewürztraminer; chicken tikka with a Pinot Grigio.

 MATCH WHITE MEATS WITH FULL WHITES OR LIGHT REDS

The flavors in white meats are, on the whole, much more subtle than those in red meats, and so chicken, pork, and turkey dishes in which the meat is roasted, poached, or grilled in quite a simple style, rather than heavily flavored or richly sauced, work really well with more subtle wines, such as light reds. However, over the last few years, there has certainly been a trend for whites to become fuller and more opulent, especially the big, oaky-fruity New World wines, and these heavier whites have also proved good partners for white meat dishes, probably because their complex aromas and oily opulence balances and harmonizes with the mellow flavors in the meat.

TRY Roast chicken *(above)* or pork or turkey escalopes with Australian Chardonnay from Margaret River; roast loin of pork with a white Châteauneuf-du-Pape; chicken breast with girolles mushrooms with a chilled New Zealand Pinot Noir; roast partridge with Barbera d'Asti.

8 RED MEATS CAN TAKE ON STRONG TANNINS

For lamb cutlets or shepherd's pie, I'd choose a fruity Merlot-based wine, but heavier fare gives bigger-bodied reds a chance to shine. Protein-rich food softens the tannin in red wine so that the fruit flavors are able to come to the fore more easily. Red meats can therefore be successfully matched with big, strong reds with firm tannins without your having to worry that the fruit in the wine will be overpowered. Cheese also has a similar effect on wine; the tannins are absorbed and the wine tastes more mellow and easy to enjoy. The more austere tannic wines can be made much more food-friendly by decanting; temperature helps, too—serve them slightly warmer than usual.

TRY Rare steak *(below)* with a Côte-Rôtie Syrah; spicy sausages with Cahors; confit of duck with a Barolo; mature Comté cheese with Napa Valley Cabernet Sauvignon; steak and kidney pie with Spanish Ribera del Duero; Pauillac or Coonawarra Cabernet with roast leg of lamb.

TEN GOLDEN RULES

WINE: A USER'S GUIDE

9

MATCH WINE TO SAUCES, NOT WHAT'S UNDERNEATH

The maxim "red wine with dark meat, white wine with light" is a little misleading; most wines can, in fact, be served with most meats. When trying to make the perfect wine and food match, it is much more likely to be the sauce served with the meat, be it chicken or beef, that takes precedence. Lemon chicken, for example, goes well with a Chablis from Burgundy, but the same wine would never be a good match for coq au vin, which needs a fruity, unoaked, lightly tannic red. Similarly, a steak au poivre needs a medium-bodied, low-tannin red, but a beef goulash can be matched with a ripe, full-bodied, fruity white. With wine-based sauces, it's often true that the wine you cook the dish with makes the perfect accompaniment to the meal, which makes life a little easier.

TRY Beef bourguignon with earthy Pinot Noir from Gevrey-Chambertin in Burgundy or an Australian Cabernet–Merlot; beef stroganoff with Brunello di Montalcino; venison casserole with a Gigondas Syrah; duck à l'orange with a St-Èstephe or an Australian Shiraz from the Hunter Valley.

10

MATCH DESSERTS WITH THEIR WEIGHT IN WINE

The weight and sweetness of a dessert wine needs to match the weight and sweetness of the dessert. It's obvious, really—would you want to drink the same wine with raspberry mousse as you do with sticky toffee pudding? It may sound unlikely, but it's true that the intensity of sweetness in a cinnamon bun can be enhanced by a really rich, sweet dessert wine; if you tried to drink a light, flowery wine with it, you can easily imagine that the flavors in one would destroy the flavors in the other. Don't forget, however, that sparkling wines can also be perfect matches for fruity summer desserts, particularly the semidry and sweeter styles. And strawberries have an affinity with red and rosé wine, particularly if the wine also has strawberry flavors. Try them with a light Beaujolais, a blush Zinfandel, or even a sweet, sparkling red Lambrusco.

TRY Sticky toffee pudding with a Hungarian "5 puttonyos" Tokaji; apple strudel with a Bonnezeaux; chocolate brownies with a chilled Maury or a Rutherglen Muscat; pear tart *(facing page)* with Moscato d'Asti; summer bread pudding with a German or Austrian *Beerenauslese.*

MAJOR WHITE WINE GRAPE VARIETIES

The most important white grapes are undoubtedly Chardonnay, Sauvignon Blanc, Sémillon, and Riesling, followed by Muscat, Gewürztraminer, and Viognier. But one of the most versatile white grapes is hardly ever seen on a wine label. The Chenin Blanc grape is made into every style: dry, medium-dry, sweet, sparkling, and dessert, from workaday wines best drunk soon and forgotten just as quickly, to glorious, lusciously sweet wines that will seemingly keep and improve forever.

GRAPE	OTHER NAMES	COMMENTS
Albana		A key variety of the Emilia-Romagna region, it makes one of the finest full Italian whites, although is difficult to grow well.
Albariño	Alvarinho (Portugal)	The Albariño grape makes juicy, aromatic, peachy, Viognier-like wine in Spain (Galicia) and also in Portugal; fresh and expressive, it is a good alternative to Loire Sauvignon Blanc.
Aligoté		Enjoying increasing popularity, especially in Eastern Europe, Aligoté produces crisp, light, lemony wines that are a key ingredient in the famous Burgundian aperitif Kir *(see p.90)*.
Arneis		A dry and delicate wine, Piedmontese Arneis has characters of juicy apple, almond, and citrus, and balanced acidity.
Chardonnay	Morillon; Feinburgunder (Austria)	A very versatile grape, especially in cold climates, Chardonnay makes refreshing, crisp light wines, including the French classic, Chablis, with notes of minerals, green apple, citrus, and grapefruit. It is also the ultimate full, opulent white wine variety, producing wonderful wines from Burgundy, such as Meursault and Montrachet, as well as the finest New World whites. It is also the essential sparkling-wine grape, at its best in the coolest regions of its range, where the resulting wines express lemony and green apple aromas and a yeasty character, with complex but elegant notes of almond, warm bread, and biscuit. It is expensive to grow, but widely planted, extensively so in the New World.
Chasselas	Gutedel (Germany); Fendant, Dorin, Perlan (Switzerland)	Grown worldwide; some of the best Swiss wines are made from this grape. The wines are crisp, with apple and citrus aromas.
Chenin Blanc	Steen (South Africa); Pineau de la Loire	A major grape of the Loire Valley in France and in South Africa, making white wines in every style. Crisp, dry whites, lean and light, have notes of apple and citrus, while the fuller styles can be quite austere when young. Sparkling wines tend to be less aromatic than those from other grapes. In the Loire, it makes great botrytized sweet wine with intense aromas.
Clairette		Makes sparkling wines that are subtle, elegant, fruity, but never too fizzy. Clairette de Die, made in the Rhône Valley, is a less expensive but enjoyable alternative to Champagne.

GRAPE	OTHER NAMES	COMMENTS
Gewürztraminer	Traminer	Gewürztraminer makes off-dry aromatic white wine, with charming notes of exotic fruit, such as lychee, and a spicy character. As a sweet wine, it offers intensity and lots of fruit.
Grecchetto		Often used in a blend, Grecchetto is becoming more important in full, Umbrian white wines, such as Orvieto and Torgiano.
Greco		In Italy and Greece, this grape makes a dry white wine that is full-bodied and, despite its weight, very elegant.
Grenache Blanc		Grown in southern France and Spain, Grenache Blanc makes wines that express oiliness, with good acidity and a nutty finish.
Grüner Veltliner		Austria's most important grape makes classic juicy, aromatic wine, elegant and characterful, with floral and spicy notes.
Len de L'elh		This grape makes juicy, perfumed, aromatic wines with notes of apple, pear, and citrus, but it lacks acidity, so they can be flabby.
Loureiro		Makes a crisp, lightly structured wine that is slightly fizzy, zesty, and clean. In Portugal, it is used to make Vinho Verde.
Malvasia		Grown in Italy to make the famous dessert wine Vin Santo. When blended with Trebbiano to add complexity, wines compare with the Sauternes blend of Sémillon and Sauvignon.
Marsanne	Ermitage Blanc (Switzerland)	Makes, full, opulent wine of amazing complexity; ranks among the finest grape varieties in the world.
Müller-Thurgau	Rivaner (Luxembourg)	The quality of this cool-climate grape is fast improving. At its best, it is crisp, fresh, aromatic, and expressive.
Muscadet	Melon de Bourgogne	Makes crisp, dry wine; refreshing, not strongly flavored; known as Melon de Bourgogne in the Muscadet region itself.
Muscat	Moscato (Italy); Moscatel, Muskateller	The dry white wine of the Muscat grape is juicy, aromatic, delicate, and full of grape, exotic fruit, and floral aromas. The grape is also used for light sparkling wines, most popular in the Asti area of Italy. Sweet wines are vibrant with pronounced grape character, and range from light in weight to much darker and stickier, all with intense flavors. Their lack of strong acidity means that they do not age well beyond a few decades, but fortified styles, such as Madeira and Setúbal, age for centuries.
Pedro Ximénez	PX	This Spanish grape is becoming better known thanks to improved vinification. It is used to make fortified wines, notably sweeter styles of sherry, that are sticky, intense, and flavorsome, but beautifully balanced. Also grown in Australia.

GRAPE	OTHER NAMES	COMMENTS
Pinot Blanc	Pinot Bianco (Italy); Weissburgunder (Germany and Austria)	Wines made from Pinot Blanc, chiefly grown in France, northern Italy, Germany, and Austria, are generally unoaked, and at their best are crisp, fruity, and well balanced.
Pinot Gris	Pinot Grigio (Italy); Pinot Beurot (Burgundy, France); Malvoisie (Switzerland); Ruländer, Grauburgunder (Germany)	Grown in Alsace and the Loire, in France, and also in New Zealand, Pinot Gris can make fantastic, well-balanced, juicy wine with intense color and distinct aromas, and with complex fruit and good texture. Grown in Italy as Pinot Grigio, it makes a crisper, drier wine with little aroma, but refreshing lemony acidity—the perfect easy-quaffing dry white.
Prosecco		This grape produces a light, refreshing, sparkling wine in northeastern regions of Italy, lower in flavor than many fizzes, but elegant and subtle with notes of almond, pear, and flowers.
Rhoditis		Pink-skinned, making crisp white wine often blended with other grapes. It is used as the base for the Greek wine Retsina.
Riesling		The classic, versatile German grape variety with great floral and lime characters, Riesling is used for dry, sweet, and sparkling wines in both the Old and New World. Dry white Riesling is aromatic, expressive, elegant wine that is flinty and smoky and among the longest-lived of white wines, thanks to its perfectly balanced acidity and fruit. Riesling is also used to make some of the finest and rarest dessert wines in the world. These again age well, improving over decades, thanks to the grape's high acidity. Sekt, German sparkling wine with a slightly sweet character, is also made from this variety.
Rivaner		The flagship variety of Luxembourg, Rivaner makes juicy, clean, pure, and expressive wine with great complexity and balance.
Robola		One of the finest grapes in Greece, Robola makes lemony, minty, and flowery wine that is dry with a juicy structure.
Rotgipfler		The Rotgipfler grape makes very distinctive Austrian wine—full-bodied, spicy, and full of character.
Sauvignon Blanc		Sauvignon Blanc makes juicily refreshing, aromatic white wine, with high acidity, medium alcohol, a mineral character, and citrus flavors. In France, this important grape makes the superb Sancerre and Pouilly Fumé.
Savagnin		This grape of northern Europe makes a full, nutty, and lemony wine that can be austere, but has great complexity.
Schonburger		This pink-berried variety is limited in production, but its lack of acidity makes it produce surprisingly full wine in a cool climate.

GRAPE	OTHER NAMES	COMMENTS
Sémillon		Used for both full, dry wines and intensely sweet dessert wines. Dry wines are robust, with an appealing exotic fruit style in Australia, compared with the more reserved but complex Bordeaux style. It is often blended with Sauvignon to balance its oily, rich texture. The key grape in Sauternes, Sémillon supports noble rot extremely well. The resulting sweet wines are very fine, with delicate and intensely complex aromas. They age superbly, revealing their true personality after many years. In the New World, sweet Sémillons tend to be stickier, and are ready to be enjoyed sooner.
Sylvaner	Silvaner	Sylvaner makes wine that is crisp, dry, and steely, with citrus flavors. This variety is also grown in Germany, Austria, and Switzerland.
Torrontés		The Torrontés grape makes wine that is subtle, juicily aromatic, and not too heavy, with Muscat-like aromas underlined by soft, lemony acidity.
Trebbiano	Ugni Blanc (France)	Trebbiano is known for its acidity, even in hot climates. The crisp wine it makes is increasing in popularity in the world market.
Verdejo		Juicy, aromatic Verdejo has floral and citrus characters, with notes of pear, peach, and mango.
Verdicchio		Crisp Verdicchio has a naturally high level of acidity. The best wine from this grape is Italian Verdicchio dei Castelli di Jesi.
Vermentino		Increasingly popular, Vermentino makes juicy, charming, floral wine with a good balance between acidity, fruit, and alcohol.
Vidal		Thick-skinned, heavy-yielding Vidal is used to make a rich ice wine that has helped revolutionize the Canadian wine industry.
Viognier		Viognier makes a fabulous summer wine—juicy, highly perfumed ,and floral but with clean acidity—but also a much fuller, muscly style, rivaling a big Chardonnay, with notes of exotic mango, peach, and pineapple.
Viura	Macabeo	The most-planted grape in northern Spain, Viura makes crisp floral wines with citrus and a balanced acidity. Under its alternative name, Macabeo, it is also a highly productive sparkling wine grape, fairly neutral in character, with high acidity. Macabeo is often blended with other grapes, including Chardonnay, to add a fresh, light touch to Cava.
Zierfandler	Cirfandil (Hungary)	This Austrian variety is gaining popularity in the world market. Its finest, fullest wines are made in a blend with Rotgipfler.

MAJOR RED WINE GRAPE VARIETIES

Cabernet Sauvignon is the most widely planted grape in the world, which will hardly surprise anyone who has browsed among a wine merchant's or supermarket's shelves. But while inspection of those same shelves might well lead you to conclude that second place must surely go to Pinot Noir, Merlot, or Syrah/Shiraz, in fact that honor belongs to Grenache, or in Spain, Garnacha. Other key red grape varieties include Tempranillo, in Spain, and Sangiovese, in Italy.

GRAPE	OTHER NAMES	COMMENTS
Agiorgitiko	Nemea, St George	The Agiorgitiko grape makes rich, dense Greek red wine with dark fruit aromas, but sometimes lacks acidity; ages well.
Aglianico		This grape variety makes the great, rich, full-bodied, and intense wines Taurasi and Aglianico del Vulture from the south of Italy; it also makes good red wines in Greece.
Aleatico		A particularly aromatic red grape that makes lively, fruity, and highly appealing wines in Italy.
Barbera		This widely planted Italian grape, an alternative to Gamay, produces lively wines with lots of fruit flavors and elegance, good acidity (freshness), and low tannins.
Blaufränkisch	Lemberger (US); Kékfrankos (Hungary)	An up-and-coming Central European variety, Blaufränkisch produces ripe, smooth wines with intense soft, red fruit, sweet spice, and good color. In the US, it is known as Lemberger, and is used to make a distinctive Washington State wine.
Brunello		This Tuscan grape makes a rich, dense wine that is well structured, with good color and acidity, and balanced alcohol.
Cabernet Franc	Bouchet (St-Émilion, France); Breton (Loire, France)	Cabernet Franc likes a cool climate, and is used to make the fruity, lively reds of the Loire Valley, such as Chinon and Saumur. In the New World, it produces wines with good structure, fruit flavors, and hints of pepper.
Cabernet Sauvignon		The tiny black berries of this variety produce rich, dense wines with high color, tannin, acidity, alcohol, and fruit. The finest examples have power and elegance and benefit from oak-aging. This is a key variety for the great wines of Bordeaux, and is also very widely grown in the New World; it is especially successful in California and Australia.
Canaiolo		This grape produces light and fruity, lively wines on its own, but is better known as the secondary grape in Chianti.
Carignan		Largely grown in France and also in Italy and Spain, Carignan produces rich, dense wines that are high in tannin, acidity, and alcohol, but need time to develop their character.

GRAPE	OTHER NAMES	COMMENTS
Carmenère		Originally from Bordeaux, this grape has found a new home in Chile. Its ripe, smooth wines show great complexity, with dark fruit aromas and flavors, and a clean, dry finish.
Castelão Frances	Periquita	Castelão Frances is a Portuguese grape variety that produces smooth, ripely fruity, well-structured wines.
Cinsault	Cinsaut	This is a workhorse grape for blended reds from southern France, but it can make good rosés, aromatic, fruity, light and fresh. It is often blended with Grenache.
Dolcetto		This key grape from the Piedmont region of Italy ripens early and prefers a temperate climate. It is charming in character, producing lively but soft, easy-drinking, aromatic, fruity reds with good balance.
Dornfelder		Dornfelder is a German variety of grape that makes ripe, smooth, fruity wines with a medium texture.
Gamay		The classic fruity, lively grape of Beaujolais, Gamay is also grown well in the Loire and in Switzerland. Its wines are very aromatic, with soft tannins, high acidity, and low alcohol. Made mainly by the carbonic maceration vinification method *(see pp.42–3)*, they are ideal for early drinking.
Grenache	Garnacha (Spain); Cannonau (Sardinia, Italy)	One of the most widely planted of all varieties, Grenache makes some real blockbuster wines, rich and dense, with lots of flavor and good aging potential, in the Rhône Valley and elsewhere in southern France, and also in Australia. It is known as Garnacha in Spain, where it makes a fine, medium-bodied, fruity wine. It is also one of the most popular red grapes for making fortified wines around the Mediterranean, unusually fresh in taste and possessing delicate bouquets. Rosés from Grenache have intense color, and lovely ripe fruits with spice and good structure.
Klevner		This Swiss grape thrives in a cool climate, and makes very light and lively but complex, world-class wines.
Lambrusco		Wines from this Italian grape should be drunk when young. Well made, they are simple but lively and full of fruit, and are very appealing, with touches of red berries and spice.
Malbec	Auxerrois (Cahors, France); Côt (Loire, France)	Malbec makes full-bodied, intense, dark-colored, long-lived wines, largely in Cahors, France, but also in Argentina.
Mencía		Widely grown in Spain, Mencía makes light, fruity reds ideal for early drinking. It is famous for Bierzo DO and Galicia wines.

GRAPE	OTHER NAMES	COMMENTS
Merlot		This fine grape variety, planted worldwide, is consistently excellent in quality and style. It produces well-colored wines full of soft, smooth, ripe fruit, and velvety on the tongue. Merlots may be very rich, and these grapes are used to produce some of the finest wines of Bordeaux.
Mondeuse		Wine from the Mondeuse grape is ripe and smooth, with black currant and pepper notes. It is similar to a light Syrah.
Montepulciano		Montepulciano is an Italian grape that makes wines that are ripe and smooth, well-perfumed and complex, with good structure and distinctive fruitiness. These wines age well.
Moristel		The light, fruity wine from this Spanish grape is often blended and should be drunk young, since it oxidizes quite quickly.
Mourvèdre	Monastrell (Spain); Mataro (New World)	This grape makes big, rich, powerful, tannic wines, the best from southern France, Spain, and California, with plenty of black fruits and sweet spices. It is often used as a blend.
Nebbiolo	Spanna (Piedmont, Italy); Chiavennasca (Lombardy, Italy)	Grown in small quantities in Italy, Argentina, and California, this grape produces rich, dense red wine with high acidity, balanced alcohol, high tannins, and lots of fruit. It needs time in the bottle to develop its superb bouquet.
Pinot Meunier		Pinot Meunier is part of the classic Champagne blend, adding fruit intensity to the wine. It is usually blended, but on its own it produces some charming peachy and apple-rich styles that have less finesse and elegance than Champagne, but are great as aperitifs! Also grown in Italy and as far afield as Canada.
Pinot Noir	Pinot Nero (Italy); Burgund Mare (Romania); Spätburgunder (Germany and Austria); Blauburgunder (Austria and Switzerland)	At its finest in Burgundy but also excellent in North America, Pinot Noir grapes produce light and fruity, silky red wines with light color, and highly and delicately perfumed. It ages well and displays a wide range of characters, from black cherry to leather and spice, as well as vanilla and smoke. Grown in Germany as Spätburgunder, it makes elegant and slightly lighter wines than those of Burgundy. In Sancerre, in the Loire Valley, it is used to make elegant and sought-after rosé wines, lightly colored and refreshing, with good fruit intensity. This grape also provides the "backbone" for many Old and New World sparkling wines, holding together their structure, and bringing body as well as intensity and freshness. It is part of the blend of grapes used to make most of the great names in Champagne, including the finest, Dom Pérignon and Cristal.
Pinotage		A South African cross between Pinot Noir and Cinsault, Pinotage makes light reds with soft tannins.

GRAPE	OTHER NAMES	COMMENTS
Poulsard	Plousard	A large, thin-skinned, long-ripening grape of the French Jura, this makes pale but fruity, lively, relatively perfumed wines.
Rossese		This grape, which is widely grown in Liguria, Italy, makes distinctively flavored ripe, smooth wines.
Sangiovese	Nielluccio (Corsica, France); Sangioveto, Brunello, Morellino, Prugnolo Gentile (Italy)	This classy grape, which is often blended, makes some of the most famous Italian DOCGs, such as Chianti and Brunello—ripe, smooth wines whose success can depend a lot on vintage and winemaker. It is also used to make Tuscan rosés, light in color with marked acidity, balanced alcohol, and plenty of flavor. Also planted in California and Argentina.
St-Laurent		The deeply colored but light and lively wines from this grape, planted in Germany, Austria, and Eastern Europe, taste of crushed red berries, have soft tannins, and age very well.
Syrah	Shiraz (Australia and South Africa)	One of the finest red grapes in the world: in France's Rhône Valley its tiny berries make ripe, smooth wines with firm tannins and acidity, balanced alcohol, and good aging characteristics. In Australia and South Africa, as Shiraz, it makes world-class wines with a rich and opulent character that are typically warming and "jammy." Syrah rosés have an intense, deep pink color and are very fruity and refreshing; some of the best come from California.
Tannat		A "monster" grape, but making elegant wines in Uruguay, Argentina, and Madiran in France, Tannat produces big, intense, rich wines, with high levels of tannins, that age well in wood.
Tempranillo	Aragonez, Tinta Roriz (Portugal); Ull de Llebre, Tinta de Toro, Cencibel, Tinto del Pais, Tinto Fino (Spain)	Tempranillo is one of the finest Spanish red wine grapes. It makes complex, well-structured, ripe, smooth wines that can handle long aging; even the more basic Tempranillo wines are elegant and fruit-driven.
Teroldego		Famous for making the charming, elegant Teroldego Rotaliano from Italy, Teroldego makes wine that is ripe and smooth, with deep colors, fragrant fruits, and soft tannins.
Touriga Nacional		This Portuguese grape has tiny black berries that make a rich, deep wine, full of flavors and tannins, with balancing acidity.
Zinfandel		A full-flavored Californian grape making top-class plummy and peppery reds with high alcohol and long aging potential, and easy-drinking rosés, whites, or nearly-white "blush" wines.
Zweigelt		This variety, which produces excellent ripe, smooth reds, is widely planted in Austria, but little-known internationally.

GLOSSARY

ABV Alcohol by volume. The alcoholic strength of a drink measured as a percentage of the whole volume.

ACIDITY The "spine" of a white wine; this is essential for a refreshing flavor and to allow the wine to age well.

AGING The process of maturing wine, usually in wooden containers, especially oak. It develops character and complexity.

ALCOHOL The by-product of the fermentation of sugars by yeast.

ANAEROBIC In the absence of oxygen.

ANGELS' SHARE A term used to describe the wine that evaporates through the wood of barrels that contain aging wine.

AOC Appellation d'Origine Contrôlée. The highest classification of French wine, assuring that it has reached a set quality standard *(see also pp.64–5).*

APERITIF A drink taken before a meal to stimulate the appetite.

APPELLATION A French geographically designated wine-production area; often used more loosely to describe wine from a particular area.

AROMA The perfume or smell of a wine, often used interchangeably with "bouquet."

AROMATIC Usually associated with fruity and appealing grape varieties such as Riesling, Sauvignon Blanc, and Muscat.

AUSTERE Wine in which the fruit is dominated by tannin or acidity. Such wine usually needs time to age and improve.

BALANCE The harmonious relationship between fruit, acidity, tannins, and alcohol in a wine.

BLUSH Very pale pink rosé wine.

BODEGA Spanish for cellar or domaine.

BODY The weight of a wine's flavors in the mouth, usually related to its fruit and alcohol content.

BOTRYTIS CINEREA The fungus that causes the benign disease "noble rot" on grapes. *Botrytis cinerea* is important in the production of sweet wines, such as Sauternes, because it concentrates the sugars in the grapes. Grapes affected by this fungus are referred to as botrytized.

BOUQUET The smell of a wine, reflecting the ingredients and aging or maturity.

BREATHING The interaction between wine and the air, leading to the release of aromas.

BRUT French word for "dry," commonly applied to sparkling wines such as Champagne.

CARBONIC MACERATION A technique of fermenting grapes without crushing them, producing well-colored and fruity wine; typically used in the Beaujolais region.

CAVA Spanish sparkling wine, made using the same techniques used to produce Champagne (the *méthode traditionnelle*).

CHÂTEAU Literally French for castle, but used to describe the domaine of origin of some French wines.

CIGAR BOX A descriptive term for the aroma of older wines matured in wood, especially red Bordeaux.

CLARET An English term used to describe red Bordeaux wines. This term is no longer in popular use.

CLASSICO The Italian term for the central or classic part of a DOC or DOCG region. This is often considered to be the part of the region where better wines are made.

CLOS French term for a small, wall-enclosed vineyard, or for a small area within a larger vineyard.

COMPLEXITY Term used to describe the many different flavors or aromas found in a high-quality wine. Very desirable.

CORKED WINE Wine that smells moldy and damp, caused by mold or chemicals in the cork that have tainted the wine.

CÔTE The French term for the ridge or slope of one contiguous hillside, the most famous being the Côte d'Or in Burgundy.

CÔTEAUX French term for noncontiguous slopes and hillsides.

CRÉMANT French term for a sparkling wine.

CRIANZA Spanish classification for wine that has spent six months in oak barrels and 18 months in the bottle before release.

CRU French word for "growth," used to define wine quality, as in *grand cru* and *premier cru.*

CRU BOURGEOIS A classification that applies only to French wines from the Médoc. It was established in the 1930s to promote the region's lesser-known quality wines, which were not included in the first Bordeaux Classification of 1855.

CRU CLASSÉ French term for a classified vineyard.

CUVE CLOSE Production method for making sparkling wines in which secondary fermentation takes place in large tanks, before bottling under pressure.

CUVÉE French term, meaning the juice from the wine press. It is often used to refer to a blend, or the special production of a particular wine.

DECANTING Separating wine from its natural sediments by pouring into a decanter before serving. Decanting also puts the wine into contact with air, releasing its aromas.

DO Denominación de Origen *(see also p.67).* A quality standard for Spanish wine similar to the French classification AOC.

DOC Denominazione di Origine Controllata. With DOCG (Denominazione di Origine Controllata e Garantita), the top classification of Italian wine *(see also pp.65–7).*

DOMAINE French term for wine estate.

DOSAGE The final addition of sugar in the Champagne-making process.

EISWEIN German term for sweet wine made from grapes harvested when frozen, a process that helps to concentrate the sugars in the grapes. It is called ice wine outside Germany, especially in Canada.

FERMENTATION The process by which sugars are broken down by the action of yeast, forming carbon dioxide and ethyl alcohol.

FINISH The taste that lingers in the mouth after a sip of wine has been swallowed.

FIRMNESS A measure of the structure and acidity of a drink, as in "firm tannins."

FLOR A scumlike yeast deposit that covers the top of some sherries as they mature, and seals them from the air.

FORTIFICATION Adding spirit, usually grape spirit, to a wine such as port or sherry to increase its strength and character.

FRIZZANTE Italian expression for a lightly sparkling wine.

GRAND CRU French term meaning "great growth." This is the top classification of wine quality in Burgundy, but in other regions of France lies just below *premier cru*.

ICE WINE see *Eiswein*

LATE BOTTLED VINTAGE (LBV) Port from a specified vintage that has been matured for between four and six years in wood before bottling.

LEES The remains of grape seeds, yeast, and sediment that settles after the fermentation process of making wine. Also called *lie* in French. In Muscadet, *sur lie* is wine that has deliberately been left in contact with the lees to add character.

LENGTH The amount of time that the flavor of a wine makes an impression, both on the palate and after swallowing. See also *finish*.

MACERATION The process of steeping grape juice with the crushed skins and seeds to extract flavor and color.

MÉTHODE TRADITIONNELLE Sparkling wines made by the same production process as is used to make Champagne (*see also p.44*). In this production method, secondary fermentation takes place in the bottle the sparkling wine will be sold in.

MICROCLIMATE A special and distinct climatic condition within a small area, such as on a particular part of a hill that faces the sun, or a sheltered spot within a valley.

MOUTH FEEL Term used to describe the texture of a drink in the mouth.

MUST The mixture of crushed grapes—including their juice, and sometimes also their seeds, skins, and stalks—that will undergo fermentation in the winemaking process.

NOBLE ROT see *Botrytis cinerea*

NOSE The aroma of a wine.

OXIDIZED Wine or fruit that has been overexposed to air.

POMACE The remnants of stalks, seeds, and crushed berries left after the juice has been pressed from grapes. It is often used to make basic brandies, such as marc and grappa.

PREMIER CRU French term meaning "First Growth"; this is the top classification for châteaux or producers in some regions of France; in the Burgundy region, however, it ranks just below *grand cru*.

RANCIO Rich, earthy, and desirable aroma of dried fruits, chocolate, and spice that appears in some fortified wines, such as Tawny port.

SEC French wine term meaning dry; demi-sec is semidry or medium-dry.

SEDIMENT The dead yeast produced during bottle-fermentation of wine; also the tannins and color pigmentation deposited as solids in very old red wines.

SEKT The German term for sparkling wine.

SOLERA SYSTEM The system used in sherry-making whereby younger wine is gradually blended with older, through a special arrangement of barrels.

SPUMANTE Italian term meaning sparkling.

SUR LIE see *lees*

TANK METHOD see *cuve close*

TANNIN A substance contained in the skins of red grapes, which enters the wine during maceration and fermentation, and is a key part of the aging process. It gives a dry feel in the mouth, rather like green apples.

TERROIR A French word describing the character of any given area in a vineyard, including soil, climate, and aspect. Some include the grower in this evaluation.

TRADITIONAL METHOD see *méthode traditionnelle*

VDQS Vin Délimité de Qualité Supérieure. French wine classification that falls below AOC but above Vin de Pays (*see also pp.64–5*).

VENDANGE French term for the grape harvest. *Vendange tardive* is "late harvest."

VIN DE PAYS French term meaning "country wine"; a classification of French wines that falls between the most basic Vin de Table and the higher-quality AOC and VDQS (*see also pp.64–5*).

VIN DE TABLE French term meaning "table wine"; the lowest classification of French wine (*see also pp.64–5*).

VINIFICATION The process of turning grape juice into wine.

VINTAGE A wine from a single year. Also used interchangeably with the word "year" in describing wine.

YEAST A microscopic fungus, which converts sugar to carbon dioxide and alcohol and is used in the fermentation of wine.

YIELD The total amount of wine produced by a vine or vineyard in a particular vintage.

INDEX

Page numbers in *italics* refer
to illustrations.

ACKNOWLEDGMENTS

AUTHOR'S ACKNOWLEDGMENTS Writing my second book has been an amazing and rewarding experience, and I could not have written it without the support of many people, to all of whom I give sincere thanks. First of all, a very special thank-you to my wonderful and beautiful wife, Amy, for her continuous support and understanding, and to my lovely and fantastic children Émilie, George, and Louis. A big *merci* to my lovely Maman, Brigitte, for all her encouragement through the years and her sacrifices for her five sons. Also, a massive thank-you to Mary & John Fisher, who once again have totally supported me throughout this book.

A huge thank-you to all my family, both in France – especially Thierry, Valerie, Pierre, my goddaughter Julie, Matthieu, Fabrice, Corinne, Lolo; Laurent, Cecile, Maxime, Camille, Ludo, Aurore, and Oceane – and in England, especially Alex, Tanya, Hollie, Alice, William, and Auntie Maureen, who have been with me all the way. Thanks also to Karen & Graeme Souness, wine-lovers and business partners, for their support, faith, and valued friendship over the years. To Robin Hutson, for all the very special years at Hotel du Vin; Nick Jones, Charlie Luxton, and Jonathon Brackenbury at Soho House, for all their support, trust, and kindness; and all at the Soho House units, in particular Pierre, for letting me use Soho House, and David, for all their help. To Simon & Carol Foderingham and Mike Mason for their constant support as well as their great advice; and to Andy & Loukie Gair, Rob, Gemma, Stu, Holly, and Father Ted for the many intense but enjoyable tastings.

To the amazing team at Dorling Kindersley, especially Mary-Clare Jerram, John Roberts, Simon Tuite, Sara Robin, Antonia Wilkinson, Adèle Hayward, and Stephanie Jackson; to Gary Werner and Ruth Arnold; and to the "A team" at cobalt id: Marek, Paul, Kati, Lloyd, Maddy, Louise, Claire, Annika, and Darren, for making this book so wonderful. Thank you to Ian O'Leary, for his stunning photos, and to all my friends and work colleagues, especially Julian Rigotti, Joel Lauga, Christophe Jandeau, Christophe Rollet-Manus, Georges Barbier, John Elliot, and Charlie Monro, Emma & Hubert Pelletrat, our neighbours Rachel & Duncan Saunders, and Lucy at Spiral Cellars.

To all my personal and private clients and friends, especially Tracy & Ashley Levett, Mrs & Dr Garnett, Alistair & Michelle Collier, Chris & Anne-Louise Akers, Matthew Tawse, Danny & Diana Desmond, Anthony Ward, Kate & Georges Digweed, Peter Sherrard, Mrs & Mr McCue, Ron Carlier, Jim & Anne Roberts, Hassan & Farah Alaghband; and Harry & Sandra, Jamie & Louise Redknapp, Joy & David O'Leary, Lanya & Alan Shearer, Louise & Michael Owen, and all my friends in the football world. And to my very good friend and agent Luigi Bonomi, for all his trust and belief in my passion; to my teachers, Vincent Courseau and Alain Dussetour; to my superb and amazing mentors Philippe Bourguignon and Gerard Basset; and to Brian Julyan and all my friends and colleagues at the Master Sommeliers' Court. Thanks to you all! VG

PUBLISHER'S ACKNOWLEDGMENTS Cobalt id would like to thank the following for their help with this book: Ruth Arnold, Gary Werner, Steve Setford, and Judy Barratt for invaluable editorial assistance; Christine Heilman for Americanization; and Hilary Bird for indexing. Our thanks to Ian O'Leary, and to photography assistants Laura Forrester, Kerry O'Sullivan, Steve Ambrose, and stylist Kim Jackson, all at Ian O'Leary Studios.

We gratefully acknowledge the assistance of the following individuals, organizations, and companies, who provided guidance, resources, images, and products without which this book would not have been possible:

A. Racke GmbH + Co.; Addison Wines; Alivini Company Limited; Andrew Chapman Fine Wines; Australian Wineries LLP; Barrels & Bottles; Baton Rouge Wines; Berkmann Wine Cellars Ltd; Bodegas López de Heredia; Bortársaság; Boyar International Ltd; Brown Brothers; C & D Wines Ltd; Cachet Wine; Chalie, Richards & Co Ltd; Champagnes & Chateaux Ltd; Charles Hawkins; Château du Cléray-Sauvion en Eolie; Château Palmer; Chateau Rives-Blanques; D.A.D. (Didier Absil Développement); Dalmacijav; d'Arenberg; De Trafford Winery; Domaine Laroche; Dromana Estate Ltd; Du Toitskloof Wine Cellar; Edward Cavendish & Sons Ltd; Eurowines; First Drinks Brands; Folly Wines; Freixenet UK; Gentilini Winery & Vineyards; Georges Barbier; Goedhuis & Company Limited; Great Western Wine Co Ltd; H & H Bancroft Wines; Hallgarten Wines; Harrison Vintners; Hatch Mansfield Limited; Hayman Barwell Jones Ltd; Howard Ripley Ltd; HwCg Ltd; Jean-Claude Raspail; John E Fells & Sons Ltd; Julian Baker Fine Wines; Kendall-Jackson Vineyard Estates; Lane & Tatham Wine Brokers; Lay & Wheeler Group; Le Bon Vin Ltd; Lea and Sandeman Co. Ltd; Les Caves de Pyrene; Liberty Wines; Matthew Clark Wholesale Ltd; McDowell Valley Vineyards; Meridian Wines Ltd; Michael Hall Wines; Mistral Wines; Morgenrot-Chevaliers PLC; Morris & Verdin; Negociants UK Ltd; O W Loeb & Co Ltd; Perez Barquero, S.A.; Peter Lehmann Wines (Europe) Ltd; Pol Roger; Potocki Spirits America; Quinta do Portal; Richards Walford & Co Ltd; Richmond Towers; Richmond Wine Agencies; Saintsbury; Simon Maye & Fils; Southcorp Wines Europe Ltd; Stevens Garnier Ltd; Storm Communications; T & W Wines Ltd; The Vintry; Umberto Cavicchioli & Figli; Val d'Orbieu Cordier Wines; Western Wines; Wine Importers Edinburgh Limited; Yapp Brothers Ltd.

PICTURE CREDITS The publisher would like to thank the following for their kind permission to reproduce their photographs:

Abbreviations key: t = top; b = bottom; l = left; r = right; c = centre; rh = running header; pictures in rows are numbered left to right.

ANTHONY BLAKE PHOTO LIBRARY: Norman Hollands 40bl. **ALAMY:** AllOver photography 59; Andy Christodolo/Cephas Picture Library 25b; Art Kowalsky 13; Bernager Elie/Stock Image 296bl; Bernd Mellmann 54b; Bobo 310tr; Cephas Picture Library 153tr, 34b, 86bl, 87tl, 259tl; Chloe Johnson 312bl; Craig Lovell - All Rights Reserved 51bl; Danita Delimont 50; David Noton Photography 70br; Diana Mewes/Cephas Picture Library 18bl, 22br; Eye35.com 66; Foodfolio 5c, 80–81, 82–83rh; Guy Moberly 14bl; Helmut Ebner/WoodyStock 23b; Ian Shaw/Cephas Picture Library 305, 42t, 57b, 83tr; ImageState 77bl; Jeffery Drewitz/Cephas Picture Library 24bl; John Ferro Sims 193tl; Kevin Judd/Cephas Picture Library 275tl, 33; Martin Jenkinson 53; Martin Norris Travel Photography 68t; Mary Steinbacher 131tl; Mick Rock/Cephas Picture Library 166bl, 19, 218bl, 26t, 31, 44br, 45, 49; Mike Long 43b; Neil Phillips/Cephas Picture Library 297t; Nigel Blythe/Cephas Picture Library 192bl, 22bl; Oleg Boldyrev 283tl; Per Karlsson-BKWine.com 104bl, 25t, 29b, 32bl; Peter Huggins 60, 62–79rh; Robert Holmes/AGStockUSA, Inc. 141t; Thomas Hallstein 35b; Tim Graham 65t; TNT Magazine 28t; Wilmar Photography.com 267tl; WoodyStock 21t. **CEPHAS PICTURE LIBRARY:** Kevin Judd 55b; Mick Rock 30bl, 48bl, 62bl, 152bl, 213tl, 233tl, 258bl; Nigel Blythe 304bl; Ted Stefanski 52br. **CORBIS:** Cameron 58b; Charles O'Rear 39; Krista Kennell/ZUMA 14br; Owen Franken 5cl, 10–11, 23tr; Photocuisine 324b, 326; Reuters 300bl. **DIGITAL VISION:** 85tr, 273tr. **GETTY IMAGES:** Ian O'Leary 83bl, 83br; Johnér Images 296br, 303t; Justin Sullivan 56; Rita Maas/The Image Bank 331b; Romilly Lockyer 15t; Sebastian Willnow/AFP 274bl. **ISTOCKPHOTO:** Bluestocking 316tr; Carlos Lozano 27; Daniel Gilbey 191tr; Danny Yates 117t; Diane White Rosier 35tr; Elena Elisseeva 165tr; Fotosav 129tr; Gabrielle Chan 151tr; Grapegeek 36bl; José Carlos Pires Pereira 6bl; Olga Vasilkova 37t, 38bl; Stephen Walls 46, 46, 48–59rh. **JUPITERIMAGES:** E. Jane Armstrong/FoodPix 83tl; Sang An/FoodPix 330t; Simon Watson/FoodPix 5cr, 294–295; Steve Cohen/FoodPix 329.

Every effort has been made to trace the copyright holders. The publisher apologizes for any unintentional omissions and would be pleased, in such cases, to place an acknowledgment in future editions of this book.

THE FOLLOWING IMAGES © DORLING KINDERSLEY: 1c, 2, 4, 7, 8bl, 9, 12–45rh, 12bl, 16, 17tr, 18tr, 20b, 20bl, 24tr, 30tr, 32tr, 36br, 38tr, 40tl, 41, 44tl, 47tr, 51br, 52bl, 61tr, 62tr, 63, 64b, 64br, 67tr1, 69br, 69t, 69tl, 71, 72bl, 72br, 72c, 72c, 73, 74bl, 74tr, 75, 76bl, 76cr, 77br, 79bc, 79bl, 79tr, 82bl, 84, 86–101rh, 87tr, 88cr, 89bc, 90b, 92, 93t, 93tl, 93tl, 94bl, 97, 98bl, 98br, 98tl, 98tr, 99t, 99tr, 99tl, 99tl, 101, 102, 103tr, 104–127rh, 105tl, 105tr, 106, 107bl, 110bl, 110br, 110tl, 110tr, 111t, 111t, 111tl, 111tl, 112cr, 114bl, 115br, 115t, 116ff, 117tr, 118, 119tl, 120, 122cr, 124, 125t, 125tl, 126bl, 126t, 128, 130–149rh, 130cl, 131tr, 132, 133bl, 134, 135t, 135t, 135tl, 135tl, 137bc, 138bl, 138tr, 139b, 140, 141tr, 142cl, 144, 145cr, 146, 147t, 147tl, 147tl, 148b, 150, 152–163rh, 153cr, 154, 155bl, 158bl, 158br, 158tl, 158tr, 159t, 159tl, 159tl, 161tr, 162b, 164, 166–189rh, 167cr, 167tl, 168, 168tl, 170t, 171bl, 171, 172bl, 172br, 172tl, 172tr, 173t, 173tl, 173tl, 174trl, 175bl, 175t, 177, 178, 179t, 179tl, 179tl, 181bl, 181t, 184, 185t, 185tr, 186c, 187t, 189b, 189t, 190, 192–215rh, 193cr, 194, 197br, 198bl, 198br, 198tl, 198tr, 199t, 199tl, 199tl, 201, 202bl, 204, 205t, 205t, 205tl, 205tl, 208bl, 209cr, 212, 213tr, 215bl, 215t, 216, 217tr, 218–255rh, 219tl, 219tr, 220cl, 222bl, 224bl, 224br, 224tl, 224tr, 225t, 225tl, 225tl, 226, 228bl, 230bl, 232, 233tr, 234, 236, 237cr, 237tl, 238c, 239b, 239tc, 240, 241t, 241tl, 241tl, 241tl, 242bl, 243bl, 243t, 244cr, 248, 249t, 249tl, 249tl, 251c, 253tr, 254b, 254c, 256, 257tr, 258–271rh, 259cr, 260bl, 261bl, 261cr, 262bl, 264c, 264r, 266, 267tr, 271r, 272, 274–293rh, 275cr, 276b, 279bc, 280bl, 280t, 281, 282, 283tr, 284t, 285b, 285r, 286bl, 286t, 287, 289c, 290bl, 290br, 290tl, 290cr, 291t, 291t, 291tl, 291tl, 296–305rh, 298, 299tr, 300tr, 301, 302bl, 304tr, 306, 307tr, 308–317rh, 308tr, 309, 310bl, 311, 313, 314b, 315b, 316bl, 317, 317tr, 318, 319tr, 320–333rh, 320bl, 321, 322bl, 322br, 325t, 333.

For further information see www.dkimages.com